Crisis of Command

Crisis of Command
Australian Generalship and the Japanese Threat, 1941-1943
D. M. Horner

Australian National University Press
Canberra A.C.T. and Norwalk, Conn., 1978

First published in Australia 1978

Printed in Australia for the Australian National
University Press, Canberra

National Library of Australia
Cataloguing-in-Publication entry

Horner, D. M.
  Crisis of command.

  Index.
  Bibliography.
  ISBN 0 7081 1345 1.

  1. Australia — Army.
  2. World War, 1939-1945 — Oceania. I. Title.

940.5401

Library of Congress no: 78-52595

United Kingdom, Europe, Middle East and Africa:
Eurospan Ltd, 3 Henrietta St, London WC2E 8LU,
England
North America: Books Australia, Norwalk, Conn.,
USA
Southeast Asia: Angus & Robertson (S.E. Asia) Pty
Ltd, Singapore
Japan: United Publishers Services Ltd, Tokyo

For
Sigrid and Jolyon

Acknowledgments

The initial research for this book was made possible when the Australian Military Board approved my appointment as a postgraduate student in the Faculty of Military Studies of the University of New South Wales. Although I subsequently travelled to the United States at my own expense and continued work on the book in my own time in both Canberra and Townsville, as part of my studies the Army provided me with the means to spend ten days walking and driving over the battlefields of New Guinea, and enabled me to visit Adelaide, Melbourne (twice) and Sydney (five times) so that I could interview retired generals and study in various libraries. I would like to record my appreciation to the retired officers who gave generously of their time in replying to letters and sitting through long interviews. Their names are recorded in the bibliography.

I wish to express my gratitude to Mr A. J. Hill, Senior Lecturer, Department of History in the Faculty of Military Studies, University of New South Wales, and Dr R. J. O'Neill, Head of the Strategic and Defence Studies Centre, Australian National University. I have benefited greatly from their wisdom and advice while undertaking this study. I also wish to thank Mr J. R. Robertson of Duntroon who read the manuscript and offered sound advice.

I received valuable assistance from the staff at the Australian War Memorial, particularly Mr Geoff McKeown, the staff at the Australian Archives, and from the staff of the National Library of Australia. Mr Robert Vasey allowed me to photocopy and use his father's letters. The late Sir Sydney Rowell allowed me to use some of his wartime files, and his daughter generously allowed me to use additional letters. I must also thank the Trustees of the Australian War Memorial for permission to quote from the official histories.

Whilst in the United States I was given great help by the staff at the

MacArthur Memorial, the National Archives, and the National Records Center. I thank Professor Jay Luvaas of Allegheny College, Pennsylvania, for his hospitality and for allowing me to take away copies of General Eichelberger's dictations and letters. I am indebted to the United States Department of the Army for permission to reproduce the maps taken from the *Reports of General MacArthur, The Campaign of MacArthur in the Pacific,* Vol. 1, and from S. Milner, *Victory in Papua.*

Many others have given me assistance at some stage. Their goodwill has helped make the last four years enjoyable. Finally I must thank my wife Sigrid who helped me with research in USA, attempted to correct my expression with more necessity than I would like to admit, and in many ways supported the project throughout.

Townsville, 1977   D.M.H.

Abbreviations

AAF	American Air Force (strictly USAAF, see below)
AA & QMG	Assistant Adjutant and Quartermaster-General
ADMS	Assistant Director Medical Services
AG	Adjutant-General
AHQ	Army Headquarters
AIF	Australian Imperial Force
AMF	Australian Military Forces
ANGAU	Australian New Guinea Administrative Unit
AWM	Australian War Memorial
Bde	Brigade
BGGS	Brigadier-General, General Staff
BGS	Brigadier, General Staff
CCRA	Commander, Corps Royal Artillery
CG	Commanding General
CGS	Chief of the General Staff
CIGS	Chief of the Imperial General Staff
C-in-C	Commander-in-Chief
CMF	Citizen Military Forces
COSC	Combined Operational Services Command
CRA	Commander, Royal Artillery (of a division)
DA & QMG	Deputy Adjutant and Quartermaster-General
DAQMG	Deputy Assistant Quartermaster-General
DDMS	Deputy Director Medical Services
DCGS	Deputy Chief of the General Staff
DMI	Director of Military Intelligence
E-in-C	Engineer-in-Chief
G1	Shortened version of GSO1
GHQ	General Headquarters
GOC	General Officer Commanding

GOC-in-C	General Officer Commanding-in-Chief
GSO1	General Staff Officer, Grade 1
GSO2	General Staff Officer, Grade 2
HQ	Headquarters
LGA	Lieutenant-General in charge of Administration
LHQ	Allied Land Forces Headquarters
L of C	Lines of Communication
MGO	Master-General of the Ordnance
MGGS	Major-General, General Staff
MGRA	Major-General, Royal Artillery
NGF	New Guinea Force
NLA	National Library of Australia
PIB	Papuan Infantry Battalion
QMG	Quartermaster-General
RAAF	Royal Australian Air Force
SO-in-C	Signals Officer-in-Chief
SWPA	South-West Pacific Area
USAAF	United States Army Air Force
USAFIA	United States Army Forces in Australia
USASOS	United States Services of Supply
USN	United States Navy
VDC	Volunteer Defence Corps

Contents

Maps

Plates

All photographs are reproduced by courtesy of the Australian War Memorial

Introduction

GENERALSHIP: For what art can surpass that of the General? — an art which deals not with dead matter but with living beings, who are subject to every impression of the moment, such as fear, precipitation, exhaustion — in short, to every human passion and excitement. The general has not only to reckon with unknown quantities, such as time, weather, accidents of all kinds, but he has before him one who seeks to disturb and frustrate his plans and labours in every way; and at the same time this man, upon whom all eyes are directed, feels upon his mind the weight of responsibility not only for the lives and honour of hundreds of thousands, but even for the welfare and existence of his country.

A. von Boguslawski[1]

After over twenty years of a policy of forward defence, Australian strategic planners are once again examining the problems of continental defence. Following the decades of commitment to Japan, Korea, Malaya, Borneo and South Vietnam, the Australian services have a new task — the defence of Australia, its island territories, marine resources zone and sea and air approaches. The re-orientation of thinking required by the defence chiefs is no more abrupt than that required of the defence chiefs in late 1941 and 1942 when the threat was real rather than hypothetical. How well did the generals then deal with the threat to the Australian homeland? The Japanese threat in 1942 posed the greatest danger to Australia that the young country had hitherto faced. At no other time have the performances of the Australian generals weighed so heavily upon the question of national survival.

No true analysis of Australian generalship has yet been produced although a number of superficial studies of Monash have appeared. John Hetherington's fine biography, *Blamey, Controversial Soldier*, stops short of an analysis of Blamey's military achievements. The performances of the Australian commanders have rarely come under closer scrutiny than that provided by the official histories.[2] These have usually been limited by an unwritten charter requiring the official historian to provide a multi-strata picture of the Australian war effort with emphasis on the actions of the private soldier. In the opinion of Professor Encel they are democratic war histories.

The great strategic decisions, the historic battles, the political conflicts, the personal rivalries of generals and admirals in search of glory, are no more than a distinct back drop for hundreds of personal dramas taken from regimental diaries. It is the kind of history that would have commended itself to Tolstoy.[3]

This is a little unfair to Gavin Long and Paul Hasluck, but the point is made.[4]

Liddell Hart believed that if military history was to be of practical value, it 'should be a study of the psychological reaction of the commanders, with merely a background of events to throw their thoughts, impressions and decisions into clear relief'.[5] In other words the heart of the military problem is the personality of the commander, for it shapes the battle, and in turn, the battle affects the psychological state and effectiveness of the commander. The field of command relationships is the least studied in Australian military history, and one which needs cultivation. In no period have personalities played a more significant role than in 1942.

The period from December 1941 to January 1943 marked a time of great development in the Australian Army. Not only did the shock of Japan's outward thrust cause fundamental changes in Australia's attitude to foreign relations, defence, and to the army, but from this period onwards Australians no longer looked to Britain for protection, but rather to the United States. It is not the intention here to investigate the changes in foreign policy, national government or the economy, but rather to examine closely the impact of these changes on the army commanders, and to discuss their performance when faced with these extraordinary pressures.

It is important to note that the changes forced on the army by the rapidity with which the nation was catapulted into total war coincided with organic developments within the structure of the army during the first two years of war. In 1911 the Australian Government had established the Royal Military College at Duntroon. By 1942 those officers who had been in the first classes at Duntroon were reaching the rank of general. In July of that year there were eleven generals who were graduates of RMC; a year earlier there had been only one.[6] For an army with a strong tradition of citizen soldiers in high positions, this development brought tension in some quarters.

With the split between regular and amateur, there was to be yet a further division within the ranks of the army. This was between the 2nd AIF, the volunteers who had served with distinction in the Middle East and who were now returning home to defend their country, and the conscripts of the militia (CMF), who were restricted to service within Australia. This 'two army' system was one of the great mistakes of the Australian war effort.

Unlike the previous fighting in South Africa, Gallipoli, France and the Middle East, the fighting of 1942 and 1943 took place on Australia's doorstep. This imposed on the commanders pressures that they had hitherto escaped, for they now became subject to the interference of politicians, who in their turn were keeping an anxious eye on their electorates.

Unable to defend herself adequately, Australia looked anxiously to America for support. The bulk of the initial fighting, however, was to be done by Australians. The delicate task of co-operating with the American forces added a further complication to the problems of Australian commanders during this period. Despite the fact that it was Australia which was being defended, Curtin, the Prime Minister, had no hesitation in placing all of his forces under American command. It is remarkable that such an arrangement worked at all.

For the fighting man, the complexion of the war changed considerably. With the exception of the small expedition to German New Guinea in World War I, the army was faced, for the first time, with war in the tropics — war in the terrain and climate of Australia's immediate neighbours. This demanded a change in tactical technique at the lowest level, paralleled by the development of combined air, land and sea operations to a pitch hitherto not achieved in English speaking forces. The paradox of this new warfare was that it required a flexibility of thought and a standard of leadership not always found in the professional soldier, but it also required a technical skill which could be gained only by considerable study and application.

These then were the types of problems faced by Australian military commanders in 1942 and 1943. The roots of many of these problems lie in the history of the army during the preceding fifty years and in many ways are bound up with the development of the nation. The conflict with Japan was the catalyst which was to make these problems apparent, and although the 'pressure cooker' atmosphere of the following year — the need to produce much in a short time — helped resolve a good number of them, many of these problems still exist today.[7] Thus, just as the problems of 1942 and 1943 have their roots in the military tradition preceding that period, the problems of today are in many ways a reflection of those brought to notice by Australia's war with Japan.

It is against this background that the command relationships are to be examined. Clausewitz wrote: 'The difficulties [in war] accumulate and produce a friction which no man can imagine exactly who has not seen war'.[8] Another writer has taken this a step further and noted that 'the higher direction of war would in fact be far simpler than a game of chess if it were not for (externally) the opposition of the enemy and (internally) the friction that is unavoidable in the operations of any military force and which increases rapidly with the size of the force'.[9] This book is about the internal friction and its effect on the commanders, and in turn its effects on the conduct of the war in the South-West Pacific Area.

How is the historian, the final master of the battlefield, to go about examining this effect? To look carefully at the facts of each battle or incident, to weigh the possibilities and to examine the results in the cold light of retrospect is not satisfactory. Men are not automatons and their decisions are governed as much by emotion as logic. It can be argued that Napoleon lost at Waterloo because of an agonising attack of haemorrhoids. Yet of even greater effect on a commander than physical discomfort is the mental strain which is the inevitable companion of command in war. One way of getting into the mind of the commander and understanding this strain is to read his personal correspondence. Personal correspondence has been used extensively as evidence in this work. It reveals elation and depression, suspicion and confidence, frustration and satisfaction, fortitude and trepidation. It also reveals the intense pressure of command.

Field Marshal Lord Wavell, in *Generals and Generalship*, discerned various qualities which he saw as being essential to a good commander. The first essential, he believed, was 'the quality of robustness, the ability to stand the shocks of war'.[10] Montgomery called it 'toughness'.[11] Napoleon had the same idea: 'The first qualification of a general-in-chief is to possess a cool head, so that things may appear to him in their true proportions and as they really are. He should not suffer himself to be unduly affected by good or bad news'.[12]

There are two types of pressures to which a commander is subjected. There are those imposed by enemy action, and those imposed by other forces, for example interference from superior commanders. Both of these pressures play upon the psychological well-being of the commander. Colonel J. F. C. Fuller wrote that 'the enemy does not attack [the commander] physically, but mentally; for the enemy attacks his ideas, his reasons, his plan. The physical pressure directed against his men reacts on him through compelling him to change his plan, and changes in his plan react on his men by creating a mental confusion which weakens their morale'.[13]

On the other hand the pressures from areas other than the enemy are more insidious and can be even more damaging. The superior who shows a lack of confidence in his subordinate, by implication, and often directly, reminds him that if he makes even an apparent mistake, he will be disgraced and fall into oblivion. Sir Francis Tuker noted that commanders venture themselves in command in battle. He says ' "ventured" because the commander stakes his reputation, his career, all that he is and may be in his profession, on the issue of a fight in which his instinct must derive so much that is unknown and his science weigh all that is imponderable: above all, he stakes the coin he values most — the trust that his officers and men have in him'.[14] Field Marshal Dill maintained that 'in war you must either trust your general or sack him',[15] and if neither is done then an atmosphere is created which may lead to disaster and which certainly will not promote the bold stroke that invariably wins a great victory.

The higher the rank of a commander the more open is he to criticism from all sides. Furthermore the closer the fighting comes to the homeland, the more intense is the criticism from civilians. Political leaders, fearful of their own positions, tend to interfere with superior commanders who then apply pressure to their subordinates. Generals Blamey and Rowell were to discover this harsh reality in 1942.

The detail of the study and the necessity for a great deal of evidence to ensure that reputations are not disparaged unfairly has caused the examination to concentrate on a limited number of generals, namely General Sir Thomas Blamey, and Lieutenant-Generals S. F. Rowell, V. A. H. Sturdee, J. D. Lavarack, I. G. Mackay and E. F. Herring. To support the conclusions it has been necessary to look at the performances of the subordinate commanders and staff officers, but in this respect their actions are discussed only where they affect those of their superiors. The Americans, Lieutenant-General R. L. Eichelberger and Major-Generals E. F. Harding and R. K. Sutherland, and the Australians, Major-Generals A. S. Allen, F. H. Berryman, C. A. Clowes, B. M. Morris, J. Northcott and G. A. Vasey, and Brigadiers J. R. Broadbent, R. N. L. Hopkins, H. G. Rourke and G. F. Wootten, appear prominently in the narrative.[16]

A commander cannot always choose his subordinates, and their conduct often affects that of the commander. Conversely, a commander has no control over the selection of his superior. In the case of Blamey this was General Douglas MacArthur. The performances of the Australians can only be measured if it is understood that they were operating in a framework in which the major decisions were made by MacArthur. For example, MacArthur's lack of knowledge of the conditions on the Kokoda Trail and of the tenacity of the Japanese led directly to Blamey's and Herring's decision to replace Allen.

In addition to the requirement for robustness it is worthwhile remembering some of the other qualities required by a commander. Almost on a par with robustness, Wavell stressed the aspect of administration. The principles of tactics and strategy are simple, but it is another matter to marshal the resources to execute the tactical plan. It was easy for MacArthur to give Rowell a brigade to capture Kokoda. It was another matter to transport the brigade to New Guinea, feed and supply it along the Kokoda Trail and put it into the line in a condition fit to fight. The general must, therefore, have a knowledge of the mechanics of war — the principles and practice of military movement and administration. It was their inaccurate appreciation of the logistical problems which led the Japanese to their defeat on the Kokoda Trail.

The personal factor in war should never be overlooked. The attributes required of a commander in the days of Wellington and Napoleon, such as courage, leadership and a personal presence on the battlefield, are just as relevant today. While the general should no longer have to lead his troops personally into battle, he should at least have a detailed knowledge of conditions in the forward areas and he must be seen by his troops. General Eisenhower said,

I found that it did a great deal of good to get down to troops in the combat area. My presence relaxed them and made them feel more comfortable about the situation. But I was not deceived as to the reason, I knew what was running through their minds. They were saying to themselves, 'There must be less danger than we thought or the old man wouldn't be here'.[17]

Few more stirring examples of leadership in modern war can be found than Eichelberger at Buna. Vasey's leadership of the 7th Division was equally outstanding. Other generals rarely saw the front line for themselves, and their performances suffered accordingly.

Modern warfare, however, demands more from its generals than wars of old, for now they must know how to handle air and naval forces, armoured vehicles, radio communications and the more intangible influences of propaganda and public relations. To be successful in battle with these instruments the general must have a creative intelligence and imagination, coupled with technical skill learned from years of study and training. The latter can dull the former, for as Archduke Albert said, 'When war arises, the small minds, worn out by attention to trifles, are incapable of effort, and fail miserably. So goes the world'.[18] Perhaps the answer is to combine the two as was often done in the Australian Army during World War II, when, in many cases, citizen soldiers commanded divisions and Staff Corps officers led the operations and administrative staffs.

Fuller saw three pillars of generalship, courage, creative intelligence and physical fitness, and observed that they were the attributes of youth rather than of middle age.[19] After the battle for Greece, General Rowell suggested to Blamey that Australia should aim at having no division commanders over 50, no brigade commanders over 40 and no battalion commanders over 30.[20] At that time the average age of the Australian division commanders was 55 years and 6 months, while that of the commanders of the overseas divisions was 55 years and 1 month. By March 1943 the average ages were 50 years 9 months and 40 years 4 months respectively.[21] Nevertheless the early success of the Australian commanders, and the gradual reduction in size of the Australian Army from 1942 onwards,[22] meant that there was not the rapid promotion that was evident in the Canadian and British Armies.[23] Fuller took the ages of one hundred generals from Xenophon (401 BC) to Moltke (1866) and discovered that on the average the period of most efficient generalship lay between the years 30 and 49, and that the peak was reached between the years 35 and 45.[24] It is always possible to find examples of the successful general in his sixties, but there is no doubt that a good young general will usually have the advantage over a good old one.

These then are some of the qualities required in a general. Sir Basil Liddell Hart listed a good number of additional qualities. His list included mental initiative, a strong and positive personality, an understanding of human nature, a capacity for ruthless determination, an ability to express his thoughts clearly, the power to grasp the picture instantly, and a combination of exceptional ability and commonsense. His supreme requirements were creative intelligence and moral courage.[25]

It is against a background of such premises that the performances of the commanders of the South-West Pacific Area can be examined. It must be remembered, however, that there were very few commanders with completely independent commands, and it is arguable whether it is only with a completely independent command that a commander can realise his full potential. Clausewitz wrote,

For each station, from the lowest upwards, to render distinguished services in War, there must be a particular genius. But the title of genius, history and the judgment of posterity only confer, in general, on those minds which have shone in the highest rank, that of Commander-in-Chief. The reason is that here, in point of fact, the demand on the reasoning and intellectual powers generally is much greater.[26]

Despite this it is still valid to examine the performances of the commanders in the South-West Pacific Area, for not only had they the burden of command in terrain for which they were largely unprepared, but also that of being a subordinate, or at best having to co-operate with another commander of a foreign ally. In this way, the problem of co-operation required the additional qualities of tact, sympathy and modesty.

It is possible, therefore, to link the study of problems of command with that of the study of generalship, or the ability to overcome these problems. Yet it should never be forgotten that it is the little things which go wrong that compound the problems and determine the psychological effectiveness of the commander. For as Liddell Hart has said:

it matters little what the situation actually was at any particular point or moment; all that matters is what the commander thought it was.[27]

1
Preparing for the Imperial War, 1934–1941

By the beginning of 1933 the Australian defence system had reached its lowest ebb for twenty years. Not only had the Depression taken its severe toll, but the generally widespread belief that disarmament was the key to world peace had negated the desperate pleas of the few far-sighted strategic thinkers in the country. It was easy for money-starved politicians to cling to the secure notion of Imperial Defence with which they had been preoccupied since World War I. Many politicians and indeed a number of service officers agreed with Senator Pearce when he declared during the year that 'Australia's defence policy "must dovetail with the Imperial defence policy" '.[1] For the serviceman whose main point of discussion for three years had been who was to be retrenched, the increased defence expenditure announced in the October budget was welcome news.

Nevertheless there were a number of senior army officers who were disturbed by the government's continued reliance on Imperial Defence. As early as 1926 Lieutenant-Colonel H. D. Wynter had delivered a lecture to the United Services Institution of Victoria pointing out the dangers of the policy. The following year the text of the lecture was published in the *Army Quarterly* of London and Wynter stated that 'The security of Great Britain — the heart of the Empire — is the primary consideration of Imperial Defence'. He concluded with the belief that 'Australia should provide in her own territory, within the area which is defensible by her local land and air forces, a first class naval base capable of undertaking the maintenance of the British Battle Fleet'. He stressed that this base should not be a substitute for Singapore, which was being presented as the cornerstone of Imperial Defence in the Far East.[2] Another officer, Colonel J. D. Lavarack, the Commandant of the Royal Military College, held similar views and in January 1933 published 'The Defence of the British Empire with Special Reference to the Far East and Australia' in the *Army Quarterly*.[3]

Clearly the army was determined to maintain its views, for when in 1932 Cabinet instructed the Chief of the General Staff (CGS), Major-General Sir Julius Bruche, to prepare to despatch an expeditionary force within three months of a declaration of war, he preferred to spread the defence vote on fixed defences rather than on the weapons necessary for the expeditionary force.[4]

This rumbling of discontent had little effect on the government, and in 1934 Sir Maurice Hankey, the Secretary of the Committee of Imperial Defence, visited Australia. Naturally Sir Maurice was an advocate of Imperial Defence, and in November he pointed out that as Australia could rely on the naval base at Singapore to protect Australia the army could be rationalised and reduced to two divisions and seven brigades.[5] Major-General Bruche, the tall, impressive and articulate CGS, disagreed with this assessment and argued that, whilst Sir Maurice Hankey's opinion should be respected, 'the direct responsibility for military advice upon the problem of the defence of Australia rests upon the naval, military, and air advisers of the Australian Government'.[6] Colonel Lavarack, who was now Chief of Staff designate, reinforced Bruche's comments and in March 1935 pointed out that the Royal Navy could not guarantee Australian security. Australia would have to develop her own defence under her own control. Lieutenant-Colonel Wynter was now the Director of Military Training at Army Headquarters and at a meeting of the United Services Institution in Melbourne in August 1935 he revived the arguments that he had put forward nine years earlier: Australia would only be attacked when Britain was occupied elsewhere and therefore Australia should rely on her own resources.[7]

In October 1934 Sir Archdale Parkhill had become Minister for Defence. Although he lacked the experience and technical knowledge to formulate an adequate defence policy, Parkhill pursued his task with enthusiasm, relying on advisers such as Sir Maurice Hankey. Nevertheless the army's arguments gained a significant boost with the replacement of the 62-year-old CGS by the 49-year-old John Lavarack. The appointment of Lavarack on 21 April 1935 to the top position in the Australian Army, to which all ambitious regular officers aspired, was a radical step, for not only did he disagree with Parkhill over the Singapore strategy but he was promoted over the heads of five permanent officers.[8] Indeed when in June 1935 Lavarack was promoted to substantive major-general he superseded the other two members of the Military Board, Major-General Sir Carl Jess, the

Adjutant-General, and Major-General O. F. Phillips, the Quartermaster-General.

Yet Lavarack was a man of considerable achievement. Brilliant, charming and unpredictable, he was a highly trained and most capable officer, and had been a lieutenant-colonel during World War I as GSO1 of the 4th Australian Division. It was not, however, until his appointment to CGS that he had become a substantive colonel. General Rowell has noted that whilst Lavarack had a fine brain, wrote brilliantly and spoke convincingly:

> He did not possess the most equable of temperaments and could be a difficult master. But at other times he was a delightful character with a wide range of interests. Nevertheless, I am glad that I did not play either bridge or golf with him. If there was a fault in Lavarack's military philosophy it was the idea that the CMF was the medium by which the Regular officer was trained rather than the reverse, that is that the Regular officer existed to serve the CMF.[9]

Lavarack knew that he had a violent temper and attempted to control it, but it sometimes got the better of him and this resulted in some unwise actions. Moreover, he was always imagining affronts, although he rarely bore malice.[10]

The four years of Lavarack's tenure as CGS leading up to World War II did not prove to be an easy time. Not only did he disagree with government policy but he was bedevilled by Parkhill's interference in military affairs. It will be recalled that Colonel Wynter had spoken against Hankey's recommendations, and at the request of Parkhill, Wynter had sent him a copy of the lecture. Senator H. C. Brand also asked for a copy and later he distributed copies to other parliamentarians including the Leader of the Opposition, John Curtin. Later Curtin used the paper to attack Parkhill in the House and Parkhill reacted by having Wynter removed and posted to an inferior appointment. Although the Military Board did not concur with this decision, nor recommend any disciplinary action against Wynter, it could not amend or alter the minister's decision.[11] Wynter's request for a court martial could not be granted.

When another highly qualified and experienced officer, Lieutenant-Colonel L. E. Beavis, was moved to a junior posting after expressing views unacceptable to the government, resentment against the government began to be felt amongst regular officers.[12] The feeling was worsened by the belief that some very senior officers had not supported their more junior colleagues. The senior army officers were in a difficult position, and General Rowell has written that 'there were some curious cross-currents at Army Headquarters in those days: great enthusiasm and drive on the lower levels, but some reaction to progress and reform on the higher'.[13]

The development of army policy and training was also hindered by the severe under-manning of the regular staff. In December 1935 Sir Archdale Parkhill stated in the House of Representatives that 'There are 52 officers of the Australian Staff Corps who are carrying out higher duties than is commensurate with their rank. Rates of pay are dependent on substantive rank held'.[14]

General Squires, the Inspector-General of the Army, in his report to the government in December 1938, found that the health of a number of officers had been affected by overwork and mental anxiety:

I cannot speak too highly of the keenness, devotion, and efficiency with which the majority of the Staff Corps officers carry out their duties. But the present conditions of service are such that not only do they fail to attract in sufficient numbers, candidates of the type that is needed, but owing to the slowness of advancement under the present system, they have created among the officers now serving — and particularly among those who are now approaching the higher ranks — a feeling of despondency which cannot but be detrimental to the best interests of the service.[15]

Not only had the regular officers of the Staff Corps been required to forfeit one day's pay per week during the Depression, but they had also suffered in comparison with the officers of the militia.

It is true that the militia officers had shared the hardships of the lean years. It had needed a real enthusiasm or a firm belief in the likelihood of another war for the militia officers to strive to maintain the militia. Units lacked arms, tanks and anti-aircraft guns and seldom had sufficient soldiers to allow their commanders to develop their powers of leadership and command. But the permanent officers who administered these units required a similar dedication, for the defence cuts of 1923 thwarted their hopes of early promotion after World War I, whilst their opposite numbers in the militia not only kept their war-time ranks, which the permanent officers generally did not, but continued to be rapidly promoted.

Gavin Long quotes the case of G. Vasey, who graduated from Duntroon in 1915 and had been a major in the AIF on the Western Front from September 1917, but was promoted to the rank of substantive captain on 1 March 1923. On 31 March 1923 K. W. Eather was commissioned as a lieutenant in the 53rd Infantry Battalion (Sydney militia) at the age of 21. On 1 July 1935 he reached the rank of lieutenant-colonel commanding the 56th Battalion. Vasey was promoted to substantive lieutenant-colonel only after the outbreak of World War II.[16] Another example of the apparent inequalities of the system and the resultant injustices to the Staff Corps officers was the case of C. E. Prior, who graduated from Duntroon on 23 April 1916, fought on the Western Front, and at the end of 1918 was Adjutant of the 3rd MG Battalion. At the outbreak of World War II he was Brigade Major of the 3rd Infantry Brigade which was commanded by Brigadier A. R. Allen. Allen had fought on the Western Front and had been promoted to substantive captain in April 1924. Fifteen years later he was a brigadier while Prior was only a major. The latter was, however, a brigadier by early 1941, as was Vasey.[17] In his report of 1927 General Sir Harry Chauvel found that 'disparity of opportunity and stagnation in promotion, with retention in subordinate positions, cannot lead to the maintenance of the active, virile and efficient staff that the service demands'.[18]

The disparities between the Staff Corps Officers and the militia officers sometimes led to bitterness and suspicion. Some militia officers criticised publicly the ability of the permanent officers, but when officers such as Brigadier S. G. Savige, commanding the 10th Infantry Brigade, declared that all new Duntroon officers should command platoons, he overlooked the fact that there were simply no platoons to command except in the militia.[19] In a similar vein Major-General Gordon Bennett wrote: 'Experience has proved that citizen soldiers can handle our citizen army more efficiently than permanent officers. Our permanent officers are trained as staff officers and not as active soldiers'.[20] This statement was not strictly true, and aroused the ire of permanent soldiers like the fiery Major H. C. H. Robertson, who during World War I had commanded a Light Horse Regiment in battle. The jealousy of the permanent officers was matched only by the suspicion of the citizen soldiers and although these disagreements were not present at every level and in every unit, they existed in pockets and amongst the higher ranks.[21] This discontent was, of course, only a reflection of the parsimony and lack of understanding of a series of governments between the wars.

The tensions within the higher echelons of the army were exacerbated when, after Germany's seizure of Austria in 1938, the Prime Minister, J. A. Lyons, announced the appointment of a British officer, Major-General E. K. Squires, as Inspector-General of the Army. Considering the government's appointment of Lavarack three years earlier, the selection of a British officer came as a considerable shock, particularly to the CGS. John Hetherington concluded that:

They did not question his military sagacity or doubt that, technically, he was probably the best soldier in Australia, but some ministers had begun to suspect soon after he became CGS that his reports were framed to tell them less what they should know than what he believed they would like to know . . . The appointment of a British officer to this key post was freely criticised then and later; what the critics did not know was that the Government was trying to solve a difficult situation while at the same time sparing Lavarack's *amour-propre* as much as possible.[22]

This serious charge is not supported by any evidence and since Lavarack disagreed with government policy perhaps he had been guilty of telling the ministers too much of what they did not wish to hear. General Rowell claims, however, that Squires was invited to Australia because of a clash of personality between Lavarack and Sir Carl Jess, the Adjutant-General.[23]

Another point of view is worth considering. Lavarack had expressed views similar to those of Wynter, namely that it was wrong to rely upon Singapore for the defence of Australia since there was no guarantee that a fleet would be stationed there, and Australia should, therefore, concentrate on developing her ability to resist a large-scale attack on her shores.[24] This was a view which was closer to that of the Labor Party than to that of the government. It does appear that Lavarack was frightened by the Wynter affair, and other senior officers resented what they thought was the abandonment of Wynter. The result was that Lavarack began to feel that the other officers were against him, and this irritated his already prickly personality and made it more difficult to work with him.

There was perhaps another side to Squires's appointment, which was the result of vigorous reforms by the new Minister of Defence, Brigadier G. A. Street MC.[25] At the time of Lavarack's appointment there were no graduates of Duntroon with sufficient experience to be promoted to the position of Inspector-General or CGS. Australia was still suffering from the long-term effects of her limited pre-World War I army, and there were now few officers available with the necessary qualifications for senior appointments. Most of the officers who had held senior positions in the AIF had either retired or were in the militia. Despite this, the appointment of Squires revealed a continuing dependence on Britain and the maintenance of the Imperial connection. Of the three services, only the army had challenged the validity of the reliance upon Singapore and the consequent heavy expenditure on the navy to the detriment of the other services. Now, with the appointment of a British officer to the most senior position in the Australian Army, this opposition viewpoint was further stifled. This view is supported by J. J. Dedman, a Labor Government minister during the war, who has claimed that he had information from top ranking service officers that Squires would have 'gone along with' government policy.[26]

Whilst Street instituted measures to increase the militia, he ordered Squires to investigate the needs of the army and to prepare a series of reports. The first of these was submitted at the end of 1938 and was presented to Parliament in an expurgated form in March 1939. Despite Dedman's claims that Squires would go along with government policy, the report confirmed the army's 'equipment first' policy and measures to defend vital areas, and also recommended the formation of two regular brigades with an establishment of 7,500 men. These troops would assist the militia with training, and would be available immediately at the outbreak of war. Furthermore they would afford the officers of the Staff Corps much needed opportunities for gaining experience in the command of troops. The government accepted the report, which included recommendations to improve the size and efficiency of the militia, and decided, as the first step, to raise a permanent force of 1,571 troops during 1939 and 1940. At that time the establishment of the regular army was 3,572.

The most important aspect of the report concerned the organisation of the army, for at that time the six military districts, six militia divisions and various independent brigades were all commanded directly from Army Headquarters in Melbourne.[27] Squires proposed to reorganise the army into four commands based in Brisbane, Sydney, Melbourne and Perth, with an independent garrison at Darwin. The commands, named Northern, Eastern, Southern and Western, would be responsible for all units in their areas, with the exception of some training establishments. Southern Command would include South Australia and Tasmania. As this change required an amendment to the Defence Act, it could not be implemented until October 1939. Squires also made recommendations concerning the conditions of service for permanent officers. He lowered the retirement ages for officers, made promotion above the rank of major by selection rather than seniority, ensured that officers held the rank required for their posting, and made recommendations on pensions. Unfortunately most of these proposals came too late for the vacillating government to institute them before the outbreak of war.[28]

The respite of a little over two years, from the time when the Prime Minister, R. G. Menzies, declared Australia at war with such alacrity that Parliament was not consulted, until the time when Australia's shores were threatened, was critical for the successful defence of the country. Although during this period Australian troops fought in five bitter campaigns, for the people at home it was 'business as usual'. The 'phoney war' in Western Europe was broken by the German invasion of France and Holland in May 1940: in Australia the 'phoney war' lasted until Japan's attacks on Pearl Harbour, Malaya and the Philippines catapulted the Australian homeland into total war.

There is little value in speculating what would have happened if Japan had entered the conflict in September 1939, but it is indisputable that at that time Australia was not, in any way, prepared for war. The years of 1940 and 1941 were therefore a period of preparation, albeit fitful, for the Australian munition industries and defence forces. In 1939, faced with the prospect of a European war, few senior politicians were clear how the country could contribute to the Allied war effort. Plans were, however, in hand for the reorganisation of the defence machinery, and on 15 September 1939 the Australian War Cabinet was established.

With the Prime Minister as chairman, and including senior members of the government, War Cabinet became the controlling body for the higher direction of the war. It was, in effect, an executive subcommittee of the Cabinet in matters relating to the active conduct of the war. The secretary was F. G. Shedden, aged 46, who had been Secretary of the Defence Department since 1937. He had joined the department in 1910 and had been a student at the Imperial Defence College.[29] A later Chairman of the Chiefs of Staff Committee, Lieutenant-General Sir Sydney Rowell, has written that Shedden 'had an unrivalled knowledge of matters associated with Commonwealth defence and he was a tireless and meticulously accurate worker'.[30] The War Cabinet secretariat was controlled by Shedden, who was supported by five assistant secretaries responsible for Civil, Navy, Army, Air and War Book Coordination matters.[31]

The War Cabinet did not incorporate service representatives, although these could be called upon when required. Two defence bodies, however, did provide advice to the War Cabinet. The Chiefs of Staff Committee, which was created on 4 September 1939, consisted of the chiefs of staff of the three services, and it gave advice in regard to operational matters and strategic appreciations. A larger body, the Defence Committee, which included the chiefs of staff and officers of the secretariat of the Department of Defence, and on occasions the Controller-General of Munitions, the Controller of Civil Aviation, and the chairman of the Principal Supply Officers' Committee, gave advice on defence policy as a whole. In October 1940, as a gesture to the opposition, another body was constituted to offer advice to the War Cabinet. This was the Advisory War Council, which included members of all the parliamentary parties. The party system continued to function as in peace-time, but the Council gave increased stability to the government and enabled Parliament to function more smoothly, and as in the case of the War Cabinet, the Prime Minister was chairman and Shedden was secretary.

At the outbreak of war the Department of Defence Coordination was established to control the newly formed departments of Navy, Army, Air and Supply and Development. The Prime Minister became the Minister of Defence Coordination and Shedden became the Permanent Head of the Department. This system of controlling the national war effort continued throughout the war under the various Prime Ministers — Menzies, Fadden, Curtin and Chifley. Paul Hasluck has explained how the various groups worked together:

The Department of Defence Coordination (and, after April 1942, the Department of Defence) was in fact the central and, in some respects, the supreme component of the machinery for the higher direction of the war because, throughout the war, the Prime Minister himself held the portfolio of Defence Coordination or of Defence; the department was the Secretariat of War Cabinet and all business flowing to and from War Cabinet passed through it; and its organisation embraced the Defence Committee and the Chiefs of Staff Committee, for both of which it provided the secretariat, as well as being represented on the Defence Committee. [32]

Since 1904, control of the military forces of the Commonwealth had been exercised by the Military Board. This consisted of the Chief of the General Staff (CGS), [33] who was responsible for operations and training, the Quartermaster-General, who was responsible for supply within the army, the Master-General of the Ordnance, who was responsible for procuring arms and equipment, the Adjutant-General, who was responsible for personnel matters, the Finance Member, who was a civilian from the public service, and the President of the Board. The latter was the Minister of Defence or Army and, as a rule, did not attend meetings, and in his absence the Chief of the General Staff acted as chairman. It can be seen, therefore, that although the CGS was responsible for advising the minister or the War Cabinet on the general conduct of military operations, including strategic policy and, as Chairman of the Military Board, for advising the minister on matters of military policy affecting the security of the Commonwealth,[34] in no sense was he a commander-in-chief. The supreme authority was, after all, the Military Board.

It was to the Military Board that the government now looked for advice on the organisation and development of the army. Since May, Lavarack had been on an inspection tour in Britain and Europe. The second member was the Adjutant-General Sir Carl Jess, aged 55, who had commanded a brigade in France and had occupied his position since December 1934. The two positions of Quartermaster-General and Master-General of the Ordnance had been amalgamated, and were filled by Major-General O. F. Phillips.[35] Aged 57, he had commanded the artillery of the 2nd Australian Division at the end of World War I. The Finance member was J. T. Fitzgerald. Although the Inspector-General was not usually a member of the board, in May he had been gazetted as acting CGS in Lavarack's absence.

The Commonwealth War Book had laid down the measures to be taken at the outbreak of war, and on 5 September the militia was called out for war service in successive drafts of 10,000 to serve for sixteen days continuous training, and to provide guards on 'vulnerable points'. Much work had already been done on war plans, and included in the War Book was 'Plan 401', which was a scheme to prepare an expeditionary force for service overseas.[36] The government, however, had considerable difficulty determining the size and shape of Australia's contribution to the war, for as well as domestic considerations there was the uncertainty of Japanese intentions. On 8 September 1939 the British Government summed up the dilemma in a cable to the Australian Government, stating that if Japan 'adopted an attitude of reserve towards the democratic countries' it would be unwise for Australia to send an expeditionary force to Europe, but if Japan was friendly then Australia could send brigades to Singapore, Burma and India as they became available, or wait until complete divisions could be sent to the main theatre.[37] Japan followed this by declaring that she would remain 'independent' and eventually, after some discussion and a decision by New Zealand, on 15 September the Prime Minister announced that 20,000 men would be enlisted for service at home or abroad, 'as circumstances permit'.[38] This force was to be known as the Second Australian Imperial Force (2nd AIF).

One problem that had to be faced by the new War Cabinet was the selection of an officer to command the new volunteer division (6th Division AIF). There were seven substantive major-generals on the army's active list. The most senior was H. Gordon Bennett, aged 52, a militia officer who had commanded a brigade in France in World War I. Although a man of considerable leadership ability, he had not commanded a division for seven years, and had occupied his time since then sniping at the Staff Corps, the Military Board and the government. The second most senior officer, Major-General Sir Thomas Blamey, aged 55, had been Monash's Chief of Staff in 1918, the Victorian Police Commissioner from 1925 to 1936, and since 1938 had been the Chairman of the Manpower Committee as well as Controller General of Recruiting. He had, however, relinquished command of the 3rd Division (militia) in 1937, and had been on the unattached list since then.

Lavarack, who was third in seniority, had high claims to the position. Two years younger than Blamey, he had remained in the army when Blamey had chosen to leave. The next senior was Jess, followed by Phillips. Sixth was Judge E. A. Drake-Brockman, a militia officer of 55 and on the bench of the Commonwealth Arbitration Court. He had commanded a brigade at the end of World War I, but was now not completely fit. Seventh was I. G. Mackay, 57, the headmaster of Cranbrook School and a militia officer who had also commanded a brigade in France.

Nevertheless there was never really much discussion about the selection of a commander for the 6th Division. Menzies, supported by R. G. Casey and Sir Henry Gullett, was convinced that Blamey was the most suitable candidate.[39] The selection had been facilitated when the Secretary of the Department of Defence, Frederick Shedden, had secured Blamey the position with the Manpower Committee in the previous year, thereby rescuing him from the obscurity of semi-retirement and once again familiarising him with the workings of the Defence Department.

Blamey had proved his ability as a staff officer under Monash, but had commanded a battalion for only three weeks and a brigade for six weeks. He had a temper, but unlike Lavarack always kept himself under control. Although he was a domineering man who did not suffer fools gladly, he remained loyal to lesser men such as those who had stood by him after he had resigned from the Victorian Police. The previous Prime Minister, Joseph Lyons, who felt that Blamey lacked the moral qualities to lead Australia's soldiers in battle, had to agree after meeting him that 'He's really somebody'.[40] Major-General L. E. Beavis, who was Blamey's chief ordnance officer throughout the war, has written:

I had the greatest admiration and respect for him as a commander. He had his shortcomings, such as aspects of his personality which affected some of the personal clashes in which he became involved, evidenced in a degree of ruthlessness when he felt sure he was right.[41]

Gavin Long noted that:

He had a mind which comprehended the largest military and politico-military problems with singular clarity, and by experience and temperament was well-equipped to cope with the special difficulties which face the commander of a national contingent which is part of a coalition army in a foreign theatre of war.[42]

Yet he was out of touch with recent developments in military technology and it was unlikely that he would have the time to regain this expertise. He was more suited to command the 2nd AIF as a whole than to a field command. He was rarely able to inspire loyalty and trust amongst the soldiers. He enjoyed life to the full in the manner which soldiers understood, but which they did not expect of their commanders. Sensitive to criticism, relentless in pursuit of personal enemies, perhaps his greatest failing was his lack of understanding of the importance of public relations; in short, he lacked tact. Amongst some Staff Corps officers there was an enmity towards Blamey which, in some cases, for example with Lavarack, dated back to World War I.[43] Others felt that Blamey's performance as Police Commissioner had let down the Staff Corps. The selection of Blamey came, therefore, as a savage blow to the Staff Corps, and when it was reported that Menzies had 'announced (*without reference to anybody*) that the commands in the division would go to militia men',[44] the bitterness within the Staff Corps became intense. Indeed Gavin Long believed that Menzies's statement had the effect of making 'the corps more firmly resolved than ever to defend its interests — in fact to make it to a greater degree a compact and defensive group within the army as a whole'.[45] Early manifestations of these feelings were the obstructions placed in the way of the new staff of the 6th Division by Lavarack who had been replaced by Squires as CGS and was now GOC Southern Command.

The brigadiers for the 6th Division were chosen from the militia, which remarkably contained only four brigadiers who were substantive colonels — J. L. G. Johnstone, aged 58, F. P. Derham, 54, L. J. Morshead, 50, and A. S. Allen, 45. The two youngest were chosen. The third to be chosen was Blamey's friend, S. G. Savige, who had stood by him in his difficult days after he left the Victorian Police, and Colonel E. F. Herring of the 3rd Division became the Artillery Commander (CRA). The reason for this last selection is not quite so clear cut for at least two militia CRAs were younger and one other was the same age, that is, 47.[46] Herring had known Menzies for twenty years, but there is no evidence that this was the deciding factor. He was, however, a prominent barrister, had been a Rhodes Scholar, and had been awarded a DSO and MC during World War I. His militia record had been first class. The two senior staff postings went to Staff Corps officers. Lieutenant-Colonel S. F. Rowell, who until recently had been the staff officer to General Squires, was promoted to the appointment of Chief Operations Officer (GSO1) of the division, and Lieutenant-Colonel G. A. Vasey, who had been GSO1 (Training) at AHQ, became the Chief Administrative officer (AA & QMG).

Whilst implementing these changes the War Cabinet also took the opportunity of carrying out the reorganisation recommended by Squires. The details of the changes are outlined in Appendix 3, but the important appointments were those of Squires to CGS, Lavarack to Southern Command and Sturdee to Eastern Command, all as lieutenant-generals. It was clear that as the army expanded there would have to be more senior officers and that with the increased pressure of work some of the incumbent officers would prove to be too old. Consequently by the end of October 1939 there were four new major-generals at AHQ and three other newly appointed generals. Lavarack's dissatisfaction at being removed from a position which he had held for over four years can well be imagined. Furthermore, it confirmed again the reliance placed by the government on the United Kingdom for advice on defence policy. By early 1940 all three chiefs of staff were officers seconded from the United Kingdom.[47]

During the two years and two months from the outbreak of war to the entry of Japan, the Australian Army underwent a considerable transformation. By the end of 1940 the AIF had expanded to four infantry divisions, with the 1st Armoured Division yet to be formed. The 6th Division was commanded by Major-General I. G. Mackay, and Lavarack stepped down to command the 7th. After the death of Squires in March 1940 General Sir Brudenell White was recalled from retirement to become CGS. Then, in August 1940 when White was killed in an aircrash along with three government ministers, Sturdee became CGS. Sturdee had been the commander of the 8th Division and now Bennett received the command.[48] One significant aspect of White's tenure as CGS was his determination to ensure that Staff Corps Officers received commands during the war. After being 'banished to the wilderness' by Parkhill, General Wynter had returned to command the Command and Staff School and then Northern Command. By October 1940 he was GOC of the 9th Division but in

February 1941 he was forced to relinquish his command through illness and Brigadier Morshead was promoted to replace him.

Throughout 1941 the troops of the AIF distinguished themselves in campaigns in Libya, Greece, Crete, Syria and Tobruk. Their contribution to the war in the Middle East was decisive and their training for the future war in the Far East was invaluable. But the AIF remained an organisation completely separate from the remainder of the army, and Blamey, the Commander of the AIF in the Middle East, was responsible directly to the Minister for the Army in operational matters. Not only was the AIF removed from the operational control of the Military Board, but it had its own seniority list, its own establishment, and its own *esprit de corps*. The army, which had previously been divided between citizen and permanent soldier, now became split between the volunteers and the militia; or as the AIF called them, the 'chocos' (chocolate soldiers).[49]

The AIF also had its own problems, and in the Middle East Blamey experienced the difficulties of co-operating with a more powerful ally. For a while the Australians provided the majority of the fighting troops in the Middle East, yet despite Blamey's appointment to Deputy Commander-in-Chief in the theatre, he had little say in the control of operations. For the Australian commanders the experience was invaluable, but although the successive Menzies, Fadden and Curtin Governments took a firm line, at Blamey's behest, over the relief of Tobruk, the politicians did not grasp fully the importance of obtaining a role in military decision-making. By late 1942 these same difficulties had recurred and then the government supported an American rather than their own military leader.

Thus Australia threw her forces into the campaigns beyond the seas. The raising of these forces had placed the army under considerable strain and had demanded the services of the more active commanders and the attention of the staff officers at home. The question remained: how much had this effort detracted from the preparations for the defence of Australia?

2
Planning for the Defence of the Homeland, June 1940–7 December 1941

Whilst the commanders and men of the 2nd AIF were gaining valuable experience overseas and were helping to hold the forces of the Axis at bay, the military leaders in Australia were faced with mounting problems.

The foremost military position in Australia, the mantle of Sir Brudenell White, had now fallen on the shoulders of the 50-year-old Vernon Sturdee, who a year earlier had been a Colonel and Director of Staff Duties at AHQ. In October 1939 he had been promoted from colonel to lieutenant-general to command Eastern Command, but he had stepped down a rank to raise and command the 8th Division. He had not held this position for two months before White had been killed. By training and experience he was well suited for the position of CGS. Sturdee had joined the Australian Engineers in 1908 as a sapper, and by 1914 he was the adjutant of the 1st Divisional Engineers. For most of 1917 he commanded the 4th Pioneer Battalion as a lieutenant-colonel. Then after four months as CRE of the 5th Division, he joined Field Marshal Haig's staff until the end of the war. This gave him a broad view of the BEF and gave him experience which was to help him when in later years he had to co-operate with British and American forces. During World War I the British Army provided the logistic support for the Australian units. Consequently few Australians were in positions to grasp the problem of logistics. Yet during World War II Australian forces became responsible for their own administration. For this reason, General Berryman felt that the choice of a commander for the 2nd AIF rested between only three officers, Blamey, Lavarack and Sturdee.

Between the wars Sturdee had attended the Staff College at Quetta and the Imperial Staff College, and he served for a number of years in England. From 1933 to the outbreak of war he was DMO & I and then

DSD at AHQ. General Rowell, who served with Sturdee for part of this time, wrote later:

> To those of us working with him then, Sturdee displayed those characteristics which he retained all his life. He had a very precise mind — he had a great sense of the need for priorities — he saw the problem very clearly — he was able to give orders which left no doubt as to what was wanted and he then left people to get on with the job. When it came to the answer he was kindly and constructive in criticism. But he didn't suffer fools gladly and told them so, while, at the same time, he was unerring in picking out the one who was dragging his feet and who needed encouragement or something stronger. But above all, he knew how to laugh, and thus was a great help to people who . . . were asked to work beyond the normal.[1]

General Wilton, who served under Sturdee later in the war, found him to be able, balanced, courteous and fair. He never lost his temper.[2] General Hopkins found him to be 'quite unflappable',[3] yet others were never greatly impressed by him as a commander. His forte seemed to be as a first rate staff officer.

While Sturdee had been DMO & I at AHQ, he had been vitally concerned with the development of the Plan of Concentration for the defence of Australia. This plan will be described shortly, but Sturdee had quite early discerned that Japan would pose the major threat to Australian security. In 1933 he told senior officers that the Japanese would act quickly, 'they would all be regulars, fully trained and equipped for the operations, and fanatics who like dying in battle, whilst our troops would consist mainly of civilians hastily thrown together on mobilisation with very little training, short of artillery and possibly of gun ammunition'.[4] Sturdee was soon to be faced with the responsibility of handling such a situation.

Meanwhile the militia organisation of four infantry divisions and the nucleus of a fifth, with two cavalry divisions, remained. In June 1940 it was decided to raise the Home Army to 250,000, although the full-time strength was to be increased to only 22,000. The remainder were to be trained by raising units for three months and then disbanding them. It was a fragmentary and unsatisfactory system. Gavin Long pointed out:

> Thus the Government's desire to maintain a force in a main theatre of war and yet retain a home army for defence against Japan, combined with the objection to conscription for overseas service and the fact that such a large number of volunteers had enlisted, had led to the establishment of an army of

twelve divisions, five fully-maintained and seven for the present partly-maintained. Before the war the army staff had contended that Australia could not support more than seven or eight divisions at full strength in active operations, and events were to prove them right.[5]

The problems of dividing the military effort between the requirements of the Middle East and the defence of Australia provided considerable difficulties for military leaders in Australia. For the past ten years Australian defence had hinged on the security of Singapore. Japan had been perceived as a threat, but while Singapore was held it was believed that Australia would be safe.

It is now generally agreed that the Australian defence policy between the wars and until the fall of Singapore was at the best, naively optimistic, and at the worst, some might say, close to treason.[6] The outcome was that with the bulk of her well-trained forces occupied overseas Australia was faced with the real prospect of the invasion of her shores. But although this prospect had seemed highly unlikely when the AIF had been despatched to the Middle East Australian military leaders, with perhaps more responsibility than their political counterparts, had for some years been considering plans for the continental defence of Australia.[7]

In early 1931, in the midst of the Labor Government's cut-backs in defence spending, officers at Army Headquarters had noted the possibility of an attack by Japan: 'It may be assumed [they concluded] that Japan will make war only when she is reasonably certain of comparatively minor opposition at sea for a time long enough to enable her to establish command in the Western Pacific'.[8] They saw the possibility that Japan might either raid or carry out a 'definite invasion', of Australia. The likely objectives were Sydney, Newcastle, Darwin, Fremantle and Albany. The strength of the attack would be about three divisions and the main objective would be the Sydney area.

It is interesting to note the manner in which Army Headquarters planned to defend Australia. It was assumed that the Japanese would attack Newcastle and Sydney and that the Australian forces would have time to concentrate to meet this threat. In these circumstances the invasion would be met by an Australian Army commanded by a General Headquarters and consisting of two corps, each of two infantry, plus two independent cavalry divisions and corps troops. I Corps and the 1st Cavalry Division would be responsible for the defence of Newcastle, II Corps and the 2nd Cavalry Division would be responsible for the defence of Sydney, and a mixed brigade with a light horse regiment would be assigned to each of Brisbane, Melbourne, Tasmania and Fremantle.[9]

Two faults are immediately apparent in this plan. Firstly, none of the troops were regular soldiers and there would have to be a long warning period to enable the divisions to be mobilised, equipped and trained. Secondly, it assumed that the enemy would attack Sydney. There seemed no way in which an enemy could be prevented from seizing Perth, Darwin or Townsville. Furthermore one is left with the impression that the magnitude of the threat was selected to correspond with the Australian order of battle as it then existed. In 1931 the problem was hypothetical. Ten years later it was not, and with the majority of the trained soldiers and their equipment deployed overseas, the state of the militia was not substantially improved on that of 1931.

In March 1940 there were 4,000 permanent soldiers, 3,000 militia permanently called up and 5,000 in garrison units. The militia numbered 62,300. Half had done three months training and the second half were about to begin; after that they were to revert to the pre-war system — that is a 12-day camp plus home training. With 20,000 national servicemen also being trained, the defence of Australia rested on about 75,000 men.[10]

When the fall of France foreshadowed a growing aggressiveness on the part of Japan, Australian and British authorities became concerned. On 16 June 1940 it was decided to raise a larger home defence force with the aim of reaching 250,000 men, 30-40,000 of whom would, at any time, be AIF in training in Australia. Initially there would be a call up of 40,000 men for 18 days and then two successive groups for three months. The crucial factors in training these men would be the lack of facilities and equipment.

On 28 June 1940 the United Kingdom Government asked if the Australian Government could provide a division for the defence of Singapore, pointing out that:

. . . we can no longer concentrate upon the defence of Singapore Island entirely, but must consider the defence of Malaya as a whole, particularly the security of up-country landing grounds. For this reason, and because we cannot spare a fleet for the Far East at present, it is all the more important that we should do what we can to improve our land and air defences in Malaya.[11]

At a time when Australia had only one division (6th) in the Middle East and with the others not yet trained or equipped, this proposal was resisted, but it should have served as a warning to the Menzies Government. J. J. Dedman has noted that: 'The whole issue of the relative importance of home defence, now aligned with the holding of Singapore as against assisting the United Kingdom to retain control of Egypt and the Suez Canal were here brought to a head'.[12]

When in August 1940 the UK Government requested the despatch of troops to Singapore 'in view of the urgency of the problem', the Australian Chiefs of Staff became alarmed and even began to consider the possibility of a medium-scale attack or an invasion. Cabinet was still not convinced.[13] Finally, however, after the elections in October 1940, Menzies decided to journey to London to press the case for the reinforcement of Malaya. In addition it was decided to send a brigade group to Singapore, although it was only to be stationed there temporarily before concentrating in the Middle East. The government continued to rely on Singapore. Plans were to be made to resist raids and landings, but not an invasion.[14]

Despite the government's reliance on Singapore, military authorities in Australia continued preparing a plan for the defence of the continent. 'Such a plan', the military planning staff noted. in April 1940, 'therefore does not purport to raise questions of major policy, and it is consequently assumed that little or no expenditure can be incurred to implement it'.[15] The commanders of each command were responsible for the field troops within their areas and also for the defence of their areas. It should be remembered that the majority of their soldiers were the part-time soldiers of the militia. Of the militia permanently called up, many were in coastal defence units, and others were in garrison battalions. An appreciation by the intelligence staff of Eastern Command noted, in December 1940, that the garrison battalions included men who, although returned soldiers, were likely to prove of very poor fighting quality. 'There are some very fine soldiers amongst them, but also many of the type who in civil life could be described as unemployable'.[16]

As in 1931, it was still considered that if the Japanese attacked Australia they would go for a 'knock-out blow' and would attack the Newcastle-Sydney-Port Kembla area.[17] Consequently two infantry divisions and one cavalry division were located near Sydney, and the bulk of two infantry divisions and one cavalry division were located near Melbourne.[18] There were two infantry brigades and one cavalry brigade in Queensland, but there were few troops in the other states. Of course since these were militia units they had to be located near the main centres of population. In all, the home forces consisted of two cavalry and four infantry divisions. There were various independent brigades which could form a fifth division, and there were corps troops, garrison battalions and coastal defences.

These forces sound impressive, but as recruiting for the AIF continued they became less so. They lacked equipment and training and their best men left for the AIF. There was no co-ordinated plan for the defence of Australia. General Jackson of Northern Command, which at that time included New Guinea, described the situation:

No plans for the defence of Northern Command were in existence when I took over command in May 1940. Approximately half of the troops to be raised in Queensland were to leave the State, and proceed to New South Wales, in the event of invasion of Australia in accordance with long standing plans. [Presumably he meant plans similar to the 1931 plan.] The main activity in the command was the raising and reinforcing of the Australian Imperial Force.
Up to the end of 1940 Government Policy did not permit of consideration by the military authority of defence against raids. Authority was then given to consider defence against invasion without increase of forces. In November 1940, General Sir Brudenell White, then Chief of the General Staff, impressed on me while down in Melbourne, that in the event of anything happening in this country of ours, I was the fighting commander of the north. I proceeded on those lines but unfortunately for Australia, Sir Brudenell was killed shortly afterwards, and complacency ruled in his stead.[19]

The latter comment was unfair to Sturdee, the new CGS, and was probably the result of a long-standing feud between Jackson and Sturdee. But the problem of the continental defence of Australia does not appear to have been discussed by the government until early 1941.

During February 1941 the Australian Chiefs of Staff produced a Far Eastern Appreciation which was based on one produced by the UK Chiefs of Staff. This was to meet the threat imposed if Japan entered the war. The Chiefs of Staff concluded that it was unlikely that Japan would undertake an invasion of Australia until they had secured Malaya and the Netherlands East Indies and had, in some way, dealt with 'the possibility of American intervention from Hawaii'. This appreciation led to the opinion that it was necessary to reinforce Malaya and strengthen the Netherlands East Indies.[20]

Yet only the AIF could be used to reinforce Malaya as the AMF could not be sent out of Australian territory. It was not possible to increase the AIF as there was insufficient equipment for further units. The 22nd Brigade Group of the 8th Division, which in February 1941 was arriving in Malaya, was not yet fully equipped. Eventually it was decided not to send the 8th Division to the Middle East but to retain it for the defence of Australia with one battalion being sent to Rabaul to secure forward airfields. Other forces were held in readiness to go to Timor and Ambon.[21]

These matters were discussed at a meeting of the War Cabinet in Sydney on 14 February 1941. Sir Robert Brooke-Popham, the British C-in-C in the Far East, was present and he stated that he was not pressing for the rest of the 8th Division to be despatched to Singapore. He told the meeting that he thought that Singapore could defend itself for six months until a fleet arrived to protect it. It has now been revealed that Brooke-Popham had private doubts about the security of Singapore and apparently he gave the Australian Government 'a less than comprehensive survey of his view of the situation'.[22] General Sturdee stated that there was no need to increase the AIF for local defence as such action might have the effect of delaying the production of equipment. The 7th and 8th Divisions of the AIF were at that time not fully equipped. If the AMF in Australia were called up for service it would not be possible to equip both the AMF and the AIF remaining in Australia.[23]

Nevertheless, soon after the meeting AHQ issued an instruction that there was now a possibility of war with Japan. As a consequence,

The military forces in Australia will be disposed to provide a greater degree of preparedness in relation to defence requirements.
AIF units in Australia, less those for overseas, will be used for operational roles.
Approximately half the AMF at a time will be maintained in camps of continuous training. All camps will be of 90 days duration, those at present current being extended from 70 to 90 days.

Coastal defences and existing AA armaments were to be manned continuously to War Establishment plus 20 per cent and deficiencies were to be rectified by calling up additional troops. The 49th Battalion was to be raised for service at Port Moresby.[24]

Therefore the local defence of mainland Australia remained substantially in the hands of the part-time soldiers of the AMF. It is clear that the defence chiefs did not envisage the rapid Japanese successes between December 1941 and February 1942, and they assumed that when Japan decided to attack there would be many months for the militia to mobilise.

Twelve months before the surrender of Singapore, Australia's pre-war defence policy of relying upon a British fleet stationed at Singapore had been revealed as being totally inadequate. Yet short of putting it in these terms Menzies could not rouse the population to the seriousness of the position. Since he had, in Disraeli's words, 'climbed to the top of the slippery pole', and had become Prime Minister in 1939, Menzies had been faced with a multitude of problems. The Country Party had refused to join his UAP Government in a coalition, but the greatest problem was that imposed by the circumstances of the 'phoney war'. J. J. Dedman sympathised with his political opponent:

Perhaps [Menzies] use of the phrase 'business as usual' on one occasion was unfortunate but the fact is that the people were not then ready to submit to that high degree of direction by the government which is a *sine qua non* of an all-in war effort. Only under a dictatorship could the tempo of the war effort have been greatly accelerated at that time. No leader in a democracy can pursue a policy very far in advance of public opinion; if he does he will soon be displaced and in Australia an election was due towards the end of 1940.[25]

Following the election Menzies was forced into coalition with the Country Party and he maintained power with the support of two independents.

Nineteen forty-one was an unfortunate year for Menzies. Attacked in the press and in Parliament, he 'was unable to overtake the losses he suffered by detraction'. Hasluck noted that:

He was . . . unable to establish positively a different reputation for himself by either the attractiveness or the force of his own nature. He thus did not have and could not command the trust or seize the imagination of the people and hence inspire them to an undivided war effort under his leadership. It is a debatable point whether any man in Australian politics could have done so.[26]

In August Menzies was ousted. His successor, Arthur Fadden, ruled for, in his own words 'forty days and forty nights' and on 7 October 1941 the Labor Party Leader, John Curtin, formed his government. Curtin, aged 56, had led the party since 1935, had restored coherence to it and prepared it for war-time responsibility. Loyal to the party, politically skilful, honest and approachable, he, like most of his party, lacked experience in government. Fifteen of the nineteen new ministers had not held office before.[27] Sir Percy Spender believed that while Curtin was austere and detached, he 'stood above' all of his ministers: 'A kindly, warmhearted man, despite a rather prim and somewhat cold appearance; he was an outstanding wartime leader'.[28]

It is paradoxical that during the 1930s the defence policy of the Labor Party had followed more closely the thinking of the army leaders than had the UAP and had subsequently been proved more

valid, for since the turbulent days of the anti-conscription campaign the Labor Party had represented all that these army leaders mistrusted. Few of the new ministers had served in the forces, most were anti-conscriptionist and unsympathetic towards the military, and a number held beliefs which the Staff Corps found threatening to their position in the army. Not only was the new ministry unsuited by training, experience and prejudice to control the armed forces, but the background of the new ministers found them unsuited to tackle matters of foreign policy and world affairs. Few ministers held university degrees, but they were all hardened politicians, sensitive to the electorate, and often ruled by principles established by years of class struggle.

The new government faced a deteriorating situation. In August 1940 American cryptoanalysts had broken the Japanese diplomatic code and had developed a machine to decode the messages relayed by the Japanese encrypting machine, known as PURPLE.[29] In January 1941 the Americans had exchanged one of these machines for a British machine which could decode top level German cyphers.[30] One writer noted that soon afterwards information began to be passed to Australian Intelligence authorities.[31] The American ability to read Japanese diplomatic messages in the months leading up to Pearl Harbour has been well documented.[32] It is surprising therefore that the UAP Government did not express more concern at these developments. It is even more surprising that, despite their record of attacks on the Lyons and Menzies defence policies, the new government maintained the policies established by their predecessors. Indeed, the month before the Japanese attack saw increasing optimism that a clash in the Far East could be averted and J. J. Dedman, who was then the Minister for War Organisation of Industry, observed that: 'So long as [the government] thought there was a possibility that Japan would not go to war, [it] was unwilling to weaken the British position in the Middle East where the second western desert offensive was about to be launched'.[33]

Yet by the end of November the developments were ominous. On 1 December 1941 the Combined Operational Intelligence Centre in Melbourne reported that Japan was

ready to strike in any direction from Indo-China at any moment . . . New naval concentrations in the South indicate that preparations have now been completed to strike against the Philippines or NEI (particularly Borneo) or Malaya at an opportune moment and one or more of these moves must be considered possible.[34]

Three days later Sir Charles Burnett, the Chief of the Air Staff, received news from Vice-Admiral C. E. L. Helfrich, the C-in-C of the Netherlands Navy in the East Indies, that the Japanese Navy had begun to move.[35] The Dutch cryptanalysts had also broken the Japanese codes.[36] That evening Burnett told the Cabinet this, and R. G. Casey in Washington was ordered to take the intelligence to the White House.[37]

The events of this period show that the government was unprepared to face the pressures of total war. General Rowell, the DCGS, recalled that Lieutenant-Colonel W. R. Hodgson, the Secretary of the Department of External Affairs, told him on the evening of 8 December that until two days before the attack they thought that war in the Far East could be averted.[38] Rowell wrote that Army Headquarters was 'forbidden to issue any instructions to Commands that war with Japan was inevitable', but that he wrote personal letters to the GOCs warning them of approaching war. Furthermore, Evatt, the Minister for External Affairs, would not allow the Japanese representative's quarters in Melbourne to be 'bugged'. In Rowell's words, 'the whole prospect was frightening'.[39]

During 1941 Sturdee had found his task as CGS increasingly difficult, for although he had no operational control over the AIF he was responsible for the training of the AIF for both the Middle East and Malaya, their resupply, the administration and training of the militia, and the defence of Australia. The growing threat to Australia revived the matter of determining an appropriate command structure to organise this defence. As early as 1935 Lavarack had suggested that at the outbreak of war a Commander-in-Chief should be appointed with AHQ to become GHQ and another officer be appointed to command the principal field army. The GOC of this field force would be subordinate to the CGS who would become C-in-C.[40] This topic was raised on a number of occasions during 1940, but General White could see a necessity for a C-in-C of the AMF only when war seemed imminent, and in no circumstances could he see a need for a C-in-C of the Home Forces.[41]

In April 1941 the Minister for the Army, P. C. Spender, recommended to the War Cabinet that Lieutenant-General Sturdee should be appointed as Commander-in-Chief of the AMF, that Major-General Northcott should become CGS, and that the Military Board should be abolished. On 9 May 1941 the War Cabinet agreed in principle and directed that proposals for the necessary organisation to give effect to this decision should be submitted to War Cabinet.[42] Later that month Spender explained that it was unworkable to have a GOC-in-C of a field army as well as a C-in-C, and submitted 'that on psychological grounds affecting both the Military Forces and the general public, a GOC-in-C in supreme command of all the military forces in Australia should be appointed'.[43] In June War Cabinet again discussed the matter and there was disagreement over the necessity for a C-in-C. The result was that the appointment of a GOC-in-C was deferred to give the minister an opportunity for further consideration.[44]

It appears that the example of the British system in which their equivalent of the Military Board (Army Council) and the CGS (CIGS) continued to exist, and a separate GOC-in-C Home Forces was appointed, carried particular weight with the War Cabinet.[45] Despite the reservations of the army about the efficiency of this system, on 5 August 1941 Major-General Sir Iven Mackay, the commander of the 6th Division, was appointed GOC-in-C of the Home Forces.[46] He already had a distinguished military career, having commanded a brigade in France in 1918, and the 6th Division in Cyrenaica and Greece, and he was a gallant and capable soldier, but he was not equipped to handle the complex political matters demanded by this appointment.[47] His instructions placed him equal in rank to the CGS, but subordinate to the Military Board and the authority delegated to the GOC-in-C Home Forces was not clearly defined. In spite of this grandiose title, the responsibility for the defence of Australia rested with the CGS.

On 1 September Mackay took up his appointment, but from the outset he operated through Army Headquarters rather than from his own headquarters. He was concerned with two matters — the training of the militia and an appreciation of the methods of defending Australia with the resources available. The *Daily Telegraph*, on 5 September 1941, pointed to the problems likely to be faced by Mackay claiming:

that an attempt is being made to water down Sir Iven's jobs, to whittle away his authority and to limit his scope to the training of the home defence army . . . Why bring him back if he is not to have the complete authority that should go with his new command. The truth may be that Federal Cabinet made a familiar political compromise, hoping that nobody's feelings would be hurt.[48]

Despite his own reservations, General Sturdee reaffirmed that the appointment was 'based on the organisation which was introduced into England in June, 1940, when General Sir Alan Brooke was appointed

GOC-in-C Home Forces', and he emphasised that he and Mackay were old friends and that there would be no friction.[49]

Mackay's instructions stated clearly that:

Subject to the general responsibilities of CGS for the military policy affecting the security of the Commonwealth, the GOC-in-C, Home Forces, will exercise operational command over all military forces . . . allotted to the defence of the mainland of Australia and Tasmania, except such as may from time to time be withdrawn from his control by the CGS.[50]

The instructions continued that Mackay was responsible for co-ordinating defensive plans of each of the GOCs of the Commands. These plans were to be formulated in the light of a policy outlined by the Secretary of the Military Board to the Minister for the Army on 20 September 1941, and this stated that the task of the army was:

a. To secure the bases necessary to the Navy and Air Force in their role of:
    (1) Defending sea communications
    (2) Preventing the Japanese establishing bases from which to threaten Australian interests.
b. To provide, with Naval and Air Force co-operation, final opposition to raids or invasion.[51]

Obviously Mackay's concern was with the second situation.

The problems of defending the vast area of Australia are illustrated by an appreciation made by the new GOC of Northern Command, Major-General J. M. A. Durrant, at Brisbane on 23 September 1941.[52] His plans were based on deductions made by his predecessor, Major-General R. E. Jackson, who had improved on the situation which he had found when he took over in May 1940. Jackson wrote later that by December 1940 he had secured 'an organisation adequate for the defence of Southern Queensland, the Brisbane Line, this being the farthest point north where troops from southern states might be used'. He also prepared plans for creating obstacle belts throughout Queensland, for the reorganisation of Northern Command, and for the improvement of road and rail communications to the far north. He recommended that an additional brigade should be raised in north Queensland for use at either Port Moresby or Rabaul. He later commented acidly on the success of these plans. 'None of my proposals were even replied to. Such complacency is hardly conceivable'.[53]

After he took over Durrant deduced that it would be very difficult to defeat an enemy who landed in north Queensland, but, he added 'we must never give up hope of aiding the North which would be a policy of despair. This points to the necessity of maintaining a complete Infantry Brigade Group in N. Queensland'. In north Queensland he had the 11th Brigade, in central Queensland, around Maryborough, the 29th Brigade, and near Brisbane the 7th Brigade and the Brisbane Defences. The 1st Cavalry Brigade was south of Brisbane. His appreciation was a realistic assessment of capabilities and he concluded:

The most important area of Queensland, by far from a defence point of view, as has been previously deduced, is the Brisbane area. Therefore we must be as certain as we can of retaining this in our hands by allotting the bulk of our forces to its defence. Should this area not be attacked, these troops could be regarded as a general reserve for eventual use further north, but only after adequate steps have been taken to secure Brisbane.[54]

If this was the plan to which E. J. Ward was referring in 1942[55] then undoubtedly he was right in his allegations of a Brisbane Line, but there is no evidence that this concept was approved by the government.[56] Yet in a situation where most AIF troops were overseas, and where the CMF was called up for short periods, GOCs of Commands had no option other than to produce plans envisaging the defence of the main areas of population. It would therefore have been equally valid to speak of a Newcastle Line or a Perth Line.

The GOC of Eastern Command, Lieutenant-General C. G. N. Miles, followed a similar policy to Durrant, deploying his forces to protect the vital Newcastle-Sydney-Port Kembla area.[57] In all he had the equivalent of three infantry divisions and one cavalry division. In Southern Command Lieutenant-General E. K. Smart followed the same principle with one infantry and one cavalry division.

In organisation, the forces available to Mackay were little different from those existing soon after the outbreak of war,[58] except that command was now exercised by the Northern, Eastern, Southern and Western Commands with independent garrisons at Darwin and Port Moresby. At the end of August 1941 the militia numbered 173,000 men, of which only 45,000 were serving full time.[59] Their training had been fragmentary, they were short of equipment, and their efficiency was impaired because the most energetic and capable of the younger officers and men had gone to the AIF. The remainder included those who were too old or too young for overseas service, those who for some moral or social reason thought that the place to defend Australia was from the homeland, and those who were retained because they were employed in 'essential' industries. Of prime importance in maintaining the standard of these forces was the calibre of their senior officers.

It will be recalled that in the reorganisation following the outbreak of war Squires had become CGS, Lavarack had assumed command of Southern Command and Sturdee of Eastern Command, all as lieutenant-generals. New appointments amongst the staff at AHQ had followed. During the first two years of war many of the commanders were changed, and generally speaking the first echelon of commanders, those who were generals and in command positions at the beginning of the war, were replaced by a second echelon of commanders who had been colonels in September 1939. This was to be expected, for before the outbreak of war Squires had recommended that a number of generals should be retired as they were approaching their ages for retirement.[60] The problem of the age and ability of the senior commanders was one which exercised the mind of the government during the early months of the war, and on 11 July 1941 the War Cabinet directed that: 'The Military Board is to furnish particulars of the Divisional Commanders of the AMF including their ages, and qualifications of their potential successors'.[61] Many of the generals were simply too old, while others lacked the drive, initiative and knowledge to command in modern warfare. Nevertheless in October 1940 it was noted that: 'the serious inroads on the best militia officers for service overseas and in Australia [necessitated] the calling on retired officers to fill duties where a lower standard of physical fitness in the officer can be accepted . . . '[62]

The confusion in Australia over how to employ a number of officers who had been returned from the Middle East because they were too old is revealed by the case of Lieutenant-Colonel T. S. Louch. Louch had commanded the 2/11th Battalion in Libya, but in Greece he had been injured and had to return to Palestine. In June 1941 he and another battalion commander were returned to Australia because of age. Louch was 47, the other was 50. Brigadier Vasey, who was in the Middle East, wrote to his wife: 'They cannot fail to be of some help at home for as we see it nothing could be worse'.[63] On 19 October 1941 Louch wrote to Vasey of his experiences on returning to Australia, and he included extracts from his diary:

11 Aug:	Appointed G2 Northam and given a fortnight's leave.
25 Aug:	Appointed G2 Western Command and given a week's leave.
4 Sep:	Told I was to be either CO Northam Camp or 13 Bde.
7 Sep:	Ordered to administer comd 13 Bde forthwith and formally posted to command on 29 Sep.

27 Sep: Previous instructions cancelled — appointed G2 Northam.
29 Sep: Interview with [Colonel O.V.] Hoad [i/c Administration Western Command].
1 Oct: Transferred to R of O to take effect on 7 Oct.
6-10 Oct: Resumed practice as a solicitor.
10 Oct: Ordered to report to AHQ.
17 Oct: Reported to AG [Adjutant-General] and ordered to report to school for junior leaders AFV [Armoured Fighting Vehicles] to be trained by courses in D & M — wireless etc. with a view to ultimate apptmt to a *cavalry* command.

I start tomorrow — thus is my experience as an infantryman in the recent campaigning made available to the benefit of the AIF and AMF in Australia . . . I offered to return to AIF as a batman or a Legal Staff Officer in that order of preference — but Sid [Rowell] seemed to think I ought to qualify as a tank Sgt . . . if ever there was a bloody fool when it comes to anything mechanical I am he . . . Sid [*sic*] mentioned vaguely something about a job on the personal staff of the Lion of Bardia [Mackay] and I struggled manfully — and I hope with success — to conceal my emotion. I have never felt so completely unworthy.[64]

On 4 December 1941 just before Japan entered the war Louch was promoted to brigadier to raise and command the 29th Infantry Brigade.

The majority of the soldiers in Australia were militiamen, and until further troops were enlisted for full-time service it was obvious that the defence of Australia rested in their hands. As a result the government had, in 1940, decided that there should be 'direct militia representation on the Military Board or at Army Headquarters'.[65] Sturdee, the CGS, was most unhappy with this decision but chose Major-General J. H. Cannan, the Commander of the 2nd Division, to become QMG on 24 October 1940. Major-General E. K. Smart, the previous QMG, became the commander of Southern Command, replacing Lieutenant-General J. L. Whitham who was one of the permanent officers whom Squires had recommended for retirement. Cannan, aged 58, had had a most distinguished record during World War I and had commanded a brigade in France for over two years. Although he had not served in the militia for most of the inter-war period, he brought to his position considerable managerial skills, for after World War I he had become a successful businessman. Furthermore, his position as a citizen soldier meant that he was not subject to the normal constraints of the Staff Corps officer. One of Cannan's senior staff officers, Colonel G. Drake-Brockman, found him to be 'a man of great personality and charm with tremendous drive'.[66]

He believed Cannan's administration was outstanding and characterised by very good forward planning. In his opinion: 'Cannan's contribution to the defence of Australia was immense, his responsibility for supply, transport and works, a giant-sized burden; his acknowledgement — nil'.[67] General Berryman described him as the 'soul of rectitude', and he served unobtrusively but effectively in his position to the conclusion of the war.[68]

On the same day that Mackay took up his appointment, Major-General S. F. Rowell, who had been Blamey's Chief of Staff in the Middle East, became Deputy CGS, enabling his predecessor, Major-General J. Northcott, to take over the command of the 1st Armoured Division. Rowell had been recalled at Sturdee's urgent request, as Northcott had been unable to devote his full attention to either his job as DCGS or to the problems of the raising of the Armoured Division.[69] This appointment probably came as a disappointment to Rowell. As Vasey observed: 'Isn't it just too awful. I consider it a tragedy for the AIF and for Syd too. As you know he didn't see much of the last show [World War I] and here he is being defeated this time'.[70] On the other hand Rowell and Blamey had not seen eye to eye, particularly after Greece, when Rowell had written to Vasey: 'The Lord is established in Cairo with his son as personal assistant. We are rarely consulted. I prefer it this way as we are now not tuned to the same wave length and are never again likely to be'.[71] After Rowell's appointment Blamey commented, 'I think Rowell will like that'.[72] The appointment had little to do with personal acrimony, despite the fact that Rowell had written to Sturdee that he would never again serve under Blamey in the field. Vasey summed up the situation to his wife:

there is no doubt that if there is any threat to Aust. a number of us must go home. When all is said and done the brains of the Staff Corps are over here and if anything important is to be done at home some of us will be wanted. I know that is Syd's view and I know that if anyone is asked for it will be me.[73]

By September 1941, of the sixteen generals in Australia only three, and these were commanding militia divisions, had been generals at the outbreak of war. Of those who were permanent officers, two had been brigadiers, four colonels and three lieutenant-colonels. Of the remainder, three had been promoted from the Reserve of Officers or from the Unattached List, and one had been a CMF brigadier.[74] At this time, the younger, and now, after the recent fighting in the Middle East, more experienced officers, were still serving with the AIF in Syria and Palestine. In their ranks was the third echelon of commanders; those who had been majors and lieutenant-colonels at the outbreak of war and who would be promoted as those of the second echelon were tested, and in some cases found wanting, when they were faced with the increased pressure of a war for the nation's survival.[75]

3
The Outbreak of War with Japan, 7 December 1941 – 17 March 1942

The news that Japan had attacked Pearl Harbour and Kota Bharu on 8 December 1941 came, to most Australians and their government, as a tremendous shock, but initially there was little dismay. Singapore was impregnable, and two large British warships had been sent as reinforcements to the Far East. The attack on Pearl Harbour assured the USA's entry into the war. There is, however, evidence to indicate that the government, or at least the Prime Minister John Curtin, realised that the country would soon be fighting for its life in 'the gravest hour of our history'.[1] Curtin spoke of 'a complete revision of the whole economic, domestic and industrial life' of the country, and declared, on 16 December, that the government would act ruthlessly. He claimed that he would be too busy with the war to worry about introducing a new social order.[2]

It took two months for Australia to come from complacency, or confidence, to the threshhold of fear for her own survival. Despite the fact that Japanese planes bombed Rabaul on 4 January, on 16 January there was the news that the Australians had done well in the first battles in Malaya. It was not until 23 January, with the fall of Rabaul, that the fear began, and recriminations against Great Britain, whom a number of leading politicians claimed had let Australia down.

During these early months the government grappled with a large number of problems on different levels. There was what might be termed the civilian problem; that is the changes in industrial, commercial and social life brought about by total war. The problem of defence had, in itself, many levels. At the highest level was the matter of a world-wide strategy for the conduct of the war. At a lower level was the problem of determining the strategy to be followed in the defence of Australia, and interacting with the overall world strategy was the decision over the employment of I Australian Corps. A further problem was that of organising the Australian Army to meet the increased threat.

The Japanese attack provoked immediate concern for the defence of Australia, and on 8 December the Chiefs of Staff were requested to prepare an appreciation covering defence capabilities and the likely forms that an attack on Australia might take. This appreciation was submitted to the War Cabinet on 11 December, and it stated that the attack on Malaya 'might well be a first step in the Japanese plan for a major attack on Australia', and that 'the possibility of a direct move on Australia via the islands to the north and North East must now be considered'.

This attack would start, it was argued, by attempts to occupy Rabaul, Port Moresby and New Caledonia; from these bases the attack on Australia could be launched. Therefore the Chiefs of Staff recommended that to hold these areas a minimum of a brigade group with anti-aircraft and coastal defences should be stationed in all three localities as well as on Timor. If Singapore and the Netherlands East Indies were occupied, and the bases to the north were captured, then the Japanese would be in a position to invade Australia. All these situations were possible and the Chiefs of Staff advised that it was 'necessary to establish and train now the forces that would be required to prevent and to meet an invasion'. One would have thought that this would have been an admirable aim a year earlier.

The appreciation recommended that proposals for a joint US-Australian effort to defend Rabaul should be accelerated. Furthermore it was recommended that 114,000 personnel of the AMF should be called up for full-time duty, with a further 53,000 to be called up to complete full-scale mobilisation, and that approval was to be granted to separate the operational and administrative functions of Northern, Eastern and Southern Commands.[3]

War Cabinet approved all measures recommended by the Chiefs of Staff, with the exception of the despatch of forces to the outlying islands, and on 12 December Cabinet asked for a supplementary appreciation on the disposition of Australian Forces to defend: a. Newcastle, Sydney, Port Kembla and Lithgow; b. Darwin, Port Moresby and the islands to the north-east of Australia including New Caledonia.[4] This supplementary appreciation was submitted on 15 December, and it noted that the Newcastle, Sydney, Port Kembla, Lithgow area was 'of such importance that its defence, to the limit of our capacity, must not be compromised by detachments which we can not subsequently concentrate'.

As a result the Chiefs of Staff recommended that Darwin should be retained as a fleet operational base, that the garrison of Port Moresby should be increased to one brigade group, that Rabaul should be left with its existing garrison of one battalion group and that an Independent Company should be sent to New Caledonia 'to enhance the morale of the [French] . . . and for demolition purposes'. The Chiefs of Staff realised that the Rabaul garrison of one battalion would be too small to resist an invasion successfully, but they considered it essential: 'to maintain a forward air observation line as long as possible and to make the enemy fight for this line rather than abandon it at the first threat'.[5]

It is important that the strategic situation as it appeared to the Chiefs of Staff should be completely understood. In the latter part of 1941 the Naval and Air Forces available in the Australian area were almost non-existent as the bulk of the limited resources were deployed in other areas. The only aircraft available for offensive operations were a limited number of Hudsons and Catalinas which, in the first few months of operations against Japan, were continuously employed, until their ultimate destruction, in daring and effective operations against Japanese advances to the north-east of Australia. These aircraft operated from available airfields in Papua and, even had large numbers of additional aircraft been available for offensive operations, their use would have been restricted to those which could have operated from the limited airfields available. No engineer organisation or equipment was available to construct the additional airfields.

In the previous chapter it was described how the seven CMF divisions consisted largely of part-time soldiers. It would not be until January or February that the drafting of these units and formations would be completed and they would be able to settle down to steady training. In the meantime the Armoured Division, which had no tanks, and the 23rd Infantry Brigade at Darwin, destined to garrison Timor and Ambon, formed the only trained units in Australia. There was one mobilised militia battalion in Port Moresby.

The equipment situation was comparable with the standard of training. Even as late as February 1942 such items as Bren guns were being allotted to formations on a priority basis direct from the small arms factories. It was not until June 1942 that the whole of the CMF could be said to be on a reasonable basis of equipment and that by no means the full battle requirement.

In view of these crippling limitations, the decision of the Australian Chiefs of Staff not to reinforce the north-eastern approaches seems unchallengeable. The movement of large army garrisons to the north-eastern approaches to protect advanced bases, even had trained troops been available, would have served no useful purpose. Whatever the numbers of troops deployed, the effective defence of bases to which they would have been moved would not have been possible without naval and air forces sufficient to support the land forces in this defence, and keep open the lines of communication to these bases from Australia. These naval and air forces were not available and to reinforce the bases would therefore have resulted only in the investment of the garrisons concerned and their defeat. There is no reason to believe that such a course would have delayed Japanese operations against the mainland had that been their intention. It would only have reduced the forces available in Australia for defence against a Japanese attack.

The U.S. defence attaché in Melbourne showed a lack of understanding of the situation when, in early January 1942, he advised Washington that:

the major idea among Australian chiefs of defence departments, except the Navy, is that the first mission of defence personnel and equipment is to protect areas not at present threatened, instead of forwarding them for offensive operations in areas already under attack or threatened.[6]

That the Australian Chiefs of Staff were fully alive to the need for strengthening the north-eastern approaches is indicated by their appreciation of 15 December 1941. It was as a result of this paper that the garrison of Port Moresby was increased to a brigade group, which was the limit of the maintenance capacity, and the decision was taken neither to reinforce nor to withdraw the Rabaul garrison.

While the overall strategy outlined in the appreciation has withstood the test of events, certain aspects proved unfortunate. With respect to Rabaul the Chiefs of Staff saw three options open to them. These were:

a.   To reinforce the garrison to meet the scale of attack likely to be directed against Rabaul.
b.   To withdraw the garrison and abandon Rabaul.
c.   To retain the existing garrison.

They considered that a. was not possible. The argument that b. was not possible because of the psychological effect it 'would have on the minds of the Dutch in NEI' was not decisive, but the persuasive argument was for the maintenance of 'a forward observation line'.[7] Colonel Keogh saw the possibility of a fourth option; that there should have been a plan to fight a withdrawal action and in the process inflict damage and delay on the enemy.[8] He pointed out that no instructions to that effect were issued by either AHQ or HQ 8th Military District. Rowell said later that they had the scale of attack all wrong. The Japanese employed a division against a battalion. It was bad luck for the battalion that the Japanese intended making Rabaul their main base.[9]

One is left with the impression that this token contribution to forward defence, and it was repeated in Ambon, Timor and New Ireland, was merely grasping at straws. Army Headquarters must be indicted for failing to assess realistically the chances of these garrisons. After the fall of Rabaul Rowell said: 'It's not the first time a few thousand men have been thrown away and it won't be the last'.[10] Furthermore, it is clear that Army Headquarters was not organised to control operations. There was confusion over orders, roles and equipment, leading, in the case of Ambon, to the replacement of the commander.[11] One problem faced by Rowell and Sturdee was that there were no young and experienced officers in Australia.[12] The new commander on Ambon was by some years the oldest battalion commander in the AIF.[13]

The fate of the garrisons can be attributed to the fact that the army leaders now found themselves caught in the cleft stick of Singapore and the defence of Australia. It is not the intention of this work to investigate the Singapore strategy,[14] but certain points must be mentioned. If Singapore held firm with a substantial naval force ready to strike at the Japanese, then there was little need to strengthen the garrisons in the islands. All that was needed was a force sufficient to ward off the Japanese while the British reorganised their naval forces to send a fleet to Singapore.[15] But when the *Repulse* and *Prince of Wales* were sunk soon after Japan entered the war the Singapore strategy lost its validity. Indeed, in the appreciation of 11 December, the Australian Chiefs of Staff noted that the 'defeat of the *Allied Naval Forces* or the capture of Singapore and the Netherlands East Indies' would enable the Japanese to occupy bases to the north-east of Australia.[16]

The disasters in the islands therefore appear to have been caused by a number of factors. Firstly, in late 1941 the government and their military advisers found themselves locked into reliance upon the Singapore strategy. Secondly they were caught off guard by the speed and power of the Japanese thrusts. Thirdly, the army was not ready for war, neither with respect to the training of troops, organisation of headquarters for command, supply of equipment, nor possession of young experienced leaders. It is not certain that all of these short-comings were the fault exclusively of the army leaders. What is clear is that the disasters jolted the army into the acceptance of a changed situation. The policy of continental defence, rather than forward defence, became a reality only after the complete failure of the latter.

While Australian military planners were deciding how best to defend Australia, leaders in Britain and America were considering the problem of south-east Asia, where the Japanese were advancing rapidly in Malaya and the Philippines. On 17 December the Chief of Staff of the US Army, General George C. Marshall, approved General Eisenhower's plan to establish an air base in Australia to be commanded by Lieutenant-General G. H. Brett, and to support the operations north of Australia.[17]

This did not, however, resolve the problem in Malaya, and on 25 December Curtin cabled both President Roosevelt and Winston Churchill in Washington that he was very concerned about the situation. 'It is in your power', he said, 'to meet situation. Should United States desire we would gladly accept United States command in Pacific Ocean area'.[18] Eventually at the end of December it was agreed to set up a combined command under Field Marshal Wavell to be known as ABDACOM (American British Dutch Australian Command), but Australia was to have no direct representation on the controlling body.[19]

Curtin's concern can be understood, for on 23 December he had received the United Kingdom Chiefs of Staff appreciation of the situation in the Far East. This stated that the position in Malaya was 'very serious' and that 'the best possible delaying action' should be fought in Malaya. 'Unified direction and closest co-operation of all allied forces should be secured as soon as possible'. On the other hand the appreciation noted that:

Limited United States Naval support can be expected in the Atlantic where our mutual interests coincide and from the United States Asiatic Fleet but *not* elsewhere . . . Apart from the question of fighter protection we ourselves can *not* provide a balanced fleet at Singapore at once. Therefore unsound to send capital ships there at present.

The Australian Chiefs of Staff found this situation 'most un-satisfactory'; 'In other words', they wrote on 29 December,

the United States Pacific Fleet on which we had based great hopes is unable or unwilling to assist . . . As the protection of the interests of both America and Great Britain is identical and depends solely on our regaining control of the sea by the defeat of the Japanese fleet [the inability of the British and Americans to co-operate in the Pacific] is difficult to understand.[20]

Meanwhile on 22 December 4,500 American troops of field artillery and administrative units arrived in Brisbane on route to the Philippines. By this time, however, the Philippines had been almost isolated, and Brigadier-General J. R. Barnes took command of the United States Army Forces in Australia (USAFIA).[21] General Brett became commander of USAFIA on 31 December, before in early January becoming deputy to Wavell.

On 3 January 1942 the first conference between the American Forces in Australia and the Australians took place at Victoria Barracks in Melbourne. Present were the Australian Chiefs of Staff and their deputies, Shedden, and the American Generals Brett, Barnes and Brereton, the commander of the U.S. Air Forces. General Brett explained that his main interest was to achieve close co-operation with Australia and to establish bases to support operations to the north. It was agreed that a Joint Planning Committee, consisting of the Australian deputy Chiefs of Staff and General Barnes, and an Administrative Planning Committee should be established.[22] The U.S. headquarters was to be set up in Melbourne.[23]

In mid January 1942, with the situation becoming grimmer each day, Churchill cabled Curtin that the USA would be willing to reinforce Australia with 40,000 to 50,000 U.S. troops: 'Do you think you are in immediate danger of invasion in force'.[24] Curtin put this question to the Chiefs of Staff and on 16 January they submitted their reply. They reiterated their argument of 11 December, that while Malaya held there was little danger of a major attack on Australia, but that Japan was likely to continue her advance towards New Guinea and New Caledonia to sever the sea communications to the United States and to be in a position to attack Australia when the situation in Malaya and the Netherlands East Indies allowed. Therefore the danger of invasion remained until either the enemy advance in Malaya was held, or until the U.S. Pacific Fleet secured supremacy over the Japanese fleet. The Chiefs of Staff welcomed the suggestion of U.S. reinforcements as they would increase the defence capability of Australia and would be well placed for an offensive northwards against the Japanese. They assumed that if U.S. troops came to Australia they would be subject to the Australian CGS in respect of training and operations.[25]

There was little that the Australian Chiefs of Staff could do at this stage about the fighting in Malaya, but they were determined to improve the naval situation off Australia's east coast. When Churchill proposed the establishment of a joint naval ANZAC area covering New Zealand, eastern Australia and north to the equator, the Chiefs of Staff prepared a reply on 20 January 1942 which was approved by the War Cabinet. This pointed out the value of Australia as an offensive base, but that the American 'capacity to launch a counter offensive might be frustrated by inadequate naval strength in this region'.[26]

The next day Curtin showed his concern in an urgent message to Roosevelt:

We are now, with a small population in only white man's territory south of the equator, beset grievously. Because we have added to our contribution in manpower so much of our resources and materials we now lack adequacy for our forces of our homeland on our own soil.[27]

The fall of Rabaul on 23 January to a Japanese division, as had been anticipated in the Chiefs of Staff appreciation of 15 December, alarmed Australia as nothing else had to that time. Curtin agreed to establish the ANZAC Area under U.S. command, and soon afterwards Vice-Admiral H. F. Leary of the U.S. Navy assumed command. At the same time the ABDACOM area was enlarged to include Darwin. Thus the security of Australia became a matter for Allied concern. Nevertheless with the Allies involved in desperate actions to the north, the defence of the Australian homeland remained chiefly in the hands of the Australian defence planners.

While the Allies sought to develop a system of Allied Command, and the battles raged on around and over Australia's protective screen of tropical islands, Lieutenant-General Sir Iven Mackay, the GOC-in-C Home Forces, had been examining the problem of defending Australia with the forces available. on 4 February he produced a memorandum for the Minister for the Army, F. M. Forde, seeking direction and government concurrence in regard to the area which they considered vital to hold in the event of an attempted invasion. Mackay pointed out that the Chiefs of Staff, with the agreement of the government, had decided that the area most vital to the continuance of the war effort was the Port Kembla-Sydney-Newcastle-Lithgow area. With the decision to develop an important base for U.S. forces at Brisbane, and with the economic and military importance of Melbourne, Mackay noted that it was vital to hold the area stretching some 1,000 miles from Brisbane to Melbourne. This area contained a force of barely five divisions.

Mackay explained that all other areas must be looked upon as isolated localities and that Tasmania and Townsville should not be reinforced, although 'for reasons of morale and psychology' it was undesirable to withdraw troops from these areas. He stressed that this plan was based purely upon the assumption that he could only use the troops at that time in Australia.[28]

Forde, whose electorate was in north Queensland, was not happy with this appreciation and he asked General Sturdee whether it was possible to move an additional division to Queensland, and also that the forces in Queensland should be more heavily armed. Sturdee's reply of 6 February was to the point:

The problem is . . . not what can we move out of the vital area to protect say, north Queensland or Tasmania or Western Australia, but whether we may not have to, or should not now, take troops away from these areas to increase our strength at the decisive place.

Sturdee concurred generally with Mackay's views with the qualification that if it became established that the main threat was to the flanks the 'problem would become an entirely different one and the main field army' would be disposed to meet it.[29]

This was not just theorising on the part of the military commander, for the army order of battle corresponded roughly to Mackay's plan.[30] In Northern Command General Durrant had 25,800 troops. In Eastern Command General Wynter had 105,000, and in Southern Command General Smart had 82,750 troops. There were 20,400 troops in South Australia and 12,400 in Tasmania. The troops in Northern, Southern and Eastern Commands formed Mackay's Second Army. General Plant in Western Command came directly under the command of Army Headquarters. He had one brigade group and a total number of 14,300 troops. Civic leaders in Perth were very perturbed and indignant about the lack of troops in their area.[31] General Blake in Darwin also came directly under Army Headquarters. He had two brigade groups with 6,670 troops. General Morris in Port Moresby had one brigade group with 6,500 troops.[32]

These troops had been deployed in accordance with a War Cabinet instruction of mid-December. Early in December the government had laid down that the area of top priority was the Newcastle-Sydney-Port Kembla-Lithgow area with second priority to Port Moresby and Darwin. Accordingly, Port Moresby had been reinforced to a brigade group.[33] One problem in deploying the troops was a widespread feeling in the country that forces raised in a particular area were designed particularly for the defence of that area.[34]

In the fortnight after Mackay submitted his memorandum the situation changed greatly. The Japanese seized Ambon and landed in Sumatra, Java and Timor. Singapore surrendered, and with it 17,000 Australians of the 8th Division marched into captivity. It was now certain, beyond any doubt, that the policy of forward defence which had been unsoundly based in the 'Singapore Strategy', had failed. The government was now forced to grapple with the realities of Mackay's appreciation. Yet Forde still found the situation described by Mackay quite unacceptable, and on 17 February recommended to War Cabinet that:

the policy of the government should now be defined as a determination to defend the whole of the populated areas of Australia to the utmost of our ability, and to prevent the enemy by every means within our power from obtaining a foothold on our shores.[35]

The next day, the Chiefs of Staff were ordered to prepare another appreciation. They were to take into account the fact that the bulk of I Australian Corps, which had been destined for Java, and then for Burma, would be returning to Australia, and that there had been suggestions for reinforcements from America and Canada.[36]

Although the War Cabinet asked the Chiefs of Staff to work on the assumption that I Australian Corps would be returning, this was not yet certain. Since early February there had been disquiet in military circles about the plan to send the corps to Java. After arriving in Java on 27 January, the corps commander, Lavarack, and his BGS, Brigadier Berryman, had reconnoitred southern Sumatra and central Java. On 2 February Lavarack's senior intelligence officer, Lieutenant-Colonel K. A. Wills, prepared a paper in which he forecast Japanese intentions and concluded that if part of the corps arrived before the Japanese attacked it could be lost; and that 'by attempting to bring 6 Aust Div, 7 Aust Div and Corps troops to southern Sumatra and Java, under the circumstances and bearing in mind the time factor, the defence and safety of Australia itself is being jeopardised'.[37] Lavarack was not yet ready to press these views on the Australian Government, but on 6 February he wrote to Sturdee and warned him that the defences in the Netherlands East Indies were not adequate. He declared that

The policy . . . may have to be changed. After all the first flight of the Australian Corps convoys can hardly arrive in less than about three weeks from now, though one ship, I understand may arrive sooner. By the time the main body does arrive the Japanese may already hold S. Sumatra. If they do it will be hopeless to try to land and eject them, under present conditions of sea and air power. Therefore I envisage the possibility that before the arrival of the first flight a decision may have to be taken to alter its destination, either to Java or some other vital area . . .

Presumably the government possesses knowledge of future intentions which is denied me, and in default of which I must act in the dark.[38]

Lavarack's letter was carefully worded. He described the situation as grim but he awaited instructions from the government.

Wavell's Deputy Intendant-General (chief administrative officer), Major-General C. E. M. Lloyd, had no such reservations. He felt that Lavarack was not strong enough in the 'Alice in Wonderland situation in Java'.[39] Two days later he wrote to Sturdee's deputy, Major-General Rowell, condemning the proposal to keep the corps in Java as completely unsound. In characteristic fashion he concluded:

The successful concentration of the whole party in Australia would do more to cramp the JAP plan than the high class bush ranging which will result here . . .

You must be very busy these days and I hope I have not unduly added to your burdens but I'd hate to see the party spoilt on the altar of ABCDZYZ or whatever this outfit here is.[40]

Finally, on 13 February Lavarack prepared an appreciation to send to Sturdee, but Wavell asked him to delay it while he sent a similar one to the Combined Chiefs of Staff and the War Office.[41]

Meanwhile Sturdee acted on his earlier information. On 15 February, the day Singapore fell, he produced a comprehensive paper pointing out that the troops in Java would probably be lost, and even if they were not lost Java did not provide a continental base suitable to build up Allied strength for an offensive. Unlike Java, Australia had the shortest sea route to the United States of any large area of land in south-east Asia. He concluded that:

Its extent is such that it cannot be completely overrun by the Japanese if we concentrate our available resources for its immediate protection whilst American strength is arriving . . . Its Northern shores are sufficiently close to Japanese occupied territory to make a good 'jumping off' area for offensive operations, whilst its southern areas are sufficiently far from Japanese bases to ensure a reasonable degree of immunity from continuous sea and air bombardment bearing in mind the growing strength of USA Naval and Air forces.

These views foreshadowed a great allied offensive based on Australia, and indeed the previous day the United States had reversed an earlier decision and had decided to send the 41st Infantry Division to Australia.[42] Sturdee's paper gives the lie to allegations that the Australian Army planned to give up the north of Australia to the Japanese. What Sturdee was saying was that there was the possibility that this plan might be forced on the government if the AIF were not diverted to Australia. Furthermore he recommended that a British armoured brigade in the AIF convoy should come to Australia, and that the 9th Division in the Middle East should be returned as early as possible.[43]

Cables from Lavarack and Wavell arrived after Sturdee had completed this paper, but they confirmed his views. The official historian noted that:

Sturdee and Lavarack had the advantage, when preparing these and later appreciations, that they were reproducing proposals and arguments which they had been expressing during the last decade . . . The Australian leaders belonged to a school of thought which had long contended that the situation of February 1942 would come about.[44]

The defence correspondent of the *Sydney Morning Herald* agreed with this assessment, and on 24 February 1942 wrote that: 'With Singapore in Japanese hands and an enemy temporarily commanding the sea, Australian Army leaders face a situation which they long predicted and have long been planning to meet, with the slender means at their disposal.[45]

It was these convictions which steeled Sturdee to press his views on Curtin. Indeed he threatened to resign if the government did not press the British government for the return of the AIF.[46] This resulted in the exchange of cables between Churchill and Curtin. On 18 February the War Cabinet confirmed Curtin's stand, and on 23 February after further cables Churchill informed Curtin that the convoy would head towards Australia.[47] At the same time the Combined Chiefs of Staff accepted Wavell's recommendation that ABDACOM should be dissolved. On 12 March the Allied force in Java surrendered.

Having cut their losses in the islands to the north the Chiefs of Staff could now turn their full attention to an examination of the likely areas and methods by which the Japanese could execute their expected attack on Australia. On 27 February they completed the new appreciation which the War Cabinet had ordered on 18 February. The Chiefs of Staff began by noting that after her successes in the Netherlands East Indies, Japan was 'now at liberty to attempt an in-

vasion of Australia should she so desire'. They saw three lines of approach open to the Japanese, and these were:

a.   Southward from the Mandated Territories.
      This would involve, as an essential pre-requisite to success, the capture of
      Moresby and New Caledonia and control of Torres Straits.
b.   South-eastwards from occupied Netherlands East Indies on Northern
      Australia.
c.   Southwards from the Netherlands East Indies on South-Western
      Australia.

Dealing with the first possibility the Chiefs of Staff indicated that
the Japanese had two alternatives:

a.   Attack Port Moresby, thence the mainland of Australia, or
b.   Proceed via the Solomons and New Hebrides to New Caledonia.

Since U.S. forces were being sent to New Caledonia the appreciation
concentrated on the first alternative, and the Chiefs of Staff recommended that it was not possible to reinforce Port Moresby without
depleting the east coast defences, and that the garrison would have to
hold out 'and exact a heavy toll from the enemy if he should attack it'.
There was no prospect of reinforcing Port Moresby until the sea lanes
from Australia were secure. Rowell and Sturdee later wrote:

As the Australian Chiefs of Staff saw the position at this stage of the war (and
it is suggested that the events of history amply confirmed their judgement) the
problem of the defence of Moresby was not so much an increase in its land
garrison, as the provision of adequate naval and air support.[48]

The Chiefs of Staff noted in their appreciation that the east coast of
Australia was not defended adequately and if the Newcastle to Port
Kembla area was to be held, then it was not possible to reinforce
Townsville which was protected by a brigade group. This was not
adequate but, as in the case of Port Moresby, it would have to hold
out.
    The Chiefs of Staff then turned to the problem of a Japanese attack
from the Netherlands East Indies. There were two brigade groups in
Darwin, but this force could not be increased without a resumption of
sea traffic or an improvement to the overland route. It was realised
that Darwin was untenable as a fleet base. It had been heavily bombed
on 19 February.[49] There was considerable concern for Fremantle as it
was a potential fleet base and it was difficult to reinforce rapidly the

forces in Western Australia. For this reason it was recommended that the garrison should be increased.

This appreciation of 27 February was based on the assumption that only the troops available in Australia could be used. However, it was realised that there would soon be in Australia two AIF Divisions (6th and 7th) and one U.S. Division (41st) and it was suggested that these troops would allow the garrison in Darwin to be increased from two brigade groups to one division, that in Western Australia to be increased from a brigade group to one division, and that in Tasmania to be increased from one to two brigade groups.

This account has dealt only with the army measures, but the lack of naval and air protection can be gauged by a statement in the summary of the appreciation:

If there were adequate Naval and Air Forces for the defence of Australia, an army of the numbers that would be required could nearly be met from Australia itself although a great deal of equipment would be required from abroad. Until such time as adequate Naval and Air Forces are available, it is estimated that it would require a minimum of 25 divisions to defend Australia against the scale of attack that is possible. This would mean that 10 fully equipped divisions would have to be supplied by our Allies.[50]

An earlier appreciation had mentioned a possible Japanese invasion force of eight divisions,[51] but these, of course, would be concentrated in one area.

The appreciation of 27 February was presented to the Advisory War Council on 5 March, but the Council was not satisfied.[52] The minute noted that there was 'inadequate treatment in this appreciation of strategic possibilities'.[53] The government had been attempting to develop a strategy covering the whole South Pacific area. On 26 February the Australian and New Zealand Chiefs of Staff had reviewed the situation in the Pacific and had recommended the establishment of an 'Anzac Area' with an American as Supreme Commander. This was to replace the naval 'Anzac Area' and was to be extended to include most of the Western Pacific, New Guinea, Ambon, Timor and the sea to about 500 miles around Australia. These proposals were transmitted to London and Washington on 1 March,[54] and a few days later the Australian Government decided that it would welcome General Brett, who had recently returned to Australia from ABDACOM, as Supreme Commander.

The receipt of the Chiefs of Staff's appreciation of 27 February lent support to Curtin's requests to London and Washington, and he cabled the Dominions Secretary that 'The Advisory War Council representing all political parties in Australia regard the whole matter as one of overriding urgency'.[55] Yet this was not just a last plea for help in a desperate situation. It is true that Curtin pointed out that Australia was threatened, but the main argument was that if Japan was to be defeated, then Australia and New Zealand were 'the only bases for offensive action by the Allied nations against the Japanese from the Anzac Area'.[56]

In anticipation of his appointment General Brett, who believed that the main threat to Australia was from the north-west,[57] now requested another appreciation from the Australian Chiefs of Staff on probable immediate Japanese moves in the proposed new Anzac Area. This appreciation was produced by the Australian DCGS, General Rowell, on 5 March, and he disagreed with Brett. He reiterated many of the statements of the appreciation of 27 February and concluded with a number of startling forecasts. These were that the Japanese might attack as follows.

a.   Upon Port Moresby in the middle of March,
b.   Upon Darwin in early April,
c.   Upon New Caledonia in the middle of April,
d.   Upon the east coast of Australia in May.[58]

That is, Rowell saw the main threat as coming from the north-east of Australia.

In this regard Rowell had gauged correctly the Japanese intentions, for on 2 February the Japanese Imperial General Headquarters had ordered the capture of Lae and Salamaua, and at the proper time Port Moresby. On 8 March Japanese forces landed at Lae and Salamaua. On 15 March Imperial General Headquarters debated whether to attack Australia. The result was a decision to capture Port Moresby and the Southern Solomons, and then 'to isolate Australia' by seizing Fiji, Samoa and New Caledonia.[59] Japan was now poised to strike at the islands to the north-east of Australia, but events elsewhere were to divert her attention until May. The Japanese High Command never really agreed to invade Australia.[60]

All this was not, of course, known at the time, but the prospect raised by Rowell alarmed the Americans in Australia. Brett had already radioed Washington: 'successful defence Australia doubtful unless immediate efforts made to formulate and implement detailed plans'.[61] General Barnes, who was acting as Brett's deputy, later wrote:

The entire situation in the South West Pacific area had reached the stage where successful defence of Australia itself was questionable, considering the force which the enemy could concentrate against it as soon as the situation was cleared up in the Netherlands East Indies, as compared with the defensive forces and equipment in Australia at that time.[62]

The American opinion of the situation can be gained from a memorandum written by Brigadier-General Patrick J. Hurley to General Marshall on 21 February. Hurley, a former Secretary of War, and an old friend of General Douglas MacArthur, had been sent to Australia to lend his 'energetic support' to attempts to get supplies to MacArthur who was the American commander in the Philippines.[63] Hurley found that there were two opinions of the situation. The first was that the operations north of Australia were to protect the Japanese flank before attacking through Burma towards India. The second was that after finding 'the opposition in Malaya and Netherlands East Indies so soft' the Japanese might include an all-out attack on Australia and New Zealand, while at the same time continuing operations in Burma. He continued:

I am convinced that if the Japanese should make an all-out attack on Australia before deciding the issue in Burma the situation would be immediately critical. It may be pointed out by the optimistic that Japanese landings in New Zealand and Australia would over extend long supply lines and thus enable us to break them, but when I stated this proposition to one of our Generals, he replied: 'Break them with what?' Unfortunately, his question is significant . . . it is essential that the Commonwealth and Dominion Governments of Australia and New Zealand recognise that the territories, for whose defense they are responsible, cannot be regarded any longer as their own strategic responsibilities, but that they constitute the arena in which the United Nations must stage their joint defense and offense. The paramount issue is still the defeat of Japan.[64]

The United Kingdom Chiefs of Staff had by this time produced another appreciation of the situation in the Far East. They believed that the immediate object should be 'to stabilise the situation so as to ensure the security of bases and points vital to our prosecution of the war'.[65] This was submitted to the Australian Advisory War Council on 11 March, which called for the observations of the Australian Chiefs of Staff.[66] By 14 March these observations had been produced and they stressed that the British appreciation laid 'too great an emphasis . . . upon stabilising our present position rather than taking the initiative from the Japanese'. They recommended sea and air harassment of the Japanese force at Rabaul and air attacks on the Japanese in the Netherlands East Indies as the best means of defending Port Moresby and Darwin. In particular the Chiefs of Staff called for an *Allied* force of British and U.S. naval units to conduct an offensive policy.

In our opinion . . . it is necessary to use such forces as we have to attack the Japanese, with a view to:
(i)   paving the way for future offensive operations on a large scale;
(ii)   preventing them from consolidating their present positions; and
(iii) preventing or hindering any further advances.[67]

In the light of this information, on 18 March the Advisory War Council reviewed again the defence of Australia.[68] They affirmed that Darwin and Port Moresby should be defended to the fullest possible extent, and that every effort should be made to provide forces for these areas. They also decided to move troops from Victoria to south Queensland, reinforce Fremantle and increase the tempo of building up the air force, especially in northern Australia.[69]

It is clear from this that Australia's intention was to carry the fight to the Japanese just as soon as forces became available to do it. At this stage, however, only the first troops of the 7th Australian Division had arrived in Australia. The 41st U.S. Division had not yet arrived but a further U.S. division had been offered to replace the 9th Australian Division which was to remain in the Middle East. Until these forces and American air forces arrived, Australia would have to remain on the defensive. This did not mean, as Eddie Ward and MacArthur later claimed, that the Australian Army planned to withdraw behind a Brisbane Line. Indeed on 3 June 1943 Mackay wrote to General Vasey: 'Did you ever hear of the "Brisbane Line" till lately . . . my letter to the Minister of 4 February 1942 has been pulled about by one Eddie Ward and is now used as a political weapon by the government against the opposition'.[70] The next day Mackay told Gavin Long that he thought: 'MacArthur's statement, inferring that there had been a defeatist policy in Australia until MacArthur took over and began to fight the Japanese in the islands, as a piece of skite'.[71] The true Australian position is revealed by a letter written by Vasey to an American general, possibly Barnes, on 20 March 1942.

I hope you realised from our conversation that what we told you was our *present* plan; but that as more troops become available we shall continually revise it. Like your colleague of yesterday I feel that we are only deluding ourselves if we make and *count on* future plans which we have not the means of carrying out.[72]

Yet if the evidence that Australia intended to set up a Brisbane Line is tenuous, there is evidence that some Americans were thinking along those lines. In the 7th Fleet History File for 1942 there is what appears to be a USAFIA appreciation written in early or mid March 1942. This appreciation began that:

a major offensive by Japan against the Australian continent is likely before the combined resources of Australia and the United States in the area can be materially increased, *and therefore that the defence must be planned and carried out with the resources actually available now*

The appreciation considered tentative locations for defensive positions which could be organised in depth and strongly and resolutely held. These were:

a. In the east. Along the general line west from Maryborough in Queensland.
b. In the centre. Along the MacDonnell Range north of Alice Springs.
c. In the west. Along a general line north of the line Lowlers-Mt Magnet-Geraldton.

It was realised that this view would be opposed by those who believed that the outer areas should be held for use by aircraft, and that there were political considerations. The appreciation came to the following conclusions.

a. That Darwin was indefensible and forces there should be engaged in a delaying action only.
b. That reliance on Brisbane was unjustified.
c. That Sydney should be the base for the USAFIA and that activities in Brisbane should be transferred there.
d. That the extended development of air bases, except for landing fields, outside of the vital areas should be discontinued for the time being. Bases for heavy bombers should be built in vital areas and remote from the coast.
e. Joint Staff action between Australian and U.S. air, ground and naval forces should be indicated to co-ordinate defence.

It is not known what happened to this appreciation but it would not have been welcomed by the Australian Chiefs of Staff. The suggestion to form a defensive line in the MacDonnell Range showed an abysmal knowledge of Australian geography.[73]

On 20 March the government received a reply from the United Kingdom to a cable detailing the Australian Chiefs of Staff's comments on the UK appreciation. This reply advised that the UK Government did not feel that it was justified in disregarding other risks and duties to undertake a naval offensive operation[74] and confirmed that Australia would simply have to hold on until American support arrived. On a number of occasions the government had expressed its willingness to accept an American Supreme Commander in the area, and had pressed London and Washington to appoint one. Then on 7 March Earle Page, the Australian representative, cabled from London that the British and Americans had tentatively reached agreement to divide the world into areas of strategic responsibility. Two days later the government agreed to send Dr Evatt to Washington. Meanwhile Australia held her breath.

The Americans in Australia now expected an attack in the Darwin area by three enemy divisions before the end of the month,[75] and the Australian Chiefs of Staff forecast an attack on Port Moresby during the same period.[76] By the middle of March an air of panic or desperation hung over some quarters of the Australian population.[77] On 11 March Ek Dum of the *Bulletin* wrote: 'War has ceased merely to be on Australia's doorstep. It is on the mat reaching for the knocker'.[78] The Sydney *Daily Mirror* discovered a 'reputed tremor of civilian morale through some sections in Australia', and Federal ministers were perturbed at what they considered to be a lowering of public morale.[79] This panic was not, however, peculiar to Australia. In America some government officials 'suggested establishing battle lines in the Rocky Mountains'.[80]

The Japanese played upon these fears.[81] On 3 March a Japanese radio announcement was heard in Townsville:

Many thanks to the Americans for having hot water laid on in the Queen's Hotel, for building a new aerodrome and headquarters; we will soon be using them . . . We also know of 70 bushmen going to Townsville from Melbourne.[82]

Actually seventy-four men of an anti-aircraft battery had just been transferred from Melbourne. When on 8 March Japanese forces landed on the north coast of New Guinea schools were closed in north Queensland. A government report noted that: 'a hurried exodus followed, and it is estimated that Cairns and Townsville each lost between five and seven thousand residents'.[83] It was against such a background that the government decided to restructure the Australian and Allied command systems.

4
Restructuring the Command System
7 December 1941 –
17 April 1942

Japan's attacks on 7 December, and her swift advance to Australia's doorstep, not only accelerated plans for the defence of the Australian continent, but it also caused the government to reconsider the problem of providing commanders for the rapidly expanding army. One of the first considerations was the distribution of commanders and staff officers between Australia and the Middle East, and it was felt that there should be a review of personnel holding high command and staff appointments in Australia.[1]

It will be recalled that in July 1941 the War Cabinet had asked for the particulars of the potential successors of the division commanders, but it had been recognised that the younger, more able and experienced commanders were in the Middle East. The process of returning selected officers to Australia had already begun. Mackay and Rowell had returned in September, Brigadier B. M. Morris, who had commanded the Australian Overseas Base in the Middle East at the beginning of the war, had become the commandant of the 8th Military District (New Guinea) in May 1941, and Major-General E. J. Milford, who as a brigadier had commanded 7th Division Artillery in Palestine, had become MGO in January 1941.[2] Major-General H. D. Wynter, who had commanded the Australian Force in Britain, but had relinquished command of the 9th Division because of ill health, had become the Chief of Staff of Eastern Command in July 1941. When on 19 December 1941 Lieutenant-General C. G. N. Miles had retired, Wynter had become GOC of Eastern Command.[3]

Nevertheless, with the exception of Mackay and Rowell, no commanders with battle experience in the current war had been returned to Australia. Faced with the problems of the defence of Australia and the training of the militia, the government now determined to bring home a number of senior and experienced Staff Corps officers to bolster the home forces. Brigadier G. A. Vasey, aged 46, the commander of the 19th Brigade, returned to Australia as a Major-General to become Chief of Staff to General Mackay, Brigadier H. C. H. Robertson, 47, who had commanded the 19th Brigade in Libya and was now commander of the AIF Reinforcement Depot, returned and was promoted to command the 1st Cavalry Division. Brigadier E. C. P. Plant, 51, the commander of the 25th Brigade returned and was promoted to become GOC of Western Command,[4] and Brigadier C. A. Clowes, 49, the artillery commander of I Australian Corps, returned and was promoted to command the 1st Infantry Division. These four officers were all from the Staff Corps, and three had graduated from Duntroon. The defence correspondent of the *Sydney Morning Herald* noted that:

They do not come to a problem that is new to them, because since the last war they have been discussing and planning to meet a situation like that which now threatens . . . Australia . . . In Australia key command and staff appointments are now being allotted to a long list of Duntroon-trained soldiers, who will be doing a job they have been preparing to do for 20 years or so.[5]

In October 1941 General Blamey had recommended the recall of Brigadiers S. G. Savige, aged 51, and J. J. Murray, a rather overweight 49, to conduct a recruiting campaign — 'he felt this would be a graceful way of retiring with honour two officers who had done useful work in the Middle East but seemed to him unequal to the severe physical trial of fast moving modern warfare'.[6] In the crisis, and realising the psychological value of promoting two militia brigadiers from the AIF, the government promoted Savige to command the 3rd Division, and Murray to command the Newcastle Covering Force (later the 10th Division).[7]

There were a number of other appointments from within Australia. Brigadier W. J. M. Locke was promoted to command the 2nd Australian Division, and Brigadier W. A. B. Steele was promoted to be the Base Commandant of Southern Command. Both of those officers were Duntroon graduates, but had not served overseas during the war. In addition Brigadier B. M. Morris, the Commander in New Guinea, and Brigadier D. V. J. Blake, the commander in Darwin, were promoted to Major-General.[8] All these changes were completed by the end of the first week of January.

These promotions meant that a number of senior officers had to be retired.[9] In announcing the new appointments, Forde pointed out that they were made in accordance with the government's policy of replacing senior commanders and staff officers by younger officers, and, where possible, by those who had had active service experience in the war. Referring to the retired officers he continued:

The Government appreciates the sterling work and long and honourable service of those officers who are being replaced. They all devoted close attention to their duties and achieved excellent results in the war of 1914-1918, in the process of training and administration of the militia between 1920 and 1939, and finally in the expansion and training of the military forces since the outbreak of the present war.[10]

Ek Dum of the *Bulletin* answered the critics in the more excitable press when he noted that one paper

raised a triumphant scream of 'Four Generals Sacked'. All that had happened was that older men, with splendid records, three of whom had given up important positions in civil life to which they were anxious to return, had been replaced by men whose age advantage had made it possible for them to gain 1941-42 war experience.[11]

The replacement of a number of senior officers did not solve the command problems in the army. Soon after he returned to Australia General Savige told newspapermen:

The basis of our training must be that every man is a master of the weapons he handles, and that non-commissioned officers are trained to the highest possible standard, because leadership devolves on the junior leader in modern war to a much greater extent than in the last war.[12]

At that time lieutenants were not commissioned in the AIF (except for good service in the field) unless they were under 30 years of age. Captains had to be under 35 and majors under 40 when first appointed. Yet in the militia the limits were 10 to 15 years higher. The experience of the Middle East proved the value of younger officers. One AIF battalion had gone into action at Bardia with about fifty returned soldiers. After the capture of Tobruk the only returned soldiers still with the unit were the commanding officer and three or four non-commissioned officers. The others had not been able to stand up to the severe conditions.[13]

At the end of March 1942 Gavin Long compared the ages of the brigadiers of the 1st Division of the 1st AIF and the corresponding divisions of the 2nd AIF and the AMF:[14]

| 1st AIF | 2nd AIF | AMF |
(1st Division)	(6th Division)	(1st Division)
36	47	52
43	42	46
31	38	45
39	37	48

He urged that the new commanders for the AMF should be selected from those who had given evidence that they were the best men for the job, regardless of age and seniority. General Savige reiterated the problem of finding commanders in early 1942 when he wrote later: 'Strong pressure was exerted to find a job for a middle-aged departmental manager in a large emporium who had risen to the rank of Major at HQ since his enlistment after the outbreak of war'.[15] All this was valid criticism, but until the convoys of the AIF returned, young, experienced leaders were not available. Until then, elderly World War I veterans were still better equipped to train the newly formed units than the young inexperienced officers who had not joined the AIF.

Parallel with the problem of finding younger commanders was that of organising a command structure suitable for the situation. On 11 December 1941 the Prime Minister discussed this matter with the Minister for the Army, and the points covered included the return of General Blamey, the appointment of a C-in-C of the army and the status of the Military Board, and they considered the possibility of the C-in-C also commanding the Air Force.[16]

For a while, however, nothing was done in the matter of higher direction. On 22 December General Mackay opened his headquarters,[17] but not to exercise command of the Home Forces as detailed in his instructions of September 1941, for early in the new year it was announced that the defence of Australia would be divided between Mackay, who would be responsible for Queensland, New South Wales, Victoria, Tasmania and South Australia, General Plant, who would be responsible for Western Australia, Brigadier Blake, for Northern Territory, and Brigadier Morris for New Guinea. This immediately raised a storm of protest in the press, and the editorial of the *Sunday Telegraph* claimed on 11 January 1942 that:

At a time when unified, central and vigorous command was never more necessary we have taken a step backwards towards disunity, more muddle and red tape . . .
A fortnight ago we seemed to be moving forward to a sane and modern conception of what an Australian Home Army should be. There were fifteen

major changes in the personnel of the Army Command. Six senior officers were brought from the Middle East to make army training thoroughly realistic.

The latest move is completely retrograde . . . This is no time for finicky politeness. If Mackay is a better man than Sturdee, he should be made GOC — a real GOC — over Sturdee.

If Sturdee is the better man, make him GOC, with power really to command. But let's do it now, not wait till the fight is on us.[18]

The defence correspondent of the *Sydney Morning Herald* was also concerned.

We have then a picture of an Australian facing the near approach of a remorseless enemy, frantically striving to make up lost time in the last hours given her to arm herself — facing this situation with neither a single army nor a single commander; but with at least two separate and basically distinct organisations of incompletely trained soldiers, a sharply divided command, and, as supreme directing authority, a committee or board, partly departmental and almost wholly lacking practical knowledge of modern warfare.[19]

Nevertheless this unsatisfactory situation continued, and the *Bulletin* even found 'the scheme sensible enough' provided that the commanders were able to make quick decisions and take responsibility without undue interference from 'come-by-chance Ministers, State Governments and pea hen editors'.[20]

A month later the *Sydney Morning Herald* again attacked the scheme, reviving the argument that there should be unity of command and asserting that it was wrong that the commanders of the field forces should be subordinate to the Military Board. The editorial concluded:

The remedy, surely, is to appoint a commander-in-chief without delay and invest him with complete powers. General Sir Thomas Blamey is the Australian soldier best fitted for the post. His appointment would overcome duality of control, and give to the home defence forces a homogenity [*sic*] of command which at this crucial moment is dangerously lacking.[21]

The argument for a C-in-C had been discussed since the outbreak of war, and indeed at the Imperial Conference in 1937 the Australian Government had declared that: 'The experience of war also proves that the direction of military operations by a Board is unsound. Such a form of control has either failed with disastrous results, or has been abandoned under the force of circumstances.'[22] Before the appearance of the *Sydney Morning Herald* editorial the government had, apparently, already decided on a course of action, for on 20 February Curtin had cabled Blamey requesting him to return to Australia 'as speedily as possible'.[23] On 5 March the Advisory War Council agreed in principle that Sir Thomas Blamey should be appointed C-in-C of the Australian Army, but that any appointment of an Acting C-in-C should be deferred until General Blamey's arrival because of an unsettling effect that this could produce.[24] The appointment was discussed again on 11 March and it was decided that:

In view of the gravity of the Japanese threat to Australia and as the date of return to Australia of General Sir Thomas Blamey is uncertain, action should be taken forthwith to appoint an Acting Commander-in-Chief of the Australian Military Forces.

It was therefore agreed that Lieutenant-General Sir John Lavarack, the commander of I Australian Corps, who had arrived in Australia from Java on 23 February, should be appointed to this position.[25] Apparently Lavarack was not considered for the position as C-in-C. Gavin Long later wrote in his diary that Curtin appeared to harbour a lack of faith in Lavarack because in September 1939 Lavarack had given him the impression of being a man in despair because the long expected war was on him and Australia was not ready.[26]

Meanwhile Sturdee was thinking about a suitable organisation for the defence of Australia. In February he proposed that the Home Forces should be redesignated First Australian Army, Eastern Command, II Corps, South Command, III Corps, Northern Command, 5th Division and the Newcastle Covering Force, 10th Division. The changes were designed to clarify responsibilities and make it clear that Mackay was no longer to be considered GOC-in-C for the defence of Australia.[27]

These proposals were not introduced at that time, but they indicate the manner in which Sturdee was thinking, and this is confirmed in the details for the reorganisation which he presented to the minister following the decision to appoint a Commander-in-Chief. He argued that the C-in-C should be responsible to the government until the time that a Supreme Commander of the ANZAC Area was apppointed to whom he would then be responsible. Until this Supreme Commander was appointed, the Military Board would temporarily cease to exist and its members would become the principal staff officers on the staff of the C-in-C. The CGS would continue to exist and would represent the C-in-C at meetings of War Cabinet. Following the appointment of a Supreme Commander the Military Board would be reconstituted to look after the 'Home Administration' and to advise the government, although its responsibilities would be restricted, leaving the C-in-C free to devote his time to operations and war training. It was proposed that the forces under the C-in-C would be divided into:

a.   First Army under Lieutenant-General Sir John Lavarack.
b.   Second Army under Lieutenant-General Sir Iven Mackay.
c.   Port Moresby.
d.   New Caledonia.

The First Army would include Northern and Eastern Commands and consist of three corps, and the Second Army covering the remainder of Australia would have a corps in Victoria and South Australia and independent forces in Tasmania, Western Australia and Northern Territory. The First Army staff would be created from that of I Australian Corps and the Second Army staff from that of HQ Home Forces.[28]

While Sturdee was preparing plans for the reorganisation of the army, the government was considering whom to promote to fill the new positions. Major-General Gordon Bennett, who had just escaped from Singapore, met the War Cabinet on 2 March,[29] and although it was not discussed at the meeting he felt that after his experience in Malaya he should be named the Australian Commander-in-Chief.[30] Forde was impressed with Bennett,[31] but did not act immediately. Finally on 11 March, after the decision to appoint Blamey had been decided, Bennett was appointed to the position of Acting Inspector-General of Training so that he could visit training centres and pass on his knowledge of Japanese tactics.

Unaware of the government's decision to recall Blamey, and afraid that either Bennett or Lavarack would be appointed as C-in-C, a number of officers had been pressing for a young charismatic military leader. Three officers, General E. F. Herring and Brigadier C. S. Steele, who had recently returned with I Australian Corps, and General Vasey, proposed to Forde that Major-General H. C. H. Robertson — 'Red Robbie', who had commanded the 19th Brigade at Bardia and Tobruk — should be appointed. As an afterthought they suggested that all generals over the age of 50 should be retired. This would have disqualified not only Blamey, whom they imagined had been overlooked, but Lavarack, Morshead, Bennett, Mackay, North-cott, Sturdee and Savige, and a number of other generals, while most others were within a few years of that age.[32] Forde knew that Blamey had already arrived in Perth and he offered no encouragement. Robertson had, however, been urging his own chances, and had told Forde that he was prepared to take any post offered to him, even that of C-in-C.[33]

Of more importance to Forde was the matter of finding officers of division commander level, and earlier in the week he had discussed this with the acting C-in-C, General Lavarack.[34] Forde was already considering Robertson, Vasey and Steele, but while recognising their qualities and being willing to accept Robertson as a division commander and Steele as Engineer-in-Chief, Lavarack did not feel that they were the best men available. In the first bracket he placed Rowell and he wrote to Forde that:

This officer has had no experience in actual command during this war, mainly because his services as a staff officer, both to Blamey and myself, have been indispensable. I should have no doubt myself about taking him either for command or high staff work, as I hold him in the greatest esteem for his strength of character, intelligence, judgement and loyalty. I should be glad to accept him in any capacity including a Corps Command or Lieutenant General on the General Staff.[35]

Next Lavarack placed Brigadier F. H. Berryman, his BGS of I Australian Corps, and Brigadier J. E. S. Stevens of the 21st Brigade.

Both good strong fighting men of real experience in successful battle, and both equipped with forceful character, brains and loyalty. Berryman in addition has the advantage of being a highly trained and experienced staff officer. Either could fill a Divisional Command at once and would probably go higher after that experience. Berryman, in addition, could fill the appointment of Major-General, General Staff, to an Army Commander.[36]

Lavarack then went on to suggest Brigadiers W. Bridgeford, H. B. Sewell, V. C. Secombe and I. N. Dougherty.[37]

In the light of the representations made by Bennett and Robertson, and the news of the intentions of Herring, Vasey and Steele, which he heard from Rowell,[38] Lavarack found it necessary to add a warning to his letter to Forde:

I think it very necessary to stress the loyalty aspect in assessing an officer's value. Without this quality in its officers any Army must eventually break up into cliques. Therefore, other things being equal, I place an officer whom I know to be reliable in this respect above one of whom I am not sure.[39]

Blamey arrived in Melbourne on Thursday 26 March and met the War Cabinet in Canberra the following day, where he received his instructions. Basing his plans upon those already prepared by Sturdee and Lavarack, by 31 March he was able to submit his proposals to War Cabinet. These proposals followed, in outline, those prepared by Sturdee,[40] but Blamey increased the force in Western Australia to one corps and placed the forces in Western Australia and Northern Territory under Army Headquarters, which he called General Headquarters. The First Army was to have two corps instead of the three proposed by Sturdee. As had been intimated in the appreciation of 27 February, one of the AIF brigade groups (19th) recently arrived in Australia was to be despatched to Darwin immediately. On 27 March Major-General E. F. Herring left Adelaide for Darwin to assume command of Northern Territory Force.[41] These proposals were accepted with one condition. Blamey proposed that General Wynter should go to Washington as the Army Representative, General Northcott should become Lieutenant-General-in-charge-of-Administration (LGA) and General Smart the commander of II Corps in Lavarack's First Army.[42] If Wynter was found fit enough, however, it was planned that he should become LGA, Smart should go to Washington and Northcott to II Corps, and this was how it eventuated.[43]

As Lavarack had foreshadowed a week before, Rowell, at the age of 47, became a lieutenant-general and commander of I Corps. Berryman became Lavarack's MGGS, Steele became E-in-C, Stevens became a division commander and Bridgeford became DA & QMG of the First Army. In all six brigadiers were promoted to major-general.[44] This new organisation drew immediate praise in the papers, as had the announcement of Blamey's appointment five days earlier. The editorial of the *Sydney Morning Herald* noted that:

In his choice of the soldiers who are to fill the new posts, General Blamey, with the endorsement of the Government, has followed a policy long advocated in these columns of giving the best jobs to the best men wherever they are to be found . . . The foundations of planning and organisation on which General Blamey will work can be assumed to have been soundly built by General Sturdee, whom General Blamey retains as his Chief of Staff.[45]

Blamey was now faced with an immense and complicated task. The technical problem of defending Australia with very limited forces was just one of his many problems. He must have been aware of the jockeying amongst the senior officers that had gone on in Australia before his arrival. Not only was there the so-called 'revolt of the generals', and the machinations of Robertson and Bennett, but

Lavarack too must have felt resentment that his old rival, Blamey, had been successful. They would all be waiting for a false step. For a while Forde harboured some doubts about Blamey's suitability, but he consulted General Douglas MacArthur, the new American Commander-in-Chief, who replied that he was quite satisfied with Blamey. 'He is an experienced military officer; he is very courteous and comes to see me whenever I want to see him immediately; nothing seems to be a trouble to him and my wish would be that you would not take any action to remove him'.[46]

Blamey returned to a situation in Australia that had been developed under the control of his new subordinates. He was not completely happy with some of the details of the proposed organisation, or with some of the new commanders; but for the time being he would have to make do and wait for an opportunity for readjustment. Nevertheless he could not appear to falter, nor did he. His decisions were rapid, sure and to the point. Yet under the gruff exterior and despite the assurances of the government, he could not but have felt the precariousness of his position.

The announcement that Blamey was to be Commander-in-Chief of the army followed soon after a more startling and even more welcome announcement. On 18 March it had been announced that General Douglas MacArthur was to assume supreme command in the ANZAC Area.[47] On 17 March MacArthur had arrived in Darwin, and on that day, at the direction of President Roosevelt, Brett had telephoned Curtin with the news that MacArthur was to command all U.S. forces in Australia. It was suggested that MacArthur should become Supreme Commander of all Allied forces in the South-West Pacific.[48]

This information was welcome news for the government, for that morning the Australian Chiefs of Staff had completed a report in which they had agreed that the supreme commander of the proposed South-West Pacific Area should be an American, and that he should be located in Australia.[49] The War Cabinet meeting of that day concurred and 'felt that General MacArthur's leadership of the Allied Forces in this theatre would be an inspiration'.[50]

While MacArthur made his way slowly by train from Alice Springs to Melbourne, the Australian newspapers were jubilant. The editorial of the Brisbane *Courier-Mail* said that: 'The arrival in Australia of General Douglas MacArthur . . . is stirring news, the best news Australians have had for many a day'.[51] The *Bulletin* commented that:

in sending their national hero to Australia [the Americans] have charged themselves with the responsibility of saving it as a free white English speaking

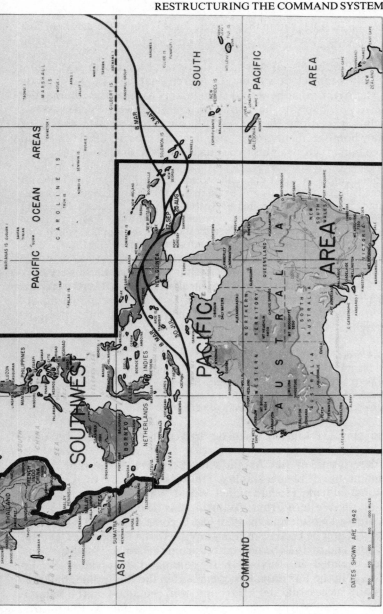

Map 1   The boundaries of the South-West Pacific area and the extent of the Japanese advance. From *Reports of General MacArthur*, Vol.1, p.32.

nation, as far as it lies within their power, for it is not in the nature of that great people to let MacArthur down.[52]

Unknown to the rest of Australia, however, MacArthur was feeling that he had been let down. On 18 March Marshall in Washington cabled MacArthur that he would assume duty as supreme commander of an area 'probably to be known as the Southwest Pacific Area'. MacArthur was informed that his U.S. air forces were to consist of two heavy bombardment groups, two medium groups, one light group and three pursuit groups plus two squadrons. Marshall continued:

U.S. ground forces in Australia, aside from field artillery and anti-aircraft units already there or enroute, will be limited to the 41st Division except that this country has agreed to dispatch to Australia another division in the event Australia permits an additional one to remain in the Middle East . . . These limits on U.S. forces are definitely fixed by shortages in shipping, which is of the utmost seriousness, and by critical situations elsewhere.[53]

Simultaneously with this news, MacArthur learnt that there were only about 25,000 American troops in Australia, and that there were not enough troops in Australia to defend it, let alone to conduct an offensive to regain the Philippines.[54] MacArthur was bitterly disappointed by these revelations. One biographer has written:

This news literally stunned MacArthur. He turned deadly white, his knees buckled, his lips twitched. An officer who had known him for 20 years said later, 'I have never seen him so affected. He was . . . heartbroken'. After a long silence, McArthur whispered miserably, 'God have mercy on us'. Unable to sleep, he spent the whole night pacing the train.[55]

Next morning (21 March) when he arrived in Melbourne, his confidence had returned.

This description of MacArthur's reaction gives some hint of the emotional nature of his personality. He was already one of America's outstanding soldiers. He had ended World War I as a division commander on the Western Front; following this he had become Superintendent of West Point, and by 1930 had become Chief of Staff of the U.S. Army. Later he became military adviser to the Philippine Government. At the end of 1937 he had retired from the American Army, but had been recalled in July 1941 to command the United States Army Forces in the Far East. His command in the Philippines had not been signally successful, and his troops, who remained on the Bataan Peninsula, were shortly to face a disaster exceeded only by that of the

British at Singapore. The defeat rankled deeply within him, and he vowed to return to the Philippines.

When Forde met MacArthur at Melbourne railway station on 21 March, he was tremendously impressed. Although MacArthur was aged 62, 'he did not look it', recalled Forde, 'He seemed to have black hair; he was well proportioned and kept in the very best physical form and cameramen were always glad to photograph him'.[56] Aloof, highly intelligent, widely hated and also loved throughout the American Army, MacArthur believed it was his destiny to lead an Allied force to victory in the Pacific. General Brett wrote of him:

a brilliant, temperamental egoist; a handsome man, who can be as charming as anyone who ever lived, or harshly indifferent to the needs and desires of those around. His religion is deeply part of his nature . . . Everything about Douglas MacArthur is on the grand scale; his virtues and triumphs and short-comings.[57]

MacArthur shunned publicity unless it would personally assist him, then he used all means available to him. He was suspicious of other generals, particularly of Marshall, who believed that MacArthur thought everyone had ulterior motives about everything.[58] MacArthur also heartily disliked the navy, and the feeling was mutual. Some sailors called him 'the Brass-Hatted Bastard'.[59] General Herring, who served with MacArthur from October 1942 throughout 1943, found him a very remarkable man with a great presence, yet terribly vain. Gavin Long, after an interview with MacArthur, wrote that he was 'a man of mind and feeling rather than a man of iron'.[60]

In late 1943 Colonel G. H. Wilkinson, the British liaison officer, reported of MacArthur:

He is shrewd, selfish, proud, remote, highly-strung and vastly vain. He has imagination, self-confidence, physical courage and charm but no humour about himself, no regard for truth, and is unaware of these defects.
He mistakes his emotions and ambitions for principles. With moral depth he would be a great man: as it is he is a near-miss, which may be worse than a mile . . . his main ambition would be to end the war as pan-American hero in the form of generalissimo of all Pacific theatres . . . he hates Roosevelt and dislikes Winston's control of Roosevelt's strategy . . . [he] is not basically anti-British just pro-MacArthur.[61]

Yet for all his faults MacArthur gained the confidence of Australia and of the government. The Deputy Prime Minister, Frank Forde, commented that faced by 'the greatest catastrophe that could have happened' the country looked to America. The government 'felt that General Douglas MacArthur was the man who would influence his government along the right lines'.[62]

On 26 March MacArthur addressed the Advisory War Council. He said that there were two schools of thought on the strategy to be followed in the war. The first regarded the European theatre as dominant, the second was that the Pacific was more important. He believed, and asked the Australians to stand firmly by the view, that the first step 'was to make Australia secure' after which a counter-offensive would be organised. He doubted whether the Japanese would undertake an invasion of Australia, but they would attempt to secure air bases.[63]

During the next few days discussion continued about the form of MacArthur's command. He had not yet been officially designated Supreme Commander, and on 1 April he wrote that he was functioning with the Australians by 'co-ordination and co-operation'.[64] Finally, on 3 April, he received his directive from Washington. He was ordered to 'hold the key military regions of Australia as bases for further offensive action against Japan, and in order to check the Japanese advance towards Australia and its essential lines of communication'. That is, although he was ordered to 'prepare to take the offensive', it was primarily a defensive directive. MacArthur was also told that he could not directly command any national force.[65] At this stage, however, the Australian Government had not ratified this directive.

MacArthur now began to organise his headquarters. Fourteen officers had come to Australia with MacArthur and these, who were known as 'the Bataan Gang', resented the intrusion of outsiders,[66] particularly those who were from the original USAFIA staff. It was clear from the beginning that 'the Bataan Gang' was to form the nucleus of MacArthur's new headquarters. He had brought with him his Chief of Staff, Major-General R. K. Sutherland, his deputy Chief of Staff, Brigadier-General R. J. Marshall, and a number of other senior officers. MacArthur proposed to promote a number of these to fill important positions on the Allied headquarters staff. When he put this to Washington, General George C. Marshall, who had been astonished that MacArthur had taken most of his staff from the Philippines, leaving no senior staff officer with General Wainwright,[67] replied:

The situation in the new Southwest Pacific area has so developed that the supreme commander, his Chief of Staff, the air commander, and the naval commander, will probably all be officers of the United States forces. In this situation the President feels that a number of higher positions on your staff should be occupied by Dutch and particularly by Australian officers.[68]

This made little impression on MacArthur, who explained later that there were no 'qualified Dutch officers' in Australia and that the Australians did not have enough staff officers for their own rapidly expanding army. 'There is no prospect', he told Marshall flatly, 'of obtaining qualified senior staff officers from the Australians'.[69]

Major-General Richard Sutherland continued as MacArthur's Chief of Staff throughout the war, and had a major influence on relationships between MacArthur and his subordinate commanders. He was a brilliant, hardworking officer, but his egocentricity and arrogance made him universally disliked. He was brusque, short tempered and autocratic,[70] and was an exacting taskmaster, but even 'his worst enemies . . . never questioned his professional competence'.[71] Brigadier Rogers, who was on the staff of GHQ, as MacArthur's headquarters was known, and who later became Blamey's Director of Military Intelligence, noticed that Sutherland was rarely helpful to General Vasey, or later to General Berryman, when they were Blamey's DCGS.

It was not just the Australians and the American naval and air officers who found it difficult to deal with Sutherland. He alone remained able to talk freely to MacArthur. Brigadier-General Willoughby, MacArthur's Chief of Intelligence, who had come out from the Philippines, found Sutherland to be a hard man, an indefatigable worker who kept his difficult temper under control.[72] Major-General R. L. Eichelberger, who later became a corps and then an army commander under MacArthur, wrote of Sutherland:

Nothing remarkable about Sutherland — he was a natural climber trying to advance his own interests at the expense of the other fellows. He told me personally with great pride of how he had managed to get rid of Eisenhower and become MacArthur's Chief of Staff . . . Sutherland was a smoothie and I had to be something of one myself in dealing with him.[73]

On another occasion Eichelberger wrote of Sutherland's relationship with MacArthur:

He knew how to work on General MacArthur like Paderewski playing the piano. He could bring out in MacArthur any latent jealousy and envy in his nature . . . Sutherland had a strange control over MacArthur. He knew all of MacArthur's little failures, weaknesses and foibles, and he could manoeuvre him and play on these characteristics like an expert plucking the strings of a fine violin.[74]

The Australian Government had not yet agreed to President Roosevelt's directive to MacArthur, and on 7 April asked that it be amended so that MacArthur could only move Australian troops out of Australian territory with the consent of the Australian Government. Curtin, however, already considered that MacArthur was the Supreme Commander,[75] and that General Blamey, as well as being C-in-C of the AMF, was Commander of the Allied Land Forces.[76]

In anticipation of assuming command of the Allied Land Forces, on 9 April Blamey issued orders detailing the reorganisation of these forces into a Field Army and Lines of Communication Areas. Blamey was to command from General Headquarters (renamed Land Headquarters in May) and this was located in Melbourne. The Military Board was abolished and the members became Blamey's principal staff officers. Sturdee continued as CGS and Vasey became deputy CGS.[77]

The new groupings meant that the 7th Division, which had just arrived in Adelaide with a strength of about 18,000, was to move immediately to northern NSW. The move was to be completed by 27 April. To build up the strength of the two brigades in Western Australia to a full division (4th) the 2nd Brigade and divisional troops, totalling 6,000, were ordered from Melbourne to Perth.[78] Command was to pass from the GOC-in-C Home Forces to the two army commanders on 15 April, and the headquarters of the various commands and military districts were to cease operating on the same date.[79]

By 14 April the Australian Government was happy with the terms of MacArthur's directive and on 17 April Curtin wrote to MacArthur that the next day he would hand over the combat elements of the Australian defence forces in the Australian area to him, and that all orders and instructions issued by him were to be considered by Australian commanders as emanating from the Commonwealth Government.[80] On 18 April MacArthur issued his first general order and this specified the following commands:

a. Allied Land Forces, Southwest Pacific Area. Commander: General Sir Thomas Blamey, KCB, CMG, DSO, Australian Army.
b. Allied Air Forces, Southwest Pacific Area. Commander: Lieutenant General George H. Brett, United States Army.
c. Allied Naval Forces, Southwest Pacific Area. Commander: Vice Admiral Herbert F. Leary, United States Navy.

d. United States Forces in the Philippines. Commander: Lieutenant General Jonathon M. Wainwright, United States Army.

e. United States Army Forces in Australia. Commander: Major General Julian F. Barnes, United States Army.[81]

The next day MacArthur named the staff of the combined Allied General Headquarters. Of the eleven senior positions, all were filled by American Army officers, and of these eight had come out of the Philippines with MacArthur.[82]

Of all the senior positions in the SWPA only one was held by an Australian. Not only was Blamey Commander Allied Land Forces, but he continued as Commander-in-Chief of the AMF. On 14 April Curtin detailed the machinery for the higher direction of the war. He explained that he would be the link between the government and MacArthur, and that the Department of Defence Co-ordination would revert to the Department of Defence. The advisers to the government on Australian defence would be the C-in-C of the AMF, the Chief of the Naval Staff and the Chief of the Air Staff. These would attend the Advisory War Council and War Cabinet meetings as required, although the CGS (Sturdee) could represent Blamey. MacArthur was not responsible for the internal administration of the respective forces under his command.[83]

Blamey felt that he should be able to communicate directly with Curtin if necessary, and on 23 April Shedden informed him that this was allowed.[84] Then on 25 April Curtin explained the situation in detail to Blamey. He reiterated that the government would not interfere with army operations. As adviser to the government on Australian Army policy Blamey was to have direct access to the Prime Minister, but all matters of administration were to be dealt with by the Minister for the Army.[85]

From a point of despair in mid March the government had now secured the assured help of the USA, and had established a system of command to utilise the considerable forces now to be arrayed. It was with a sense of relief that the government handed over the resources of the country to a foreign general, fully confident that he would handle them with skill and judgment. Yet the situation faced by MacArthur in mid April was scarcely less daunting than that faced by the Australian Chiefs of Staff, Sturdee, Burnett and Royle, a month earlier.

5
From Defensive to Offensive
27 March – 20 July 1942

By the end of March 1942 the Japanese had occupied the main areas of the Netherlands East Indies and they had established footholds on the north coast of New Guinea. Although the American forces in the Philippines were still resisting, the initial objectives of the Japanese High Command had been achieved. Australia stood on the defensive, expecting an attack any day. Yet during that month the first AIF troops began returning to Australia from overseas.

Three months later the forces in Australia began to prepare for an offensive through the islands to the north against the Japanese occupiers. The changes in Japanese and Allied strategy which brought about this reversal of initiative have been adequately dealt with elsewhere.[1] But the changes within the army in Australia helped make possible the plan for the offensive. It was a fine achievement by General Blamey and the newly promoted officers of the AIF to weld the different elements of the AIF, militia and U.S. forces into one army by June 1942. There were many problems, and they were not all solved, but the major problem, that of defending Australia with troops who were completing elementary training, was overcome, within the limits of the defensibility of the continent.

The main argument during the period revolves around MacArthur's later claims that the Australians had planned to defend the country from the Brisbane Line, and that it was he who decided to take the fight to the Japanese in New Guinea. The events of the period, and in particular MacArthur's plans for defending Australia in April 1942, reveal the over simplification of this notion.

The fragile nature of Australia's defences in early 1942 is emphasised by the impact made by the returning AIF officers and units. The first direct impact was made in Darwin. The Japanese attack on Darwin on 19 February 1942 brought home to the Australian people that the front line in the war had now reached their shores.[2] To civilian and soldier alike in this 'northern station' the attack seemed to presage a Japanese landing. The rapid and unseemly evacuation of the city by some civilian and military elements indicated the morale-lowering effect of the attack and the necessity for the reinforcement of the area. Not only was Darwin the first line of Australia's defence, but also the most forward base for air attacks on Japanese installations in the Netherlands East Indies, and it had to be held.

The military garrison in Darwin consisted of the Darwin Fortress Area, and two infantry brigades under the command of Major-General D. V. J. Blake. Aged 54, Blake was a regular officer and had commanded the 3rd Squadron AFC during World War I. He had ended the war temporarily commanding 15 Wing RAF, but he had not seen overseas service during World War II. One of his brigades, the 23rd commanded by Brigadier E. F. Lind, was nominally an AIF brigade, but Lind had been forced to watch as each of his battalions was systematically destroyed at Rabaul (23 January), Ambon (3 February) and Timor (23 February). The 2/4th Pioneer Battalion, the 2/14th Field Regiment and various ancillary units were all that remained of the AIF units of the 8th Division.

In December 1941 the 27th and 43rd Battalions (militia) from Adelaide had joined the 23rd Brigade to replace the battalions sent to Ambon and Timor. Then in January the 18th Light Horse Machine Gun Regiment had replaced the 2/4th Machine Gun Battalion which had been sent to Malaya. Also during this time the 147th and 148th U.S. Field Artillery Regiment had arrived. In February the 7th and 8th Battalions (militia) reached Darwin. By mid March Blake's force had been organised into the 3rd Brigade (Brigadier A. R. Allen) consisting of the 27th and 19th Battalions, the latter being the old Darwin Infantry Battalion, and the 19th Machine Gun Battalion (19th LH [MG] Regt); and the 23rd Brigade (Brigadier Lind), consisting of the 7th, 8th and 43rd Battalions. This force numbered some 14,082 Australians.[3]

Therefore of the troops in Darwin, five battalions (7th, 8th, 27th, 43rd, 19th MG) had been called up after the outbreak of war with Japan. One militia battalion (19th) had served in Darwin for most of 1941, and there were two AIF units, the 2/14th Field Regiment and the 2/4th Pioneer Battalion. The standard of the troops, who had only recently been mobilised, can be imagined but the unfortunate fact was that those who had been there for most of 1941 were little better. The AIF units complained of their retention under monotonous conditions in a military backwater when they had enlisted for service overseas, and the militia units regarded service in Northern Territory as banishment, and even as punishment. There was a higher-than-average incidence of psychiatric cases among men reporting ill. Colloquially they were diagnosed as 'going troppo'.

During March General Mackay visited Northern Territory and on 21 March reported that:

Preparations for meeting an invasion are reasonable as far as wiring and other defence works are concerned, but the alertness of the personnel is not up to the same standard. Readiness of the garrison for immediate attack is not sufficient.

He continued that there were considerable supply and transportation difficulties which he thought might be rectified if General Blake was made responsible for the Northern Territory Lines of Communication Area. He concluded:

A commander with fighting experience in the present war should take over operational control. I consider also that this commander should control the personnel of the Navy and Air Force and USA troops in the area.[4]

Three days after this report Major-General E. F. Herring, who had just returned from the Middle East, was ordered to Darwin, and at 9.30 in the evening of 27 March he arrived with the nucleus of the 6th Division HQ staff.[5] He had been given command of all AMF units in Northern Territory, and once an attack had begun he was to command all naval, military and air forces.[6] Herring was appalled by what he found. There was too much beer, morale was low and the 19th Battalion was in a 'miserable condition'. Few units could be relied upon. One reliable unit was the 2/14th Field Regiment. The supply situation was chaotic, which meant that the 19th Brigade, which had just arrived in Adelaide from the Middle East, could not be accommodated in Darwin. The tactical deployment of the force was unsound with most units scattered along the coast in the vicinity of Darwin. Chances of a successful counter-attack rested on the unlikely event of an enemy landing in a particular area. The American Air Force units under Colonel Wurtsmith were doing all that they could, but the Americans told Herring bluntly that they would send no more troops to Darwin until the situation improved.

Herring brought considerable military experience to his new command, but of more importance, this small quiet man brought to the area a strength of character and devotion to duty which hitherto appeared to be lacking. He had begun the war as CRA of the 6th Division. His performance in Libya and Greece had not been outstanding, but he had a trained mind and he leant heavily on his Staff Corps Brigade Major.[7] It is always difficult to know to what degree opinions are coloured by personal prejudice. Berryman, the GSO1 of the 6th Division at Bardia and Tobruk, was critical of Herring's performance in Cyrenaica. Savige was highly critical of Herring in Greece,[8] as was Allen. However, Brigadier Vasey, who commanded the 19th Brigade in Greece, and who had been AA & QMG of the 6th Division in Libya, welcomed the appointment of Herring to the command of the 6th Division, although he suspected that there was some connection between the fact that Herring was a prominent Melbourne barrister and Blamey's son was a new lawyer in Melbourne.[9] On 15 August 1941 Vasey wrote to his wife: 'The real news of the week is Ned Herring's appointment. As far as we are concerned it is grand'.[10] On 29 August he wrote:

Don't be so disappointed about Ned. He is really first class. He has ideas, nearly always good ones, and has the power to have them put into execution as well as being very pleasant.[11]

On 12 September Vasey again wrote to his wife about Herring's appointment:

I think he realises his limitations but I feel as you do. Of that type of person he is quite the best. Educated, pleasing personality, able to deal with his seniors and quite willing to learn, are qualities which go a long way towards making up for other deficiencies. Also he does direct and control the business. Even mediocre direction is better than none.[12]

As commander of the 6th Division Herring leant heavily on the advice of his two senior staff officers, Colonels R. B. Sutherland and R. Bierwirth, and also on Vasey. Few commanders would have been happy with Sutherland and Bierwirth,[13] but it was a measure of Herring's personality and ability to work with people, that he got on well with his staff.

During the voyage from the Middle East to Australia Herring spoke on 4 March 1942 to the troops on board HMT *Andes*. The speech was recorded in the 6th Division war diary.

In this fight [said Herring] we are going to be alongside the AMF. I shall be quite honest with you. Perhaps I have said as many rude things as you about the militia. But we must forget about that now. We must help them. We must get a united people in this hour of crisis. We must not only put away all recrimination but we must help them in every way, in battle and out of battle. We have to show what an Australian soldier should look like and how he should behave. You fellows have to remember that you have something to be proud of in the AIF and have to make the best of yourselves and not the worst. If we set the right example, people will stand firm, there will be no panic, and Australia will be safe. If we do not, then God help Australia![14]

Herring was to have an immediate opportunity to put these principles into operation.

The new commander of Northern Territory Force arrived in Darwin at the height of the expectations of an invasion. Three days earlier the Central War Room in Melbourne had warned that 'an attack on Australia from the Netherlands East Indies area may occur by the end of the month'.[15] The moon and tide would be right for an attack in about one week. One observer said later, 'We wrote what we thought were to be our last letters home'.[16] Herring would have to act quickly.

Only General Blake and Brigadiers Allen and Lind knew officially that Herring was coming, and Allen and Lind had been told two nights before that they were being replaced. Colonel E. L. Sheehan, the GSO1 of the Force, became commander of the 3rd Brigade for a short while before being replaced by Brigadier R. King and Brigadier I. N. Dougherty took over the 23rd Brigade. King and Dougherty were both outstanding AIF officers with experience in Libya and Greece. Dougherty had also commanded his battalion on Crete, and King had commanded his battalion in the Syria Campaign. The bulk of the 7th Military District Headquarters went to Katherine to form the Headquarters of the Lines of Communication Area with Blake in charge. Some time later this organisation was disbanded when Herring advised 'that they were a nuisance more than anything else'.[17] Other AIF officers took over the 7th, 8th, 19th and 2/4th Pioneer Battalions. Dudley McCarthy, who was present at the time, recorded that 'Although the wholesale replacement of officers represented by such appointments as these . . . was ruthless, and certainly unduly harsh in some cases, the effect was electric, particularly as it was accompanied by corresponding staff changes'.[18]

The morning after his arrival Herring drove around the area while his GSO1, Colonel Sutherland, talked to Colonel Sheehan about the disposition of the units. At 4 o'clock that afternoon Herring gave his orders. He altered the tactical plan, disposing his forces in depth with defended company localities, each self-contained with food and ammunition. The 3rd and 23rd Brigades were deployed along the main road south of Darwin from where they could attack the enemy wherever he landed. The bases were to be used for counter-attack and there were to be aggressive fighting patrols. After the conference one observer reported that 'People went away with a happy look. Lift in morale at the conference was immediate. Something was being done at last'.[19] The following day Herring established his Headquarters about eighteen miles south of Darwin, and the Air Headquarters was moved next to it.

The garrison lived each day in expectation of a Japanese attack. Indeed between 28 March and 5 April there were nine Japanese air attacks in the Darwin area.[20] On 31 March the first night attack took place. To raise morale Herring arranged for demonstrations of fire power in the brigade areas. After each demonstration he spoke to the officers of the brigade. While he was speaking to the 23rd Brigade a formation of fourteen aircraft came over from Darwin some ten miles away. Herring went on talking. Numbers of officers stood up ready to go to shelter, but as Herring went on talking they sat down again. This had a great effect on morale, and the aircraft dropped their bombs about eight miles away. Four days after their arrival the diarist of the HQ 6th Division recorded with pride:

Units are settling into new positions and a new spirit noticeably pervades the area. Units feel they have a plan which they can understand, and which offers them great hopes of success in the event of a Japanese landing in force. GOC is concerned with the question of morale. Troops display undue fear of air raids, and the spectacle of troops running for cover when an air raid is taking place 20 miles distant is frequent. The energies of all members of the staff of 7MD are directed towards this problem. Already the forces are being compelled to throw off the inertia which tropical conditions and lack of drive on the part of commanders has produced in them.[21]

Throughout April Herring and his staff drove their troops relentlessly, improving their physical fitness, revising minor tactics and rehearsing the counter invasion plans. By the beginning of May these efforts were showing results and the troops were gaining confidence in their ability and were more alert. The supply system finally began to work efficiently. In the opinion of a number of observers Herring performed outstanding work in Darwin during this tense period. On 17 May the 19th Brigade (less one battalion) began to move from Adelaide to Darwin.[22] By 30 May Herring could report that while individual training of soldiers was still far from satisfactory, 'Brigade and battalion exercises are being carried out with the object of practising movement in enclosed country and increasing the physical fitness of personnel'.[23] But by this time the Battle of the Coral Sea had made it clear that the enemy's main area of interest had shifted to the north-east approaches.

Despite MacArthur's post-war claims that immediately upon arriving in Australia he changed the defence policy from one of defence of continental Australia to one of taking the fight to the enemy in New Guinea, his defence plans for March and April 1942 suggest otherwise. Herring's efforts in Darwin were part of a scheme which MacArthur succinctly summed up on 26 March 1942 when he told the Advisory War Council that his first step 'was to make Australia secure'.[24]

Indeed before the appointments of MacArthur as Commander-in-Chief and Blamey as Commander of the Allied Land Forces had been made official, they had been turning their minds to the immediate problem of the defence of Australia. Herring and his staff had been sent to Darwin, but for the time being little more could be done directly for the area. Meanwhile the Joint Planning Staff under the chairmanship of Major General J. F. Barnes was examining the situation.[25] They concluded that the scale of attack was unlikely to exceed two divisions against either Darwin or the north-east coast of Australia, but that the attack on Darwin could take place at any moment and on the north-east coast not before 15 April. They believed that to defend the Brisbane-Melbourne area adequately then the area north of Brisbane should be held to ensure air security. They concluded that Townsville should be developed as a fortress area and that the forces there should be increased to one division as soon as possible after the arrival of the 41st U.S. Division in Australia. They also suggested sending an AMF brigade group to the Hughenden-Cloncurry area in case the Japanese landed in the Gulf of Carpentaria.[26]

A little later, on 4 April, the Australian Chiefs of Staff and MacArthur's Headquarters produced a joint estimate of the situation. They expected a Japanese attack on 'Australia's supply line and against Australia itself' in the very near future. They recognised that the 'critical point' was Port Moresby, and that if sufficient naval and air forces could be found Australia could be defended there.[27] There was nothing new in this theory, for the Australian Chiefs of Staff, in their appreciation of 27 February, had indicated that Port Moresby was the key to the north-eastern defences of Australia. When they had recommended that Port Moresby should not be reinforced, they were acting realistically, for at that time the forces were not available.[28]

With the arrival in Australia of the four brigades of the AIF in late March, and of the 41st Division in early April, ground forces were now available to bolster the forward defences. Despite later claims by MacArthur that he decided from the time of his arrival to defend Australia from New Guinea,[29] with his concurrence these forces were deployed in southern Australia. Blamey's reorganisation of 9 April was, in effect, a preliminary defence plan. The salient points were that the First Army, with the bulk of the forces, including the 7th Division (AIF), was located in New South Wales and Queensland, the 19th Brigade (AIF) was to be sent to Darwin, and the troops in Western Australia were to be brought up to a full division (4th).[30] In addition U.S. anti-aircraft and engineer troops were sent to Darwin, a squadron of heavy bombers and a U.S. anti-aircraft regiment were ordered to Perth, a U.S. anti-aircraft regiment and an additional Australian infantry brigade went to Townsville, and the remainder of the U.S. anti-aircraft troops were grouped in Brisbane. The air force concentrated most of its striking force in the Townsville-Cloncurry area, where airfields were becoming available.[31]

On 10 April Blamey issued his first Operation Instruction to the GOC of the First Army. While recognising that the retention of the Newcastle-Melbourne area was vital to the continuance of the war effort, Blamey did not, however, think that it was likely that the enemy would attack the area on a major scale because they were occupied in Burma and the Netherlands East Indies, and because of the growing air and naval strength in Australia. He considered that the enemy's first southward effort would be directed at capturing Port Moresby, and this would be followed by a landing on the north-east coast of Australia with a view to advancing southwards covered by land based aircraft. It followed from this that Brisbane had to be held since its occupation by the enemy would give them suitable airfields for land based aircraft to attack Newcastle and Sydney. It was important to hold Townsville because it was opposite a gap in the Barrier Reef, it had good port facilities, it was to be developed as a submarine base, it was an important air base, and it was an important port on the alternative route to Darwin. It was recognised, however, that it was not possible to hold the area between Brisbane and Townsville, although 'as our resources increase it is intended to hold progressively northwards from Brisbane'. In the light of this appreciation the tasks of the First Army were listed as follows:

a. Defence of Thursday Island with the existing garrison.
b. Defence of Townsville by a garrison which is to be built up to one division at an early date.

c. Defence of the east coast from inclusive Brisbane to the Army Southern boundary [that is, the New South Wales-Victoria border].[32]

While these dispositions were being made, the Australian Government received the full text of the UK Chiefs of Staff's comments on the Australian Chiefs of Staff's view of the UK appreciation.[33] The UK Chiefs of Staff began by acknowledging that the Australian Chiefs of Staff were better placed than they to judge Australian requirements, but they continued that they felt that the invasion of Australia did not form part of the Japanese plans at that time. Only after they had consolidated in the southern Pacific, and when the situation with regard to Russia had become clear, would Japan decide whether to invade Australia. The UK Chiefs of Staff considered that the defence of Fremantle was as important as the defence of the Australian east coast. As the U.S. main fleet could not be expected to remain in eastern Australian waters, they concluded that:

The allied aim should therefore be to build up the land, air and local Naval Forces in Australia and New Zealand to a point where they can stand without the immediate support of the United States Fleet, and can ensure that they will not be defeated before the United States Fleet is able to return to sever the enemy's communications with her invading forces.[34]

Two days later the government received further comments from the UK Chiefs of Staff. They recognised the need for an offensive in the Pacific, but said it was not possible before adequate forces were gathered to defend the Indian Ocean area, before Australia and New Zealand were secure, or before the U.S. Pacific Fleet had gained superiority over the Japanese. Until then, they considered that it was 'necessary to remain strategically on [the] defensive'. In the meantime offensive action should be limited to raids in the Pacific and Indian Oceans.[35]

These appreciations were discussed by the Advisory War Council on 16 April, and Curtin said that on 20 April he would be discussing with MacArthur 'the fundamental basis of the strategical appreciation to which it should be our objective to obtain the assent of the United Kingdom Chiefs of Staff, the Combined Chiefs of Staff and the United States Chiefs of Staff'.[36] As a result of the discussion between Curtin and MacArthur, Curtin sent a cable, with which MacArthur agreed, to Evatt in Washington, repeating the argument of the UK Chiefs of Staff that for the present the Allies were forced to remain strategically on the defensive in both the Indian and Pacific Oceans.[37]

It is important to remember that when he agreed to this initially defensive strategy MacArthur did so with the advantage of a detailed and accurate knowledge of Japanese intentions. The extent of the intelligence available to MacArthur in late March and early April is still not certain, but since his time in the Philippines he had been served by two excellent intelligence organisations. These were the Army Signal Intelligence Service unit, under Lieutenant-Colonel J. R. Sherr,[38] and the USN OP-20-G unit under Lieutenant-Commander R. J. Fabian. Each unit was devoted to decoding intercepted Japanese messages. These organisations had been formed before Japan had entered the war and by the time of Pearl Harbour the navy was able to decode a fair proportion of the Japanese fleet cryptographic code, known as J25b.[39] The army had not been so successful because they had had fewer messages to practise on during 1941. Fabian, however, had another trump, for he possessed a PURPLE machine which enabled him to read the Japanese diplomatic messages. Fabian moved from the Philippines in February, and Sherr accompanied MacArthur to Australia in March.

It is not known when, and with what frequency, MacArthur began to receive top level decoded messages, but it is likely that the information from the PURPLE machine, known as MAGIC, would have indicated that the Japanese had no immediate intention of invading Australia. MacArthur therefore could base his plans on information which Marshall said was not 'merely "authentic and from a reliable source" but was actual truth'.[40] There is some doubt, however, that MacArthur received all of the available MAGIC. General Willoughby later wrote that:

the Navy has shrouded the whole enterprise in mystery, excluding other services, and rigidly centralising the whole enterprise. At this date [8 May 1945] for example, this same system is still in vogue: as far as SWPA is concerned, the crypto-analysis is made in Melbourne, forwarded via 7th Fleet DNI; the Melbourne station is under direct orders of Washington, is not bound by any local responsibilities, forwards what they select, and when it suits them. The possibility of erroneous or incomplete selection is as evident now as it was in 1941. The only excuse the Navy has is that its field is primarily naval intercepts, but there is a lot of Army traffic or other incidental traffic. This collateral traffic is not always understood or correctly interpreted by the Navy, in my opinion.[41]

That MacArthur, therefore, had definite information that Japan was not planning to invade Australia is speculation, but there is no doubt that during April Allied Intelligence began to receive more definite information about Japanese intentions. On 16 April 1942 MacArthur's Chief of Staff, General Sutherland, warned General Brett: 'Information obtained indicates hostile movement by sea (strength unknown) will be made from Rabaul area about 21 April and that attack may be made on Port Moresby from SE about 21 April'.[42] Four days later he revised his estimate:

The absence of dangerous concentrations of enemy shipping or air strength in New Guinea and New Britain area, together with other information available, points to a postponement of any enemy attack against Port Moresby until later in the month.[43]

A Joint Staff appreciation of the same day reveals a clarity of thought which to date had been lacking in some of the American appreciations. The appreciation listed the courses open to the enemy. These were:

a. A direct attack on the Brisbane-Adelaide area. This was considered unlikely.
b. A direct attack on Fremantle. This was more favourable to the enemy than a., but was still unlikely.
c. A direct attack on the supply lines to Australia, especially New Caledonia. This was not likely until the Rabaul area was secure.
d. The occupation of Port Moresby. It was considered that the enemy might soon attempt this, in conjunction with an attack on north Queensland.
e. The occupation of the Darwin-Broome area. The enemy was withdrawing air units from Koepang to Ambon, so this was unlikely.
f. To stand temporarily on the defensive with perhaps carrier raids on the main bases.

It was considered that the probable enemy action would be to stand temporarily on the defensive and to consolidate their position for about a month before attempting a large-scale amphibious attack. A further appreciation, two days later indicated the order of probability of this attack as being 1. Port Moresby. 2. New Caledonia. 3. Darwin.[44]

On 25 April MacArthur warned General Patch in New Caledonia of a likely enemy offensive against north-east Australia in the period 29 April-3 May.[45] On 30 April Marshall radioed MacArthur:

Press despatch in Wash. Papers under dateline Allied HQ Aust. 27 Apr states a Jap naval concentration is in Marshalls apparently preparing for new opn. Jap well aware that submarines scouting would be ineffective for obtaining information for such conclusion and justified in believing their codes broken — which would be disastrous.[46]

MacArthur replied: 'No release such as your 4#30 Apr made from any HQ, nor given out by communique, inference or discussion. Knowledge indicated known to very few and concealed from most mil'y personnel'.[47] It is clear from this that the forces in Australia were no longer fighting in the dark. Having broken the Japanese codes the Americans were able to lay their plans accordingly. Thus with the knowledge of the approaching Japanese offensive MacArthur ordered his forces to remain on the defensive.

On 25 April MacArthur's headquarters (GHQ) issued Operation Instruction No. 2 detailing the role and responsibility of the Allied Land Forces. This directed that:

a. The Allied Land Forces, South West Pacific area will prevent any landing on the North East coast of Australia or on the South West of New Guinea.

b. The Allied Land Commander responsible for the areas in the vicinity of Port Moresby and along the North East Coast of Australia to include Brisbane will immediately perfect plans for the co-ordination of all the defensive forces in their respective areas and will implement the necessary machinery for assuming command when the necessity requires.[48]

It can be seen that MacArthur's instructions were basically defensive and indeed envisaged holding the area with the troops already deployed. These instructions were based on 'Plan A' for the defence of the north-east coast of Australia and Port Moresby which had been issued the previous day.[49]

There is no doubt that MacArthur was far from satisfied that the forces available to him in Australia were adequate for the defence of the country, let alone for an offensive. He hoped to obtain more troops from America, but the Japanese gave him no breathing space to amass these additional forces. During April the Japanese continued their advance southwards through the Solomons. Plan A, issued on 24 April, indicated that it was likely that a Japanese force of three aircraft carriers and five cruisers might strike the north-east coast of Australia between 28 April and 3 May. Naval forces of the SWPA and SOPAC (South Pacific Area) were concentrating to meet this threat, and land based aircraft from Townsville were preparing to attack the enemy convoy. The land forces' instructions were identical to those quoted from the GHQ Operation Instruction No. 2 above,[50] and a few days later General Milford in Townsville was warned: 'An early attack on Port Moresby is probable and this may be followed by a landing on the northeast coast with a view to a progressive advance southwards covered by land based aircraft'.[51]

Even if it was MacArthur's intention to base his defence on New Guinea, he was not able to reinforce substantially that area before the Japanese were ready to strike. Furthermore his orders contrast markedly with his later statement that 'It was never my intention to defend Australia on the mainland of Australia'.[52] On the other hand it was not easy to reinforce Port Moresby, for the Allies had not yet secured control of the sea, and the air bases in Port Moresby were very inadequate. In an attempt to rectify this situation, in early April an Australian light anti-aircraft battery from the Middle East arrived. In late April U.S. engineers and anti-aircraft units were ordered to Moresby, and also by late April U.S. bombers based in Townsville were using Moresby to attack Lae, Salamaua and Rabaul.[53]

In anticipation of a victory in the Coral Sea, on 1 May MacArthur suggested to Blamey that there might be a chance of taking 'a limited initiative' by raiding Lae and Salamaua.[54] Tentative plans for such a raid had already been made. On 17 April the 2/5th Independent Company had arrived in Port Moresby. When Generals Brett and Vasey had visited Moresby from 21 to 24 April they had decided to set up Kanga Force, to include the 2/5th and the various units in the Markham Valley and around Wau. Kanga Force was to operate against Salamaua and Lae.[55]

During the period MacArthur made repeated requests to Washington for additional forces, but Roosevelt eventually made it clear that Europe was to be the decisive theatre. This did not daunt either MacArthur or the Australian Government. They continued their plea that the Pacific should not be forgotten for the remainder of the year. The government stressed the need to defend Australia and MacArthur urged that the Pacific should be the decisive theatre.[56]

Yet while MacArthur continued to press for additional forces, he felt confident that the Japanese task force could be defeated by the Allied air and naval forces.[57] General Blamey was also confident, and in a press conference on 1 May he said that the Allies were in a much better position to resist the Japanese than previously. Acknowledging the importance of Port Moresby he said that if it were lost then a later offensive would be made more difficult.[58] What he did not say was that the ground forces in Port Moresby were not adequate to defend it, and that the defence depended on the air and naval forces.

In early May the Japanese invasion force expected by MacArthur left

Rabaul and headed for the Coral Sea.[59] On the morning of 7 May, after receiving news of the Allied fleet, the Japanese transports turned back for Rabaul, and on 8 May the main battle was fought. Although it was not a tactical victory for the Allies, it was a strategic victory, and the Japanese were prevented from moving on Port Moresby and from attacking Townsville.[60] For the troops in Port Moresby the battle was a reprieve, and the Australian official historian noted that:

So hesitant had General MacArthur and General Blamey been to send reinforcements to New Guinea that on 10th May, the day on which the Japanese planned to land round Port Moresby, the defending garrison was not materially stronger than the one which General Sturdee had established there early in January.[61]

The bulk of the garrison consisted of the 30th Brigade commanded by Brigadier N. G. Hatton. The 49th Battalion of the brigade had arrived in New Guinea in early 1941, and the other two battalions, the 39th and 53rd, had arrived after Japan had entered the war. They were militia units whose members had been drafted at short notice. Of the new soldiers who had arrived in Port Moresby, many were under twenty years of age. Their training was poor and they had little opportunity to improve it as they were involved in developing the base. In July 1941 Sturdee had told Morris, the commander in New Guinea, that the 49th Battalion was the worst in Australia.[62]

The way in which these units were formed demonstrates the lack of appreciation of the value of regimental pride. They were formed not by handing over a cadre from a trained and established battalion and filling it up with reinforcements, but by obtaining batches of men from a number of units. The units concerned often gave their worst and not their best, and one battalion selected those with the longest crime sheets. The 53rd Battalion was formed originally for service in Darwin, and in 1941 it was regarded as a punishment to be sent to the northern station. On the other hand those units which remained in the south spent three months in camp and three months out of it, while those who went to Darwin stayed there. Gavin Long has asked the rhetorical question, 'To what extent was the comparative failure of the militia battalions in New Guinea a product of the blunders in army policy for which the Cabinet was responsible'.[63]

After the early February air raids there had been looting in Port Moresby, and morale had been very low.[64] On 14 February civilian administration in the territory ceased. About the same time the AOC NE

Area, Air Commodore Lukis, warned the Air Board of the poor morale in Port Moresby.

This does not mean that troops will not fight but they cannot overlook the lack of naval, air and political support. An impression is growing rapidly that the policy of the government is to let the garrisons at Moresby and Thursday Island go, in the same way as that at Rabaul and that no serious assistance will be given . . . .[65]

Since that time, with the increase in Allied air activity, morale had risen. Nevertheless the reaction during the battle of the Coral Sea was alarming. Commander R. B. A. Hunt, the naval officer-in-charge (NOIC) in Port Moresby has written that

When the Coral Sea Battle was at its height . . . the army evacuated Moresby, retiring hurriedly overnight to the area of Rouna Falls. At this time I was not advised by anyone whatsoever, so that when morning came, my small Naval Staff, a few Ack Ack gunners, and caretakers of the two first World War 6" naval guns on Paga hill, and the RAAF crews at the 'Three Mile' remained as the sole defence of Port Moresby.[66]

Throughout this period the commander in New Guinea was Major-General Basil Morris, aged 53, who had been at Port Moresby since May 1941.[67] A solid, unassuming professional soldier, and a 'gentleman of courtesy and honour',[68] he readily admitted that he had no pretensions to being a tactician.[69] He realistically assessed the chances of his small force in New Guinea and courageously faced the prospect of fighting to hold Port Moresby, which he realised was important to Allied strategy. He felt that the few troops that he had should be used to develop an air base, as control of the air would be decisive. Morris wrote later that the troops under his command 'were hardly trained at all and I am quite sure that they did not look forward with any confidence to meeting the enemy'. On the other hand he had some reason for optimism. He believed that the Allied fleet would protect Port Moresby from seaborne invasion, and that the Owen Stanley Range would prevent movement from the north. [70]

In the opinion of Sir Kingsley Norris, Morris was just an 'ordinary, mediocre fellow'.[71] General Vasey was more caustic. In July 1943 he wrote to his wife that Morris was 'a very good scout — no brains but very honest and stout hearted'.[72] Blamey was aware of Morris's weaknesses,[73] but he also realised that he could not be blamed entirely for the situation in New Guinea.[74] The answer was to send a new commander to New Guinea and leave Morris to run the administrative

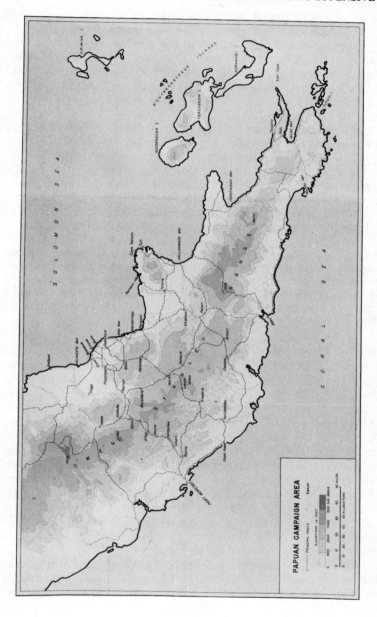

Map 2   The Papuan campaign area. From S. Milner, *Victory in Papua*.

elements, and in particular the Australian New Guinea Administrative Unit (ANGAU). The remarkable thing was that Blamey delayed so long in making this change, but until the number of troops in New Guinea increased he could not really do so without hurting Morris's feelings. Blamey always felt a certain loyalty to those officers who had served their country long and well, and through no fault of their own found themselves in situations that they were not equipped to handle.[75]

It was some days before the results of the Battle of the Coral Sea were known fully in Australia, but they led to little jubilation, for it was realised that Japan might attempt such an invasion again. On 12 May MacArthur gave Curtin a gloomy estimate of the general strategic situation in the Pacific. He pointed out that the Japanese successes had continued in Burma and that they were now able to release the divisions that had been occupied in the Philippines. The Americans there had surrendered on 6 May. MacArthur continued:

Despite the reverse suffered in their recent move against New Guinea the Japanese Navy has not been opposed in force and is in a position to undertake further offensive efforts. The availability of these forces makes possible a strong enemy offensive effort of the most dangerous possibilities. The entire history of the conduct of the war by the Japanese leads to the belief that the Japanese will continue their offensive action.

He believed that the next Japanese offensive would be in the South-West Pacific Area and that this was where a Second Front should be opened. He concluded by emphasising the need for haste in developing a 'defensive bastion' in Australia. 'We have . . . in this theatre at the present time all the elements that have produced disaster in the Western Pacific since the beginning of the war'.[76]

The next day the Advisory War Council discussed the recent events, and disappointment was expressed that heavy losses were not inflicted on the enemy. It was felt that not enough land based aircraft had been concentrated in the north-east.[77] When he heard of this criticism, MacArthur wrote to Curtin that he felt 'a sense of disappointment' with the Council. He thought that it had been 'a very brilliant effort . . . which undoubtedly saved Australia from a definite and immediate threat . . . '. He did admit, however, that he was a little disappointed with the effort of the air force.[78]

On 14 May Curtin made yet another plea to Washington for further reinforcements, but was unsuccessful. Meanwhile more U.S. troops continued to arrive. On that day 6,200 personnel of the 41st Division and 15,850 of the 32nd Division, under Major-General E. F. Harding, arrived. This brought the total strength of U.S. Army personnel in Australia to 60,822 and with the 20,495 Air Corps and anti-aircraft units, a grand total of 81,317.[79]

The arrival of these additional troops, and the obvious Japanese interest in the area, meant that Blamey could now afford to concentrate more of his force in north Queensland and New Guinea. On 13 May he told the Advisory War Council that he was moving the 7th Brigade (CMF) to Townsville, bringing the strength in the area to two brigades, but 'the main preoccupation of the Army was to strengthen the defences of New Guinea'. Anti-aircraft defences were being increased and he planned to send an additional brigade as soon as shipping and escorts were available.[80] Indeed on 7 May he had put the 14th Brigade of the 2nd Division, located around Greta, on 24 hours notice to move from 12 May,[81] and on 15 May the brigade headquarters left Townsville for Port Moresby. The remainder of the brigade followed, but it was not concentrated in Port Moresby until late June, and its service troops did not arrive until late July.[82]

Considerable controversy has surrounded the selection of the 14th Brigade to reinforce New Guinea. At that time the seasoned 7th Division (AIF) was in southern Queensland, and both its commander, General Allen, and the commander of I Australian Corps, General Rowell, felt that it would have been better to send the AIF to New Guinea. Rowell recalled that the decision made his 'headquarters weep at the time'.[83] After visiting Darwin, Townsville and Port Moresby in July 1942, Gavin Long wrote in his diary that the ignorance at LHQ of the quality and morale of the troops was inexcusable 'and the decision to keep the best troops until last was "criminal" '.[84]

It is difficult to establish the exact reason why the 14th Brigade was chosen, but a number of reasons may be offered. The brigade was one of the units of the 2nd Division commanded by Major-General H. W. Lloyd. Lloyd, a former regular officer, had a fine record from World War I and had attended the staff college at Quetta. He had left the army in the mid 1920s and had rejoined in 1940. He was not universally popular,[85] but he was a close friend of Blamey,[86] and he had a very high opinion of the troops in his division. General Hopkins recalls that 'all his geese were swans'[87] and Rowell recalled that Lloyd thought that the 14th Brigade was 'absolutely marvellous' and that Brigadier W. E. Smith, the commander, was 'very good'.[88]

Blamey inspected the brigade at Greta on 14 May. Chester Wilmot was present and thought 'it was a poor show'. When he asked Blamey whether he thought that the brigade would fight, the Commander-in-

Chief had replied that he hoped so.[89] On the other hand it might have been expected that the 2nd Division was at a higher stage of training than the other divisions of II Corps. The 1st Division, which had formerly been the Sydney-Port Kembla Covering Force, and the 10th Division, which had formerly been the Newcastle Covering Force, had both been involved in the construction of defence works, while the 2nd Division had had more time for training.

On 13 April 1942 Major-General Vasey, the DCGS, wrote to the subordinate army commanders requesting that monthly reports be submitted on the operational efficiency of headquarters and formations down to brigade and detached units.[90] Brigadier Hopkins, the Director of Military Operations and Plans, followed this on 29 April with an instruction that the reports were to be classified as follows:

A.   Efficient and experienced for mobile offensive operations.
B.   Efficient as a formation for mobile offensive operations but not experienced.
C.   Individual brigades are efficient for mobile offensive operations, but higher training has not been completed.
D.   Individual brigades are efficient in a static role. Additional brigade and higher training is required.
E.   Units have completed training. A considerable amount of brigade and higher training is required.
F.   Unit training is not yet complete.[91]

Shortly afterwards reports began arriving at GHQ (Australia).[92] These reports are difficult to evaluate since the commander of a division might have had an inflated opinion of his troops, or he might have been a harsh realist. Some trends, however, can be detected. As the year progressed there was an increase in realism, and with it a marked decrease in listed efficiency.

A provisional operation report by GHQ (Australia) in late April or early May found that most brigades were at the standard of classification D, but that some units, including the 30th Brigade in New Guinea and the 2nd Division, were at standard C. Only the 7th Division (AIF) and the 19th Brigade (AIF) were at standard A.[93] During May formations submitted their reports, and all recorded that the standards were lower than those estimated by the GHQ (Australia) report. On 2 June HQ First Army reported that at 15 May, with the exception of the 7th Division (A) and the 2nd Division (D) all formations were at standard E.[94]

During this period the 14th Brigade arrived in New Guinea, and General Morris found that it was at standard E, and that the 30th

Brigade was at F.[95] Therefore on 2 June the First Army, in the eyes of the commander of the 2nd Division, recorded the 14th Brigade as D and two days later Morris found it to be E. Furthermore, GHQ (Australia), which had not yet received Morris's report, recorded the 30th Brigade to be at standard D.[96] Finally in July GHQ, now called LHQ (Land Headquarters), caught up with the assessment of the formations and classified the 14th Brigade as E and the 30th Brigade as F, although by this time most formations in Australia, including the 2nd Division, were at standard C. The 7th Brigade, which by this time was at Milne Bay, was at standard D.[97]

These reports indicate that by early June the Allied command could be under no illusion as to the relative merits of its troops. Those in the most threatened area, New Guinea, included a brigade with the lowest possible combat efficiency rating, and with the exception of Kanga Force, the troops with the highest standard were still at efficiency level D. Meanwhile the 7th Division (standard A) remained in southern Queensland, and most formations in Australia had a higher efficiency rating than those in New Guinea.[98]

At the Advisory War Council on 19 May concern was expressed at the youthfulness of the militia soldiers sent to New Guinea, but the CGS replied that the 7th Division would have to remain in Australia for training in combined operations as it 'was the only available force of seasoned troops which could be used for offensive operations, for example against Rabaul and Java'. On the other hand members of the Council felt that in view of the strategic importance of Port Moresby and the imminent Japanese threat, well-trained and experienced troops should be sent to the area.[99] Apparently, however, they declined to interfere in this matter of detail in the deployment of the army.

There is no doubt that General Lloyd of the 2nd Division was a very able trainer of soldiers,[1] but the varying reports on the 14th Brigade suggest that he tended to have an over-optimistic view of his division. The reports also indicate that in early May GHQ was having difficulty determining exactly the relative merits of the different formations.

If Blamey expressed doubts about the training of the 14th Brigade at Greta on 14 May, these doubts were soon confirmed. Indeed, the previous day he had told the Advisory War Council that the discipline of the Australian troops was not good because of a lack of trained and experienced officers.[2] After the 14th Brigade was ordered to New Guinea a large number of soldiers went absent without leave. The danger was not only that this indicated a breakdown in discipline, but also that the information of the impending move was spread over a large part of New South Wales. On 21st Blamey wrote bitterly to Generals Sturdee and Wynter that the movement was 'carried out in such a manner as to leave a very painful impression as to the quality of the staff work and the discipline of the forces involved'. Blamey added that it had been found necessary to relieve one of the battalion commanders of his command.[3] Later on 1 July, at an Advisory War Council meeting, W. M. Hughes referred to the incident, and Blamey told him that disciplinary action had been taken.[4]

The fault did not lie with only one battalion, although one had 60 per cent absent without leave while another had about 10 per cent. In the opinion of one of the officers of the brigade, Brigadier Smith was largely at fault, for while his troops were training in the Hexham area he worked them fifteen hours per day for weeks and gave no leave, although other units had leave. Then on the eve of embarkation he gave a weekend's leave. It was impossible for men living in areas like Bega and Crookwell to get home and return in time, so they took a few days extra.[5] Blamey must have realised this situation for on 18 May Sturdee sent Lavarack a peremptory message that no leave was to be granted, but by then it was too late.[6]

This incident throws into relief the problem of preparing the militia for war. The situation whereby there were two armies in Australia, the AIF and the militia, was, in the opinion of a number of senior officers, the great tragedy of the war.[7] The political problems were immense, but will not be dealt with here.[8] The military problems were almost of the same magnitude, although a political decision to make one army would have resolved the difficulties.

It has already been mentioned in Chapter Two how the standard of the militia deteriorated as the younger and more able soldiers left for the AIF. With the entry of Japan into the war the militia was mobilised and began preparing for operations. Unit strengths were at less than half of the establishment and new 18-year-old recruits were arriving in big batches.

A good number of senior militia officers had distinguished records from World War I, but were now too old or unfit. A further proportion of officers in militia units had served with the AIF in the Middle East and had been returned as unsuitable.[9] This was the situation faced by the new commanders from the AIF when they returned to Australia in 1942. Blamey was determined to prepare these militia units for combat and he sought out experienced soldiers from the AIF to train the militia. Brigadier J. Field of the 7th Brigade remembered how when he was at Milne Bay and later at Port Moresby he made strong representations, with support from General Clowes, to get the assistance of AIF officers. When Blamey called at Port Moresby he asked Field what his officer position was. Field replied that it was fair but that he would like some AIF captains. Blamey said 'Very well' and the *next day* four captains from the 7th Division arrived.[10] Blamey ordered, 'Promote corporals to lieutenants if necessary',[11] but these measures needed time to take effect. One problem was that officers returning from the Middle East often found that their contemporaries, who for some reason had not joined the AIF, had been promoted to higher ranks than they had whilst they had been overseas.[12] Blamey, of course, had no hesitation about replacing officers, but in many instances he had to rely on reports which were coloured by personal feelings. An example of one of Blamey's letters to a brigadier with a DSO and an MC is as follows:

I regret that it has been found necessary to terminate your services in the Active Military Forces and to transfer you to the Reserve of Officers. I know that this will be the cause of considerable disappointment to you, but trust that you will readily realise that with the return of younger officers with experience in the present war it is in the best interests of the service that their services be utilised to the best advantage.[13]

A number of instances of poor discipline can be found to indicate the lack of training and inexperience of the officers in the militia units. In early June General Savige of the 3rd Division found it necessary to write to his subordinate commanders:

At the time of my return from overseas, the general demeanour of troops in our Home Forces was of such a low order that it shocked one's accustomed habits of good discipline and turnout. This was painfully evident in the prevalent 'undress' appearance of troops in the streets, and the many sights of completely intoxicated troops. In camp, discipline, to the point of normal self-respect, was evident by its non existence. I saw this in three of the largest states and, though our Division compared most favourably with other Units, that fact brought no comfort.
I have found, and still find, a feeling with the public that our Home Forces will fail in battle. That opinion has been formed by contrasting the appearance and behaviour of returned AIF personnel and American troops. I think you, too, have experienced this public alarm and noted the differences mentioned.[14]

General Rowell estimated that it would take about one year from their call up before the militia would be ready for combat.[15] Yet during this period nine militia battalions saw action. Of these two performed very well, three were adequate and four were not up to standard.[16] This proves at least that there was nothing inherently wrong with the militia soldier, and that with training and leadership he could perform well. Indeed the four regiments of the U.S. divisions which fought at Buna and Sanananda performed no better than the militia units. The problem of two armies was not one that could be swept under the carpet. In I Corps Rowell arranged for sub units of the 7th and 3rd Divisions to be exchanged to give each element some idea of the capacity of the other.[17]

After speaking to an AIF officer in Townsville in June 1942 Gavin Long recorded:

The discipline is bad. No compliments. The GG [Governor General] and Milford [GOC of the 5th Division] walked through the town the other day and the men looked at them — not one salute. It's the CO's fault. They say half the men are not interested and just don't want to be in the war, we used to say the AIFs discipline was bad — it wasn't.[18]

In August 1942 Brigadier T. S. Louch, commander of the 29th Brigade in Townsville, wrote to General Vasey:

The last six months has nearly broken my heart. I have never had a show before in which I could take no pride at all. That so many young men in [good] health and in the pink of physical condition should have so few guts is a biological phenomona that is beyond me.[19]

Despite this criticism the official historian was of the opinion that for a number of reasons the militia was unfairly disparaged. He believed that the reasons were that there was a traditional Australian prejudice against conscript forces, and that they were unfairly compared with the AIF, or British regular units. MacArthur and the Australian ministers were attempting to persuade Washington of the need for reinforcements, and their argument was strengthened if the efficiency of the militia units was played down.[20]

In the militia units experienced AIF officers worked around the clock training militia officers in their duties. In Darwin General Herring, who was faced with the possibility of an early invasion, found it necessary to set up a thirty-hour officer training school to teach the essentials to his officers.[21] Brigadier S. W. H. C. Porter, who in April went to Port Moresby to assume command of the 30th Brigade, later commented that 'No one except we who were sent to command militia brigades know how we had to work like coolies'. Porter described how when he arrived at Port Moresby he asked the

Above I Brigadier C. E. M. Lloyd, Lieut-General V. A. H. Sturdee, CGS, General Sir Thomas Blamey, the new C-in-C of the Australian Army, and Major-General E. F. Herring, GOC 6th Division
Below II General Douglas MacArthur with the Prime Minister, John Curtin, Melbourne, 17 April 1942

Left III The Minister for the Army, F. M. Forde, and General Blamey at the 1st Armoured Division review, Puckapunyal, June 1942

Below IV Major-General E. F. Herring in Cairo soon after his appointment as GOC 6th Division

Intelligence Officer for the fire plan, but had received the reply from the Intelligence Officer that he did not know what he meant. Finally he said, 'The battalions may have one, sir, we haven't'.[22] In such a fashion the militia was brought to combat readiness.

The Battle of the Coral Sea underlined the Allied weakness in New Guinea, and in particular the lack of a forward air base at the south-eastern tip of the island. MacArthur felt that the Japanese would strike again at Port Moresby with at least a division of troops and with carrier and land based aircraft 'anytime after June 10',[23] therefore on 14 May he wrote to Blamey asking if he could supply troops to defend an air base to be established near Milne Bay. Blamey replied on 16 May that he could supply the 7th Brigade of the 5th Division.[24] This militia brigade, which had just moved to Townsville, was at a higher standard of training than most, but it had been somewhat unsettled and had just received a new commander. He was Brigadier John Field. Field has left his impression of his arrival in Townsville:

When I went to command 7 Bde I went alone, without one other returned AIF officer. It took me several days to get from S. Queensland to Townsville, and there Gen. Milford was away and I saw Col. Fullarton the GI. I was still wearing the badges of a Lt-Col. not having the time to get any others.

Of his new soldiers, Field concluded that 'they had had some good preliminary training. They knew their weapons and they were in good heart, but it would have helped if I had had a handful of AIF captains to help me.[25]

Field, an engineer in civilian life, was well suited to the task of developing the air base at Milne Bay. The proposed area for the air-field had not been reconnoitred properly, and on 12 June GHQ authorised the construction of the airfield closer to Milne Bay, but it was not until early July that the bulk of Field's forces arrived in the area. Despite the delay, this bold strategical move was to prove valuable during the months ahead. 'Fall Creek', as the project was known, came directly under the command of GHQ, and so the Allied forces in New Guinea were under divided command. Morris in Port Moresby remained responsible for the 30th and 14th Brigades, and Kanga Force, and in turn reported to LHQ. In conjunction with these moves MacArthur ordered additional fighters and light bombers to Port Moresby, and increased the anti-aircraft troops in north Queensland to enable more aircraft to operate from that area.[26]

Despite the reinforcement of New Guinea, concern continued to be expressed about the defence of the north-east coast of Australia. The 5th Division under General Milford was now concentrating around Townsville, the 7th Division was deployed north of Brisbane, and the 3rd Division under General Savige was arriving in the area south of Brisbane from its original training ground in northern Victoria. One of the brigades of the 1st Motorised Division was also stationed in southern Queensland. The remainder of the division was stationed in New South Wales where Northcott's II Corps (1st, 2nd, 10th Divisions) was defending the Sydney-Newcastle area. Lavarack felt keenly the lack of armoured forces to support his troops around Brisbane, but they were not yet fully equipped.[27]

Norman Stockton, a press correspondent in Townsville, reported on 18 May that of fifteen experienced war correspondents questioned all believed that the Japanese would attack Port Moresby within a month, and most believed they would attack within a fortnight. Twelve of the correspondents believed that the Japanese would simultaneously attack northern Queensland. They all believed that the next Japanese attack would be larger and better prepared than the one prevented by the Battle of the Coral Sea. Only one correspondent felt that the Battle of New Guinea would be the turning point of the war, but five thought that the Battle of Australia would be the decisive action of the war.[28]

The military commanders were not so pessimistic but it was necessary to take all precautions. Lieutenant-General Sir John Lavarack, who was responsible for the defence of this vast area, felt that he lacked information about the Japanese, but he also felt that he was not fully aware of Allied air and naval strengths and dispositions. On 21 May he wrote to Blamey: 'The nearest approach to a reliable appreciation of the situation was "Plan A", but even that contained no information as to our own sea and air strength and disposition'.

Lavarack recognised that it would not be possible for a unified command of air and ground forces to be effected, but he felt that the headquarters of the forces should be co-located as there would have to be close co-operation between the two, not only in the defence of Australia, but in the advance through the islands. Looking ahead to future operations, Lavarack proposed that in the case of special task forces, there should be a sole commander. This was a situation which MacArthur could not countenance except under threat of attack, but as Lavarack pointed out, the force commander should at least have the machinery to facilitate a joint command if it were necessary. Lavarack explained to Blamey that he had 'no means of exercising this command'.

Lavarack pointed to a further problem. The government had still not detailed any firm policy on the evacuation of civilians, and he suggested that local commanders of threatened areas should be empowered to initiate evacuation if the presence of the civil population were judged to impede seriously the operation of the defending forces.[29] The next day Lavarack wrote again to Blamey:

I want to make it quite clear to you that I am not myself apprehensive at the present time of any attack by land on the N.E. coast of Queensland. I have believed ever since I was in Java, that any Jap operations into an area would be preparatory and/or diversionary and not in the shape of a definite attempt at invasion until he has settled matters to his satisfaction in areas more decisive from his point of view. This opinion was not shaken even by the operations that took place in the Coral Sea a while ago.

Since I don't want to be caught napping with a whole division fighting in area not very well provided with communications and water it seemed to me desirable that I should ensure at least a partial evacuation of that area.[30]

Lavarack's concern can well be understood. Brigadier Field, whose 7th Brigade was defending the area north of Townsville, recalled that, 'one problem at Rollingstone was the sugar farmers. We had to clear fields of fire in the cane and clear scrub away. There were always protests, sugar inspectors, inflated claims for so much timber destroyed. This at the time of the Coral Sea battle'![31]

Throughout the early part of 1942 there had been considerable discussion in War Cabinet and the Advisory War Council about denial of resources to the enemy or as some put it, a 'Scorched Earth Policy'.[32] On 4 February the War Cabinet had decided that: 'undue emphasis should not be placed upon evacuation measures as this would be detrimental to morale and to the maintenance of essential production'.[33] On 27 March H. L. Anthony, the former Minister for Transport and a member of the National Security Regulations Committee, informed the House of Representatives 'that officers of the Metropolitan Fire Brigade are at present in the Casino district organising a scorched-earth policy'. He continued: 'The time has arrived for the Government to make an authoritative declaration particularly on the subject of the disagreement between advocates of the "standfast" policy, and those of the "run" policy'.[34]

On 1 April War Cabinet considered a directive to local commanders of all three services outlining the denial policy which would be implemented if the military were forced to withdraw from an area. In cities and towns where the civilian population was evacuated, a 'total denial' policy was to be implemented. This entailed 'the complete and total removal or destruction of everything likely to maintain or assist the enemy in his operations'.[35] This directive was not issued pending further discussion with MacArthur. From Lavarack's letter it is clear that by late April the policy was still not firm.

In the month after the Battle of the Coral Sea the Australian commanders were not thinking only of defence. On 19 May Blamey wrote to Bennett in Perth that he was 'keeping in mind the possibility of an eventual offensive to the North from the area of your command'.[36] Then on 1 June 1942 Blamey and the Chiefs of the Naval and Air Staffs conferred and put the case for an offensive policy against Japan. They concluded that: 'The land forces in Australia are forced at present into a completely passive role. The effect of this is to contain approximately 12 Divisions in Australia while the Japanese forces are almost completely freed for operations elsewhere'. They believed that some of these forces should be employed in a limited offensive as soon as practicable.[37] MacArthur and the Australian Chiefs of Staff now agreed that a large-scale Japanese invasion of Australia was unlikely.[38] During this period Blamey had been turning his mind to the possibility of an offensive against Timor, but had been resisted by MacArthur.[39] These tentative plans for an offensive were now overshadowed by more important events.

The decisive defeat of the Japanese fleet at Midway on 4 June marked a turning point in the war in the Pacific. When the results became known in Australia MacArthur realised that his dreams of an offensive could now become reality. On 11 June Curtin told the Advisory War Council that he had received a communication from MacArthur to the effect that Australia's defence position was now assured.[40]

On 17 June MacArthur addressed the Advisory War Council and reaffirmed these views. In his opinion there had been a complete transformation of the war situation as it affected Australia. Internally there had been a tremendous accomplishment, not only in the services, but in the general war effort. He stated that the army 'had been transformed from a non-organised Militia, only partly trained and ill-equipped, to a sound and efficient force. In three months' time it would be ready for any task, defensive or offensive, that it might be called upon to undertake'.

After surveying the improvement in the air force, navy and productivity, MacArthur then turned to the external situation. He claimed that the Battle of the Coral Sea had been

the most crucial incident of the war insofar as Australia was concerned . . .
Australia was in grave danger up to the time of the Coral Sea action. The
results of that action and the successes gained at Midway Island has assured
the defensive position of Australia.

From the strategical point of view, we should take the initiative and not wait
results in other theatres. Our aim should be to strike at Japanese bases in the
islands to the north and throw the enemy bomber line back 700 miles.

The greatest weakness of the present set up is that there is too much
strategical control in London and Washington. General MacArthur said that
if the decision were left to him he would attack now, even in the face of a tactical defeat, in order to destroy the Japanese psychology of initiative.

The remainder of MacArthur's speech was, in essence, a plea for support for his theory that the Second Front should be initiated in the
South-West Pacific Area, and if given the necessary troops and arms,
he would undertake an offensive to retake Rabaul and New Guinea.[41]

It was probably after this meeting that Menzies told Sutherland,
who had been present, that he would like to 'throttle MacA' because
of his exaggerated praise of the government. He agreed that Mac-
Arthur had stiffened morale and had gained considerable equipment
when people had turned a 'nasty colour', but he felt that the 'Germany First' decision was the right one.[42]

While the government must have welcomed MacArthur's statement
that Australia was secure, they could not afford to tell the public.
They could not allow the tempo of the war effort to slacken. On 11
June, after speaking to Blamey, Forde said that Australia was about
to enter the worst period of the war.[43] On 17 June, in a national broadcast, Curtin said that it was possible that Australia could be lost,[44] and
on 25 June he again spoke to the nation and said that Japan still had
the initiative.[45]

Meanwhile MacArthur and his staff were busily preparing plans for
the capture of Rabaul. As early as 8 June MacArthur had suggested to
Marshall that he should be given amphibious troops and naval craft
for the operation.[46] By 27 June GHQ planners had completed a plan
called Tulsa I to capture Rabaul in two weeks. Chamberlin thought
that this was unrealistic and prepared a revised plan, Tulsa II, which
envisaged seizing Rabaul in eighteen days.[47] These plans were grandiose and fanciful and one of MacArthur's biographers has written
that:

For a while in June it seems that euphoria was unrestrained both in
Washington and Melbourne probably because of the Midway triumph and
the desire to follow up quickly before the Japanese recovered their balance.[48]

Despite requests by Morris during June for additional troops,[49] no further infantry units were ordered to New Guinea until August.[50] Apparently MacArthur considered that there were sufficient troops to ensure the safety of Papua, the springboard for his offensive.

In Washington arguments continued between the army and the navy over the strategy to be followed in the Pacific.[51] Four valuable weeks were lost through this bickering, and the unpreparedness for a victory at Midway, and it was not until 2 July that the Joint Chiefs of Staff issued their directive. This ordered offensive operations with the ultimate object of seizing and occupying the New Britain-New Ireland-New Guinea area. Three tasks were given:

a.   Task One. Seizure and occupation of Santa Cruz Islands, Tulagi, and adjacent positions.
b.   Task Two. Seizure and occupation of the Solomon Islands, of Lae, Salamaua, and Northeast Coast of New Guinea.
c.   Task Three. Seizure and occupation of Rabaul and adjacent positions in the New Guinea-New Ireland Area.[52]

Task One was to be achieved by the South Pacific Area with naval assistance from the SWPA, and Tasks Two and Three were to be achieved by the SWPA.

The Australian Army also began to prepare for an offensive. On 6 and 7 July Blamey held a conference of his senior commanders and staff officers.[53] General MacArthur was present for the first item on the agenda and Blamey gave his appreciation of the strategic situation.

[He] emphasised the task of all formations now was training for mobile offensive operations. Defensive preparations are of secondary importance and valuable time was not to be wasted in digging and wiring. Physical fitness and intensive preparations for offensive action were our immediate objective.

Later Blamey mentioned that an Advanced HQ Allied Land Forces would be opened in Brisbane 'at an early date'.[54] This move was to follow that of MacArthur's GHQ which was to open in Brisbane on 20 July in preparation for the offensive. In addition the 41st and 32nd Divisions were ordered from Melbourne and Adelaide respectively to Queensland to form a U.S. Corps.[55]

On 8 July Admiral Ghormley of the South Pacific Area and MacArthur objected to the early date (1 August) set for Task One, but nevertheless they threw themselves into the preparations. The revised version of Tulsa II had mentioned the necessity of establishing bases near Milne Bay and Buna. Milne Bay was already under way, and MacArthur now ordered a reconnaissance of the Buna area. This was completed on 11 July and the report recommended the establishment of an airfield at Dobodura. On 15 July plans were issued for the occupation of the Dobodura area by Australian infantry and U.S. engineers.

'Operation Providence', as it was known, had barely been ordered, when on 17 July news was received of a Japanese convoy which appeared to be moving towards Buna. This news caught GHQ at a most inconvenient time as they were preparing to move to Brisbane. General Willoughby[56] said that there was no evidence that the ships were heading for Buna,[57] but he was soon proved wrong. Frustrated at Coral Sea and Midway, the Japanese Imperial General Headquarters had, on 11 June, instructed the 17th Army commander, General Hyakutake to determine whether it was possible to capture Port Moresby from the north coast of Papua, and if so, carry it out. Hyakutake decided eventually to carry out the operation without a reconnaissance,[58] and on the night of 21 July about 1,800 Japanese landed at Buna. MacArthur's plan to establish a base north of the Owen Stanley Range had been forestalled.

While plans were going ahead for an offensive, events elsewhere were causing Allied leaders around the world to have grave fears. The German U-boats in the Atlantic were engaged in their most successful battle so far. With the fall of Tobruk and Sevastapol there was concern lest the Germans would link up in the Middle East. General Marshall thought it was 'a very black hour',[59] and Curtin was 'very disappointed' with the unexpected reverses in the Middle East.[60]

In contrast to these events, the Japanese landings marked an acceleration of activity in a theatre where there had been little action since early June. At the beginning of June Japanese midget submarines had attacked Sydney Harbour, and a week later a submarine had shelled Sydney and Newcastle. These attacks had been accompanied by an increasing air offensive against northern Australia,[61] but as June had progressed the activity had died away.

This pause gave Blamey the opportunity to carry out a reorganisation of the Australian Army that the victories at Coral Sea and Midway, and the increasing flow of equipment made both possible and necessary. On 29 June Blamey wrote to Curtin detailing the changes in organisation which he found necessary to ensure:

(a) A properly balanced force.
(b) A force that is adjusted to meet the flow of equipment now arriving.

(c)   A force within the capacity of the population of the country, having due
      regard to other requirements.

The army at this time consisted of ten infantry divisions, one armoured division and two motorised divisions, but most of these were
incomplete, lacking men and equipment. Blamey proposed to reduce
the force by one infantry division and to convert the two motorised
divisions to armoured divisions. The three armoured divisions would
be given a low scale of organisation, each consisting of one armoured
and one motorised brigade. He concluded his letter in characteristic
fashion:

I would be grateful, therefore, for an early conclusion of the determination of
the powers requested for the Commander-in-Chief.
In the meantime the circumstances demand that I proceed with the
reorganisation policy with all possible speed, and I propose to do so unless
you direct to the contrary.[62]

The next day War Cabinet approved the proposals in principle.[63]
  Blamey's plans for the reorganisation were discussed in detail at his
conference for commanders on 6/7 July,[64] and soon afterwards orders
were issued.[65] These orders confirmed that the 32nd and 41st Divisions
now came under the command of the First Army, that the 10th
Division was disbanded, and that the 1st and 2nd Motorised Divisions
were to become the 2nd and 3rd Armoured Divisions.[66] In addition to
the disbandment of the 10th Division, a number of other divisions
were reduced to two brigades. The 2nd Division, which had lost the
14th Brigade (to Port Moresby), now had two brigades and was sent to
Western Australia to bring Bennett's III Corps to two divisions (2nd
and 4th). In Savige's 3rd Division, which had just moved to southern
Queensland, the 10th Brigade was disbanded and split between the
other two brigades in the division. At Townsville Milford's 5th
Division, which had lost the 7th Brigade (to Milne Bay) now had two
brigades. The reduction of nine battalions was achieved by linking
units to others on a state basis.
  This reorganisation meant that a number of changes had to be made
in the command system. The two U.S. divisions in the Second Army
had been ordered to Queensland,[67] and the 1st and 2nd Motorised
Divisions with the 1st Armoured Division became part of LHQ Reserve. This left very few combat troops in the Second Army area. In II
Corps area of the First Army (NSW) the 10th Division had been
disbanded and the 2nd Division had been ordered to Western

Australia. On the other hand there would now be five divisions in Queensland.[68] It was decided, therefore, that the headquarters of the II Corps, located at Parramatta, would move to Queensland (Rockhampton area) and that the Second Army would take over responsibility for all of New South Wales, as well as for Victoria, Tasmania and South Australia. The headquarters of the Second Army would move from Melbourne to Parramatta.[69]

The disbandment of the 10th Division meant that Blamey had to find employment for its commander, Major-General J. J. Murray. Furthermore, Blamey had been concerned that the Australian Army representative in London, Brigadier J. K. Coffey,[70] was not senior enough, and this set off a chain reaction through the higher command levels. Blamey decided that Lieutenant-General E. K. Smart, the army representative in Washington, should go to London and that Sturdee, the CGS, should replace him.

This new posting for Sturdee did not signify that Blamey or the government had lost confidence in him. Nor did it mean that Blamey was getting rid of a potential rival. Sturdee had worked exceedingly hard since taking over the position of CGS on the death of General Sir Brudenell White, and he needed a rest. In the opinion of F. M. Forde, Sturdee had performed very well at a time when there was no glamour attached to the position: 'He had very responsible duties and had to be a sort of a go-between between other officers who did not get on so well with one another'.[71] It was now obvious that the important decisions of the war were being made in Washington, and it was vital that Australia should have a representative who not only held a high rank,[72] but who also was thoroughly conversant with the problems of the Allied Forces in Australia. Rowell wrote that Sturdee 'had an unrivalled knowledge of the strategy of the area and he knew as well as anyone its needs in men and material'.[73]

Sturdee had an added advantage: 'A first class staff officer, a patient and pleasant negotiator and a trained and qualified technical engineer', he was most suited to get Australia the best deal in innumerable equipment orders when often on-the-spot judgment was the only answer.[74] He accepted the appointment on the condition that after one year he should return to a command position in Australia.[75] Sturdee's appointment left the CGS position vacant and Blamey proposed that it should be filled by Lieutenant-General Northcott.

John Northcott, aged 52, had already obtained considerable experience of the duties of the CGS. He had been the Director of Military Operations and Plans at the outbreak of war, and had then been promoted to become the Deputy to the new CGS, Squires. When

Squires had become ill he had acted as CGS until, after Squires's death, Sir Brudenell White had been appointed. In many respects Northcott was suited to his new task. He had attended the Staff College at Camberley and the Imperial Defence College, and was a highly trained staff officer. He gave a solid, confident impression, and was good at running a team. Brigadier L. C. Lucas, the Deputy Engineer-in-Chief, thought that he was a brilliant man, calm and collected, if a little 'stuffy'.[76] General Eichelberger has written that he was 'a very frank, natural person with whom I could get along for the rest of Time'.[77]

Northcott's reaction to the appointment may well have been mixed. In mid 1940 when the 8th Division had been formed he had been worried that his career might be jeopardised because he had not served overseas during the war. He asked that it be noted that he had volunteered for service with the AIF and that because of the appointment of a new CGS at the time (Sturdee), he was required to continue as DCGS.[78] Eventually he obtained a command. When Wynter, the GOC of the 9th Division, became ill in early 1941, Blamey asked for Northcott, but Sturdee told him that Northcott was earmarked for command of the Armoured Division,[79] and he became GOC of it in September 1941. Then in April 1942 he had been given command of II Corps, but now with his appointment as CGS it was clear that he was not to have an active command during the war.

General Berryman, who ended the war as Blamey's Chief of Staff at Advanced Land Headquarters, has claimed that Northcott wanted to swap places with him, but General Hopkins was sure that Northcott was happy to remain as CGS.[80] He believed that Northcott was a little afraid of command.[81] Brigadier MacArthur-Onslow, the commander of the 1st Armoured Brigade, believed that Northcott failed in the Armoured Division. He had been obstructionist and negative.[82] Northcott had never had any great experience of command. He had been severely wounded at Gallipoli and after periods in hospital had returned to Australia. After World War I he had been recognised as a transport expert, and had prepared a transport study for the government in the mid 1920s.[83] His lack of command experience made a staff appointment more appropriate. Sturdee later wrote that he did 'a magnificent job as CGS without consideration of his own personal interests'.[84] Major-General L. E. Beavis, who as war-time MGO worked closely with Northcott, has written that 'Blamey had complete confidence in Northcott's wisdom, tact and loyalty and relied on him increasingly to present the army's problems and proposals to the War

Cabinet, and to maintain a friendly liaison with the rear echelon of GHQ'.[85]

To replace Northcott as commander of II Corps Blamey proposed to promote Major-General E. F. Herring, who had performed very well as GOC in Northern Territory. Major-General J. E. S. Stevens, the GOC of the 4th Division, became the new commander in Northern Territory, and Murray took over his old division. In addition Blamey proposed to abolish the Melbourne District Command, which would make its commander, Major-General F. P. Derham, aged 57, surplus. On 12 July Blamey wrote to Forde and explained that 'This officer has rendered excellent service', and that he proposed to place him on the Unallotted List.[86] At the end of July, however, Blamey decided to send Clowes of the 1st Division to New Guinea and Derham took over the division.[87] In this way Blamey reorganised and prepared the army for the approaching battles.

6
Focus on New Guinea,
20 July –
26 August 1942

The Papuan campaign was shaped from the beginning by inaccurate strategic assessments by MacArthur's headquarters. This placed all commanders under great strain during August and September. It is therefore worthwhile to investigate MacArthur's strategy, for it forms the background to the tensions which culminated in the command crisis in late September.

General MacArthur, in his *Reminiscences*, wrote that in anticipation of the Japanese attack in New Guinea, he 'moved headquarters forward to Brisbane and then to Port Moresby. If I could secure Moresby, I would force the enemy to fight on ground of my selection — across the barrier of the Owen Stanley Range'.[1] Apart from his apparently faulty memory of the date of his move to Port Moresby, this statement is a distortion of what actually happened. As A. J. Sweeting noted, 'the truth surely is that the early conduct of the Papuan operations was dictated by the enemy with the Allied forces under General MacArthur responding sometimes belatedly, to known enemy plans'.[2]

It is clear that MacArthur saw his haphazard reinforcement of New Guinea as no more than the strengthening of a defensive bastion which he thought was unlikely to be attacked by the Japanese. His claims, that he wanted the Japanese to attack across the mountains, do not correspond with his orders for the capture of Buna. If the Japanese were to be in sufficient strength to attack Port Moresby, it should have been obvious that they would be in sufficient strength to protect Buna from a landward assault. The answer is that MacArthur refused to believe that the Japanese were in sufficient strength either to attack or even to hold Buna. He under-estimated his enemy.

Nevertheless, the news that the Japanese had landed on the north coast of Papua near Buna and Gona on 22 July did not come as a complete surprise to the staff of MacArthur's headquarters.[3] They knew that the Japanese were interested in the area, and in June GHQ had asked General Morris what his plans were for the protection of 'the vital Kokoda area'.[4] Morris had replied that he was patrolling the area with native troops and that he was preparing to move forward the remainder of the PIB.[5]

Morris's resources were very meagre, consisting of two militia brigades and service troops, and he had no wish to fight the Japanese away from his main base. However, he had been ordered to send the 39th Battalion to Buna to secure a forward air base. This move had barely begun when the Japanese landed, and he was therefore instructed to concentrate the battalion at Kokoda immediately. Hence, on orders from LHQ in Melbourne, Morris found himself committed to fighting at the end of a tenuous line of communications over the Owen Stanley Range. He had hoped that the mountains would have hampered the Japanese advance.[6] That he was not unmindful of these difficulties is indicated by his signals to Landops. On 17 July he radioed Melbourne:

One company already at Kokoda. Second company leaves Moresby 18 July. Fear physical condition troops and native track may result in numbers arriving Kokoda fit for action being reduced as much as 33 per cent . . . request urgent advice aircraft for troop carrying to Kokoda.[7]

Despite the rapid Japanese advance inland to secure the important airfield at Kokoda, and despite Morris's appeals to GHQ for air support, in Australia MacArthur remained unconvinced that this Japanese attack marked a new offensive. Since the American success at Midway, MacArthur had been determined to advance his air bases into New Guinea, but he was not yet ready to move. There was some justification for this attitude. The original plan had been that after the landing by South Pacific forces at Guadalcanal on 7 August, MacArthur would occupy the Buna area. The Japanese had beaten him to it, but he felt that the landing of the marines might cause the Japanese to withdraw troops from New Guinea, thus allowing him to continue his plans for an amphibious advance along the north coast of Papua. It is true that the amphibious forces were not yet available, but MacArthur's reluctance to be forced to conform to the Japanese movements can be understood. To Curtin in Sydney, however, he did not rule out the possibility that he might be compelled to move larger forces to New Guinea.[8]

The unwillingness of GHQ and LHQ, at this stage, to reinforce New Guinea, and their lack of knowledge of conditions, is reflected in the message sent from LHQ to Port Moresby on 28 July: 'Disturbed by enemy penetration in Kokoda area. Most vigorous action must be taken to establish block as far east as possible. Passes over range must be secured'.[9] Morris was being ordered to hold, but he was not to be given the necessary troops, supplies or transport to do so.

Although GHQ viewed the Japanese landing with confidence, there was disquiet in a number of quarters in Australia. In particular, the staff of the First Army, located at Toowoomba, was becoming increasingly concerned. The GSO1 (Int.) was Colonel K. A. Wills, who had been Lavarack's intelligence officer in I Corps. A keen amateur soldier, Wills had served with a British regiment in World War I. His comfortable financial circumstances (he was a company director in Adelaide) probably enabled him to be more outspoken than the majority of Staff Corps officers.[10] He had been studying the situation, and early on the morning of 30 July he produced an appreciation.[11] Calculating the Japanese strength on the north-east coast of New Guinea at about 10,000, he went on to compare the tactics being employed in the area with those used by the Japanese in Borneo. There, after naval reverses in the Macassar Straits, they had abandoned the direct seaborne attack and had advanced overland across most difficult terrain from Balikpapan to capture Bandjermasin. Only when they had almost reached their objective did they make a seaborne landing at Bandjermasin.

Wills was convinced that the immediate Japanese objective was to capture Moresby with an overland attack, probably in conjunction with a seaborne attack.[12] He therefore took this appreciation to the Chief of Staff of the First Army, Major-General Frank Berryman, who in turn took it down to General Sutherland in Brisbane. Wills's appreciation differed markedly from that of the same date by MacArthur's Chief of Intelligence, Brigadier-General Charles Willoughby. He believed that the enemy would 'limit himself to the development of a fighter air-base', and an advance to Moresby in strength was 'not imminent by any indications' even though occupation of the Gap was probable.[13] Sutherland therefore disagreed entirely with Wills's assessment and Berryman wrote on the paper: 'The recent op [operation] is regarded as the last of his purely defensive ones. New facts NOT mentioned indicate more Jap attention Aus. area'.[14]

From the mass of information which flows into any intelligence centre it is the task of the intelligence officer to extract the important material. In this regard Wills had proved reliable. Willoughby's record was not so consistent, but he was faced with the problem of making his assessment fit MacArthur's strategic concept. (This view will be discussed later.) Apparently, with the help of recently arrived, although not necessarily valuable information, Willoughby and Sutherland managed to persuade Berryman to accept their assessment. Yet surprisingly, with much less information at his disposal than Wills or Willoughby, Ek Dum (M. H. Ellis) of the *Bulletin* came to a similar conclusion to Wills. On 29 July he wrote that 'a land attack on Moresby is both feasible and probable'.[15]

A number of politicians were also becoming concerned about the position in New Guinea. W. M. Hughes, the 'Little Digger' of World War I, and former Prime Minister, declared on 5 August that Australia would suffer the same fate as Malaya unless an offensive strategy was adopted and Buna and Gona were retaken without delay. The public may well have taken notice of Hughes, who was the leader of the UAP and a member of the Advisory War Council, when he remarked: 'There has been a lamentable lack of vision, of initiative, of co-ordination of control by our military leaders . . . They have done too little or moved too late'.[16]

The next day Curtin replied, pointing out that the Advisory War Council had had numerous consultations with the service chiefs, Blamey and MacArthur, and that Hughes had had many opportunities to indicate his proposals in the Council. That same day (6 August), at a meeting of the Council, the matter was discussed. Curtin pointed out that 'a satisfactory defensive position had been established' and he 'did not believe in castigating [the] military commanders over the operations in Gona and Buna'.[17]

Thus, a week after the Japanese landings, concern had been expressed in a number of quarters, in New Guinea, Brisbane and Canberra, that the allies had not reacted to the new threat. The longer they delayed, the more strain this would cause to the troops and commanders who would have to deal with the situation.

It will be recalled that in the previous chapter it was observed that the Japanese landing in Papua caught the staff of GHQ at a most inconvenient time as they had barely established the headquarters in Brisbane. Furthermore it caught the Allies with LHQ still in Melbourne. Blamey, of course, had already indicated that an Advanced Land Headquarters (Landops) was to follow GHQ to Brisbane. LHQ was to remain in Melbourne under the control of the CGS, Lieutenant-General Sturdee. Landops would assume responsibility for the control of the operations of the Allied Land Forces. The DCGS, Major-General George Vasey, became Chief of Staff at Landops, the Director of Military Operations was Brigadier Ronald Hopkins, and the DA & QMG was Brigadier John Chapman, soon to be promoted to Major-General.

Landops opened at the new Queensland University at St Lucia on Saturday 1 August.[18] The headquarters 'was full of disconsolate AWAS sitting on typewriter boxes'[19] and the only communication with Melbourne that day was a brief signal to say that the headquarters had opened. Vasey and Chapman were taking a few days leave and Hopkins was left to set the headquarters in running order. Hopkins believed that General Durrant at the headquarters of the Queensland L of C Area had found things moving too quickly to make proper arrangements, but in fairness to Durrant, he had been told to expect half a dozen officers while in a few days about one hundred arrived.[20]

Nevertheless Blamey was present and he was able to discuss the events in New Guinea with MacArthur.[21] Blamey, like Wills, was convinced that MacArthur was underestimating the strength of the Japanese landing, and pressed him to reinforce Port Moresby.[22] This came on top of a concerned message from Washington. Admiral King, nervous about the coming landing by the Marines at Guadalcanal, had become worried by the rapid advance of the Japanese, and had asked General Marshall to find out what MacArthur planned to do. King was 'willing to assume that MacArthur was "taking all measures in his power to deny the threat of Japanese penetration towards Port Moresby", but he doubted that the measures taken (which he described as: "airpower supported by minor ground forces north of the Owen Stanley Mountains") would be successful'.[23]

Perhaps it was these combined pressures coupled with the news of the Australian reverses around Kokoda[24] which convinced MacArthur that the time had come to reinforce Moresby. His first reaction was to send the 32nd U.S. Division to New Guinea to operate directly under the control of GHQ. This would have led to an impossible command structure with two separate superior headquarters in Australia controlling separate national forces in the one operational area.[25] Apparently Blamey talked him out of that folly.

On Friday 31 July Lieutenant-General Sydney Rowell, the commander of I Australian Corps, visited the HQ of the First Army at Toowoomba. On returning to his own HQ at Esk he received a call from Lieutenant-Colonel L. H. Lemaire, Blamey's friend and Inspector Army at Landops,[26] with the news that he was to see the C-in-C at the Queensland Club the next morning. Rowell had a good idea what it was all about, and in the morning Blamey explained that

Right V Major-General G. A. Vasey, DCGS at Landops

Below VI Lieut-General R. K. Sutherland, MacArthur's Chief of Staff, and Lieut-General Sir John Lavarack, GOC First Army, April 1943

Above left VII Lieut-General Rowell in September 1942
Above right VIII Major-General C. A. Clowes, GOC Milne Force, with his GSO1, Colonel F. O. Chilton and his AA & QMG, Colonel J. C. D. Litchfield
Below IX 7 Mile Aerodrome the day after the attack of 17 August 1942

MacArthur had decided to send I Australian Corps to undertake the defence of Moresby in the first instance, and then counter-attack. Rowell was not to discuss this with anyone other than his two senior staff officers, Brigadier Henry Rourke, his BGS, and Brigadier J. R. Broadbent, his DA & QMG.[27]

There was much to be done in the next few days. The plan was that Rowell was to go to New Guinea with the headquarters of I Australian Corps and take over the command of New Guinea Force. I Corps consisted of two infantry divisions: the 7th Australian Division (AIF) under the command of Major-General A. S. Allen, and the 3rd Australian Division (militia) under the command of Major-General S. G. Savige. That afternoon the headquarters of I Corps and the 7th Division was transferred to LHQ Reserve.[28] Major-General C. A. Clowes, the commander of the 1st Australian Division, located north of Sydney, was ordered to report to LHQ. The previous day the headquarters of II Australian Corps, under the command of Lieutenant-General John Northcott, had relinquished command in NSW to the Second Army, and now began to move to Queensland where it was to assume control of the remaining units of I Corps, and to be responsible for the defence of the Brisbane area.[29] Thus, the movement of one major unit set off a chain reaction throughout the entire military organisation, although some of the moves had been foreshadowed by Blamey in July.

On the afternoon of Sunday 2 August a team of staff officers from Landops[30] arrived at Esk with the news that advance parties were to be loaded in forty-eight hours and the main bodies a day later. It was obvious that General Allen and his staff would have to be told, and after some trouble in contacting Blamey, Rowell received approval to inform the 7th Division staff.[31] That evening Allen and his AA & QMG, Colonel George Canet, arrived at Rowell's HQ.[32] Rowell explained that the 18th and 21st Infantry Brigade groups, and part of the divisional troops, were to go to New Guinea. The movement was to begin on 5 August and be completed by 12 August. The 18th Brigade was to go to Milne Bay and the 21st Brigade to Port Moresby. The 25th Brigade, the third brigade of the 7th Division, was to follow later.[33]

During the next three days the troops bound for New Guinea hurriedly prepared to embark. It was learned that General Clowes was to command a force at Milne Bay to be known as 'C' Force, and he would have the 18th Brigade and the 7th Brigade which was already at Milne Bay. Initially it had been intended that Clowes would command the field forces in New Guinea, and on 30 July General Vasey had issued orders from Melbourne separating the functions of the command of the field troops and of the Lines of Communication Area in New Guinea.[34] Clowes had been nominated as commander of the field troops with the title of Commander New Guinea Force and Morris was to command the New Guinea L of C Area.[35] Events had overtaken these plans and Clowes had been given command of the force at Milne Bay, eventually to be known as Milne Force.

Rowell later wrote that 'It speaks volumes for the ability of the 7th Division to move smoothly and rapidly that the troops were at dockside in Brisbane at the appointed time'.[36] On 5 August he sent a message to Allen, 'I would like to congratulate you and all concerned at your HQ and in subordinate formations for the very fine effort in successfully initiating a most difficult movement problem'.[37]

Major-General A. S. Allen, known throughout the army as 'Tubby', was aged 48, and was one of the great characters of the 2nd AIF. A chartered accountant by profession, he had commanded a battalion in World War I, the 16th Brigade in Libya and Greece, and the 7th Division in Syria. 'Blunt in speech, honest as the day, choleric yet kindly, completely without affectation or pomposity, he was a leader of a kind that appeals immediately to Australians'.[38] He loved his soldiers, and his sincerity and honesty inspired great loyalty, but he could be difficult with his seniors. Rowell had not found either of his subordinates, Allen or Savige, particularly outstanding, but he now realised that Allen had achieved a great deal with the 7th Division since its return to Australia. Rowell faced the coming battles with some trepidation about Allen; not because he felt that he was incapable, but because he knew that he was a very difficult, and at times intemperate man. He felt that he was a good brigade commander who had been spoilt by being made a divisional commander.[39]

Colonel Charles Spry, who arrived at the 7th Division Headquarters late on the night of 3 August to take over from Colonel Elliott as GSO1, soon found his new commander to have a prickly personality. Allen was absent from the headquarters visiting his old friend and fellow divisional commander, General Savige. Spry brought with him the confirming orders for the move with the detailed composition of the flights for the ships.[40] In the absence of the division commander he immediately forwarded these to the brigades.[41] The next morning Allen was furious. Spry was too good a soldier to be shaken. He served Allen loyally throughout the campaign, but vowed that given the opportunity he would not serve with him again.

Although the 7th Division had performed well in Syria, it should not be supposed that it was adequately prepared for the fighting in

New Guinea. Since its return to Australia it had lost one brigade commander, its divisional artillery commander, its GSO1 and AA & QMG, three artillery regiment commanders and five battalion commanders. Immediately before leaving the Middle East two additional battalion commanders were transferred to command brigades, and one brigade commander was returned to Australia.

A number of troops were restive as they had received only seven days leave on return to Australia.[42] The division had originally arrived in Adelaide, had then gone to Tenterfield in New South Wales, before joining the defences north of Brisbane. Despite these unsettling moves, Allen felt that the division was in 'first class physical condition, as well trained as time would permit, and with its morale 100 per cent'.[43] Jungle training was not, however, adequate for the coming battle in New Guinea. There was no country near the area where the division was located in south Queensland similar to the jungle in New Guinea. No senior officers had been allowed to visit New Guinea, and the lessons of Malaya did not necessarily apply.

At midnight on 3 August, having picked up Clowes in Sydney, General Vasey arrived in Brisbane. He was completely unaware that the movement was underway. Brigadier Hopkins, who was standing in for Vasey, had been ordered by Blamey not to inform LHQ, for fear of poor security in Melbourne. This had, of course, made it extremely difficult to arrange administrative support, and Hopkins eventually found it necessary to inform the CGS.[44] Vasey described the scene at Landops on 4 August to his wife: 'Today has been busy in spots. I had Joe [Lavarack], Berry [Berryman], John N. [Northcott] and Albert [Blamey] all in my room at one stage . . . Albert seems in good form'.[45] Vasey did find that Landops had overlooked one matter of detail. They had forgotten to inform Morris, but he rectified this with a short signal: 'Syd is coming'.[46]

Morris in Port Moresby was, by this time, facing a large number of insoluble problems. With no knowledge that he was to be reinforced he must have been feeling desperate. On 3 August he signalled LHQ:

Supply situation Maroubra [the force on the Kokoda Trail] and Kanga [the force around Wau] most serious. Must repeat must have transport planes with parachutes stationed here immediately. Failing this operations will be jeopardised and forward troops liable starvation.[47]

Landops in Brisbane replied blandly that the parachutes were not yet available.[48] On 4 August a telephone line was completed to Deniki and the next day there was an experimental air drop at Myola. Morris again appealed to Landops: 'Transport planes previously made available all returned to mainland . . . Consider two machines permanently based here is minimum requirement'.[49]

Whilst Morris was struggling with inadequate resources, unaware that Rowell was heading north, MacArthur and Blamey were feeling quite confident. On 2 August MacArthur replied to Washington's request for news. He explained that plans to prevent a Japanese build-up in New Guinea had been hampered by a lack of transportation and naval assistance. He explained that it was his policy to move the forward airfields progressively northwards. The first step was to develop the Townsville-Cloncurry area. The second step was to strengthen the Port Moresby garrison, which had been completed by the movement of the 14th Brigade, begin building up the airfields in that area, and to develop airfields in northern Cape York Peninsula. The third step, which he saw as an offensive one, was to build airfields at Merauke, ' . . . secure the crest of the Owen Stanley Range from Wau southward to Kokoda; and to provide an airfield at Milne Bay to secure the southern end of the Owen Stanley bastion'.[50] MacArthur pointed out that these steps would secure New Guinea. He realised that the tasks had not been completed and appealed for aircraft carriers and a Marine Division. He could also proudly announce that he had just ordered the 7th Division to New Guinea.[51]

MacArthur's statement that the factors limiting operations in New Guinea would be shipping and naval support merely reiterated those made by both himself and Admiral Ghormley of the South Pacific Area on 8 July, when they recommended the postponement of the attack on Guadalcanal. Perhaps also MacArthur was aggrieved that the first offensive of the Pacific War was to be made by the navy.

Blamey was as confident as MacArthur. At a press conference on the morning of 4 August he said that the troops were fit and were a tough proposition for any enemy. He admitted that the Japanese had beaten the Allies to Buna, but basing his facts on Willoughby's assessment, he estimated their strength at not more than 2,000.[52] Wills had estimated the enemy strength on 29 July at about 4,500. That evening Blamey told Major-General George Kenney, MacArthur's new Commander of the Allied Air Forces, that he would capture Buna in a few weeks.[53]

The Weekly Intelligence Summary issued by Blamey's Director of Military Intelligence, Colonel John Rogers,[54] for the week 31 July to 7 August, confirmed his commander's views. From the Japanese 'moves it would appear', wrote Rogers, 'that the enemy intends establishing a series of outposts, forming a protective screen around the North Eastern Sector of Papua, thus covering their bases in Buna-Gona areas against Allied land attacks'.[55]

The Americans at GHQ believed that the Japanese moves were designed to divert attention from Japan's real aim, which was to attack Siberia. Indeed, in late August MacArthur told General Eichelberger that he expected the Japanese to attack Vladivostock in mid October.[56] However, the confidence at GHQ was more likely connected with the landings of the American Marines at Guadalcanal on the morning of 7 August. This threat to their left flank would divert the attention of the Japanese from New Guinea and so enable MacArthur to complete his strategic plan. His signal to Marshall on 2 August makes that plan clear. The plan hinged on the belief that Port Moresby could be threatened only from the sea. If Milne Bay were held and the crests of the Owen Stanley Range were picketed, then Moresby and its airfields would be secure. He would then be free to advance along the north coast of Papua with amphibious forces.

MacArthur's communique of 6 August confirmed that the New Guinea defence line 'was along the almost impassable Owen Stanley Range'.[57] His Operation Instruction of the same day laid down his plan. Having been pressed by Blamey and Washington to reinforce Moresby and faced with the Japanese capture of Kokoda, he now saw a way to turn the situation to his advantage. Although he and his staff thought that it was impossible for the Japanese to advance over the Kokoda Trail, Rowell was ordered to advance in the opposite direction, capture Kokoda and then, in conjunction with the amphibious advance from Milne Bay, prepare to capture Buna. The ultimate aim was to capture Lae and Salamaua. Nevertheless, the first mission of New Guinea Force was to 'protect the operation of Allied Air Forces operating from and through air bases in Australian New Guinea'.[58] With the exception of this mission, these ambitious plans were fanciful thinking. Since there were no landing craft in the theatre MacArthur later issued orders that as many shallow-draft boats as possible should be assembled at Milne Bay to facilitate the amphibious advance.

It is true that the Japanese were thrown off balance by the landing at Guadalcanal. On 28 July Major-General Tomitari Horii, the commander of the South Seas Detachment, had been ordered to attack Port Moresby over the range, whilst another force assaulted Samarai, near Milne Bay. This two-pronged assault was now postponed until later in August and the planned attack on Samarai was abandoned when the Japanese learnt that the Allies were at Milne Bay. Some of the troops were withdrawn to reinforce Guadalcanal while the remainder were ordered to capture Milne Bay.

During the night of 8/9 August the Battle of Savo Island was fought off Guadalcanal. It was a disastrous defeat for the Allied fleet, and when the Americans did not initially reinforce the marines, it convinced the Japanese that not only would they be able to hold Guadalcanal, but they could go ahead with their plans to capture Port Moresby.[59] It also chilled MacArthur, for he realised that Port Moresby was once again vulnerable to a seaborne assault. To attack Moresby, however, the Japanese would have to secure the area of Milne Bay. MacArthur must have congratulated himself for his strategic forethought, for with the arrival of the 18th Brigade, and including the American engineers, Clowes would have a garrison of over 8,000 troops in the area.[60]

A change had come over MacArthur's headquarters since its arrival in Brisbane. While it had been in Melbourne the headquarters had been divided into three groups of American officers. There was the group from the diverted transports, the small group that came down from Java and Singapore, and MacArthur's own party of about twenty. One senior staff officer noted that 'A sense of frustration was present in each of these groups, each of which for some reason or other looked on the others as interlopers. General MacArthur's little party remained for some time as an exclusive little coterie'.[61] It was only after the move to Brisbane that this divisive feeling began to disappear. During the months leading up to the move to Brisbane, MacArthur had been moulding his staff to suit his own requirements. The manner in which MacArthur reorganised his headquarters reveals the tensions in the command structure.

In his original instructions MacArthur had been directed that he was not eligible to command any national force. This meant that the command of the American forces remained with Major-General Julian F. Barnes, but MacArthur did not find this situation satisfactory. Undoubtedly Barnes was not suited for the command. He had been a lieutenant-colonel in the American task force that arrived in Brisbane in December 1941, and in a short while found himself commander of the U.S. forces in Australia. He told Rowell 'that he was just a "simple gunner", and that this sort of assignment was . . . "not in my bailiwick" '.[62] Furthermore, Barnes did not belong to MacArthur's Bataan clique. In early July MacArthur asked General Marshall to recall Barnes, saying that whilst he was a 'hardworking, diligent officer of exemplary personal character but of only average professional attainments' he had negated the 'potential capacity' of his staff by his 'inability to mould and co-ordinate'.[63]

This gave MacArthur the opportunity to correct what he saw as a fault in organisation. Barnes had been CG USAFIA but commanded only a fraction of the U.S. forces in Australia. USAFIA was in fact a supply echelon and MacArthur proposed to change it to that, and to call it the U.S. Army Services of Supply, SWPA. To command this new organisation he proposed to promote his deputy Chief of Staff, Brigadier-General Richard J. Marshall, of whom he had a very high opinion. Significantly, Marshall had been with MacArthur in the Philippines. This change took place on 20 July — the same day that GHQ SWPA moved to Brisbane. A by-product was that MacArthur himself became commander of USAFIA.

Lieutenant-General George H. Brett was a different proposition from Barnes. He was a former Chief of the Air Corps, and was now Commander of the Allied Air Forces in Australia. For a short while it had looked as though he might have become Commander-in-Chief of the South-West Pacific Area in preference to MacArthur. MacArthur felt that the Air Force had let him down in the Philippines and Brett represented that Air Force. Relations were always cool between the two, with neither party making any attempt to improve the situation.

Meanwhile, General George Marshall in Washington had become concerned about the problems of commanding American troops in Australia, and in late May he had ordered Major-General Robert C. Richardson to visit the Pacific and Australia to investigate this matter.[64] Richardson carried out an extensive tour of the Pacific visiting New Guinea — a place MacArthur had not yet visited. In New Guinea he discovered 'great confusion in the minds of the command' about their duties and mission.[65]

During his tour Richardson detected two disturbing facts. The first was that General Brett had organised the Allied Air Forces so that the Australian and American air forces were integrated. The result was that in some cases American units were commanded by Australians. This was particularly galling to the Chief of the U.S. Army Air Forces, Lieutenant-General H. H. Arnold, who wrote to Major-General T. T. Handy, the Acting Chief of Staff, that 'Our combat units are not being employed in accordance with War Department doctrines and principles . . . The Australians have been operating our combat units in accordance with their doctrines and no attempt has been made on our part to gain control'.[66]

The other matter was that the American ground troops in Australia were under the command of General Blamey. Richardson wrote to

Marshall that 'the present organisation was an affront to national pride and to the dignity of the American Army'.[67] MacArthur was already aware of this problem and requested that Richardson remain in Australia to command an American corps consisting of the 32nd and 41st U.S. Division. Richardson agreed, but continued his return journey to America to report to Marshall.[68] On reaching Noumea he was ordered to return to Australia, but he was determined to go on to America, and on 8 July informed Marshall:

It is most urgent and necessary that I report to you in Washington to inform you of facts that you ought to know. I am familiar with the proposed operations and in discussing them with me last week General MacArthur offered me command of the corps and wished to submit my name to you as corps commander. 1 declined his offer stating that first I must report to you. In this he concurred adding that I could return if the appointment was agreed upon.[69]

When Richardson returned to Washington it was agreed that an American corps should be set up in Australia, but Richardson again refused to accept command. He pointed out that his corps would come under the command of an Australian Army Commander who in turn was under the command of General Blamey: 'Such an organisation is inimical to the proper combat development of American Forces . . . They breed friction and resentment because human nature and national pride are involved'. He continued that American officers in Australia 'had no confidence in the Australian command and staff, and furthermore that as part of the army of a great nation, they felt that they were entitled to be under American command, and not be incorporated in an Australian army for operations'.[70] In essence, Richardson felt that the formation of an American corps would not remedy the situation since the corps commander would be 'placed under a non-professional Australian drunk'.[71] With this he was referring to Blamey. Nevertheless in his report Richardson said that, 'There was no resentment of the Australians themselves, but merely of the system of control.[72]

Richardson's point was accepted by the staff of the War Department, but they were not in agreement that it was necessarily valid, for they were confident that MacArthur would be able to handle the situation. Finally, however, it was agreed that MacArthur should be advised that one way of overcoming the problem would be to form a task force under an American commander when combat was imminent, and for the American corps to be assigned to the task force.

General Handy felt that MacArthur was aware of American policy and was sure that his request for a corps commander and staff was made with such a purpose in mind, and therefore the establishment of a corps would remedy the situation.

MacArthur has often been accused, and with justification, of undermining Blamey's authority as Commander of the Allied Land Forces by removing American combat troops from his command in operations.[73] It is interesting to note, therefore, that he was given some authority, indeed advice, to do so from the War Department. MacArthur's command was not seen as an Allied one, but as an American one which, by force of circumstances, was compelled to co-operate with other foreign forces, or as General Handy commented, 'The Australians have 350,000 troops and a little break for them seems to be necessary'.[74]

General Marshall was angry that Richardson had refused the command in Australia, but the latter was protected by the Secretary of War, Henry L. Stimson, and his career did not suffer the termination which Marshall would normally have ensured. The new officer chosen was Major-General Robert L. Eichelberger. Explaining the decision to Eichelberger, Marshall told him that he had been selected because it was believed that he could get along with MacArthur. This was felt to be necessary because MacArthur had sent home a number of high-ranking officers.

Eichelberger recalled that:

Then General Marshall launched into a tirade against General Richardson . . . With his arrival back here, he at once began to get himself out of this combat detail claiming that he did not want to fight under the Australians and particularly under General Blamey who had been selected by agreement of Americans as Chief of the Allied Ground Forces. He called Blamey the Chief of Police of Melbourne, Australia.[75]

Apparently Richardson had complained at length to Marshall about the personal life of General Blamey.[76]

Eichelberger was perplexed by Richardson's attitude. He knew him 'as a well educated officer, snappy, with a good mind, ambitious. He was a cuff snapper, well dressed and highly perfumed',[77] but only many years later did he come to the conclusion that the real reason that Richardson refused was that he was only a year after MacArthur at West Point and knew a lot about him. He felt that perhaps Richardson was afraid to come under the command of MacArthur.[78]

Probably only Richardson knew the real reason why he refused the command in Australia.[79] It is clear, however, that he was afraid that his career would be harmed by the unsatisfactory command arrangement which at that time MacArthur seemed happy to perpetuate. If no further troops were sent to Australia then Richardson would have been destined to remain a U.S. Corps Commander in an Australian Army. This was a depressing prospect; but in any army it is a bad practice to refuse command. Before the end of the war MacArthur had two American Armies under his command, one of them commanded by Richardson's successor.

Eichelberger eventually arrived in Australia in late August to take up command of I American Corps, and he established his headquarters at Rockhampton. He was particular about one detail. He had been told by Barnes that MacArthur had not liked his title as Commanding General USAFIA, and therefore when Marshall had told him he was going to Australia he asked Marshall, 'Isn't it true that General MacArthur is personally in command of our troops?' General Marshall said 'Yes'. Therefore Eichelberger asked that he be called Commanding General I Corps and not Commanding General USAFIA, 'thereby saving myself from a possible fate like Barnes'.[80]

Meanwhile MacArthur had been scheming to get rid of Brett. The matter had first been raised by Marshall but MacArthur let his feelings be known in definite terms. 'Brett is unquestionably highly qualified as an Air Technician', he told Marshall on 30 June,

He is an unusually hard worker but his very industry leads him to concentrate at times on unimportant details which tend to obscure a true perspective of more important matters; he is naturally inclined towards more or less harmless intrigue and has a bent, due, perhaps, to his delightful personality, for social entertainment and the easy way of life; he is unpopular with the Australian Administration who resent his lack of confidence of the younger or fighting elements of the Air Corps here. I would rate his service during the last three months under my command as only average.[81]

The man chosen to replace Brett was Major-General George C. Kenney and in early July he was ordered to Australia. The decision to replace Brett was confirmed when Richardson's report reached Washington and Kenney was briefed to take 'corrective action' to change the situation that had caused Richardson to complain that 'no American Commander should be placed in the position of being dependent on foreigners'.[82] Obviously Kenney was instructed to separate the command of the American and Australian air units, for as he wrote later, Marshall 'had told me in Washington that he didn't think much of mixing nationalities in the same organisation'.[83]

Kenney arrived in Australia in late July and took command of the Allied Air Forces on 4 August. He entered the offices of MacArthur's headquarters like a breath of fresh air. Short, cocky, competent, highly regarded by his men and a firm believer in air power, he was quick to grasp the situation. He knew that Brett had been sent home because MacArthur doubted his loyalty, so from the beginning he gave his new Commander an affirmation of his loyalty. This is what MacArthur wanted to hear, for Kenney knew how to flatter him. After a brief clash with Sutherland, who thought that he could run the air force, Kenney asserted himself in his position as Commander of the Allied Air Forces and as MacArthur's chief air adviser.

Kenney's importance to MacArthur should never be underrated. When he arrived in Brisbane he found MacArthur 'a little tired, drawn and nervous'.[84] but Kenney, a newcomer from outside of what Rowell called the 'Philippine performing circus',[85] was just the man to raise his confidence. Soon MacArthur began to rely on Kenney for advice on matters of overall strategy as well as conduct of the air war. More importantly, Kenney made him believe in the Air Corps, whereas previously he had mistrusted it. Kenney listened to everyone who might have ideas and was prepared to use the GHQ staff to present them to MacArthur. He knew that if his plans were presented by Brigadier-General Chamberlin, MacArthur's Chief of Operations, as his own, then they might be successfully received. After several meetings with Chamberlin, Kenney would comment to his secretary: 'Chamberlin is beginning to get a bright idea'.[86] Probably this did not fool MacArthur but it did mean that only one man was going to get the credit and that was the Commander-in-Chief. MacArthur's opinion of Kenney rose as the war continued and in his *Reminiscences* he described him in most complimentary terms:

Of all the brilliant air commanders of the war, none surpassed him in those three great essentials of combat leadership; aggressive vision, mastery of air tactics and strategy, and the ability to exact the maximum in fighting qualities from both men and equipment.[87]

Kenney was true to his instructions and acted quickly. He formed the 5th U.S. Air Force under his own command and the RAAF units were grouped together as the RAAF Operational Command under Air Vice-Marshal W. D. Bostock. He also acted with vigour. Brigadier-General M. F. Scanlon, whom Kenney found to be not up to the job, was replaced by Brigadier-General Ennis Whitehead as commander of the air forces in New Guinea and, in all, five officers of general rank were returned to America.[88]

The replacement of Brett caused some concern in the Advisory War Council and when it met in Melbourne on 13 August the question was raised as to whether an officer, to whom Australian combat forces had been allocated, should be replaced without consultation with the Australian Government. There was some concern as to whether Blamey might be similarly replaced and Curtin promised to discuss the matter with MacArthur.[89]

Curtin must already have been feeling that he was on unsure ground with MacArthur. In early July the Advisory War Council had asked for a weekly statement of operational aircraft casualties in the South-West Pacific Area. MacArthur had refused this request, pointing out that he was responsible to the Chief of Staff of the U.S. Army and was 'not at liberty to make such operational reports to other agencies'.[90] He promised to make reports of losses of RAAF aeroplanes if desired.

It was now transparently clear that except for such leverage that the Australian Government could exert as a result of supplying combat forces to MacArthur, or any influence that its resident ministers might have in Washington or London, the strategy to be employed for the defence of Australia was out of the hands of that country. The minutes of the meeting of the Advisory War Council for 9 July are illuminating: 'It was decided that the request for regular reports of operational losses in the South-West Pacific Area should not be pressed'.[91] Government leaders had been in awe of MacArthur since his arrival in Australia, and they believed that in military matters his advice should be followed at all times.

At the meeting of the Advisory War Council on 27 August Curtin explained that he had discussed the matter of Brett's replacement with MacArthur in Brisbane on 18 August. MacArthur had told him that both Brett and Admiral Leary of the Allied Naval Forces had been appointed before he had arrived in Australia. He said that the appointments of Blamey, Brett and Leary had been made by him in his capacity as Commander-in-Chief, but that the replacement of General Brett had been made by the United States Chiefs of Staff. He said that he would be glad to consult with the Prime Minister on any impending changes which might be contemplated. In the case of General Blamey there could 'be no question of any variation in his status without prior consultation with the government'.[92]

It is difficult to believe that MacArthur was being candid. Whilst it is true that the order to relieve Brett may have come from Washington, MacArthur had worked to ensure it. Furthermore, the idea of forming a task force so that the command of American troops in combat would not remain with General Blamey was definitely a 'variation' in Blamey's status. MacArthur was, however, careful not to antagonise Curtin with obvious breaches of this agreement. On 6 September he sent Curtin a message: 'U.S. Navy Department wishes to replace Admiral Leary by Admiral Carpender. Both are most excellent men. Request your approval'.[93]

With this final change of his commanders MacArthur felt that he was now surrounded by more amenable men. His position with the Australian Government was sure. He had replaced 'those incompetent, bungling nincompoop airmen who were with me in the early days of the war'.[94] All that could hurt MacArthur now was a military reverse, which he believed the Joint Chiefs of Staff in Washington would use to discredit him.

In this regard MacArthur was probably applying his own standards of conduct to General Marshall who, while he may have had good reason to find MacArthur a personal enemy, was at all times correct in his dealings with him. Others, however, were not so righteous, and Brigadier-General St Clair Street of the Operations Division expressed the opinion that the 'Chief obstacles to a sane military solution' to the Pacific 'mess' were 'the political implications that revolve around MacArthur'. He felt that 'the sooner MacArthur comes out of the place, the sounder we are going to be allowed to be in our solution of our Pacific problem'.[95]

While MacArthur was looking with confidence at the developing military picture, nevertheless he was facing the coming weeks with apprehension. It would be vital to his reputation that the operations should be successful. His headquarters, now established in the AMP building in Brisbane, was ready for action. Furthermore, since they also were in the building, close liaison with the air and naval headquarters was ensured. There was frequent liaison with the Advanced Land Headquarters at nearby St Lucia and the senior Australian commanders could become more familiar with their American counterparts. Vasey wrote to his wife of his impression of MacArthur: 'The more I see of him the more tiresome I think him. Pedantic school teacher or professor is an apt description. Incidentally when he walked up the steps here a few days ago he was blowing like a grampus'.[96]

Despite the fact that MacArthur had moulded his staff to his own liking, he still had to deal with the Australians. With the appointment of Rowell to the command in New Guinea it meant that the control of the approaching operations would be in Australian hands.[97] This was a potential weakness, but it also had advantages, for if the operations were a failure MacArthur felt that at least the Chiefs of Staff could not blame him.

On 11 August 1942 Rowell and his staff arrived in Port Moresby. Although he had been a member of the first class to graduate from Duntroon in 1914 and had served at Gallipoli I Australian Corps was his first command. After Gallipoli he had been invalided home to Australia in 1916, and had missed the opportunities that had come to his contemporaries in France and Palestine. At the beginning of World War II he had been selected as Chief of Staff of the 6th Division, and then progressed to Chief of Staff of the Australian Corps in the Middle East, where it was generally agreed that he had performed with distinction in the campaigns in Greece and Syria. In September 1941 Rowell had returned to Australia to take up the appointment of Deputy Chief of the General Staff, and had been appointed to the command of I Corps during the reorganisation in March and April 1942.

Proud, very austere and sensitive, he was high principled to the degree that one senior officer remarked 'the trouble with Syd is that he expects everyone to act like a saint'. Throughout the army he was respected for his integrity and competence. Aged 47, he was at the peak of his ability. During the inter-war period he had devoted himself to professional study, and had attended the Staff College at Camberley and the Imperial Defence College. The campaign in New Guinea was to be the first real test of his leadership.[98]

Vasey saw Rowell in Brisbane on 6 August and found him in good form. 'Syd is obviously enjoying his freedom from an office', Vasey wrote to his wife, 'and he has done a lot of good work'.[99] On the evening of 8 August Rowell and Vasey dined together and again Vasey commented that the new commander of New Guinea Force was in good form, but he detected some change in him: 'Whether it is occasioned by his promotion or whether he remembers a conversation some months ago I cannot tell. It may be it is neither but merely anno domini. I shall be sorry if he changes materially'.[1] Later in the month Vasey had lunch with Brigadier H. B. Sewell, the First Army chief of artillery. He told Vasey that Rowell 'had proved himself a bit tiresome' when he was there. Vasey wrote to his wife, 'the little I saw of him [Rowell] the other day gave me the impression that he was a bit full of himself and he has surrounded himself with people who cannot be accused of being diffident. It will be a pity if he becomes spoilt'.[2]

Accompanying Rowell when he arrived in Port Moresby was General C. A. Clowes, bound for Milne Bay, the BGS of the Corps

(Rourke), the Chief Engineer, Brigadier J. W. Main, and Colonel F. K. Norris. Colonel Norris was the ADMS of the 7th Division, but Rowell's DDMS, Brigadier W. W. S. Johnston, had been slightly hurt in a car accident in Brisbane a few days previously and Norris was deputising for him.

Rowell and his staff, seasoned officers with recent operational experience, brought to New Guinea the skill and organisation that Morris and his staff had been unable to provide. Henry Rourke, aged 46, had graduated from Duntroon in 1916 and had served in World War I. He had, however, missed the fighting in the present war. Initially he had been on the staff of I Australian Corps. Then before the Australians became involved in the fighting in the Middle East he had become GSO1 of the 8th Division in Malaya. Finally, three months before the Japanese had attacked, he had been sent back to the Middle East as the commander of the 7th Division artillery. By this time the 7th Division had ceased operations in Syria.

The DA & QMG, or Chief of Administration, was Brigadier Raymond Broadbent, who arrived in Moresby the following day. Aged 49, he had been in the same class as Rowell at Duntroon, and also like Rowell, he had been invalided home after service at Gallipoli. He left the army in the 1920s and took up sheep farming in southern New South Wales. Joining the militia just before the war, he served as the AA & QMG of the 8th Division during the fighting in Malaya. His task as DA & QMG was wideranging and demanding, requiring co-operation with ANGAU (the Australian New Guinea Administrative Unit), the American and Australian Air Forces, and the United States Services of Supply Organisation (USASOS) which was just beginning operations in New Guinea. He has been described by those who served with him as a 'very fine soldier'.

On 12 August Rowell assumed command, and the staff of New Guinea Force were absorbed into that of I Corps to form a rejuvenated HQ New Guinea Force. General Allen, who arrived on 13 August, enumerated the problems faced by the corps. The garrison was inadequate and the morale of many of the troops was dangerously low. The training of the troops was almost 'nonexistent'. The organisation of supply dumps was 'deplorable' and hygiene was most 'unsatisfactory'.[3]

Morris was not sorry to be relieved of his heavy responsibility,[4] and he moved into the old Lieutenant-Governor's residence in Port Moresby and assumed command of the Australian New Guinea Administrative Unit. Later Rowell wrote to Blamey that 'Morris has had a lot to contend with and none of my people have anything but ad-

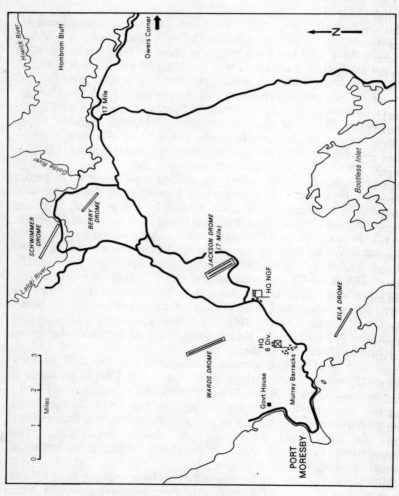

Map 3   Port Moresby area, 1943. From 1943 Army Survey map.

miration for the way he has battled along. It is all too easy to walk in with experienced people and tidy up a going concern, and we are not a bit disposed to criticise our predecessors'.[5]

On 13 August, however, in a more private letter he commented, 'What it must be to have a bad staff!! I am going over his people to see who is to be retained and will then dispose of the balance'.[6] The truth was that the headquarters in New Guinea had never been formed as an operational headquarters. Originally formed as the headquarters of the 8th Military District, it had had no substantial reinforcement when it had assumed an operational role.[7] Rowell later virtually admitted this when he discovered the appalling lack of intelligence information. Harking back to the days when he was DCGS he commented to Vasey, 'Perhaps I was to blame in not seeing that [Morris] got a decent staff'.[8]

Rowell sought immediately to gain control of the situation, but the main body of his headquarters had not yet arrived. Until it did on 17 August, he would have to rely on Morris's small staff. Morris had already ordered the 53rd Battalion and the HQ of the 30th Brigade, commanded by 'that grand AIF soldier, Brigadier Selwyn Porter',[9] to move forward to reinforce the 39th Battalion, and the first troops began to move on 12 August.

Meanwhile over the Range the 39th Battalion had, on 8 August, recaptured part of Kokoda, but could not hold it. On 13 August the Japanese drove the battalion back to Isurava, where Colonel Yokohama now waited for General Horii and the majority of the force to join him.

The size of the Allied force which could be used in the Owen Stanley Range was limited wholly by the capacity of the administrative services to maintain it. Already there were insufficient native porters, and on 9 August the dropping of supplies at Myola had begun. Rowell personally went through the figures of the supplies despatched with the senior administrative officer of the old New Guinea Force headquarters, Lieutenant-Colonel E. B. Serisier, and was satisfied that by 16 August there would be twenty-five days supply for 2,000 men and adequate small-arms ammunition at Myola. Brigadier A. W. Potts, the commander of the 21st Brigade, now arriving in Port Moresby, was ordered to have two battalions available to move forward along the Kokoda Trail on 17 August.

General Morris had believed that his main threat was from a seaborne attack, and therefore he had located his headquarters at Seventeen Mile, under the shadow of Hombrom Bluff. Rowell believed that with the defeat of the Japanese in the Battle of the Coral Sea, his main threat was from the Japanese over the Range, and that he should be in 'close touch with the naval and air commanders and reasonably placed to visit the 7th Division Headquarters. Although the latter still had responsibility for defence against a seaborne operation, each day the likelihood of this became more remote'.[10]

Rowell therefore decided to transfer his own headquarters to a new site just off the road to Seven Mile Aerodrome, four miles from Moresby. This, however, was to take some days, and meanwhile the headquarters, consisting mainly of the old New Guinea Force staff, remained at Seventeen Mile, for the bulk of his own staff were still at sea. On the afternoon of 16 August Rowell was returning to Seventeen Mile when he noticed a row of Dakota transport planes parked wing-tip to wing-tip beside a corresponding line of Flying Fortresses at Seven Mile Aerodrome. It is remarkable that the Americans, who had lost many of their planes in the Philippines through being caught with them on the ground, were not aware of the potential danger, but Rowell had seen the effect of German Stukas in Greece and was concerned. As soon as he reached his headquarters he telephoned Brigadier-General Ennis Whitehead, the new commander of the U.S. Air Force in New Guinea, and suggested the immediate dispersal of the aircraft because they offered a perfect and unnecessary target. Whitehead agreed that they had been unwisely concentrated, and promised to act.[11]

The next morning Rowell was driving into Moresby to inspect anti-aircraft defences when he almost drove into an air attack on Seven Mile Aerodrome.[12] In their first air raid on Moresby in over a fortnight,[13] but the seventy-eighth raid of the war on the town,[14] Japanese bombers and fighters carried out a successful attack, destroying or damaging all five available transports. There were no further air deliveries for five days. Initially Rowell was not unduly concerned, since he believed he had sufficient supplies at Myola, but this air raid was to have important consequences.

The shape of Rowell's operations in New Guinea was determined by the instructions from GHQ which were passed on as LHQ Operation Instruction No. 30 of 9 August 1942. This declared that there were 'no indications of an attack from seawards on Port Moresby nor of any material increase in Japanese strength in the New Britain area'. All Australian and American forces in Papua and north-east New Guinea were put under the command of New Guinea Force and the immediate task was to capture the Kokoda aerodrome and then to prepare for operations against Buna from Kokoda and Milne Bay. Plans were foreshadowed for the establishment of an amphibious force at Milne Bay and the ultimate aim was to capture Lae and Salamaua.[15]

These instructions depended upon the belief at GHQ that there was no likelihood of a threat to Moresby from across the mountains. The crux of the intelligence problem is the difference between gathering information and interpreting it. Furthermore, there is always the danger of a preconceived idea colouring the interpretation; for example when on 12 August Brigadier-General Charles Willoughby, MacArthur's Chief of Intelligence, in his daily intelligence summary said that 'an overland advance in strength is discounted in view of logistic difficulties, poor communications and difficult terrain'.[16]

Willoughby was a particularly odd character. He was part German and was the archetype of what people imagined a Prussian to be. 'Terribly boorish',[17] and single-minded, he was cordially disliked by Sutherland, but he flattered MacArthur. MacArthur had a high opinion of Willoughby's ability, he liked him, he had been with him on Bataan, and therefore kept him on. It seemed as though MacArthur delighted in employing men who lacked well-rounded personalities, as if he was then assured that he alone would be hailed as the hero and mastermind of a successful campaign. Tom Foley, who was a press censor at GHQ, wrote in 1955:

Prussian-born Willoughby always reminded me of the fictional Harley Street specialist with his immaculate dress, almost British speech, expressive gestures and pince nez glasses on a black silk cord.
MacArthur demanded the utmost loyalty from his top ranking officers. He got it to the full from Willoughby.[18]

Willoughby was a member of 'the small band of devoted men who formed a powerful buffer between MacArthur and the world outside'.[19] This is not to deny the ability of Willoughby, for under his guidance the Allied intelligence system became highly efficient.[20] He was an extremely competent linguist in German, English, Spanish and French. Eichelberger wrote that 'he was always positive in his views and usually wrong',[21] and another officer said 'Willoughby has the best hindsight of any intelligence officer in the Army'.[22] This sort of comment is a little unfair to Willoughby but he did make his intelligence fit MacArthur's communiques. Sir Kenneth Wills recalls that he kept a 'dishonest accountant's account of the numbers'.[23] Despite or because of this he remained with MacArthur until the occupation of Japan, and wrote a flattering biography of his commander.

Broadly speaking it is the business of the intelligence staff to say what the enemy might do. It is the responsibility of the commander to decide what the enemy is most likely to do. Unlike MacArthur, Rowell did not agree with Willoughby's assessment. Rowell's intelligence summary for the period ending 5 August quoted from the First Army intelligence summary, which said that 'the enemy might be considering another attempt on Moresby, this attempt to be combined with the land operations in the Kokoda area.[24] The *Bulletin* revealed outstanding perspicacity and pointed out that it was unlikely that the Japanese would attempt to cross the Owen Stanley Range before developing a base and destroying the Allied air transport, 'but he will attempt it'.[25] The raid on Seven Mile of 17 August certainly seemed to provide the second condition.

When the war correspondent Osmar White learnt that the 21st Brigade had been ordered to move over the Kokoda Trail, he questioned Rowell about the wisdom of this. He recorded that Rowell 'shrugged and said frankly: "As far as I'm concerned, I'm willing to pull back and let the enemy have the rough stuff if he wants it. I'm willing to present the Jap with the supply headache I've got. But there are those who think otherwise. We need a victory in the Pacific, and a lot of poor bastards have got to get killed to provide it" '.[26] So, like Morris, Rowell found himself committed to fighting at the end of a tenuous line of communications.

The fortnight following Rowell's arrival was a period of intense activity as he sought to develop Port Moresby as a base, began the development of an air supply system, and prepared for attacks at either Milne Bay, Kokoda or a seaborne invasion of Moresby. The resupply of Kanga Force around Wau was increasingly becoming a problem. In addition, his immediate aim remained to recapture Kokoda. Rowell was not lacking in advice from Brisbane.

On 13 August he received a signal from General Sutherland requesting:

that reconnaissance be made of critical areas of the trail through the Owen Stanley Range for the selection of points where the pass may be readily blocked by demolition and that the necessary charges be emplaced in the most forward areas and assembled for ready installation in the rear areas.[27]

This signal showed an abysmal lack of knowledge of the country by the staff in Brisbane. It has become fashionable to point to the ignorance of the Americans, yet many of the Australian commanders were equally at fault. In April and again in July Vasey had visited New Guinea. On 18 July he had actually landed at Kokoda, and had flown over the Kokoda Trail. Despite this, it was not until 7 September, after many messages from Rowell,[28] that he wrote to Blamey: 'The situation is also made more difficult by the fact that apparently, our ideas of topography in the area of the gap were all wrong'.[29]

Rowell was usually very quick to reply to all messages from Brisbane, but in the case of the direction to prepare the Owen Stanley Range for demolition, he found himself too busy to reply. Finally on 22 August he wrote:

Some parts of the track have to be negotiated on hands and knees and the use of some tons of explosive would not increase these difficulties.

It is respectfully suggested that such explosives as can be got forward would be better employed in facilitating our advance than for preparing to delay the enemy!!![30]

On 20 August Major-General J. H. Cannan, the Quartermaster-General, and Lieutenant-General Vernon Sturdee, the Chief of the General Staff, visited Rowell. Sturdee had just completed two years of intense work as CGS and was now looking forward to his new posting as head of the Australian Mission in Washington.[31] He arrived in New Guinea with a letter from General Blamey that had been written on 17 August. Blamey was full of confidence:

I don't feel any great anxiety that the Japanese groupings and concentration that are now being effected are going to be aimed directly at your force, but I do feel that as they find your resistance becoming stiffer they will not fail to reinforce their present force in Papua . . .

I am perfectly confident that you and your staff and your troops will handle the big responsibility that has been laid on you very adequately, and both myself and the Government have every confidence in the result.[32]

The lack of concern at GHQ was underlined by Willoughby's intelligence summary of 18 August, when he affirmed that 'an overland movement in strength is discounted in view of the terrain'.[33]

Ten days after arriving in New Guinea Rowell also had some reason for feeling confident. On 21 August he wrote to Blamey. 'By this evening we will have four stripped battalions on the Range, 39, 53, 2/14, 2/16; i.e. about 2,000 men'.[34] The Japanese had not advanced appreciably since the beginning of August and Potts's orders were to capture Kokoda. Meanwhile Porter and the 30th Brigade (39th and 53rd Battalions) were to continue patrolling 'so that the enemy will be pretty well shaken before he is attacked'. Rowell went on to outline his plans to take Buna and Gona adding, 'at a distance, all the above may sound very much like "counting chickens" but there are no doubts here as to the outcome . . . I am now turning over in my mind plans to capture and hold Salamaua when we have cleaned up Buna and Gona . . . We are all very well and in the highest spirits'.[35]

Yet while Rowell was optimistic he still remained cautious. Since his arrival in New Guinea, Allen had been pressing him for his third brigade, the 25th,[36] and Rowell had been pressing GHQ, but shipping was not available. Supply was always precarious and sometimes reserves were sufficient to last only about one-and-a-half days, therefore while he asked for the 25th Brigade, Rowell wrote to Blamey that he 'was not pressing for 25 Inf Bde unless you felt that direct seaborne attack was likely'.[37]

From the time of his arrival the threat of a seaborne assault had played on Rowell's mind. Allen had been given responsibility for the seaward defence as well as for the operations on the Kokoda Trail, and he found the preparations in Moresby in a 'deplorably hopeless position'.[38] Rowell realised that this threat greatly reduced the troops which he could use in the mountains, but he knew that this was 'a question only the very great can answer. But if it is at all likely [that there should be a seaborne attack], and I am still laboriously trying to build up strength on the hills to kick the Japs in the pants, then I consider 25 Inf Bde plus one Field Regiment . . . are essential'.[39]

Rowell was also aware of the precarious nature of the supply situation. On 16 August he had pressed Blamey for more transport aircraft, but Blamey was having difficulty convincing MacArthur of the need for aircraft. On 21 August Vasey wrote to Rowell that 'TAB [Blamey] has written to both MacArthur and Sutherland saying it is essential for you to have an allotment of transport aircraft. This working with Allies is becoming more and more difficult'.[40]

That same day Rowell's plans for an early advance to Buna received a severe jolt when Potts informed him that instead of the twenty days' supplies that he thought were available at Myola, there were in fact only two days for two battalions forward of Myola and five days at Myola. This meant that offensive operations had to be deferred and that the 39th Battalion would have to be extricated from the forward area.

It came as a bitter shock to Potts to find that the promised supplies were not available.[41] The staff at HQ NGF were convinced that the supplies had been despatched, but obviously this figure had not been checked against arrivals at Myola. The organisation at Myola needed straightening out, but surely the small staff in the area could have alerted Rowell to the potential problem.

Rowell had, however, sensed that the supply of Maroubra Force would be a complicated problem, and as soon as his headquarters staff arrived on 17 August, he sent his DAQMG, Major D. B. Fargher, forward to investigate the quantity of supplies at Myola and to supervise the line of communications. He was two days short of Myola when Rowell received Potts's message. With the arrival of his headquarters staff, Allen had, on 18 August, taken over responsibility for the operations on the Kokoda Trail and for the defence of Moresby. He now ordered Potts to take command of all troops in the forward area while Porter was to return to Myola to investigate the supply problem.

Rowell himself was anxious to get to the bottom of the problem and his investigations convinced him that the supplies had been sent. On 27 August he wrote to Vasey that 'I think there has been bungling here in not sending balanced rations and I'm sure a good deal of the stuff was chucked out into the jungle'.[42] Later he wrote that:

all through the New Guinea campaign cargo dropping remained notoriously unreliable. Even when experience developed much better techniques, loads were dropped miles from the target area. And this particular flight to Myola was an especially tricky business. I saw a young pilot come back one day after his second trip and he was pretty well chewed up. Besides, the pilots were mainly civilians under hire, without the sense of duty and urgency that could be expected from enlisted and trained personnel.[43]

What Rowell did not realise was that even when supplies were dropped in the correct area a large percentage was not recovered, or was recovered and found to be damaged.

Lt Fayle, General Allen's ADC, described the scene at the headquarters of the 7th Division.

The supply question was now obviously worrying the GOC as he was getting one story from NGF and quite a different story from Brig Potts. The whole fact of the matter, and NGF seemed unable to understand all through the campaign, was that recoveries were never 100 per cent of the supplies dropped and wastage was at times terrific.[44]

When on 26 August Allen received a message from Potts pointing out that the weather was good but nothing had been dropped from the air, he contacted NGF and was told that 1,500 rations had been dropped. Allen commented 'Where the hell they were dropped goodness only knows and it has been perhaps a feast for the Nips'.[45]

An indication of the problem can be gauged by a note in the GHQ G-3 Journal (the GHQ operations file) of 1 September by Brigadier

General S. J. Chamberlin. He noted that General Kenney had called and had indicated that the Air Force had delivered approximately 250,000 pounds of supplies to select localities in the Owen Stanley's and that the Air Force had transported all supplies delivered to them.[46]

On 23 August, after attempting to confirm the seriousness of the supply situation, Rowell informed Blamey:

For reasons so far unexplained I find today that reserves of rations forward is [sic] only ten thousand instead of forty thousand estimated as a result of dropping from air. This raises again question of air support. Since 17 August [the day of the big air raid] only one plane has been available and that only for the past two days. Commanding General AAF has signalled Kenney today asking for two additional aircraft at once and I would appreciate your support securing these.[47]

Rowell was already feeling the pressure of disapproval from Brisbane, and later he wrote to Vasey: 'I quite expected to be recalled after my hard luck signal about the supply situation on the Ranges'.[48] Nevertheless Blamey again tackled MacArthur, who told him that he had arranged to place at Port Moresby six Douglas Dauntless dive bombers, one Flying Fortress and two bombers.[49]

With these planes, [wrote MacArthur] it is estimated that a minimum of 20,000 pounds of supplies per day can be delivered to Kagi and Wau. There are available in Australia only thirty transport planes at the present time. Of these an average of not more than 50 per cent are available at any one time. Air supply must necessarily be considered an emergency rather than a normal means of supply. Consequently every effort should be made by the GOC NGF to develop other means of supply.[50]

Since 20,000 pounds per day was Rowell's daily maintenance requirement, he would therefore need to use carriers to increase his forces or build up reserves. No more carriers were available, and therefore an immediate offensive was out of the question. Potts was ordered to hold where he was and plan to advance on or about 1 September.

These developments did little to shake the confidence of Landops or GHQ. Willoughby reaffirmed that an overland operation against Port Moresby should be 'discounted in view of the logistical difficulties of maintaining any force in strength' on the Kokoda Trail.[51] It is remarkable that GHQ recognised all the difficulties that the Japanese would have on the Trail, yet missed the point that the Australians might have similar problems.

Rowell was now staggered by a message from Landops suggesting that while there was no indication when they would be able to move the 25th Brigade to New Guinea, the 30th Brigade would be able to return to the mainland on the same ships when they were available. Rowell replied hastily: 'With possibility one infantry brigade helping Kokoda operation, consider three infantry brigades necessary this area for reasonable security against major seaborne attack'.[52] The suggestion of returning the 30th Brigade was but a symptom of the complete lack of understanding of Rowell's predicament by the commanders in Brisbane. The supply shambles was a direct result of this lack of understanding. Not even Rowell understood fully the difficulties of supply in mountainous jungle. The inescapable conclusion is that the Allies had not, at this stage, decided to throw their full weight into the operations in New Guinea. Rowell would just have to get along as best he could.

While Rowell was struggling with his supply problems, Clowes was seeking to organise his forces at Milne Bay. On 13 August he flew down from Moresby with his new Chief of Staff, Colonel F. O. Chilton. Chilton had met Clowes only once previously in a desperate situation in Greece and he had been impressed with his new commander's courage and coolness.[53]

Until this time Milne Force had not been under the command of New Guinea Force, and the previous commander and commander of the 7th Brigade, Brigadier John Field, had laboured manfully to develop the base. Between 12 and 21 August the 18th Brigade, commanded by Brigadier George Wootten, arrived. Also on 21 August the main body of the headquarters of Milne Force arrived, and the next day Clowes took command.

Conditions were appalling. Roads sank into the mire, and Lieutenant Piper, the Intelligence Officer of the 18th Brigade, remembered seeing a bulldozer bogged in the centre of the main road.[54] The only maps were dyeline productions made by the brigade staff after pacing with a compass around the shores of the Bay.[55]

On 21 August Clowes issued an instruction detailing his defence policy, and instructed his two brigadiers to submit plans by 26 August, when he would co-ordinate them. He was not to have that much time. On 24 August coast-watchers reported that barges were moving east near Porlock Harbour. Next morning the Japanese landed at Goodenough Island. That same morning a convoy was sighted moving towards Milne Bay.

Clowes acted quickly. Under the terms of reference of his appointment, he could assume command of all land and air forces in the

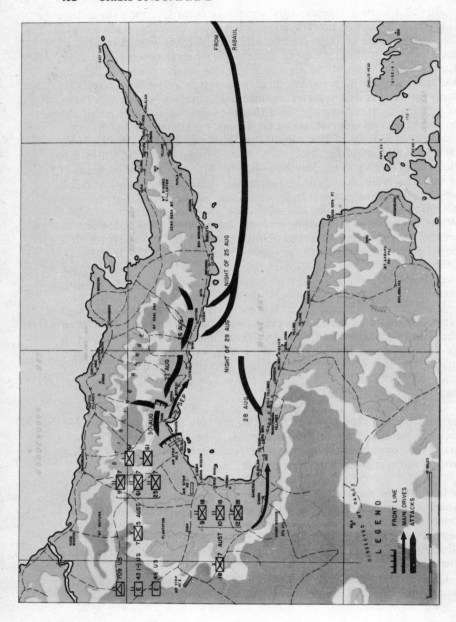

Map 4. Enemy landings at Milne Bay, August 1942. From *Reports of General MacArthur*, Vol. 1, p. 65

area when threatened by attack. He now assumed command and placed all administrative troops, engineer units and units of the USASOS under the command of the brigade in whose operational area they were located for the purposes of defence. He then gave his orders for the conduct of the defence. Not knowing at which point the Japanese would land, he decided to hold the attack with one brigade and keep the other in reserve. This was necessary since the Japanese had command of the sea and could land almost wherever they pleased.

Aged 49, Clowes had been in the same class as Rowell at Duntroon. As a young soldier in World War I he had a record of outstanding gallantry. A highly trained artilleryman, he had commanded the I Australian Corps artillery in Greece, where again his cool courage had been evident. During the early days in Palestine, however, Clowes had fallen out with Blamey after an article appeared in *Smith's Weekly* suggesting that Clowes should be appointed Commander-in-Chief. Blamey mentioned this to Rowell, who assured his Chief that Clowes was more interested in 'getting back to his little baby daughter' than in securing the position.[56]

Apart from this, Clowes was not suited to be a Commander-in-Chief. He was learned, capable, gallant and had a high sense of duty, but he was too introverted to be a forceful commander. Forde called him 'Silent Cyril' and the name stuck. To those who knew him well, he said very little; to those who did not, he said even less. Yet those who served under him found him to be a man of character and ability. Wootten, Field and Chilton all had confidence in him, but he never managed, in the short time he was at Milne Bay before the attack, to make a good impression on the soldiers. No better commander than Clowes could have been found to control the uncertain situation now developing at Milne Bay. He made his plan and stuck to it throughout the fighting. What is more, the plan was successful.[57]

Throughout August the Japanese had built up their forces in Papua, with large landings of troops at Buna on 18 and 21 August. On 21 August Allied aircraft reported that the Japanese were lengthening the emergency airstrip at Buna. As early as 15 August Willoughby had been willing to admit that a large number of troops had landed at Buna, but he had felt that their only interest was to control the Gap.[58] This latest information convinced him that the defence of the aerodrome was the reason for the landing.

Landops felt that something unexpected was about to take place. On 21 August Rogers wrote that substantial Japanese 'reinforcements have arrived in the SWPA and that the enemy is now in possession of a powerful striking force . . . It would appear that our offensive in the Solomons has goaded him into seeking revenge. There is, as yet, no clear picture as to the area on which it is intended the blow shall fall'. Rogers went on to enumerate the possibilities: an attack on Moresby by land, sea, or both, an attack on the north-east coast of Australia, an attack on Fiji, or an attack on the Tulagi-Guadalcanal area. He thought that the last course was most likely. Blamey ensured that twelve copies of this appreciation were sent to the Advisory War Council.[59]

That same day General Horii left the beachhead to direct the attack on Isurava. This did not mean that the Japanese were oblivious to the problems of advancing through the mountains. Horii's Chief of Staff, Lieutenant-Colonel Toyonari Tanaka realised that the overland campaign was not possible without mechanical power, but Imperial Headquarters had ordered it to be carried out, whatever the conditions.[159] Meanwhile, the left arm of the assault was poised to take Milne Bay. The date for the co-ordinated attack was 26 August.

Beset by innumerable supply problems, not fully supported from Australia, and indeed told by GHQ that the Japanese had no intention of capturing Port Moresby, Rowell faced the approaching battles with quiet confidence. He was confident of his commanders and of his AIF troops. Yet much of the initial blow was to fall on untried militiamen. At Isurava Brigadier Potts would have the 39th and 53rd Battalion, for supply difficulties had not enabled him to get his AIF troops forward. At Milne Bay the militiamen of the 7th Brigade were deployed to take the first shock. If MacArthur had, as he later claimed, decided to meet the Japanese on ground of his own choosing, he had certainly not deployed his forces to the best advantage.

7
The Japanese Papuan Offensive, 26 August – 16 September 1942

The battle for Milne Bay provides an example of the manner in which a battle produces pressures at many levels of command, and how these pressures have a life of their own and in turn affect the outcome of the battle. The Japanese attacks at Isurava and Milne Bay on 26 August 1942 caused immediate concern in Washington, Canberra and at GHQ in Brisbane, a concern that was in marked contrast to that displayed by the Australians of Allied Land Headquarters. Not only had all of the senior Australian officers had experience of combat in World War I, but many of them had served through the recent campaigns in the Middle East. Most of MacArthur's staff had served with him on Bataan, where they had suffered a demoralising defeat, but for others, like Brigadier-General S. J. Chamberlin, the Chief of Operations, this was to be their first battle. MacArthur refused to include any Australians on his staff, and there is evidence to support General Eichelberger's statement that the Australians regarded the Americans as 'inexperienced theorists'.[1]

Chamberlin was one of the few officers on MacArthur's staff who had not been with him on Bataan, but he was also one of the few officers to get on well with the Australians. He was fat, amiable and well-trained. MacArthur found him 'a sound, careful staff officer, a master of tactical detail and possessed of bold strategic concepts, he was a pillar of new strength'.[2] Eichelberger, who had no love for MacArthur's staff, wrote to his wife: 'Don't sell Steve Chamberlin short. Anything he says can be relied on because he is a very honest person'.[3] Despite this, Chamberlin had had no opportunity to temper his training with experience, and he told General Berryman, who later succeeded Vasey as DCGS, that he would have achieved no more than 20 per cent at the U.S. Command and Staff School.

On the night of 25-26 August the Japanese began to land troops at

Milne Bay. Simultaneously their forces on the Kokoda Trail began their attack at Isurava. It took some time, however, for both the troops at Isurava and for the commanders at Port Moresby to realise that the Japanese had been reinforced for an offensive, and therefore for a number of days the action at Milne Bay attracted the greatest attention. Here Major-General Clowes was fighting a most difficult battle. Hampered by constant rain, endless mud, and poor communications, and threatened with a landing to his rear, he was determined to stick to his plan and was wary of committing his forces to an immediate counter-attack.

By midday on 26 August the concern in Brisbane had become intense and Major-General Sutherland issued oral instructions to Major-General Vasey to take energetic action at Milne Bay to drive out the Japanese. General MacArthur repeated these instructions to General Blamey, stating that in his opinion the Japanese would reinforce this landing within seventy-two hours.[4] Although Clowes did not know it, the Japanese force at that time totalled only some 1,200 troops.

As a result of MacArthur's instructions, Landops signalled Rowell that the 'enemy landing at Milne Bay may be a prelude to landing in numbers. The landed force must be attacked with greatest vigour and destroyed as soon as possible'.[5] In Port Moresby Rowell realised that Clowes was in the best position to judge the necessity for action, and did not pass on this signal to Milne Force. Rather he sent another message to Clowes: 'Confident you have situation well in hand and will administer stern punishment'.[6] By the evening of the first day Clowes had tightened his perimeter, but because of the threat of a landing to his rear he was determined to maintain the bulk of the 18th Brigade as his reserve.

Meanwhile in Brisbane, MacArthur was becoming increasingly apprehensive.[7] Nevertheless Blamey was confident that Clowes would be able to defeat the Japanese;[8] indeed, so much so that during the day he flew to Melbourne because of the sudden death of his wife's father.

MacArthur's original strategy had been to establish bases in New Guinea from which to strike at Rabaul. Milne Bay was under construction, and the next step was Buna. He had now to alter this strategy. At a conference that evening attended by Sutherland, Admiral Leary, Kenney, Vasey, who was deputising for Blamey, and Brigadier Hopkins, Sutherland declared that if the Japanese succeeded in getting a footing and then attempted to exploit it, General MacArthur's intention was to send additional troops to Milne Bay and to 'fight it out in New Guinea'.[9]

This explains why the 25th Brigade, the remaining brigade of the 7th Division, had not been sent earlier to New Guinea. Till now MacArthur had not been convinced that he would have to fight a major campaign in Papua. His mind had been already leaping forward to his spectacular island-hopping campaign, overlooking the possibility that the Japanese might attempt to wrest control of his bases from him. Despite the fact that Admiral Leary said that he had few ships and no escorts, it was decided eventually that the 25th Brigade would be sent to Milne Bay.[10]

That same evening Clowes, in his tent at Milne Bay, was writing a hurried note to Rowell:

With information at my disposal, find it difficult to understand the Wog actions — especially as to why he didn't effect (or try to) other landings.
Spirits good here — all in good heart. Do wish, though, that the bombing were more effective. How about torpedo carrying craft — torpedoes held here.
Had assumed command of whole show early yesterday afternoon when attack seemed definitely indicated. Had no intention of letting fighters leave here, except as last resort, though they were very reluctant to stay. They have done and are doing a grand job — great lot of chaps. Am writing this in their Ops room.
Weather foul here — inches of rain daily and country and roads are foul.[11]

The next morning Clowes, who it will be remembered had not yet received Landops' signal to attack the enemy, decided to commit the 2/10th Battalion from the 18th Brigade. During the day this battalion moved forward to engage the Japanese.

That same morning Rowell, who had not yet heard news of the fighting around Isurava, wrote a letter to Vasey:

I took a lousy view of your signal telling us to be offensive as the convoy might be a prelude to further landings. That is very true but you must move slowly in two feet of mud, however much you desire to run. Again if bombers can't sink ships, what about some Navy (is there any left?) or torpedo bombers. There are torpedoes at Milne Bay, but all the Beauforts are apparently being kept for exhibition in Sydney.[12]

The lack of naval support that was worrying Rowell was also causing MacArthur some concern. Most of his navy had been taken from him to support the landing at Guadalcanal by the South Pacific Area forces on 7 August. The battles of Savo Island and the eastern Solomons had already reduced the available Allied naval vessels, and the Japanese were attacking the marines on Guadalcanal. At this time MacArthur had only one escort ship to support any reinforcement of Milne Bay.[13]

MacArthur's consternation can therefore be imagined when, during the night of 27-28 August, the 2/10th Battalion was driven back by Japanese tanks and infantry, with a loss of 43 killed and 26 wounded. This setback to experienced AIF troops convinced MacArthur that the Australians were not doing all that they might. He felt compelled to warn Marshall that the Japanese might strike at New Guinea under the cover of the Guadalcanal operation, and he would be powerless to prevent them because of the absence of the navy in the Solomons.

In the late afternoon, Sutherland called Vasey and asked whether his instructions of 26 August (to attack the enemy) had been carried out, and what further information Landops had of the situation. At five thirty that afternoon Sutherland followed this up with a curt letter to General Blamey:

The Commander-in-Chief requests that you instruct Major-General Clowes at once to clear the north shore of Milne Bay without delay, and that you direct him to submit a report to reach General Headquarters by 0800 K/29 of the action taken together with his estimate of the enemy's strength in the area . . .[14]

A signal to this effect was therefore sent immediately to Rowell, who this time had no option but to send it on to Clowes. He received it at midnight.[15] Rowell did, however, alter the signal slightly. Where GHQ required a report by 8 o'clock the next morning, Rowell altered his order to 'advice is required by earliest possible hour'.[16]

At Landops Vasey was in an awkward position, for with Blamey's absence he had to bear the brunt of the pressure from GHQ. For all his attractive characteristics, Vasey was no diplomat. Goaded by the abrasive Sutherland, he wrote to his friend Rowell in Moresby in terms that he knew would distress the Commander New Guinea Force:

The lack of information from you on the operations at Milne Bay has created a very difficult situation here. GHQ get through air sources various scraps of information . . .
Only two minutes ago I have been phoned by Sutherland asking me what reports I had, and what offensive action had been taken by Cyril. I was compelled to answer that I was unaware . . .
You possibly do not realise that for GHQ this is their first battle and they are, therefore, like many others, nervous and dwelling on the receipt of frequent messages. Hopkins told me that you had said you were not going to give a

'ball for ball' description. With this I agree in principle, but I think you might give some consideration to my statement in the previous sentence. Your wire to the C-in-C giving the situation up to 1600 hrs 26 Aug was fine. We would appreciate more of them.

I have received your G3566 of 27 August in which you say that the necessity for offensive actions is well appreciated by Cyril but I cannot impress on you too much to stress the necessity for executing that offensive action.

By the tone of this morning's conversation with Sutherland, I feel that a wrong impression of our troops has already been created in the minds of the great and it is important for the future that that impression be corrected at the earliest possible moment. [17]

Vasey was also required to keep Blamey informed and he signalled LHQ in Melbourne explaining the situation. He concluded, 'receipt by GHQ of scraps of information from air sources which indicated lack of offensive action have resulted in General MacArthur becoming very perturbed'. [18]

Later that night, Vasey, upset at his harsh letter to Rowell earlier in the day, and now in receipt of more information, wrote another message to Rowell:

If you took a lousy view of our message about offensive action, I hate to think of your reactions to my letter of this morning . . . . It boils down to the question of who is commanding the army — MacArthur or T.A.B., and it seems the sooner that is settled the better . . .

I am now awaiting the result of Cyril's activities yesterday. I'm dying to go to these bastards and say I told you so, we've killed the bloody lot.

Vasey then added a postscript: ' . . . this is a war of nerves isn't it. Let's give it to our own people too'. [19]

After a quiet day at Milne Bay on 28 August, and sporadic action on the 29th, Clowes ordered Wootten's 18th Brigade forward for an attack, but late that day aircraft reported that a cruiser and nine destroyers were heading for Milne Bay, so the attack was called off. Brisbane again signalled Moresby demanding the 'greatest vigour' to 'exterminate' the enemy immediately. [20] This was again another symptom of the anxiety at GHQ. Vasey had written earlier to Rowell that 'one of MacArthur's troubles is that all his navy has gone to the Solomons and he wants information on which to base a request, or demand, on Washington to get it back'. [21]

This view is supported by a long message that MacArthur sent to General Marshall in Washington on 30 August in which he said that:

This is the first test of Australian troops under my command. The Australians claim that the commander is excellent and rate half his troops as good. The other half from the 7th Australian Division they rate excellent . . . . With good troops under first class leadership I would view the situation with confidence unless enemy reinforcements are landed but, as I have previously indicated, I am not yet convinced of the efficiency of the Australian troops, and do not attempt to forecast results.

MacArthur went on that the failure to review the strategic situation would have a 'disastrous outcome':

Unless additional Naval forces, either American or British, are concentrated in the Pacific and unless steps are taken to match the heavy air and ground forces the enemy is assembling to launch, I predict the development within a reasonable period of time of a situation similar to those which produced the disasters that have successively overwhelmed our forces in the Pacific since the beginning of the war.[22]

Marshall was, however, unmoved, replying that MacArthur and Ghormley of the South Pacific Area would have to co-operate to meet these exaggerated dangers.[23] In essence, MacArthur would just have to get along with what he had, although the Joint Chiefs did order the return of Admiral Crutchley's Task Force 44 of three cruisers and four destroyers from the South Pacific to the South-West Pacific Area. Meanwhile Chamberlin ordered Captain Carson USN, the operations officer of Allied Naval Headquarters, to get merchant ships into Milne Bay as early as practicable.[24]

There was, however, another reason for MacArthur's message to Washington. It was the first step in shifting any blame for a disaster in the South-West Pacific Area to either the 'inefficient' Australians or the 'short-sighted' Joint Chiefs of Staff. He had recently sacked his air commander and was about to replace his naval commander and, perhaps convinced that the Joint Chiefs were conspiring against him,[25] he saw his own position as being decidedly precarious.

The root of the trouble was that MacArthur's strategy was at fault. He had based his defence of Port Moresby on the belief that a garrison at Milne Bay and a picket on the crest of the impenetrable Owen Stanley's, in addition to air and naval forces, would be sufficient, while he prepared for his spectacular forward bounds. There is no denying MacArthur's offensive spirit. This was why he had sent the bulk of his engineers to New Guinea to prepare airfields, but now this strategy was looking dangerously unrealistic. The Japanese had decimated the U.S. Navy in the Solomons and were challenging the security of Milne Bay and the Range.

There could be only one of two reasons for these setbacks. Either MacArthur had to admit that his ideas were wrong or he would have to declare that the plans were right but that the troops and commanders were not capable of executing them. It seems that he opted for the second choice but then had to produce communiques to show that in many cases there was no serious fighting. To support this, Willoughby had then to produce intelligence estimates which underrated the enemy. A third excuse, of course, was that the Chiefs of Staff were denying him air and naval resources.

In Port Moresby, the pressure on Rowell was now becoming intense. On 29 August he signalled Brisbane: 'Allen has now had good chance to see 14 Infantry Brigade and is by no means impressed with their efficiency and general standard of training'.[26] Around Isurava the Japanese were gaining ascendancy, and the 53rd Battalion was becoming badly disorganised. The poor performance of this battalion meant that neither Rowell nor Potts could have confidence in the remaining militia units at Port Moresby. Rowell therefore pressed for reinforcements of both artillery and the 25th Brigade.[27]

At 10.30 that night Captain D. C. L. Wilson, the Liaison Officer from Landops, arrived in Moresby with Vasey's letter of the 28th. Rowell was bitterly hurt, for he had just received his own Liaison Officer from Milne Bay who had told him that 'it was the nearest approach to the Somme he had seen'.[28] Rowell knew that this was an overstatement and replied immediately to Blamey in formal terms:

You will realise communications very bad and cipher personnel working to limit. Taking up to 7 hours to get messages through to and from Milne Bay depending on length. Only advice from Clowes timed 1000 this morning.[29]

The next morning Rowell gave vent to his feelings in an explicit letter to Vasey:

Let me say at once that I appreciate your position as regards pressure from above for information but I have been giving you all I have got from Cyril. This problem is an old one . . .
From Cyril's point of view, it is, I suggest, necessary to bear in mind how this HQ has been organised. It was made up of pieces from here and there and, however good they may be individually, it would be idle to expect them to be able to work as a team. I'm not making any special pleading, but the bulk of the people could no more than have landed when the attack came.
It is perilously easy to criticise a commander for his actions at a distance of 250 miles (Milne Bay to Moresby). To my regret I have not been to Milne Bay. There was too much to preoccupy me here with the situation to the north

and all the business that goes with taking over a HQ's . . . I ordered Cyril, late on 28 August to put everything in but I sincerely doubt whether in the conditions, anything but a small force can be deployed.
I'm sorry that GHQ take a poor view of Australians. In some cases this is all too true but I wish Chamberlin and Co could visit the jungle to see what conditions are instead of sitting back and criticising.[30]

He went on to explain that the fighting around Isurava was becoming difficult and that the 53rd Battalion was 'N.B.G.'. Rowell then added a note in his own handwriting:

I'm personally very bitter over the criticism from a distance and I think it damned unfair to pillory any commander without any knowledge of the conditions. It has rained for ten days at Milne Bay and it keeps on raining.
I suppose there will be heresy hunts and bowler hats soon. I hate to think what would have happened with our Allies in charge up here.[31]

Soon after, Rowell received Vasey's apologetic letter of late on the 28th and he wrote a further note:

I realise the position down there and I know how you are faced. I do hope that there is a showdown [between Blamey and MacArthur]. Taking it by and large, we do know something about war after three small campaigns; it is idle to assume that we can clean up damned good troops (as the Japs are) in five minutes.
Sorry I was a bit abrupt but I've got three wars on my hands now. (I was going to say four, but that would be uncharitable).[32]
Cyril's action, George, let me say at once that what he did has my complete endorsement.[33]

These letters throw into relief the complexity of the pressures affecting the commanders. Blamey and MacArthur were subject to more diverse influences than Rowell in New Guinea. Difficult though Rowell's situation was, he had to satisfy only one master — Blamey. So long as the correct chain of command was maintained, he should have been shielded from the direct influence of politicians, public opinion, arguments over Allied co-operation and the fears and exhortations of MacArthur.

On the other hand, both Blamey and MacArthur had to deal with such problems. MacArthur was responsible to Marshall as representative of the Joint Chiefs of Staff for the execution of Allied strategy, to Roosevelt for the safety of American troops, and to Curtin for the safety of Australian troops and for the security of Australia. Blamey had similar responsibilities: to Curtin and the Australian people for the safety of Australian troops, to Forde for the sound administration of the army, and to MacArthur for the execution of his tactical plan.

General Sir John Wilton, a former Chairman of the Chiefs of Staff Committee, has testified to the immense strain imposed on army commanders at the political-military interface.[34] It is not the intention of this work to examine this problem, but it should be noted that there is another less obvious interface — that between the generals who have to balance political and military decisions, and those who merely have to follow military instructions and whose problems are those of execution. Rowell and his subordinates in New Guinea fell into the latter category. It was important that Rowell recognise the different pressures borne by Blamey. His failure to do so may have been a result of Blamey's unwillingness to explain his difficulties to Rowell. This delicate task was left to Vasey, who could explain his own problems, but not those of Blamey. Rowell was undoubtedly well-equipped to understand Blamey's difficulties for he had been Blamey's Chief of Staff. Yet at no time did Blamey take his main operational commander into his confidence. The result was that Rowell felt that he was fighting 'four wars'. In the long run it had grave consequences for Rowell and Blamey.

The night of 30-31 August saw the fiercest action of the Milne Bay battle as the Japanese sought to cross one of the airstrips in the jungle. Next morning, troops of the 18th Brigade began to advance. It was now obvious that the Japanese at Milne Bay had been defeated, and MacArthur issued a triumphant statement, adding that the 'operation represented another ruse in the enemy's plan to capture Port Moresby. This citadel is guarded by the natural defence line of the Owen Stanley Range'.[35] Blamey, who had recently returned from Melbourne, wrote to Rowell congratulating him on the operation, although he was less than complimentary in his comments on the tactics. He wrote that 'it appeared to us here as though, by not acting with great speed, Clowes is liable to have missed the opportunity of dealing completely with the enemy and thus laying himself open to destruction . . . '.[36] At the same time Vasey summed up the feeling in Brisbane: 'GHQ is like a bloody barometer in a cyclone — up and down every two minutes. When C-in-C [Blamey] returned from there yesterday, he said one would have thought they had just won the battle of Waterloo'.[37]

And the fighting at Milne Bay was not yet over. On the evening of 1 September, while Wootten was preparing to land a battalion along the coast, MacArthur sent Clowes an urgent message through U.S. Air Force channels that the Japanese were expected to attack from the rear and would be supported by destroyers: 'Take immediate precautions'.[38] The effect at Milne Bay was consternation, and Brigadier Chilton can remember running out from his headquarters to stop the troops of the battalion.[39] Such actions could not but reinforce a circumspect approach at Milne Bay, and the operation was delayed.[40]

On the following days the 18th Brigade advanced but Clowes was continually hampered by messages from GHQ advising him that the Japanese were either going to be reinforced, or would withdraw. Each night Japanese ships entered the bay and shelled his positions. Despite these setbacks, by 8 September Clowes's troops were mopping up the remnants of the Japanese troops, the main body of which had already been taken out by their ships.

On 3 September Rowell replied to Blamey's letter of 1 September. He had just returned from a hair-raising visit to Milne Bay (2 September) during which his aircraft had spent three hours flying at heights of from 500 to 1,500 feet in an effort to find a break in the tropical clouds.[41]

You will probably have seen my letter to Vasey on the matter of Clowes' handling of the show, and after visiting Milne Bay myself, I'm sure that he was right. Inability to move except at a crawl, together with the constant threat of further landings, made it difficult for him to go fast or far.[42]

Not only was the success at Milne Bay soured by Blamey's letter, but also by an argument known as the 'communique incident'. At the height of the fighting the troops at Milne Bay heard an ABC announcement that they were in a serious position.[43] This was despite the fact that MacArthur's communique of 31 August had said that 'Australian combat troops, ably commanded by Major-General Clowes, and brilliantly supported by American and Australian air units', had 'thrown the enemy back into the narrow confines of the peninsula north of the bay'.[44] Clowes, therefore, had to issue a special bulletin to his troops to explain the position.[45] On 30 August Clowes signalled Rowell:

Desire register protest against ABC Australian broadcast tonight to effect that situation here has deteriorated and might now be regarded as grave. No repeat No ground for such statement which is considered detrimental to our operation and subversive to morale of troops and public.[46]

Rowell complained bitterly to Vasey:

Grossly misleading statements regarding land operations in NG generally and

Milne Bay in particular broadcast Cooktown [last] night and this morning by ABC and BBC. Statement obviously guess from wild imagination by individual without any knowledge natural condition NG and difficulties involved in operations. . . .[47]

Nevertheless, the controversy over the communiques continued. On 6 September Rowell signalled Landops:

ABC news broadcast presumably with approval central censorship continue give completely misleading impression NG operations . . .
Forces here hearing broadcasts feel Australian public being hoodwinked on local situation and tend disbelieve all repeat all official announcements this and other sectors. This eventually have most damaging effect on morale . . . .[48]

Vasey, who had returned from Melbourne on the night of the 4th, replied that part of the fault was that the communiques were up to 48 hours behind actual events, and he added that Lieutenant-Colonel F. J. Howard, the Australian press relations liaison officer at GHQ, had told him that MacArthur would not admit that there were any serious operations in New Guinea. 'As you probably know, all press articles must bear out the tone of the official communiques'.[49] Vasey also pointed out that the trouble was that MacArthur was writing the press releases.[50]

Later in the month William Dunstan, the General Manager of the Melbourne *Herald*, wrote to Rowell and explained that one of his correspondents had returned from New Guinea and had said to Colonel Diller, MacArthur's Chief Public Relations Officer: 'The fact is it is useless our writing anything unless it conforms to the communique though the communique be false'. Diller had agreed. Dunstan continued:

Correspondents in Brisbane hold the strong feeling that communiques deliberately falsify the position. The change from acute pessimism in reports of Milne Bay to riotous optimism bear this point . . . It all boils down to the fact that MacArthur has ruled that all reports are subject to his communiques . . . If it's any satisfaction to you to know it, the correspondents [in New Guinea] are behind you to a man. And they say the troops are too. But their reports, passed by your Field Censor, are held up for a week or more in Townsville or Brisbane — mainly Brisbane, *because they do not agree with the communiques*. Lots of our despatches are branded: 'To await release with appropriate communique'. And so the whole business of deception goes on. It's a good job the public have got reasonably reliable reports from Russia to keep them buoyed up. Stalingrad is big in the news, and that, in effect, has divided interest which otherwise might wholly be centred in New Guinea.[51]

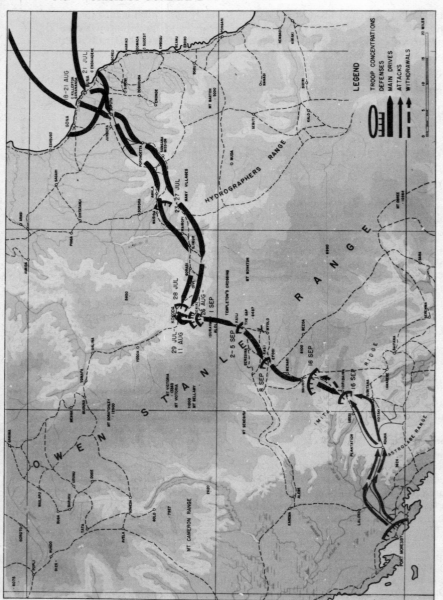

Map 5   The Japanese thrust towards Port Moresby. From *Reports of General MacArthur*, Vol.1, p.64

The communique incident had little effect on the conduct of operations in New Guinea, but it illustrates the disquieting effect that inaccurate news can have on both commanders and troops, adding unnecessarily to their burden. Furthermore it reveals the autocratic way that MacArthur controlled the release of information, much of which was designed to reinforce his position.[52]

Although Rowell could now breathe more freely over Milne Bay, Kokoda was causing real concern. By 1 September it was clear that Potts had been 'pushed out of Isurava' and Rowell signalled Blamey: 'After the experience of 53 Battalion I can have No repeat No confidence that any AMF units will stand'.[53] The only infantry units available to Rowell for operations were four militia battalions. He had already expressed his lack of confidence in these units on 29 August and again requested that the 25th Brigade, which GHQ had planned to send to Milne Bay, be diverted to Moresby. Rowell wrote later that he was convinced that 'had the troops in Moresby on my assumption of command been well trained — or had 25 Infantry Brigade been available earlier, there is no doubt that the enemy could have been prevented from penetrating the Owen Stanley Range'.[54]

Until this time Rowell had not been sure whether the Japanese in the mountains had intended to advance on Moresby but intelligence received from documents captured in the Solomons,[55] and the actions at Isurava, now convinced him that Moresby was the target.[56] In a letter to Vasey he pressed again for more troops to replace the AMF 'in whom I have no confidence and neither has Tubby who, after all, is fighting the battle'. Obviously concerned that GHQ would think that he was panicking he wrote: 'I do want to assure you once and for all that there is not the slightest thought of flap or panic over this business. Neither Tubby nor I have ever run away from a tight position and we are not starting now'.[57] Rowell was finding Allen more co-operative[58] than he had expected and on 30 August he had written, 'Thank God I've got a grand lot of blokes around me who will stick to me to the last and that, believe it or not, goes for Tubby, who has been a grand colleague'.[59] Rourke agreed with Rowell and wrote to Vasey: 'We have had some shocks but things seem to be in hand and all here are enjoying themselves. The closer one gets to the war the less "worse" it seems'.[60]

It should not be forgotten that Rowell was also responsible for operations in the Lae-Salamaua area. When he had assumed command in New Guinea, Kanga Force, under Lieutenant-Colonel N. L. Fleay, consisted of the 2/5th Australian Independent Company and elements of the New Guinea Volunteer Rifles. The 2/6th Independent Company was waiting in Moresby for air transport to Wau.

Rowell attempted to increase the air supply to Kanga Force with the aim of moving the 2/6th Independent Company once supplies had been built up. He did, however, have more pressing problems. On 27 August he wrote to Vasey that 'Fleay is screaming for No. 6 Independent Coy, but I can't get it to him. It will be too bad if the Jap sends a few hundred men to Wau or Bulolo but I can't help it. If we are to send men along every track GHQ gets a scare about, we'll want ten divisions here'.[61]

On 30 August, in conjunction with the attacks at Isurava and Milne Bay, the enemy began to advance towards Mubo. Fleay over-reacted to the threat. He realised that if the Japanese reached Wau he would be unable to hold it, and therefore carried out demolitions and withdrew. The Japanese advanced no further than Mubo, but these worries imposed strain on Rowell's HQ at a time of great activity elsewhere.[62]

Whilst Clowes was clearing the north shore of Milne Bay and Fleay was withdrawing from Wau, the situation on the Kokoda Trail was becoming increasingly difficult. By 5 September Potts had withdrawn through the Gap to Myola and on 7 September had grouped his force south of Efogi. He now had the 2/27th Battalion and Allen began to send forward the 3rd Battalion, a militia unit from the 14th Brigade.

The loss of the Gap was the first indication to GHQ that they might have been wrong about the advance on Moresby. Willoughby still discounted the possibility of an advance in strength beause of supply difficulties, but he now thought that raiding parties might reach the airfields around Moresby. With masterly hindsight he commented that 'an overland threat to Port Moresby, with the Buna landing as a preliminary, was forecast on May 23rd'.[63] On 3 September Hopkins, who was standing in for Vasey, wrote to Rowell that 'we have never for a moment considered that there was any flap or panic on your side. There may have been a little temperature at GHQ, but we've been trying to calm them. C-in-C [Blamey] does not consider your position particularly tight'.[64] Nevertheless he was willing to send Rowell both the 16th and 17th Brigade if he were to find them necessary.[65]

Hopkins was right in his judgment of the temperature at GHQ during this period, for MacArthur, after his earlier appeals, had not been impressed with Marshall's efforts to help. This was not completely fair to Marshall, for he had informed the President of MacArthur's appeals, and had put them before the Joint Chiefs of Staff. An additional infantry division had been sent to the Pacific, the South-West Pacific Area naval forces had been ordered to return from Ghormley's command, and Arnold was searching for more planes.

It was only after all this had been done that Marshall had reminded MacArthur that the defence of the Pacific area still depended mainly on his careful co-ordination with Ghormley. On 3 September MacArthur told Ghormley that he was willing to assist 'even to the jeopardy of my own safety', but saw no sense in transferring reinforcements at the time when both areas were under attack.[66]

Despite the deteriorating situation MacArthur was still not yet convinced that the Japanese would reach Port Moresby, although he recognised their advance as a threat that had to be removed. MacArthur was still confident of receiving amphibious forces, and on 4 September instructed Major-General R. L. Eichelberger, the commander of the newly-formed I U.S. Corps, to be prepared to carry out amphibious operations along the north-east coast of Papua.[67] That same day, however, Sutherland and Kenney, who were meeting Nimitz in Noumea, were informed that the navy could not spare ships, aircraft or amphibious forces. Nevertheless, the following day the I Corps, consisting of the 32nd and 41st U.S. Divisions, was assigned to the Allied Land Forces.[68] Finally, with the utilisation of these forces in mind, MacArthur sent a strongly-worded message to Marshall:

It is imperative that shipping and naval forces for escort duty be increased to ensure communications between Australian Mainland and south coast of New Guinea. With these additional naval facilities I can despatch large ground reinforcements to New Guinea with the objective of counter infiltration towards the north at the same time making creeping advances along the north coast with small vessels and marine amphibious forces. Such action will secure a situation which otherwise is doubtful. If New Guinea goes the result will be disastrous. This is urgent.[69]

If MacArthur's recognition of the threat to New Guinea was belated, at least his determination to continue with his offensive plans was admirable.

At the same time MacArthur saw another opportunity to ensure that in the event of disaster the Australians would be blamed, saying that

the Australians have proven themselves unable to match the enemy in jungle fighting. Aggressive leadership is lacking. The enemy's defeat at Milne Bay must not be accepted as a measure of relative fighting capacity of the troops involved. The decisive factor was the complete surprise obtained over him by our preliminary concentration of superior forces.[70]

By now, unknown to Landops, he had despatched his Chief of Staff, Sutherland, to Milne Bay and Port Moresby to give a personal report. The Joint Chiefs in Washington had been more impressed with his plans than MacArthur had imagined, for perhaps they realised that a landing near Buna would take the pressure off Guadalcanal. Therefore on 8 September Admiral King ordered Nimitz to release one Marine Regiment to MacArthur.[71]

It is true that the ill-trained militia of the 39th Battalion had been unprepared for jungle warfare, but aggressive leadership was not lacking.[72] Even the experienced 21st Brigade had been unprepared for jungle warfare, but their failure to hold the Japanese was a result of a lack of supplies and support, not a lack in leadership or fighting capacity. It was churlish of MacArthur to denigrate from the safety of Brisbane the fighting ability of the Australians at Milne Bay, where they inflicted the first defeat on the Japanese land forces in the war. Unfortunately there was a grain of truth in MacArthur's assertions, for in all battles it is inevitable that some troops will fail, but generally speaking, the Australians fought well. Considering the poor training of many units, the inexperience of the officers, the uncertain supply system and the lack of familiarity with the jungle, it is remarkable that so few did fail.[73]

With his exaggerated statements to Washington coupled with his optimistic press communiques, MacArthur had backed himself into a corner. There were two miscalculations which he might have admitted to himself. The first was that the Australians would not fight, and the second was that Washington would not give him the naval forces required for his offensive; but he still refused to admit that his strategy had been faulty. Now, with the loss of the Gap and the continued withdrawal of Potts's force, he became seriously worried, and in the late afternoon of 7 September he sent Brigadier-General Chamberlin to see Vasey, Blamey again being absent inspecting troops.[74] Expressing MacArthur's views, Chamberlin said that the Australians were in superior numbers and that the leadership was not sufficient to check the Japanese. He indicated that an American commander, if he allowed such precipitate retirement, would be instantly relieved and replaced by someone who would get results.[75] Vasey therefore signalled Rowell:

In absence of C-in-C I convey to you General MacArthur's grave fear that present situation may develop into one in which we shall be denied use of Moresby airfields . . . He feels that present withdrawal is wrong policy and I know it is against your instructions. He urges greater offensive action against Japs whose difficulties now considerable.

Vasey was aware of his delicate position, and added, 'I appreciate your problems but urge you take positive action and keep us posted'.[76]

That same day Vasey held a conference with the senior staff officers of Advanced LHQ. He stated that 'the situation at Kokoda was very difficult and involved possible grave complications'.[77] While Blamey had promised Rowell that he could have the 16th and 17th Brigades if necessary, he was not convinced that Rowell would need them, nor was he sure that the force that Rowell would then have in New Guinea could be adequately supplied. Vasey was not so confident and decided to play safe. He therefore wrote to Major-General A. J. Boase, the commander of the 6th Division, warning him that Blamey had told Rowell that he could have the two brigades when he required them: 'This is merely a warning but I feel sure that, when the move does take place, it will be done in a hurry and the more you and your other Commanders [sic] have considered the problem the easier it will be for you'.[78] The next morning Rowell asked for the 16th Brigade, and Vasey forewarned it for movement whilst he contacted Blamey.[79]

Vasey was unhappy about his signal to Rowell of the night before, and by way of explanation wrote to Rowell that it 'was occasioned by a visit from Chamberlin who was sent down to me, in the C-in-C's absence, by General MacArthur'. Vasey went on to point out the difficulty of finding ships for the reinforcements, but also pointed out that the reinforcements to the Middle East had priority. 'The whole situation [was] eminently unsatisfactory and I shall now speak to John Northcott to see what can be done'.[80]

During the afternoon Vasey received an unnerving signal from Rowell:

Potts is at this hour in serious trouble between Efogi and Menari, as a result of enemy penetration. Porter is being sent forward . . . to relieve Potts and take charge of all elements in the forward area. I trust you appreciate [the] gravity of immediate situation, and will produce additional troops asked for particularly infantry, with minimum delay.[81]

The decision to relieve Potts was motivated partly by a desire to obtain a first-hand account of the conditions in the mountains but also, Rowell was angry with what he saw as Potts's mishandling of his brigade. Without consulting Potts's immediate superior, General Allen, he decided to relieve him. At a conference at midday on the 8th, Allen raised no objection as he felt that, judging from the signals from Potts, the latter 'was either tired or was losing a grip of the situation'. Allen did, however, keep an open mind on the matter of whether Potts had shown lack of judgment or had been outfought, and he persuaded Rowell to hear Potts's story.[82] Later Rowell reinstated Potts, a brave, inspiring, if limited commander,[83] to the 21st Brigade. As commander on the Kokoda Trail he had not failed and had never lost heart.[84] He retained the confidence of his men throughout.

The recall of Potts underlines a serious fault in command, for neither Allen nor Rowell had been able to inspect personally the conditions in the mountains. No man could have done more than Rowell in the busy fortnight between the time he took over and the Japanese attacks. He was desperately short of transport aircraft, he lacked a good part of his signal equipment, the supply situation in the mountains was serious, and the threat of a Japanese seaborne landing was real. Under these circumstances he had little time to spare to inspect his forward troops. Furthermore, to inspect Potts's brigade, forward near Isurava, would have meant an exhausting week's journey by foot. During this time the Japanese could attack either at Milne Bay, Isurava, around Wau or by sea against Moresby. Rowell's only communications would be by a doubtful radio or by telephone via the uncertain wire that wound its way precariously along the sides of mountains and across turbulent streams.

Allen, who was concerned at the poor state of training of the militia with which he had to defend Moresby, found it equally difficult to spare the six or seven days needed to visit Potts when he was at Isurava. Later Allen wrote that

either the G1 [Colonel C. C. F. Spry] or myself would have gone forward before if I had not the added responsibility of the defence of Moresby area from a sea attack. The first I [Intelligence] report received was an even greater menace (if possible) than the attack over the mountains . . . When given the dual roles I expressed doubts to [Rowell] but at the time there appeared no alternative.[85]

In fact Spry had volunteered to go forward to give moral support to Potts and to report to Allen. Allen doubted the value of this move and referred it to Rowell, who supported his division commander.[86]

It should be remembered that during this period, corps and division commanders did not have the assistance of a chief of staff. The additional burden of co-ordinating the work of the operational and administrative staffs fell to the BGS or GSO1, and he was not always well placed to act as a deputy commander. Nor did Allen yet have the services of an artillery commander who could relieve him of some of the load. Rowell had only Allen, whose own responsibilities were heavy, and Morris, to whom he could delegate authority in an emergency. Morris had already been replaced by Rowell who, for some days, had contemplated returning him to Australia, before giving him command of ANGAU. He was not a man Rowell could regard as a deputy.

Before the battle of Milne Bay, Rowell had been unable to visit the area, which, because of the wretched weather was at that time an uncertain prospect. He was confident that Clowes would have things under control, but during the battle he had felt keenly this lack of knowledge of the area, especially since Vasey and Hopkins had visited there just before the Japanese attack.

Rowell was now faced with his most critical and trying test. On 8 September the Japanese had attacked and isolated the headquarters of the 21st Brigade, which was fighting desperately to regroup south of Efogi, about forty-five miles from Moresby. The 25th Brigade had not yet arrived and the 21st Brigade now had a strength of less than half a battalion. That evening Rowell wrote to Vasey, 'Today has been my blackest since we came, and none of the 28 days I've spent here has been free from worry'.[87] Yet, depressed though he may have been, he wrote later, 'at no time did I consider that the capture of Moresby by the enemy from the north was possible'.[88]

From his tented headquarters just off the road to Seven Mile Aerodrome, Rowell was finding the task increasingly difficult. When he had been Chief of Staff to Blamey in the Middle East, he had carefully worked out the relationship between the commander and his staff.[89] Now in New Guinea, with his tremendous resolve to do the right thing, he determined to stick rigidly to his carefully defined system. However, Brigadier Rourke was simply not capable of handling the BGS side of the arrangement, and Rowell soon found himself doing much of the BGS's work, as well as his own. Lacking complete ruthlessness and determined to give every man his chance,[90] Rowell hesitated to sack Rourke, who was taking things very seriously but was not well and had become dangerously pessimistic.[91] This lack of confidence in his BGS, coupled with the fact that the often hysterical messages from GHQ implied criticism of his performance, meant that Rowell was loath to leave his headquarters for any appreciable period. General Willoughby described Rowell's headquarters:

Scattered tentage, some attempts at camouflage; on the whole an efficient mobile campaign headquarters . . . Rowell is of dignified but amiable personality. The staff regards him with respect and affection; that feeling prevails through other command echelons. . . . There is hesitancy to change personnel in all units; there is evidently a considerable camaraderie, that has developed in the Middle East.[92]

Despite the tremendous strain, Rowell still managed to remain calm and plan for victory. His chief medical officer, Brigadier W. W. S. Johnston, wrote that he was 'amazed at his equanimity and unruffled demeanor in conditions which imposed terrific strain'.[93] Realising that Allen would have his hands full in the mountains, Rowell asked Landops for another senior officer to look after the seaward defence of Moresby. He was still convinced that his decisions had been correct and on the evening of 8 September wrote: 'I'm confident the enemy has no hope of getting Moresby from the north. His difficulties will now start and I trust we can get him on the rebound. The AAF [U.S. Army Air Force], gets into a tremendous panic and it's on their account I'm worried. They'll probably pack up and clear out'.[94]

Indeed Rowell believed that the Air Force fighters were not having the effect on the Japanese lines of communications that he would have liked.[95] He would have preferred to have had bombers at Port Moresby but despite the fact that there had been only two air raids since early August, Kenney was unwilling to risk them. Furthermore, he felt that long-range bombing attacks on Japanese airfields were of more value. The operations at Guadalcanal were having a definite effect on Japanese operations in New Guinea, for until 7 August, the major Japanese air effort had been directed towards New Guinea. After that date the main effort was in the Solomons.[96]

Lieutenant-Colonel R. R. Vial, Rowell's chief intelligence officer, identified his commander's three main preoccupations at this time in this order — the problems with Landops, keeping the Americans on side and lastly, the trouble with the Japanese. Rowell knew that he could hold the Japanese provided he controlled the air, and hence the sea, around Port Moresby. He had good relations with the U.S. Air Force commander in Moresby, Brigadier-General Whitehead, but he had to reassure him constantly to prevent him moving his planes to Australia.

On the morning of 9 September, as Potts regrouped his brigade at Menari (35 miles by air from Moresby) before handing over to Porter, Rowell freed Allen of responsibility for the sea approaches and took over the added burden himself. That same morning the troops of the 25th Brigade arrived and the 16th Brigade was ordered to New Guinea.

Now that he was no longer responsible for the seaward approaches to Port Moresby, Allen could move his headquarters forward to a position from where he could speak by telephone to his brigadier in the mountains. During this period Potts arrived in an agitated state. Spry calmed him down before he reported to Allen, who later wrote that he

had had, and looked as if he had had a very gruelling time, but he was bright and vigorous. As far as I could judge, he had saved Moresby from invasion by [the] Kokoda route by forces superior in numbers to his own and had prevented the catastrophe nearly brought about by the neglect of New Guinea by the authorities before the AIF came. He was, I think, just in time.[97]

Brigadier John Rogers, Blamey's Director of Military Intelligence, was in Moresby at this time and saw some of the troops coming back from the fighting. Rogers and the Americans, who had heard tales of the Anzacs and their fine record in Syria, were dismayed at what they saw. 'Never in my life', said Rogers, 'in the worst part of Gallipoli, or anywhere, had I seen soldiers who looked so shocked and so tired and utterly weary as those men'.[98]

If Rowell was dismayed, he did not show it and, determined to transfer his confidence to the troops, he ordered that demolitions were to be removed from equipment and public utilities. Until that time the policy had been the total destruction of everything liable to fall into the hands of the enemy. Rowell, who had been given authority to order demolitions as he considered necessary, pointed out that this policy was totally unsuitable as it would presuppose an admission that the New Guinea Force would inevitably withdraw to the hills and, when the reserves of food were exhausted, would surrender. 'This is by no means the intention', he wrote. 'While it is not possible to guarantee that the enemy will not make an initial penetration, it is intended to drive him back by offensive action once the position has been stabilised'. The plan was for each locality to hold reserves of food and ammunition and if the Japanese attacked, the 'guns must be fought to the muzzle'.[99]

One problem worrying Rowell was that he now had a large number of troops in Port Moresby, but only a relatively small number were infantry. It did mean, however, that he had a good reserve for the close defence of Moresby. On 8 September he told Vasey that 'there is a hell of a lot of power here for purely defensive purposes such as AA stations. U.S. Engineer Units and the like . . . Provided they continue to fight on their hills they provide most valuable centres of resistance from which to counter attack'.[1]

On the surface the situation looked even worse than a few days before, for by the evening of 10/11 September Porter and his scratch force were back at Ioribaiwa Ridge. However, the enemy force, now reduced by disease, had become exhausted by their hard fighting against the 21st Brigade. They lacked food and ammunition, for Kenney's planes raided daily their precarious supply route, and Porter was able to hold them until, on 14 September, Brigadier K. W. Eather arrived with the 25th Brigade. At last, imperceptibly at first, the initiative was returning to the Australians.

It is difficult to know what was going through MacArthur's mind at this time. Willoughby's assessment was full of ambiguity, for he reported that the situation was serious: 'The energetic intervention of fresh troops appears as the only immediate remedy'. He continued, however, that with increasing supply difficulties and continuous strafing attacks, the enemy advance would be slow. He concluded that the Australian reinforcements en route would hold the enemy.[2]

Correspondence from MacArthur to Blamey indicates that with Rowell calmly moving the 25th Brigade forward and Landops dispatching the 16th Brigade with all haste, the C-in-C now believed the Japanese advance could be stopped.[3] He therefore planned to hasten their withdrawal by moving an American regiment, whose training he appeared to greatly overestimate, in a bold flanking movement through the jungle to the east of the Japanese.[4] He left the choice of the unit to General Eichelberger, who decided that the 126th Regiment from the 32nd Division would be the first American combat unit to go to New Guinea.

As a professional soldier, MacArthur must have been aware of the relative merits of the fighting troops of each nation. Indeed, his staff were aware that the U.S. Corps was not yet ready for operations in New Guinea. On 8 September MacArthur's Adjutant-General, Colonel B. M. Fitch, wrote to General Eichelberger that the Corps would not be ready for amphibious jungle warfare until the beginning of 1943. 'Our present equipment is unsatisfactory for the initial offensive mission of amphibious warfare in the New Guinea area'.[5] There is, therefore, probably some validity in Kenney's claim that the American troops were sent along the Jaure trail as a psychological move to spur on the Australians.[6] Despite this, at a press conference in mid November 1942, Blamey said that after his first visit to New Guinea he discussed the matter with MacArthur and Curtin 'and we decided to make this a real go and planned to bring up the 32nd U.S. Division'.[7] Perhaps with the recent news that he could expect a Marine Regiment, MacArthur was again determined to continue with his plans, as detailed a month previously in his orders to New Guinea Force, to recapture Papua. If it was to be 'a real go' then that impression was not conveyed to HQ New Guinea Force, where Rowell saw it as another ad hoc manoeuvre.

On 10 September Sutherland, who had returned from his visit to New Guinea, reported to MacArthur.[8] He had flown over the Gap and Rowell felt that he now had the confidence of GHQ.[9] This is not at all certain, for the next day Curtin gave a confidential press conference and, after revealing that Sutherland had recently returned from New Guinea, declared that there was 'now official worry about the position there'. Curtin said that MacArthur had told him that the Allied forces had been out-generalled and out-manoeuvred. He continued, however, that the Allies had started a movement which they were confident would out-flank the enemy and that 'the Japanese, even if they are successful in the present movement, cannot attack Moresby successfully for a long time because of the difficulty of moving the large forces that would be necessary along the narrow mountain roads'.[10]

It appears from this that, while MacArthur had made Curtin aware of the seriousness of the situation, he had retained his confidence in the outcome and was willing to continue with his plan. By 11 September the details had been worked out and he wrote to Blamey that he envisaged a trek across the mountains to 'liquidate' the Japanese on the other side of the range.[11] This advance was to follow a route that MacArthur had taken completely from the map, and the orders detailed the route exactly, it was a route that was soon proved by Rowell to be completely impracticable.

Despite the cautious confidence at GHQ, panic was beginning to set in in other quarters in Australia. The rising tide of public opinion, mostly uninformed, chilled the hearts of the members of the War Cabinet who sat on the Advisory War Council. On the morning of 9 September, with Porter re-establishing the position at Menari, the 25th Brigade arriving at Moresby and the 16th Brigade preparing to leave for New Guinea, the Advisory War Council met in Canberra to discuss the operations. The three Chiefs of Staff were present. Reference was made to the military advice that the Japanese occupation of Buna and Gona posed no threat to Port Moresby as the Owen Stanley Range provided a natural defence line, but it was pointed out that the appreciation of the position had been proved wrong by the Japanese penetration of the Range. The question of the adequacy of the military leadership in New Guinea was raised and General Northcott explained that, with Rowell and the 7th Division now in New Guinea, the situation had been rectified.[12]

R. G. Menzies stressed at the meeting that either MacArthur or Blamey should visit New Guinea and the Prime Minister informed the meeting that the Minister for Army, Frank Forde, had already felt compelled to urge Blamey to journey to New Guinea to confer with Rowell and to report to the Council. Curtin said that this did not infer that there was any criticism of the commander in the area.[13] When Forde transmitted this decision to Blamey, he discovered that the latter had already resolved on this course.[14]

On 12 September, Blamey and the American Brigadier-General Hanaford MacNider, arrived in Port Moresby, the latter to arrange for the reception of U.S. troops. Rowell indicated to the American that he had little faith in the value of his task, but since he was acting under GHQ orders, there was little that the New Guinea Force Commander could do. He did, however, point out to MacNider that he could not divert any facilities from his main task, the defeat of the Japanese on the Kokoda Trail.

On the following day, Blamey and Rowell visited the headquarters of the 7th Division and, in the words of General Allen, 'all seemed pleased with the situation as proposed'.[15] One of the subjects discussed was, with the exception of the 39th Battalion, the poor performance of the militia. It was agreed that after their fine performance, the 39th Battalion should not be disbanded but that it would be best to disband the 53rd Battalion.[16] Apparently relations between Blamey and Rowell were amicable, for the next day Rowell wrote to Clowes that he had 'had a pleasant day with the little man [Blamey]'.[17]

Blamey's first trip to New Guinea had been long overdue, but although it enabled him to gain an understanding of the situation at Port Moresby, it gave him no real opportunity to learn about jungle warfare. On 13 September he gave a press conference. George Johnston reported that Blamey said 'that Moresby is in no danger and I think we shall find that the Japs will be beaten by their own advance with its attendant problems of supply. It will be a Japanese advance to disaster, an Australian retreat to victory'.[18]

Chester Wilmot astutely realised that Blamey lacked knowledge of jungle warfare. During the press conference he asked Blamey whether he thought green uniforms were necessary. Wilmot wrote that Blamey:

said they were not; that khaki had been designed in India as the ideal camouflage for the jungle; and that he had no evidence that this jungle was different from that in India. I offered to provide him with several thousand witnesses who had fought in the country and who thought otherwise. General Blamey returned to Australia and apparently told the War Council that green uniforms were unnecessary in New Guinea, even though, at that time all our troops were changing to them.[19]

It appears almost certain that Blamey did tell Curtin that green uniforms were unnecessary, for when asked by a reporter on 21 September about the criticism that the troops lacked training in jungle fighting, Curtin said that the painting of uniforms green was 'all balls'. He said that in dry patches khaki was far more effective, and after many tests it had been decided that khaki was most suitable.[20] Despite this, the 25th Brigade had gone into action on 14 September in green uniforms. It was an example of Blamey's and indeed the Australian Army's lack of knowledge of jungle warfare. There is a hint of truth in Allen's comment about Blamey and this incident: 'A simple example of apathy, ignorance and not the keenness to find out'.[21]

General George Kenney was also in Port Moresby at this time, but he spoke only to his air commanders.[22] Rowell was, of course, sensitive to the ever-present threat that the Japanese would infiltrate through the valleys to attack the airfields around Moresby. He therefore formed makeshift units to guard the approaches east and west of Ioribaiwa. The American air commanders, Whitehead, Walker and Smith, were worried about their airfields, but Rowell conferred with them almost daily, and decided that only one strip would be vacated. This one was isolated, required a battalion to defend it, and had never actually been used.

After his visit to Port Moresby, Kenney returned to Brisbane and reported to MacArthur that he believed that Moresby would be lost 'if something did not happen soon'. Despite the fact that he had not met Rowell, he 'believed that Rowell's attitude had become defeatist and that his attitude had permeated the whole Australian force in New Guinea'. Furthermore he stated, incorrectly, that Rowell was planning to give up the airfields.[23] Kenney was anxious to guard his airfields and asked MacArthur to send American troops to New Guinea to defend them, but MacArthur was reluctant to let his forces come under the direct command of the Australians in the field. He preferred the Americans to have a separate task from that of the Australians.[24]

By now MacArthur was in a difficult position. On one hand there were Kenney's bad tidings and requests, and also the news of heavy Japanese attacks on Guadalcanal. On the other hand Admiral Crutchley's squadron had returned to his command, and on 12 September he had received a signal from Marshall that Ghormley would be able to hand over to him the 8th Marine Regiment on about 1 October.[25]

MacArthur wanted desperately to continue the offensive that he had ordered over a month ago — if only to ensure that he was not outdone by Ghormley.

Finally, after 9.00 pm on 14 September, he called General Eichelberger to his hotel. Pacing the floor in his dressing gown, he outlined a plan to send one regiment over the Kokoda Trail, another over the Kapa Kapa Trail (which MacNider was investigating) and the remainder of the 32nd U.S. Division to Milne Bay, whence, reinforced by the 8th Marines, they would attack Buna and Gona. The latter group was to go by boat along the north shore by secret hops at night using luggers and landing boats. Eichelberger was to set up his command post at Abau or Milne Bay and was to be independent of the Australian High Command. MacArthur indicated that he had not yet discussed the plan with Sutherland, but that he would do so the next morning. Once again there could be no denying MacArthur's offensive spirit. He never lost sight of his desire to return to the Philippines.

Referring to the advance over the Kokoda Trail, Eichelberger asked, 'How about the Australians. Do you think they could do the job?' 'No', replied MacArthur, 'they won't fight'. Eichelberger assumed by this that he meant the Australian High Command.[26] This was grossly unfair to the Australian commanders. Perhaps MacArthur had taken notice of Kenney. Probably they were the words of a tired and exasperated man. Whatever the interpretation, MacArthur was, that night, indulging in fantasies. Air protection for such a coastal advance could not, at that stage, be provided, nor would the command arrangement have proved workable. The next morning he retreated before the opposition of Sutherland and his staff, and Sutherland told Eichelberger that the Buna plan was off.

By this time Blamey had decided to send Vasey and the headquarters of the 6th Division to Moresby. The selection of Vasey came as a severe disappointment to Major-General Boase, whom a contemporary described as a 'died in the wool, "red book", regular soldier', and who had trained the division for jungle warfare in Ceylon. Gavin Long thought that Boase was a 'keen and capable regular officer . . . ' 'but he was too silent and, at times, old womanish for the comd in Ceylon'.[27] Boase said that 'when I returned to Australia I was confirmed in command of 6th Division. When 16 Bde was warned for duty in NG I suggested to George Vasey that I should go to NG. When I got to Brisbane on 11 September TAB saw me and asked Vasey why I was here. Vasey told him he had sent for me. TAB said that he didn't want me there'.[28]

Vasey said that Blamey declared that he wanted to send one of his best fighters to New Guinea and he doubted whether Boase was the man.[29] During his visit to Moresby on 12 September Blamey asked Rowell whom he would prefer, and he replied that he wanted Vasey. The appropriate arrangements were then made. The result was that Major-General Frank Berryman, the MGGS of the First Army, replaced Vasey as DCGS, and Boase replaced Berryman.[30]

Berryman has described this tense period at GHQ. As Eather and the 25th Brigade moved forward to take over from Porter, Berryman told Sutherland that he knew Eather to be a fine soldier who could be trusted to do the right thing. The first thing that Eather did was to withdraw from Ioribaiwa to Imita Ridge, about 25 air miles from Port Moresby, and this, after Berryman's confident statement, caused the Americans to have grave fears. General Kenney told Berryman that if the Japanese reached the Goldie River, just over the Imita Ridge, then he would pull all of his aircraft out of New Guinea. The confused events which culminated in Australia's most important command crisis of the war were now moving inexorably to their climax.

8
The Command Crisis, 16 September – 1 October 1942

For MacArthur, pacing the carpet in his office on the eighth floor of the AMP building in Brisbane, this latest withdrawal by the Australians was the last straw. He was strangely reluctant to go to New Guinea to weigh the differing reports from his two most senior commanders, Blamey and Kenney. Despite the fact that Blamey, after a two-day visit to Rowell, had said in a broadcast on the evening of 15 September that he was fully confident of the result,[1] and despite MacArthur's own confidence of a few days earlier, he was now inclined to believe the reports from Kenney.

Blamey's studied lack of concern, evidenced by his trips away from Brisbane, and his determination not to interfere in Rowell's battle whilst giving him all possible support, now worked to his disadvantage. Kenney, ebullient, confident in himself and in his Air Force, was in MacArthur's office every day, and again pressed his view that Moresby would soon fall. To MacArthur, mistrustful of Marshall and his staff in Washington, the fall of Moresby would herald more than another military disaster; it would mean the end of his career. Indeed, on 15 September Marshall ordered his Chief of the Air Corps, General Arnold, to visit the Pacific and report whether MacArthur's and Ghormley's claims were true.[2] Faced with these fears, there is little doubt that MacArthur actually convinced himself that Port Moresby was in danger. Certainly he was not willing to take the risk of doing nothing.

MacArthur had already laid the groundwork for shifting the blame onto the Australians and the Joint Chiefs of Staff. He believed that the one solution to the position he might find himself in if Moresby fell was to send Blamey to New Guinea, for not only did he expect Blamey to 'energise the situation',[3] but he could then claim that he had done all that he could possibly do to save New Guinea. Furthermore, MacArthur must have been aware that the move would deprive Blamey of his powers as Commander of the Allied Land Forces. It was the first step in a scheme to resolve a situation which from the beginning of his time in Australia he had found galling.

While MacArthur hesitated to act, Blamey, against a backdrop of implied criticism in the press,[4] on 17 September addressed the Advisory War Council. He reviewed the situation, pointing out that the Japanese were making a concerted attempt to capture New Guinea. The operation at Milne Bay had been a complete success for the Australians, but the troops on the Kokoda Trail had been forced back. This had been caused partly by the air raid of 17 August which had destroyed the transport aircraft.

Blamey explained that the 25th Brigade and the 2/1st Pioneer Battalion had arrived in the forward area and were attacking the Japanese. There is no evidence, however, that he mentioned to the War Council that he had received a signal from Rowell that the 25th Brigade had been forced to withdraw south of Ioribaiwa.[5] If he did not mention this, it was a serious mistake, and it may well have contributed to the Prime Minister's subsequent lack of confidence in his Australian Commander-in-Chief.

Blamey went on to affirm that in addition the 16th Brigade was at sea and a U.S. Regiment was preparing to leave Australia. He recognised that it was imperative to hold Port Moresby, but that the Allies now had approximately 30,000 troops in the area compared to the estimated 10,000 of the Japanese. Although the Japanese outnumbered the Australians in the forward area, they would be unable to bring sufficient troops and artillery over the Range to attack Port Moresby. Blamey said that he shared with Rowell and Allen their confidence that the Japanese would 'not be able to take Port Moresby from the land'.[6]

During a heated discussion W. M. Hughes and J. A. Beasley, the Minister for Supply and Development, spoke strongly against any tendency to gloss over mistakes made by the army commanders. Blamey assured them that this would not be done.[7] Curtin said that he did not wish Blamey to have the impression that the responsibility for the mistakes and miscalculations of past commanders were being placed on present commanders, nor was there criticism of MacArthur. Blamey again assured the Council 'that all that could be done was being done and the military leaders and men were confident of success'.[8]

The matter of responsibility was not adequately determined in the minutes of the meeting. Blamey claimed that the blame for any shortcoming should be placed 'more on Army Headquarters', than on Morris.[9] Blamey had been C-in-C of the AMF since late March, and since then Army Headquarters had, in effect, meant Blamey. During the six months after returning to Australia Blamey had had ample time to correct any mistakes that Sturdee may possibly have made. The inescapable conclusion is that responsibility lay somewhere between Blamey, MacArthur and the government. As the government was unlikely to blame itself, and because it had implicit faith in MacArthur, it was obvious to Blamey that he was held responsible. Undoubtedly his address did not allay anxiety for Port Moresby. Forde was one minister who still felt that Moresby might yet fall.

It must have come as a shock to Curtin when that night MacArthur spoke to him by secraphone. He told Curtin that he was worried about the situation in New Guinea where, despite superior numbers, the Australians were still withdrawing. MacArthur had finally become convinced that 'the retrogressive nature of the tactics of Australian Ground Forces defending Port Moresby seriously threatened [the] outlying airfields'.[10] He felt that if the Japanese advance continued, 'the Allies in New Guinea would be forced into such a defensive concentration as would duplicate the conditions of Malaya'.[11]

MacArthur pointed out that the Australians were confident of their ability to meet the situation but that he was so far from sharing that confidence that he proposed sending American troops to stem the attack. This was at variance with the reason that Blamey had given the Advisory War Council, that MacArthur was sending a U.S. Regiment to New Guinea so that they 'should obtain experience in operations and in the development of supply arrangements in this area'.[12]

The 126th U.S. Regiment, the unit that was earmarked to march over the Owen Stanley Range, was due to leave Brisbane the next morning. A company had already flown to New Guinea. Kenney had, however, talked MacArthur into flying the 128th U.S. Regiment to Port Moresby, so that there were two U.S. Regiments preparing to leave Australia, not one as Blamey had claimed. This later decision, taken after the collapse of MacArthur's plan to send Eichelberger's task force to the Milne Bay area, may have been a reaction by MacArthur to Kenney's fears for the airfields. Perhaps Blamey forgot to mention this move at the War Council meeting, but more likely he had not been told by MacArthur of this latest development. Kenney, in his book, indicates that the arrangements were made directly with Eichelberger. It is also an indication of the growing influence of Kenney who, in his own words, told MacArthur, 'give me the next regiment to go, the 128th, and I'll have them in Port Moresby ahead of this gang [126th] that goes by boat'.[13]

MacArthur told Curtin that he felt that Blamey should go to Moresby to take command personally. Not only did MacArthur consider this a military necessity for Blamey, 'he thought it was a personal necessity since, if the situation became really serious, it would be difficult for the Australian leader to meet his responsibility to the Australian public'.[14] This may have decided Curtin, for he later confessed to Vasey that, 'In my ignorance (of military matters), I thought that the Commander-in-Chief should be in New Guinea'.[15] Curtin therefore agreed with MacArthur, and promised to speak to Blamey.

This shock from MacArthur came on top of a message from the Australian representative at the Pacific War Council, Sir Owen Dixon, that President Roosevelt was worried by the news from the SWPA, and that Port Moresby was a point of particular concern.[16] The ministers were worried, and Beasley said in the hearing of other ministers, 'Moresby is going to fall. Send Blamey up there and let him fall with it!'[17] The die was cast. The Commander-in-Chief of the AMF was to take personal command in New Guinea.

That night Curtin gave a confidential talk to senior newspapermen. He explained that he had had a half hour talk with MacArthur on the secraphone, but this did not mean that things were worse. In serious terms, and without the touch of humour that usually warmed his press conferences, he explained that the Japanese had a heavy fleet engaged in the Solomons. The Americans had naval strength there, which the Allies did not have in New Guinea, but if the Americans were 'beaten in the Solomons and the Japanese naval force then turned against New Guinea things would be serious'.[18]

He went on that he thought that Port Moresby could be held and steps to this effect were being taken. The important point was that Australia was now being defended 2,000 miles north of where the previous government had planned. He said that he did not feel easier, nor did he feel more anxious. He did not think the Japanese could take Port Moresby, but they might. He was not going to make definite predictions. The government could not send 100,000 men to Port Moresby because they could not get that number there nor could they supply them.

It is obvious from this that Curtin did not know who or what to believe. Yet he felt that as Prime Minister he had to do something. He did not understand the complexities of Blamey's dual appointment, and his ministers were pressing him. One minister felt that MacArthur, 'this best dressed and most handsome military leader I'd ever seen', inspired such confidence that 'there was general agreement that we should comply with what MacArthur requested in the special circumstances'.[19] Another minister, J. J. Dedman, thought MacArthur 'one of the greatest generals thrown up in World War Two'.[20] Curtin continued to the newspapermen: 'A man (Blamey) was here today whom I propose to push a long way north if I can. It would be a most effective build up and would have an important psychological effect. It does not mean, however, that I have lost confidence in Rowell'.[21]

For whom was this move to have a psychological effect? Rowell and his officers could only feel that this was a vote of no confidence. Curtin and his ministers had mixed feelings about Blamey. To those with deeply rooted suspicions of the military and personal histories of anti-conscription campaigning, Blamey was the epitome of all that they mistrusted in senior army officers. Perhaps they felt that by pitching Blamey into the fire at Port Moresby he would fight to save himself and his reputation, and in doing so save New Guinea. But if, as MacArthur implied to Curtin, the intention was to improve Blamey's personal image with the Australian people, and so reassure them by showing that their commander was at the scene of the most important fighting, Curtin was to be disappointed. It was not until 18 November, after he had himself moved to New Guinea, that MacArthur allowed it to be revealed to the press that Blamey had been there since 23 September.[22]

What catastrophe in New Guinea had caused this remarkable chain of events? On 14 September Eather had taken over from Porter at Ioribaiwa, thirty air miles from Moresby. The next day the Japanese breached Eather's line, and at 9.30 the following morning he spoke to Allen over a 'weak, spluttering' telephone line and pointed out that the enemy's strength was greater than expected and that they had penetrated his front and flanks.[23] He told Allen that he was contemplating withdrawing to Imita Ridge, about twenty-five air miles, or about thirty-five miles by road and track, from Moresby. Allen told him to act as he saw fit, pointing out the importance of holding Ioribaiwa.

At 1 pm Eather told Allen that he had decided to withdraw. Allen ordered him to fight every inch of the way.[24] Finally, Rowell sent Allen an order, laying down his view of the situation in uncompromising terms:

Stress the fact that however many troops the enemy has, they must all have walked from Buna. We are now so far back that any further withdrawal is out of [the] question and Eather must fight it out at all costs. I am playing for time until 16 Infantry Brigade arrives.[25]

At the same time Rowell moved his last available troops, the militiamen of the 14th Brigade,[26] to Hombrom Bluff as a final backstop. With professional caution, Rowell had prepared all units in the Moresby area to fight if necessary, but his order to Allen leaves no doubt that he intended that there should be no further withdrawal.[27] Nor did he expect there to be. The previous evening he had written to Clowes: 'I've a lot of faith in Eather'.[28]

The Japanese were at the end of their tether. They had been sent forward through the mountains with the minimum of supplies, relying on the tenuous support of a long line of porters, supplemented by what they could forage or capture. Now the Allied air forces exacted their toll, bombing the Wairopi bridge, and dispersing the carriers. By September the front line ration was down to less than a cupful of rice per day.

The Japanese War Correspondent, Seizo Okada, described their arrival at Ioribaiwa: 'The sea! look! Its the sea of Port Moresby! Wild with joy, the soldiers who were stained all over with mud and blood, threw themselves into each others arms and wept'.[29] Short of ammunition, hard hit by casualties and sickness, the Japanese reached Ioribaiwa with empty stomachs to find, with bitter disappointment, that the Australians had left few supplies. Osmar White wrote that:

The miserable patrols who doggedly followed the retreat of the exhausted and unsupported Australians after the fall of Isurava and Myola never constituted any peril to Moresby. Once they got within range of field artillery, they were finished. They had to die or get out — or both. In the end they did both.[30]

They had already been ordered to hold in defensive positions on the southern slopes of the Range in preparation for the advance on Moresby. Then, as a result of events on Guadalcanal, orders were issued on 18 September to defend the beachhead at Buna, and they therefore ceased their attacks. Horii and his troops were bitter at this order to withdraw, and there was a strong body of opinion amongst the hot-blooded battalion commanders advocating a desperate single-handed thrust into Port Moresby, but Colonel Tanaka remained cool,[31] and by 24 September the main body of the force had begun to withdraw.[32]

From 16 to 23 September Eather's troops patrolled the area between Imita Ridge and Ioribaiwa whilst for the first time in the campaign Australian artillery pounded the enemy. Now the Japanese faced the same problems as those faced earlier by Potts. Their supply route was long while the Australians were one day's march from their forward depot. On 21 September the 16th Brigade arrived in Port Moresby, and two days later Eather began to edge forward.

The week following Eather's withdrawal was an optimistic one for the Headquarters of New Guinea Force. Rowell could be excused for believing that his most trying time was over, and he wrote happily to Clowes: 'I feel we are now over the worst of our troubles'.[33] He was particularly pleased when, on 18 September, his old friend General Vasey arrived to assume command of the Port Moresby defences. Vasey described his arrival to his wife: 'As I expected I rather "bought into" things when I first arrived. There was a bit of a flap on and Henry Rourke had gone sick and become pessimistic so that Syd was delighted to see me'.[34] This was indeed the case. Rourke's mental outlook had become one of extreme gloom, and he told Rowell, 'I'm a complete menace'.[35] Rowell later wrote to Clowes that Rourke 'saw nothing but the worst and had, I think, given up this place as lost. I had other views'.[36] On the other hand, Rowell had found his DA & QMG, Brigadier Broadbent, to be 'a tower of strength'.[37]

With the arrival of Vasey, Rowell now felt that there was a first-class officer who could be used as a second-in-command,[38] and either because the Rourke situation had become worse, or because Vasey gave him encouragement, he decided to ask Blamey for a replacement for his BGS. The next day he wrote to Blamey and gave the letter to Brigadier H. H. Edwards, the Deputy Signals Officer-in-Chief, to take south. He followed this with a personal signal to Blamey regarding Rourke: 'Feel he is on verge of nervous breakdown and I would welcome early replacement'.[39]

On 19 September Vasey set up the headquarters of the 6th Australian Division at Murray Barracks.[40] The advance party of the 126th U.S. Regiment had arrived on 15 September, but the main body of the regiment was not due to arrive until 28 September. Meanwhile troops of the 128th U.S. Regiment (Colonel J. T. Hale) began to arrive in Port Moresby by air.

On 20 September Rowell summed up the situation for Landops. He outlined the reasons for the Japanese success, and declared that his role should be the preparation of a base for an offensive.[41] Rowell was now in a position to issue orders reorganising his forces for the coming battle. The 7th Division was given the task of re-establishing the position in the Owen Stanley's and had three brigades, the 25th, the 16th and the 14th (militia). In accordance with his appreciation, he directed that the 16th Brigade was not to be employed in attacking Ioribaiwa frontally. If the operation of the 25th Brigade was un-successful then the 16th Brigade was to be employed on the Itiki-

Jawarere track to cut the enemy's line of communication to Jaure.

Vasey with the 6th Division was given the task of defending Port Moresby from the sea and from enemy infiltration. He was ordered to send offensive patrols up the Brown and Goldie Rivers to strike into the enemy's L of C forward of Kokoda. His command included the 21st and 30th Brigades, the newly arrived 128th U.S. Regiment, the 6th Independent Company, and the remaining available field army units around Port Moresby. Rowell believed that the task for the 128th Regiment was to protect the airfields, and this is what Kenney had wanted. It had been his fear for the security of the airfields which had prompted him to ask MacArthur if he could fly the 128th north.

The 126th U.S. Regiment was committed to operations over the Jaure track by GHQ direction, and was therefore under the control of HQ NGF. It will be recalled that Brigadier-General MacNider had arrived in Port Moresby on 12 September. Rowell had explained that he could not assist the movement of the 126th Regiment and that the proposed track was completely unsuitable. MacNider quickly discovered that Rowell was right about the proposed route, and after discussing the matter with Major-General Casey, MacArthur's Chief Engineer, who was visiting New Guinea, he decided to reconnoitre two other tracks, including one proposed by Rowell — the Abau-Jaure track. Accordingly on 17 September two reconnaissance groups set out. In a signal to GHQ that same day MacNider explained what had happened:

General Rowell and his staff favour the Abau-Jaure trail to our route with its 9,000 foot divide crossing, and it is true that it presents fewer marching problems. General Casey starts reconnaissance of that route this date.
General Whitehead, Colonel Mathews and General Rowell's staff are giving active and full co-operation. [42]

It was in the evening of the day that the Americans began their reconnaissances east of the Kokoda Track that Blamey, who was in Melbourne, received his orders from Curtin to proceed to New Guinea. He later described the episode: 'One night I got a ring from Mr Curtin, who said he had been talking things over with General MacArthur and they thought I should go up to New Guinea to take command, as things had not been going very well there. I raised no question'. [43]

John Hetherington in his book *Blamey, Controversial Soldier* has described the scene at Victoria Barracks, Melbourne, the following day:

'I'm leaving for New Guinea in a few days', Blamey told Burston, his Director-General of Medical Services, on 18 September.

'Why?' Burston asked. 'Are you worried about New Guinea?'

'No', said Blamey, 'but Canberra's lost it! . . . I think highly of Rowell and I'm satisfied he has the situation under control but I feel I must go'.

If Blamey felt as strongly about not going to New Guinea as indicated by Hetherington, it is strange that in his talk with Curtin he 'raised no question'. Indeed on 20 September Blamey wrote to Rowell and explained that:

The powers that be have determined that I shall myself go to New Guinea for a while and operate from there. I do not, however, propose to transfer many of Adv. HQ staff, and will arrive by aeroplane Wednesday evening . . . I hope you will not be upset at this decision, and will not think that it implies any lack of confidence in yourself. I think it arises out of the fact that we have very inexperienced politicians who are inclined to panic on every possible occasion, and I think the relationship between us personally is such that we can make the arrangement work without any difficulty.[44]

Rowell believed that Blamey did not want to go to New Guinea, but he also believed that if Blamey felt that way he should have told Curtin that his presence was not necessary because he had complete faith in Rowell. Blamey's failure to do so was, in Rowell's eyes, an indication of a lack of moral courage.[45] This is a question that no man can answer, but it does indicate the precarious nature of Blamey's position. After the Advisory War Council meeting of 17 September he must have been aware of the hostile atmosphere amongst Cabinet ministers. MacArthur had already replaced his Naval and Air commanders and Blamey knew that the government respected the American commander sufficiently to follow his advice if he proposed to change the Land Force commander. Nevertheless Blamey dallied in Brisbane. One writer reported that when Curtin heard of this on 22 September he telephoned Blamey immediately and told him: 'If you value your position, you will not remain in Brisbane another day!'[46]

William Dunstan, who had won a VC at Lone Pine on Gallipoli, and was now the General Manager of the Melbourne *Herald*, later wrote to Rowell and explained that, at two background conferences for senior newspapermen, Curtin had discussed Blamey's position 'more or less freely — off the record, of course'. It was clear that the government was not satisfied with Blamey, and his every move was being watched. Dunstan wrote that:

To this extent we must sympathise with him . . . We must try to find every possible way to be fair to T [Blamey]. He has had to submit to the MacArthur holiness. Just how much do we know of what he has suffered under the set-up? Granted he is G.O.C. Land Forces, just how much does it mean if he took strong directive over U.S. Forces? Would he have to go cap in hand to MacArthur?[47]

When Blamey journeyed to New Guinea to assume command he was, in essence, fighting for his military life. He was a pragmatic politician. He was jealous of his own position and believed that he was the best man for the job. Indeed he had grave doubts about the suitability of some of the possible successors, like Lavarack and Bennett. A ruthless man when his own interests were at stake, it was not likely that Blamey would tolerate opposition to his plans.

The same day that Blamey was writing to Rowell, he received Rowell's letter about Rourke. Rowell asked that Brigadier C. E. M. Lloyd, the Director of Staff Duties in Melbourne, be sent north as his new BGS, but Blamey had other plans for Lloyd. He had become increasingly dissatisfied with Major-General V. P. H. Stantke as Adjutant-General,[48] and he wanted Lloyd to move to that branch. He therefore called Brigadier Hopkins to his office and told him that he would be going to Moresby as Rowell's BGS.[49]

On 21 September Rowell received Blamey's letter warning him of his imminent arrival. Rowell was upset. As he saw it, the issue was quite straightforward. Blamey would have to make a clear statement that he had confidence in his commander in New Guinea, and there would have to be an equally clear division of responsibilities. If this were not the case, then Rowell felt that a showdown was inevitable and he would have to go. The next morning Rowell wrote to Clowes:

The plain fact is that he [Blamey] hasn't enough moral courage to fight the Cabinet on an issue of confidence in me. Either I am fit to command this show or I am not. If the latter, then I should be pulled out. He comes here when the tide is on the turn and all is likely to be well. He can not influence the local situation in any way, but he will get the kudos and it will be said, rather pityingly, that he came here to hold my hand and bolster me up. Shades of Greece in April 41!!

There is no doubt that Rowell was already pessimistic about the outcome of Blamey's arrival. He concluded to Clowes: 'Once I've ironed out the difficult position between T.A.B. and myself I'll come down [to Milne Bay] if only to say goodbye'.[50]

Brigadier-General Charles Willoughby was present when Blamey's letter arrived, and he told Rowell that 'it was all political and that it would right itself'.[51] He then 'stuck his neck out' and sent the following signal to MacArthur:

Visited Corps and Division Headquarters and forward areas. Situation entirely in hand. Local offensive movement in progress, Objective Ioribaiwa. Decisive intervention expected from later employment 16 Inf Bde . . . Have just learned from Rowell of projected move here of echelon of Landops. Cannot see that any benefit is likely to arise from interposition of another headquarters at present juncture. Rowell enjoys confidence all command echelons.[52]

It is true that Willoughby was a renowned flatterer, but in this case perhaps he was being honest.[53] He had arrived in Port Moresby on 15 September[54] and on 19 September had travelled with General Allen to Owers Corner where he had been impressed by the difficulties of the terrain. The following day he had been present at a conference between Generals Allen and Vasey when they had co-ordinated their plans.[55]

On 22 September Brigadier Rourke left for Australia and the following day his replacement, Hopkins, arrived. With him came General Blamey to assume command.

The events in Port Moresby between 23 and 28 September which resulted in Blamey sending Rowell home to Australia have been described in detail in Hetherington's *Blamey: Controversial Soldier* and in McCarthy's *South-West Pacific Area: The First Year*. Their accounts of the day by day arguments and discussions are complementary, and are not greatly at variance with that of Rowell himself in *Full Circle*.[56] The incident marks the climax of the ever-increasing pressure which had been applied to both Rowell and Blamey by the 'inexperienced politicians' and by MacArthur and the staff of GHQ. Since Rowell was in the weaker position he had inevitably to give way. There are, however, a number of significant aspects of the period of five days before Rowell left for Australia.

On the evening of 23 September Rowell and Blamey had a long, frank, and 'at times acrimonious' discussion about a working arrangement to suit the circumstances. Rowell had no wish to become merely Blamey's Chief of Staff, and submitted that Blamey should establish an Army Headquarters in Moresby to control all operations, including Milne Bay and Wau, leaving Rowell to concentrate on the operations in the Owen Stanley's and the defence of Port Moresby. Blamey would not agree. Transport was in short supply and would have been further strained having to bring almost 500 personnel from Australia. Hetherington says that Blamey decided that such a headquarters 'would be redundant when the paramount need was to stop the Japanese advance on Port Moresby and turn the enemy back'.[57] This overlooked the fact that the Japanese offensive had already ceased. With the arrival of the 126th and 128th Regiments of the 32nd U.S. Division it was obvious that unless the Japanese were greatly reinforced, the coming battles would be of an offensive nature with ten brigades, as well as independent companies and army troops, deployed in Papua. Rowell was undoubtedly right in his appreciation of the need for an Army Headquarters, and before the end of November this was in fact established, with Advanced HQ NGF taking over the responsibility for operations around Buna, Gona and Sanananda.

The answer to Blamey's unwillingness to establish his headquarters in Port Moresby is given in a letter which he wrote to Curtin on 8 October 1942:

When you and the C-in-C SWPA instructed me to come to New Guinea I understood it was not your intention that I should remain permanently in the area. I know it was not General MacArthur's intention. I gathered from him that he rather felt it was necessary for someone to take a firmer hold on the situation here, and then when the present phase was completed I should return to my normal function as C-in-C. From his talk to me while he was here I gathered that was still his view . . . .[58]

It appears, therefore, that Blamey intended that he should remain in New Guinea for a short while and then return to Australia, and would not need to bring his staff. The problem was that as the force in New Guinea grew it became obvious that there would have to be an Army Headquarters in Port Moresby. Rowell, in fact, suggested that the Headquarters of the 1st Army, under Lavarack, should be brought forward. Blamey replied, 'To do that would be to bring in a commander I don't want'.[59] Rowell added that if an Australian Army Headquarters was not set up in New Guinea, then he was sure that a U.S. Headquarters would be. This was not a last-minute thought by Rowell to save his own position. Ten days earlier he had written to Clowes and complained that his command was becoming too big: 'I can't compete with the local problem and do justice to you and Kanga as well'.[60]

After the doubts that had plagued MacArthur on 17 September, and which had led to his telephone calls to Curtin and Blamey, the situation in New Guinea began to stabilise; and just as had happened before after each crisis, MacArthur returned to his plans for an offensive. This was probably the substance of his discussion with Blamey on 19 September, for the latter's actions on arrival in New Guinea give the appearance that he was acting under instructions. This point will be developed later.

Before Blamey left Brisbane, Marshall informed MacArthur that General Arnold had arranged his visit to the Pacific so that he would be in Noumea at the same time as a previously scheduled visit by Admiral Nimitz — 27 September. Marshall wanted MacArthur to attend this conference.[61] MacArthur replied:

Ghormley and myself have already conferred at length and understand completely each other's problems. It would be highly advisable if Admiral Nimitz who has not been to this area could extend his trip to Brisbane so that I could familiarise him with the general situation. Pending the completion of the operations I am developing in New Guinea I cannot leave here. I would have grave doubts about leaving at any time. The second-in-command is an Australian whose entire methods and conception differ so materially from ours that his actions during my absence would be unpredictable.[62]

Marshall then suggested that MacArthur should send Sutherland and Kenney and MacArthur agreed.

This is a perplexing message for several reasons. Firstly, MacArthur hated flying, and may not have wished to journey to Noumea for that reason. Secondly, he invariably wanted senior officers to come to him. He disliked being made to feel that he was journeying to meet a more important person. The final possibility, however, is that he was genuine when he expressed doubts about leaving his command. The message does reveal that he was developing an offensive in New Guinea. Furthermore, it reveals that he considered Blamey to be his second-in-command. Since Blamey would be in New Guinea at the time of the conference, presumably he does not mean that Blamey was his second-in-command as overall commander-in-chief of the SWPA, but rather, if he considered himself to be also the Commander of the Land Forces, then Blamey was his deputy in this context.[63] It is difficult to know whether he really distrusted Blamey's methods and conception of operations. Certainly he later praised Blamey, but it could mean that just at this time Blamey was right in believing he was walking a perilous tightrope.

Colonel E. G. Keogh in *South West Pacific 1941-45* declares that with the threat to Australia removed by the battle for Midway there was no longer any reason for the Commander of the Allied Land Forces to remain in Australia, and that MacArthur would expect him to assume personal command in the area of the main offensive. He points out that there were two complete Army Headquarters available in Eastern Australia, and the airlift of the 128th Regiment at that time proves that facilities were available to move at least part of a headquarters staff to New Guinea. He concludes that:

There is no doubt that preoccupation with his duties as C-in-C A.M.F. lay at the bottom of General Blamey's reluctance to set up his own headquarters in New Guinea. Thus the unsound arrangement by which one man was given, and accepted, heavy responsibilities which were different in nature and divergent in direction produced its first evil results.[64]

Whilst this may be true, and Blamey's comment in the letter to Curtin of 8 October of returning to his 'normal function as C-in-C' certainly supports the notion, it is not the complete answer. There can be no doubt that Blamey was sent to New Guinea for one major reason — MacArthur and the government thought that Moresby might fall or, at least, was in danger. MacArthur's secraphone call to Curtin, described in the official history, Curtin's press conference that evening, Blamey's comments to Burston, his letter to Rowell, his press conferences in November 1942 and July 1945, and Kenney's book all support this line of reasoning.

Any idea that Blamey would take command of a grand offensive followed later. It is true that from mid-July MacArthur had thought in terms of an offensive through New Guinea, but he had been forced to modify his plans progressively in accordance with Japanese movements, 'Australian unwillingness to fight', the operations at Guadalcanal, and intransigence in Washington. If he had intended Blamey to command the offensive surely he would have ordered Blamey to move permanently to New Guinea. Furthermore if that had been the intention, MacArthur's staff would have issued an instruction similar to that issued to Rowell in early August.

The *Reports of General MacArthur* are not always entirely accurate, but they are important because they reveal what his staff later believed had occurred. They maintain that, 'In order to seize the initiative while the Japanese were attempting to regroup their forces, General MacArthur rushed all available troops into New Guinea.

General Blamey moved Allied Land Forces Headquarters forward to Port Moresby'.[65]

The first claim that the troops were sent to seize the initiative is quite exaggerated. Obviously it is referring to the 16th Brigade and the 126th and 128th Regiments. It will be recalled that the 16th Brigade was sent to New Guinea as a result of Rowell's appeal of 8 September. The 126th Regiment was ordered to New Guinea on 11 September to carry out the wide sweep through the mountains, the plan for which was proved to be impracticable. Furthermore there are the claims that this unit was sent to New Guinea to provide competition for the Australians. Finally, the 128th Regiment was flown to New Guinea to protect Kenney's airfields, and the first troops were despatched the morning after MacArthur's phone-call to Curtin.

The claim, however, that Blamey moved his HQ to New Guinea is illuminating, for perhaps it reveals what MacArthur and his staff thought should have happened. Willoughby's signal of 21 September certainly imagines that GHQ's intention was to set up another HQ. If MacArthur wanted to get Blamey to go to New Guinea to set up an HQ, and consequently effectively remove him from command of the Allied Land Forces, and if Blamey were reluctant, then one method would be for MacArthur to ring Curtin, and also to let Blamey assume that he would not need to remain long in New Guinea. He knew that the eventual build-up of forces would mean that Blamey would have to set up the equivalent of an Army Headquarters.

The necessary ingredients for this theory would be a determination on Blamey's part not to set up his HQ in New Guinea — a determination which he certainly possessed — and guile on MacArthur's part — a guile which many senior U.S. officers, from Eichelberger to Marshall, recognised. Is it reading too much into events to propose this theory?[66] If the theory is true, why did Blamey not want to set up his headquarters in New Guinea? The answer is either because he did not want to lose control as C-in-C of the AMF, or because he did not want to lose his power as Commander of the Allied Land Forces.

Keogh suggested that Blamey did not want to lose control as C-in-C of the AMF, but although Curtin was mistaken he believed that New Guinea was the place for the C-in-C of the AMF. In the long run he would be the arbiter in any discussion surrounding Blamey's tenure of the position. Whilst there is certainly truth in Keogh's theory, the real answer probably revolves around the position of Commander of the Allied Land Forces.

It is an error to assume that MacArthur wished to use his nominated Commander of the Allied Land Forces in that exact role. From the

period of General Richardson's visit to Australia it is clear that
MacArthur intended that his operations should be conducted by task
forces operating under his personal control. This had been his reaction
on 1 August when he had intended to send the 32nd Division to New
Guinea under his direct control. Then again, on 14 September, he had
ordered Eichelberger to prepare to command a task force alongside
that of Rowell in New Guinea. Sutherland had talked him out of that
not simply because, like the first scheme, it would have led to a
hopeless command muddle, but also because it could have led to
Eichelberger assuming a more important role than his as MacArthur's
Chief of Staff.

Just as Eisenhower later became his own Land Forces Commander
during the advance of the Allied Armies across north-west Europe, so
too did MacArthur believe that he should be his own Land Forces
Commander. Blamey would have been aware that as soon as he
assumed command in New Guinea he became, in effect, one of
MacArthur's task force commanders. While he later resigned himself
to the fact that this was the most important role that MacArthur
would allow him to fill in the organisation of the SWPA command,
initially Blamey must have felt that not only was this a lower status of
command, but also an indication that MacArthur had lost confidence
in his assessment of the situation.

If this is the case then it would explain why Berryman felt that
Blamey was fighting for his military life and would explain why he had
no intention of staying in New Guinea longer than he could help. It
would also explain why, in a stubborn but final burst of resistance to
MacArthur, Blamey told Rowell that he had no intention of setting up
a new headquarters. He was soon to realise that MacArthur had out-
manoeuvred him, but he was too proud to admit this to Rowell.
Rowell would have to go.

On 20 September Landops had informed New Guinea Force that
MacArthur considered that the area around Wanigela should not fall
into Japanese hands, and he suggested that one infantry company
should be moved from Milne Bay to secure this area.[67] Rowell had
passed this message on to Clowes who had replied that there was no
information that the Japanese were contemplating landing at
Wanigela, but they were already on Goodenough Island. He agreed
with the need for speed to deny the north-east coast to the Japanese,
but felt that with a rising sick rate he did not have enough infantry to
fulfil adequately even his primary task of defending the air base. He
concluded that he considered that at least one battalion was necessary
to hold Wanigela, although 'If directed will organise occupation

Wanigela by one company but request full consideration situation here and due record my views'.[68]

At that time there were six battalions at Milne Bay. Clowes's argument should have appealed to MacArthur, for a month later he wrote to Blamey: 'I do not believe that the garrison there [Milne Bay] should be reduced below two brigades . . . I consider that Wanigela has no especial significance in itself. It is merely the transfer point from which troops have started a movement toward Buna'.[69] Then on 25 January 1943, after the Japanese had been driven into the sea at Sanananda, thus reducing the threat of a landing at Milne Bay, MacArthur wrote to Blamey: 'It is believed that five battalions immediately available at Milne Bay, assuming the possibility of prompt reinforcement by air, is too small a garrison for adequate security.[70] Clowes's reluctance corresponded with that of Rowell, and this was the main point of tactics over which Rowell and Blamey disagreed. Rowell wrote:

it is crass stupidity and ignorance to talk about vigorous action in this area . . . when we had no freedom of action against enemy air, and light naval forces on the north coast of Papua. The soundness of the Wanigela plan may be judged by what it actually achieved. It certainly took a lot of effort and the troops used, who later went to Buna, could just as easily have come straight from Milne Bay with their main bodies. I don't believe it had the slightest effect on the ultimate extinction of the Japanese at Buna.[71]

Blamey was, however, determined to follow MacArthur's instructions explicitly. He did not want to give MacArthur any opportunity to accuse him of dragging his feet. On the morning of 25 September he flew to Milne Bay and ordered Clowes to send a force to Wanigela by air. Apparently the air force could now supply the planes for such a move. Kenney recorded that Blamey told him that he had to '*order* General Clowes to provide the troops from Milne Bay. Clowes didn't approve of this method at all'.[72] Apparently Clowes immediately signalled Rowell to complain about this order, for when Blamey returned to Port Moresby, Rowell was already angry as he felt that Blamey had circumvented his authority.[73]

Rowell's feelings can be gauged by his letter to Clowes the next morning. He told Clowes: 'I fairly rose. I then got off my chest what I've been storing up since April 1941. Told him he'd already dumped me twice and was in process of doing it a third time and so on. In the end he rose, as I hoped he would . . . '. Blamey replied that his words to Clowes had been a suggestion: a fine distinction when the suggestion comes from the Commander-in-Chief. Nevertheless, Rowell told Clowes that with regard to Wanigela: 'I'm afraid you will have to go ahead. I'm trying to find out from Blamey when a reinforcing Bde is likely to come in'.[74]

That night Blamey outlined his plan to MacArthur, and indicated that he realised that the defensive phase was over in New Guinea. He explained that he intended to advance on three axes. The first was the present axis of advance via Ioribaiwa to Kokoda. The second was along the track through Jaure where 'a much easier route is available than the Ioribaiwa route', and the third was a sea and land route from Milne Bay. He proposed to use I Australian Corps, consisting of the 6th and 7th Divisions, on the Ioribaiwa route, troops of the 32nd Division on the Rigo-Abau-Jaure route, and Milne Force, increased to three brigades, on the land and sea route. He pointed out that there would be homogeneous national forces on the first and second axes but that Milne Force would be mixed or all U.S. troops. He suggested using all of the 41st U.S. Division, sending either the 17th Brigade or a U.S. Marine Regiment to reinforce Milne Force. He continued:

Major-General Clowes has been instructed to prepare plans to push on and has been informed that an additional brigade will soon be available . . .
So far I have had a day to look into the local position and today I have spent at Milne Bay. Tomorrow I will commence to get hold of the position in regard to General MacNider's force to get the move on the second axis under way.[75]

This letter gives the appearance that Blamey was repeating merely what he knew MacArthur wanted to read; perhaps what they had already discussed in Brisbane. It was also unfair to Rowell. MacNider's reconnaissance group was still on the Kapa Kapa trail and only that day U.S. Engineers had completed a motor road to Kapa Kapa. The main body of the 126th Regiment was not due to arrive in Port Moresby until 28 September, so it can be seen that Blamey was not able to move things any more rapidly than Rowell, although the last sentence of the letter implies this. Furthermore the letter indicates that Blamey was already thinking in terms of an organisation which would demand an army headquarters; that is, I Australian Corps on one axis, and at least a small division on each of the other two axes.

The truth of the matter is that Rowell, intent on fighting Horii at Ioribaiwa, and protecting himself from the sniping from Australia, had not realised the change in direction that had come over GHQ between 17 September when MacArthur phoned Curtin, and 23 September when Blamey arrived in New Guinea. The 128th Regiment had been sent to New Guinea for the express purpose of defending Port Moresby. That is why Kenney had talked MacArthur into allowing him to transport it by air. He was worried about his airfields. Rowell saw the movement of the 126th Regiment over the Owen Stanley's east of Ioribaiwa as a waste of time. He was not aware of GHQ's intention that all of the 32nd Division should advance over the trail, and was certain that such an advance could not be supplied. Subsequent events were to prove Rowell correct on both counts.

From Port Moresby it must have seemed to Rowell that MacArthur's reinforcements to New Guinea were merely a stop-gap. Initially, they may well have been, but MacArthur always thought in broad, sweeping terms. Blamey realised this, and in his talk with MacArthur on 19 September they no doubt discussed the plans for using these additional troops in an offensive.

Fighting a battle which changed its course day by day, Rowell never had a real opportunity to plan for an offensive, nor was he informed that he could be sure of logistical support. He has admitted that he never really made detailed plans for the reconquest of Papua,[76] and in his assessment on 20 September he envisaged a time when resources would be built up before the Japanese would be pushed back along the Kokoda Trail.

Blamey, who was privy to MacArthur's thoughts, saw the situation in a different perspective. He recognised that the immediate task was the security of Port Moresby, but in his report he declared that

the main task was to develop and set in motion plans for an active offensive against the enemy which would drive him out of Papua. Up to the date of my arrival plans for this main task had not been envisaged, the attention of the Commander having been concentrated on holding the enemy in his advance on Moresby and planning to drive him back on the Moresby-Kokoda axis.[77]

What Rowell's critics have misunderstood is that this did not mean a lack of offensive spirit on his part, but a very keen sense of the possibilities in New Guinea. His new BGS, Hopkins, shared his doubts and recognised the problems that he had forecast. 'The idea of sending a U.S. outfit over the Owen Stanley's through almost unknown country seemed crazy to me', wrote Hopkins, 'though I was BGS and had to carry it through. Of course they just disappeared and were lost to us for about two months. The Wanigela effort might have done better, but for the immense floods on the Musa River'.[78] Rowell took a realistic view of the campaign. On 14 September he had told Clowes that he was convinced that Buna could not be retaken by just an advance over the Range but Buna could be retaken 'from the sea, or by a move up the coast supported by sea and air'.[79]

On 27 September MacArthur replied to Blamey in terms which indicated that he considered Blamey to be well in command in New Guinea, and also confirmed the belief that Blamey had told him what he wanted to read. He said that he would be increasing the supply level in New Guinea to 120 days, would move AA units to Port Moresby and Milne Bay, move a tank regiment to Port Moresby, send the 17th Brigade to Milne Bay and the 127th Regiment to Port Moresby. He continued:

Your general plan of employment of forces is excellent. I am in agreement with homogeneous commands. The advance along the Ioribaiwa-Kokoda axis should be pressed at the earliest practicable date with the initial objective of securing Nauro in order to permit supply by air. The advance along the Rigo-Dorobisolo route should be co-ordinated with the advance along the Ioribaiwa-Kokoda route. Suggest that your conference with General Mac-Nider be expedited in order to determine the necessary arrangements and routes for advance. Investigations should be expedited to determine the utilisation of the Abau-Namudi route with the objective of utilising the 127 Infantry thereon.[80]

He explained that the Marine Regiment was no longer available and that the third axis would have to be confined to securing Goodenough Island and selected points south of Cape Nelson. On 23 September MacArthur had been informed by Marshall that he was not to get the promised Marine Regiment,[81] and it is surprising to learn that Blamey's plan of 25 September envisaged using it and that MacArthur did not inform him until 27 September. Perhaps MacArthur was hoping that Washington would change its mind.[82]

Meanwhile, the disagreement between Blamey and Rowell had risen to a climax. Vasey described the situation in Port Moresby to his wife in a letter on 25 September:

Albert [Blamey] is over here again — is staying for some weeks I believe. As you can imagine Syd takes a very poor view of it and a day or so ago was threatening to get out. I told him to be cautious. I'm going to see him in half an hour and will get the latest news.
Would you believe it Hoppy [Hopkins] has taken Henry's place. Syd was not impressed. Hoppy arrived the day before yesterday and I saw him for a few moments yesterday. He is very bucked as well he might be.[83]

Three days later Vasey again wrote to his wife saying that he had a visit from Syd this morning with dumbfounding news . . .

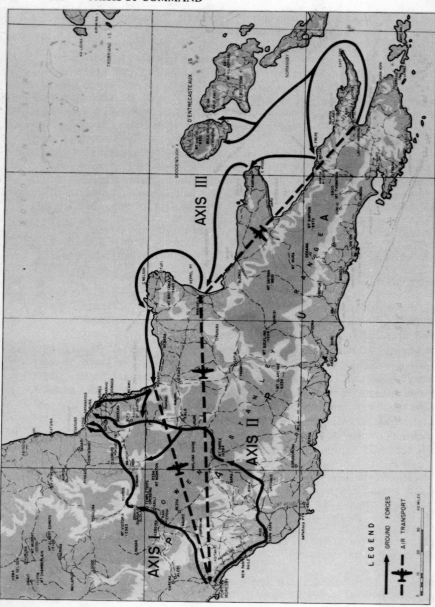

Map 6   Axes of allied advance, Papuan campaign. *From Reports of General MacArthur*, Vol. 1, p. 76.

He is to go — in fact he takes this letter with him — relieved of his command. Purely on personal grounds too — not for any failure on his part to command here. The feeling between he [sic] and Albert is really only known to themselves and this is the result. As I said in my previous letter Syd took a very poor view of Albert's arrival and conditions have got steadily worse, until this morning Syd was informed he was to go home . . . I find it difficult to assess Syd's action. He may have been precipitate. I feel that without their previous association, the situation should not have become intolerable so quickly. God only knows who will follow Syd. I trust it is not our friend G.B. [Gordon Bennett].[84]

On 1 October Blamey wrote to Curtin justifying his decision to relieve Rowell.[85] He made various charges against Rowell which, since he had left New Guinea, he had no chance to answer. McCarthy in the official history answered some of these charges and Rowell in *Full Circle* answered the others. Most of them do not stand up to close examination. Rowell concluded that the charges

were trumped up. The comment that I was not prepared to co-operate with Blamey may have had some degree of truth initially. But when I had accepted the situation and a 'modus vivendi' had been established it seemed that matters would settle down, and the discussion on 27 September appeared to confirm this.[86]

He then went on to explain that the reason he was dismissed was because Blamey wanted to get rid of a troublesome subordinate and that Rowell offered a challenge to his position. As General Lloyd said, 'This would have happened to anybody. You were getting too close to the throne!'[87]

There is a lot of truth in Rowell's assertion. On 29 September William Dunstan wrote to Rowell and explained that, when Curtin had discussed Blamey's position, it had been apparent that 'Canberra has the best possible estimation of you . . . you would almost certainly be regarded as the next man, and T [Blamey] would know it'. On the other hand, it was recognised that Blamey was in a position to denigrate Rowell's performance. Dunstan continued that there had 'been a canvass of names. You, Northcott, Herring, Morshead'. Lavarack was not considered. Herring 'would rather serve than direct', and 'I can't conceive of either of the other two being considered as against you'.[88]

On 5 October 1942 Brigadier MacArthur-Onslow, the commander of the 1st Armoured Brigade, told Gavin Long that the officers and men had lost their respect for Blamey. He believed that Blamey had 'made major mistakes in his preparation for the NG campaign', but that it was irrelevant whether Blamey was a capable soldier or not; the matter revolved around respect. Gavin Long thought that MacArthur-Onslow was reflecting General Robertson's opinions, especially when he declared that only Robertson, Berryman or Herring had the strength, brains and integrity to be Commander-in-Chief. MacArthur-Onslow felt that Rowell lacked decisiveness and experience in command.[89] Whether there was any truth in these statements cannot be ascertained, but Blamey would have been aware of these rumblings of dissatisfaction.

Rowell made much of this motive, yet he overlooked one factor — his temperament. In his book he devoted five lines to this problem, but this was the core of Blamey's complaint — 'the personal animus displayed towards me was most unexpected'.[90] Their personalities were like water and oil, and from the time when Blamey stepped onto the tarmac in Port Moresby, Rowell treated his C-in-C with less than the respect which his position demanded.[91] The night before Blamey arrived, Rowell wrote to Clowes: 'I really am sick of the whole business and hope I can keep my temper tomorrow'.[92]

In a month of deepening operational crisis, Rowell had borne intense pressure from his superiors in Brisbane, and he now found himself ill-equipped to handle the clash of personalities with Blamey. A letter to his GSO1 (Int) written on 28 September revealed his feelings:

I have had considerable heart searching during the past 48 hours as to whether I should have gone on eating dirt. But, after all, we are fighting for principles. I can hardly accept a position where my self respect is lost.
The fight is by no means over and perhaps I can do something to help cut out an evil cancer in the body of the public.[93]

The same morning he explained the situation to General Allen:

Events moved rapidly to a crisis this morning. I had accepted the situation and was prepared to bite hard for the time being, however difficult it might have been. However the C-in-C himself decided this morning that the position was untenable and that I was the cause of it through my temperament.
I have tried not to let personal matters get on top in this difficult situation, but I am not able to go beyond a certain point in eating dirt.
I'm desperately sorry to have to go away at this juncture. It almost seems to me like a retreat and I know my detractors will make it so. However my friends know the true position and I can only hope that I can do something to remove the root causes that make such actions as these possible.[94]

The truth of the matter is that however much Blamey wanted to get rid of Rowell for personal reasons, and the evidence certainly suggests that he had much to gain by doing so, Rowell made it easy for him by his attitude. Indeed on 27 September Rowell told Clowes that 'We've had three first class brawls. I would never have believed a senior officer would have taken what I said to him'.[95] Rowell despised Blamey for what he saw as a *'life-style'* not befitting a commander.[96] After Greece Rowell had lost all respect for Blamey.[97] General Willoughby, who was in New Guinea at the time, noted Rowell's uncompromising attitude towards Blamey:

If Blamey had arrived five days later the plans which Rowell and Allen had made would have been working out, and the Japs would have been pushed well back towards Kokoda.
But Blamey arrived on the first day of the advance. Rowell was a proud man — I liked him — and he bridled. I saw Rowell myself, and said to him: General Blamey is the C-in-C; he can establish an Adv HQ wherever he pleases — Milne Bay, Merauke, Melbourne or Iron Range. It doesn't rob you of your command. But Rowell — well, I understand there was a background to this — something in Crete [sic] — and words were spoken. You can't call words back.[98]

Hopkins endorsed this view. In his opinion 'Rowell sacked himself'.[99] Allen has also described the incident:

It was not just that Syd Rowell objected to T.A.B. putting his HQ at Moresby, but he used R's staff, in fact expected R to be his Chief of Staff.
I urged Rowell to grit his teeth and take it. I said: 'He won't stay long'. But it was too late. When Rowell went back from talking to me about it T.A.B. sacked him.[1]

It should not be forgotten that the pressure of the preceding weeks had been a terrible ordeal for Rowell during which time his nerves had been tested to the limit and not found lacking. During this time he was controlling forces in action on three fronts: around Wau, on the Kokoda Trail, and at Milne Bay. Japanese bombers were overhead, and there was the constant expectation of a seaborne landing. Yet Rowell never controlled a balanced organisation, for administrative troops outnumbered fighting soldiers and the latter were of variable quality.

There were perilously few transport planes. For a while there were two, then one, and for five days there were none. Moreover the pilots were inexperienced and the techniques of air dropping had yet to be

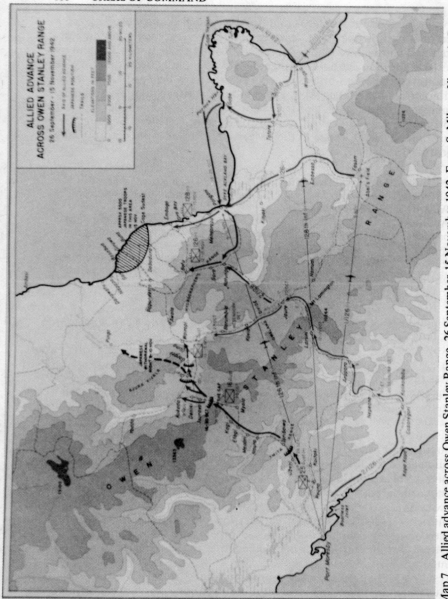

Map 7   Allied advance across Owen Stanley Range, 26 September-15 November 1942. From S. Milner, *Victory in Papua.*

properly developed. This, coupled with the formidable nature of the terrain, meant that Rowell found it extremely difficult to resupply and reinforce his troops near Wau and on the Kokoda Trail.

Rogers, Blamey's DMI, said that Blamey told him that there was something lacking in Rowell's HQ. It was not that Rowell had 'given it away', but he could not put his finger on it. Perhaps the answer was simply that Rowell lacked experience as a commander. He could not picture the problems of the men at the front and he was not assisted by his BGS, who was inadequate for the job. Yet in the long run he never lost the confidence of his commanders and staff, and this is a good test of leadership.

Hanging over his head throughout the period had been the awful knowledge that the loss of Port Moresby would be grievous for Australia. Despite this worry, and the constant pressure from Australia, Rowell had not interfered with Clowes's handling of the battle at Milne Bay, and his troops had halted the Japanese advance at Imita, thus ensuring the security of Port Moresby. As GOC of NGF Rowell had been in an invidious position. In his own words: 'It's one of the problems of a detached commander overseas that he has no one to talk to on the same plane'.[2]

Rowell did not fail as a commander in New Guinea, despite Blamey's later claims.[3] His only failure was his inability to work with a man towards whom he felt only loathing and disgust. Perhaps Rowell's equanimity had been lessened by the month of criticism and frustration before Blamey's arrival. Apparently Vasey believed that was the case, for on 8 October he wrote to his wife: 'I rather believe the job here got on his nerves and that in turn made him act as he did in the final stages'.[4]

Blamey was more culpable. It does appear that he was unwilling to risk his own position by an affirmation of loyalty and trust in his subordinate. Furthermore he did not help the situation by his actions after arriving in New Guinea. It is true that the unsatisfactory command arrangements in Australia led to the dispute in New Guinea, moreover the situation need never have arisen had Curtin been more experienced or MacArthur less worried about his own career, but a commander with more sympathy and tact than Blamey might have found his way through the shoals and rapids that became apparent once he arrived in Port Moresby. The titanic struggle which ensued between two proud and determined men could have only one result. Blamey will, therefore, be remembered as the foremost Australian general of World War II but he will never be remembered as the greatest.

9
General Blamey: Commander New Guinea Force, 1 October – 16 November 1942

The command crisis of September was followed by yet another unpleasant episode in New Guinea. If both Blamey and Rowell were victims of a situation over which they had little control, the replacement of General Allen late in October was an incident in which Blamey had a number of options.

Before discussing the Allen affair, it is worth noting the effects that the relief of Rowell had upon the command structure in New Guinea. After the replacement of Rowell, Blamey's first task was the selection of a successor. His choice was Lieutenant-General E. F. Herring, who arrived in Port Moresby on 1 October.

The selection of Herring may have surprised some observers at the time, but in retrospect it was a logical move. It will be recalled that when Sturdee had gone to Washington, Northcott, the commander of II Corps, had become the new CGS. For a short while Blamey had contemplated promoting his old friend, Major-General H. W. Lloyd, but although Lloyd had proved outstanding in World War I, he lacked experience in modern warfare and was too old (58).[1] On the strength of his performance in Darwin, Herring was promoted to command II Corps at Esk, near Brisbane. He had been there barely a month when he received the call to go to New Guinea. Before he left Brisbane he called on MacArthur, who, pacing the room, gave him a half hour lecture on the necessity of getting on with your superior.[2] He may as well have saved his breath, for Blamey had chosen his man carefully and he knew that Herring would be completely loyal. It is true that this was to be his first operational command of a formation, for as CRA he had never had to bear the responsibility of independent decisions, but for a while at least, Blamey would be at his shoulder to offer advice and encouragement.

Vasey accepted the appointment of his new commander with the view that the choice could have been worse. On 4 October he wrote to his wife:

As doubtless you know Ned is the successor. You know my views on him and I am certain I shall work pleasantly with him. Of course he has not the breadth of view on army matters Syd had and even in a short discussion I had with him yesterday I can see he wants to solve my problems without having first solved his own. However, as far as I am concerned he is amenable and I usually find that what I want is what he wants.[3]

General Allen, however, did not share Vasey's feelings. He had been promoted to the command of the 7th Division before Herring and had commanded it in action in Syria, and more recently in the fighting on the Kokoda Trail. He believed that he should have been preferred. Furthermore there was a deeply felt enmity between Herring — the smooth-talking barrister — and Allen, who was abrasive and inarticulate by comparison with Herring. Allen felt that Herring had criticised his performance in Greece[4] and Syria with clever, deprecating words which he had difficulty in rebutting.

When Herring had received command of II Corps at Esk, Allen had asked Blamey why he had been superseded. Blamey had told him that he thought that he would prefer to command a division in New Guinea rather than a small corps in Queensland. Allen said that he did, but that he wanted to know where he stood.

Now, with Herring's appointment as Commander New Guinea Force, Allen was angry. Vasey has described Allen's reactions:

Tubby's reactions to the appointment were fairly violent. He takes a very poor view of Ned — particularly as he thinks Ned was after him for his actions in Greece. He tells me he recorded his objections on paper to Albert. A most unwise proceeding. I have no doubt that aspect will compose itself; but it will never be a very cordial relationship, which will have the effect of making me more and more a second in command — which Syd thought, and was pleased about, was one of the reasons for my appointment.[5]

In his letter to Blamey Allen recalled their conversation and pointed out that he had commanded every unit of the army, from platoon to division in battle. The word 'battle' was underlined. He reminded Blamey that he had been given the job of evacuating from Greece the rearguard of the ANZAC Corps, including the remnant of the ANZAC Corps Staff. This was after Blamey, the Corps Commander, had returned to Egypt. In Gavin Long's words, 'It was a bitter and telling letter and one for which TAB [was] not likely to forgive him'.[6] Allen's GSO1, Colonel Spry, claimed that he talked Allen out of sending the letter,[7] and a copy remained in the HQ safe,[8] but after an interview with Allen in November 1942, Gavin Long gained the impression that Blamey had received the letter. Naturally this, coupled with the information that Allen had expressed to Forde views with which Blamey did not agree, hardened Blamey's attitude towards Allen.

Forde had been in New Guinea for a little over two days, but he prepared a thirty-page report which he submitted to War Cabinet on 6 October.[9] In this report he made a number of criticisms of the administration by LHQ, and commented: 'I fear that administrative authorities in Australia were caught napping by the advance into the New Guinea Area.'[10] He continued that the retreat from Kokoda was due to the numerical superiority of the Japanese and the difficulty of maintaining supplies for the troops, and he attributed the Japanese withdrawal to five reasons. These were:

a.   Their extended line of communication.
b.   Their battering by the air force, and the disruption to their supply lines.
c.   The effect of the artillery.
d.   Dysentery amongst the Japanese.
e.   The wet weather.

The point which angered Blamey, though, was the statement attributed to Allen that the temporary withdrawal was right,

and that the winning strategy of all battles is to choose the right time to withdraw and to advance as circumstances warrant. He had no hesitation in declaring that the tactical withdrawal of his troops, with the resultant extension of the enemy's line of communication, had proved to be the correct action, and has been a potent factor in the failure of the enemy to maintain his forces in this area.

It mattered little to Blamey that Forde concluded that the forces were 'efficient and well disciplined, their morale is excellent and they have confidence in their Commanding Officers',[11] nor that Forde's assertion that the Japanese had withdrawn rather than had been driven back was substantially true. He was angry at what he saw as Allen's disloyalty, and writing to Forde he complained that: 'It is the first time in the whole of my career that I have heard of a reverse on the field of battle explained away so ingenuously'.[12]

The precarious nature of Blamey's position can be gauged by the vehemence of his complaint about Forde's report:

It would have been impossible for anybody not a highly trained expert to have obtained an adequate picture of the matter in the short time at your disposal and I regret that . . . in view of [your] inadequate knowledge . . . you found it necessary to pass strictures upon the Army authorities which a more complete examination of the facts does not justify.[13]

The impact of Forde's report on Blamey's opinion of Allen was heightened because he received it in mid October, just at the time that MacArthur was pressing for a rapid advance.

Blamey's concern for loyalty was also perhaps one reason why he preferred Herring to another likely contender, Major-General C. A. Clowes, the commander at Milne Bay. Clowes's feelings about the appointment are not known, but they may be surmised. His experience in the Middle East had been at least equal to that of Herring, and he had commanded a division since January, winning an important victory at Milne Bay. There was still the remote possibility that the Japanese might attack again at Milne Bay and Blamey may have been unwilling to change the commander for that reason, but there are more persuasive arguments. MacArthur's feelings about the Milne Bay fighting have been described and Blamey tended to agree. Towards the end of the Milne Bay battle General Sutherland visited Clowes and, not understanding the latter's reticent nature, may have mistaken his silence for despondency.[14] Realising MacArthur's feelings of doubt about Clowes, Blamey was therefore unwilling to promote him. Later correspondence proved that Blamey had judged rightly MacArthur's feelings about Clowes. Clowes had submitted his report to Rowell in mid September in which he stressed the 'uncertainty existing during the whole period as to enemy strength and intentions'.[15] Rowell had then passed this on to Land Headquarters with praise for the handling of the battle.[16] When MacArthur received this report on 14 October he pointed out that GHQ had issued orders 'directing energetic offensive action', and 'that those orders should have been successfully accomplished'.[17]

In the light of MacArthur's attitude, it is hardly likely that Blamey would promote Clowes, but there were also other reasons. When Blamey visited Milne Bay on 25 September he reported that he had to *order* Clowes to send troops to Wanigela.[18] Yet Clowes's GSO1, Colonel Chilton, cannot recall that Clowes was opposed to sending troops to Wanigela, although he was very conscious of the need to defend Milne Bay.[19] If Clowes had opposed Blamey's suggestion it may have been because he felt that the order should have come from Rowell, and if this is the case then Blamey could have believed that Rowell and Clowes, great friends over 31 years, were tarred with the same brush. 'Silent Cyril' Clowes did nothing to help himself or to convince Blamey otherwise.[20]

Furthermore there was the belief amongst at least a small number of the officers at Milne Bay that the 2/10th Battalion had been sent forward with inadequate instructions.[21] Indeed the 18th Brigade War Diary notes that Brigadier Wootten was worried lest the 2/10th was encircled — 'Commander desires GOC adequately protect rear 2/10 Battalion'.[22]

It is probable, therefore, that Blamey did not even consider Clowes for the appointment of Commander of New Guinea Force, and this marks the beginning of Clowes's decline. Yet Clowes was more suited to an administrative task, for while his immediate subordinates trusted him he was never able to reach the private soldier.[23] Indeed a year earlier in Palestine Vasey had written to his wife: 'Cyril is a disappointment. Over the years he has become mentally lazy and I'm told at the moment he is very home sick'.[24] In mid November he took leave in Australia.[25] Returning in December he was found to have malaria and Milford took over the command. Clowes resumed command of the 11th Division in New Guinea in early 1943, but in October went back again to Australia to command the Victorian L of C Area.

The decision to send Herring to New Guinea immediately is interesting, for it indicates that Blamey still seemed to think that he would not remain permanently in New Guinea. On 1 October, barely three days after Rowell's dismissal, Herring arrived in Port Moresby.[26] On 8 October Blamey wrote to Curtin implying that he should return to Australia for a day or two.[27] Apparently Curtin put this to MacArthur but on 10 October MacArthur wrote to Curtin:

I believe the time of General Blamey's ultimate return to Australia might well be held in abeyance for the present pending further developments. With your permission I will be glad to inform you when I think such action appropriate and advisable.[28]

In view of Herring's lack of experience it was fortunate that Blamey was forced to remain in New Guinea for with the prestige of his rank he was more able than Herring to make MacArthur realise the problems of supply and the necessity for a sound administrative arrangement. Even at this late stage MacArthur did not realise the difficulties of supply in New Guinea, nor the tenacity of the Japanese in defence.

Despite the fact that MacArthur's signal to Blamey on 27 September indicated complete agreement with the scheme that Blamey had proposed on 25 September, it should not be supposed that MacArthur was completely convinced that this was the most suitable plan.[29] For a while he contemplated a plan which, as well as involving the advance of the Australians over the Kokoda Trail, and the Americans over the trails to the south-east, involved reinforcing Kanga Force by 'approximately a reduced battalion with the objective of holding airfields in the Bulolo Valley preparatory to employment of larger forces against Lae and Salamaua'.[30] This plan envisaged the improvement of the Lakekamu-Bulldog route for the supply of the Wau area, but it was not transmitted to Blamey.

At the same time MacArthur asked General Eichelberger, the commander of I U.S. Corps, to submit his recommendations for the use of American troops in New Guinea. Eichelberger has recorded how when he arrived in Australia he was told to have little to do with the Australian commanders, and his recommendations reveal how this policy could result in a number of misapprehensions.[31] On 29 September, one day after the Australians occupied Ioribaiwa, he wrote that:

A passive defence of Port Moresby to which so many of the Australian and American officers seem resigned will end eventually in the capture of Papua by the Japanese and with it the consequent abandonment of any offensive mission to the north west.

His plan envisaged an advance by two U.S. Regiments over the Owen Stanley Range to capture Buna and Gona, and he saw 'no great difficulties in this matter except the inertia of those who will sit and wait for the Japanese to drive them into the water at Port Moresby'.

Eichelberger was convinced that 'since this movement of American troops must not fail, a forward echelon of the I Army Corps staff should be used', and that the American troops should be under American command. He recognised however, that

The importance of American command is lessened by the fact that the Commander-in-Chief, Allied Forces [MacArthur], can direct how American troops are to be used. In this connection, as long as General Blamey has some responsibilities he may enter into the spirit of the supply for American troops more wholeheartedly than if American troops were entirely divorced from his command.[32]

This plan did not appeal to Sutherland, who had no desire for Eichelberger to assume a position more important than his, and although Eichelberger noted that MacArthur appeared delighted, it was decided later that the U.S. troops in New Guinea would remain under Blamey's control, and only General Harding, the commander of the 32nd U.S. Division, would go to New Guinea.[33]

On 1 October General Headquarters issued an Operational Instruction confirming the plan that Blamey had described to MacArthur on 25 September and which MacArthur had approved on 27 September. It is often implied that the issue of this instruction marks the beginning of the offensive in New Guinea, and this notion is supported by the fact that the Australian troops were finally advancing.[34] This exaggerates the importance of these orders. From early July MacArthur had planned an offensive through New Guinea but each successive scheme had been amended in accordance with Japanese activities. Now the reversal in Japanese fortunes meant that GHQ could lend form to the operations which were already developing. The importance of the instruction, therefore, lies not in the beginning of an offensive, for that had already begun, but that MacArthur was forced to recognise that the campaign for Papua would have to be properly organised and administered. Indeed on 29 September Blamey had signalled MacArthur: 'Allen pressing advance on Nauro by double pincers and central block. General advance almost entirely conditioned by supply'.[35] These orders are worth repeating to indicate the way in which MacArthur was now thinking:

Our Forces in the South West Pacific Area [will] attack with immediate objective of driving the Japanese to the northward of the Kumusi River line.
The New Guinea Force will:
1. Advance along the axes Nauro-Kokoda-Wairopi and Rigo-Dorobisolo-Jaure-Wairopi and/or Abau-Namudi-Jaure-Wairopi with the objective of securing the line of the Kumusi River from Awalama Divide to the crossing of the Kokoda-Buna Trail, both inclusive.
2. Occupy and hold Goodenough Island and the north coast of Southeastern New Guinea south of Cape Nelson in such force as to deny these areas to the Japanese forces.
3. Upon securing these objectives, all land forces will prepare for further advance to secure the area Buna-Gona upon further orders of this Headquarters.[36]

On 1 October, the day that he received his orders from MacArthur, Blamey went forward to Owers Corner with General Allen, A. S. Drakeford, the Minister for Air, and A. W. Coles, the Independent

MP.[37] Also that day the Army Minister, F. M. Forde, arrived in Port Moresby.[38] The visit of these parliamentarians was a symptom of the continuing concern in Australia, and at a press conference on 3 October Curtin said that 'the Ministers had been forced there through reflections on their courage. He did not like having so many eggs in one basket'.[39] Nevertheless, Blamey was now able to present his views directly to the politicians who, after all, were ultimately responsible for the conduct of the war.

It was even more important that MacArthur should understand the difficulties in New Guinea, but Blamey was soon able to explain his problems directly to his C-in-C, for on 2 October MacArthur at last arrived in New Guinea. General Kenney had been trying to get him to make the trip, but MacArthur had an almost unreasonable fear of flying; finally, however, Kenney had persuaded him.[40] The next day MacArthur, Blamey, Forde and Herring went forward to Owers Corner. Forde, in his pith helmet, told the troops of Brigadier J. E. Lloyd's 16th Brigade, some of whom had fought in Libya, Greece, Crete and Syria, that they were about to have their baptism of fire.[41] MacArthur was more eloquent and told Lloyd: 'Lloyd, by some act of God, your brigade has been chosen for this job. The eyes of the western world are upon you. I have every confidence in you and your men. Good luck and don't stop'.[42] Allen, however, was not impressed, and noted: 'MacArthur on this occasion or later insinuated that 21st Bde had not fought and I deeply resented his remarks'.[43]

Having viewed at a distance the Owen Stanley Range, and the country in which his troops were fighting, MacArthur now realised that there was 'little chance of a successful Japanese landward attack on Port Moresby, in view of the difficulty of maintaining their supply line across the ranges'. It is a pity, therefore, that he had not journeyed to New Guinea before the fighting had begun. His main worry now was that as the Allies advanced the Japanese might attempt to outflank them, and this was one of the points raised in his conversation with Blamey.[44] On 4 October MacArthur returned to Brisbane and left Blamey to conduct the campaign.

On the day that MacArthur returned to Australia John Curtin said in a radio speech: 'The enemy strikes now at Moresby. We are staging a holding fight'.[45] Either he was misinformed or was engaging in rhetoric; for this description did not correspond with the situation which Blamey now described to Curtin:

With reference to the operations which are now progressing for the seizure of the route over the Owen Stanley Range towards Kokoda; this has progressed more rapidly than we had any reason to expect . . . The difficulty is now one of supply. This must be almost entirely dependent upon our capacity to drop supplies from the air at pre-determined dropping places. The number of troops that can be maintained in the forward area is entirely dependent upon this, and our capacity to fight the Japanese is dependent upon the number of troops that we can maintain. If the enemy is very determined he should be able to produce superior forces to ours somewhere between our present position and Kokoda. All indications are at the moment that he is on the run, and it is possible that he has not planned sufficiently far ahead to do this, as our advance has been very rapid and largely unexpected by him.

It must, however, be anticipated that we will soon come to the limit of our capacity to advance on account of the difficulty of supply. We will however continue the advance as long as our resources permit. With very great luck, and if we are ahead of enemy preparation we may reach Buna, but it will be optimistic to expect to do so. In fact, except with very great luck, we can hardly hope to drive the enemy off this portion of Papua until we have obtained control of the sea.[46]

Blamey's keen awareness of the supply problem was revealed again the following day when he wrote to MacArthur:

The object of the New Guinea Force is to drive the enemy out of South-eastern New Guinea and Papua. The capacity of the force to do this is limited mainly by two considerations —

(a) communications to permit the movement of the necessary troops.
(b) supply.

Preparation of adequate communications is a matter involving the making of roads under the most difficult conditions of terrain and requires time. Supply is dependent —

(i) on the development of communications;
(ii) on the amount of sea supply which can be made available;
(iii) on the amount of air supply which can be made available.

For the moment air supply is paramount.

The first line commitments are —

(a) Wanigela — one infantry battalion (720 troops);
(b) Kokoda front — one infantry brigade (front line), total 4,600 troops;[47] one infantry brigade in reserve; 2,000 native carriers.
(c) Kanga force — 650 troops; 1,300 native carriers.
(d) To this should be added the troops of the 32nd U.S. Division advancing along the Rigo-Abau route. It is proposed to press the advance with a force of approximately 1,000 troops and 600 native carriers.

Every effort will be made by these means to press the advance on Buna on all three fronts.

The total number therefore to be supplied by air are —

(i) troops — approximately 7,000;
(ii) native carriers — 3,900.[48]

Late in September Allen had suggested that: 'in view of the enemy withdrawal it might be wise to allow me to test the enemy's intention before committing the USA Regt to the proposed flanking movement',[49] but Blamey's orders from MacArthur clearly meant that the three-pronged advance had to continue. However, Blamey pointed out to MacArthur that with the problems of supply and communication he would have to assign the top priority to the advance of the 7th Australian Division, second priority to the advance from Wanigela, and the last priority to the advance of the 32nd U.S. Division.[50] That same day (5 October) troops of the 2/10th Battalion began to land at Wanigela. Meanwhile reconnaissances of the routes to be followed by the 32nd U.S. Division continued.

In an attempt to alleviate some of the supply problems MacArthur now ordered the setting up of the Combined Operational Service Command (COSC). This was to be the co-ordinating agency between the Australian and American supply organisations in New Guinea. The main responsibilities of this organisation, which came under the command of the Commander of New Guinea Force, were all sea transport in New Guinea waters, operation of the docks, evacuation of casualties by sea, hospitals, control of the port sub-area, labour and construction in the port area and construction and maintenance of roads.[51] Brigadier-General D. F. Johns of the U.S. Army became the commander of COSC with Brigadier V. C. Secombe, formerly DA & QMG of the Second Australian Army and an engineer and staff officer of wide experience, as his deputy, and they took over on 8 October. Command of the Australian services was exercised by Secombe, and Johns issued directives with the concurrence of his Australian Deputy.[52] The success of the organisation may be gauged by the increase in cargo handling capacity of Port Moresby from under 2,000 tons to an average of over 6,000 tons daily.[53]

On 7 October Blamey again wrote to MacArthur:

Allen is pushing forward steadily and if prisoners and natives captured are to be believed, we may not have a great deal of trouble to get to Kokoda. However, whether the enemy will fight there and with what strength remains to be seen . . . Should the opposition at Kokoda not prove to be heavy, I have in mind to concentrate as much air transport as I can and land a brigade group there with supplies to push on to Buna . . .
I have, however, begun a spy system throughout the area which will give us information of Jap moves. This was a serious omission on Rowell's part not to have done this in the early stages, in as much as personnel in the shape of reliable native police have always been available to do it.

I do not, however, intend to make foolhardy advances but will endeavour to make certain of every step, unless I can be quite certain that the opposition at Buna will be feeble.[54]

The first two weeks of October were a period of great optimism at HQ New Guinea Force in Port Moresby, and at GHQ in Brisbane. The discussion of possible landings in the Markham Valley, the rapid withdrawal of the Japanese, and the injection of fresh troops led some commanders to believe that Buna would be captured quickly. The intelligence summary from Landops on 9 October estimated the enemy forces in Papua at 6,000 and suggested that they had three principal courses open to them. They could stand and fight in the general Kokoda area, they could stand and fight on the line of the Kumusi River, or they could evacuate the area. The last course was 'considered a possibility'.[55] A week later the intelligence summary put the enemy force at 3,000.[56] General Rowell, on leave in Melbourne, was under no such illusions, and on 11 October he wrote to Allen:

Its a queer position, but I can't believe that the Jap will clear out of Buna unless forced out. You will have a bag full of problems now, but the experience of the first push will be invaluable. The GHQ communique referred last week to the almost insuperable difficulties of supply. I seem to remember that we were able to maintain four or five battalions at Myola last month. However, lesser reputations were then at stake.[57]

Meanwhile, despite optimism elsewhere, Allen was facing real problems. On 6 October he signalled Herring,

Implementation of air dropping programme causing gravest concern . . . Unless supply etc. dropping of 50,000 pounds daily plus additional to build up reserve is assured complete revision of plans will have to be made and large proportion of troops withdrawn to Imita Ridge position.[58]

On 11 October, spurred by a message from MacArthur demanding to know the reason for the delay in the advance, Blamey signalled Allen:

You have been furnished with supplies as you required and ample appear to be available. In view lack of serious opposition advance appears much too slow. You will press enemy with vigour. If you are feeling strain personally relief will be arranged. Please be frank about this. Dropping arranged only at Myola 12 October. As soon as you can assure more advanced location will arrange to drop there.[59]

This signal raises a number of issues. The first is the matter of supplies. Since the days of the deployment of the 21st Brigade early in August, HQ New Guinea Force had not been able to understand that the recovery rate was always considerably less than the supplies dropped. Then there were never enough carriers to move the supplies forward to the troops. Allen's GSO1, Colonel Spry said later, 'We were living, fighting and dying on two and a half pounds per man per day, for food, ammunition, everything'.[60]

At the root of the disagreement between Allen and Blamey was the opinion of New Guinea Force that Allen was not using his resources to the best advantage. They believed that Allen would not move until he had a reserve of supplies, yet if he would only move forward they would drop the supplies at his new location. Neither Herring,[61] Allen's ADMS, Colonel Kingsley Norris,[62] nor General Vasey,[63] who replaced Allen, believed that Allen had a clear concept of how to use his divisional administrative staff, but Spry and Eather did not agree.[64] Spry pointed out that this was the first time in which an Australian divisional staff had had to operate on its feet, and that they did remarkably well in the circumstances. The headquarters of a division, which might have a strength of about 15,000 men, was itself a large organisation. Since it included signals equipment, typewriters, duplicators, files and maps, a convoy of vehicles would be required, under normal conditions, to keep the headquarters mobile. Spry's difficulties in operating the headquarters from a pack on his back can be imagined. When Vasey took over from Allen he intended to replace Allen's staff with his own. Spry persuaded him to keep the 7th Division staff, and they soon proved to be efficient enough for the demanding Vasey.[65] Norris also qualified his statement. He believed that Allen's planning was 'cautious, not brilliant, but sound and careful under extraordinarily difficult conditions'.[66]

Blamey's signal also raises another matter, for while New Guinea Force was criticising Allen's administration, its own command structure had faults. In 1944 Allen told Gavin Long: 'I sent many messages to my corps commander, Herring, and had answers to them from TAB'.[67] The question then is, who was actually commanding in New Guinea at that time? Indeed on 9 November 1942 Major-General S. R. Burston, the Director-General of Medical Services, wrote to Brigadier W. W. S. Johnston, the chief medical officer in New Guinea: 'Who do you belong to, by the way? The C-in-C or GOC New Guinea Force'.[68] Herring believed that he was in full command in New Guinea,[69] but there is no doubt that MacArthur believed that Blamey was in charge.

Brigadier R. N. L. Hopkins has described the method of command at HQ New Guinea Force:

I stayed on as BGS when Rowell left, the Chief would not let Herring bring his own staff, Roy Sutherland and Bierwirth, to replace myself and Ray Broadbent although he asked for them and later was being pressured by them to get rid of Broadbent and me . . .

The command chain worked smoothly after Rowell left and Herring took over. Each evening, I would see Herring with any papers to sign but primarily to decide the next operational move. He was a barrister and judge. His method was to work carefully round any problem, discussing factors, difficulties and courses. It took a good deal of time because he went over the same ground a good deal. But he was thorough even if I felt we had reached the ultimate conclusion twenty minutes before!

Once clear on plans, we two would walk up the hill about 200 yards to Gen Blamey's hut. Gen Herring would go through our plans with the Chief and then tackle any other matters. Herring's method at least made sure that he had his brief well discussed before he saw the Chief. Blamey never gave any impression of interfering; in my view he was outstandingly helpful. Invariably, when our discussion came to an end he asked both of us if we had anything else to bring up . . .

By the time Gen Herring and I had finished with the C-in-C, it would be midnight or later. This was the only difficulty because it kept the ops staff waiting round until I could emerge and dictate orders. Only then could they swing into action. We never overcame this but managed to live with it. Blamey's responsibilities were extensive. I'm sure he would have been better placed in Brisbane with a trustworthy commander in NG whom he could visit quite often.

New Guinea was never more than a Corps job.[70]

In the minds of the subordinate commanders in New Guinea there was never any doubt that Blamey was the ultimate commander, but perhaps it was a necessary apprenticeship for Herring. It was more force of circumstance than a desire to command which kept Blamey in charge in New Guinea. Indeed his refusal to bring his own staff and his request to Curtin to return to Brisbane are indications of his desire to leave the fighting to Herring.

General Berryman, the DCGS at Landops in Brisbane, was concerned that friction might develop between Herring and Blamey as it had with Rowell, and he secured Blamey's agreement in principle for another HQ staff to be brought forward for him. Berryman went ahead and formed a staff from the headquarters of the First Army, and these officers arrived in Port Moresby on 8 November.[71] Blamey was taken by surprise, but Berryman pointed out that he had agreed in principle, and this new staff eventually formed the nucleus of a Corps Headquarters to be commanded by Herring.[72]

Herring's BGS, Brigadier Hopkins, was one of the real personalities amongst the senior officers in New Guinea. Rowell called him 'a master of expediency and a master of side shows',[73] and Vasey wrote to his wife that Hopkins 'loves dabbling in big stuff and being secretive'.[74] Nevertheless he was a keen and able soldier with something of the flair of 'Red Robbie', without Robertson's 'complete lack of humility'.[75] Something of Hopkins' personality can be measured by his suggestion of how to get Allen to increase his rate of advance. 'After a couple of days', wrote Hopkins, 'in which the pace got slower, I thought I should really go and parachute into his HQ in order to get a first hand view of the problem'.[76]

Berryman found Hopkins to be a 'cheerful rascal', but he was convinced that he was a disruptive influence in the headquarters. One aspect which he criticised was Hopkins keeping his senior staff officers awake until after Herring's evening conference with Blamey, and then giving them instructions to be completed by morning. Hopkins admits this in his account, but one staff officer, who later became a general, was almost sacked by Blamey because he could not keep up the pace, before Berryman pointed out that it was Hopkins's fault. Vasey agreed with Berryman's assessment and wrote to his wife:

Hoppy is another complication. His treatment of Ray [Brigadier Broadbent, the DA & QMG], is similar, but even worse, than Berry's [Berryman] of me in Libya. Ray takes an extraordinarily poor view and a show down is likely to come there. In view of Ned's newness it is particularly difficult for Ray at the moment.[77]

On the other hand, Herring could not have wished for a better DA & QMG. Herring's chief medical officer, Brigadier W. W. S. Johnston, wrote later:

It was . . . indeed fortunate that the A & Q Branch was in charge of an officer with the personality, force and co-operative outlook possessed by Brigadier J. R. Broadbent. Throughout this period [mid August-mid December 1942], troublesome problems were discussed with the Medical Services in the most helpful spirit, and it was largely in consequence of this attitude that adequate solutions in a large proportion of cases were found.[78]

As was to be expected, Blamey's message to Allen on 11 October ordering him to press the 'enemy with vigour', brought a response which indicated that Allen was already feeling nettled at what he saw as Blamey's lack of understanding of his problems. He met with his two brigadiers, Eather and Lloyd, and discussed the supply problem. The troops approaching Myola had finished their rations the previous day, and with the 25th Brigade in contact with the enemy, they were 'all very worried'.[79] The next day Allen signalled Blamey:

Nothing is being left undone in order to carry out your wishes and my brigade commanders have already been instructed accordingly. The most serious opposition to rapid advance is terrain. The second is maintenance of supplies through lack of native carriers . . . This country is much tougher than any previous theatre and cannot be appreciated until seen . . . The vigour with which we press the enemy is dependent on the physical endurance of the men and the availability of supplies. Our men have been pleased so far with regard to my personal physical fitness. Am not repeat not feeling the strain. I never felt fitter nor able to think straighter. I however feel somewhat disappointed on behalf of all ranks that you are disatisfied with the very fine effort they have made.[80]

Allen reported that his 3rd Battalion was held up by enemy astride the track to Kagi, approximately two hours south of Templetons Crossing, and he again stressed 'if rations NOT repeat NOT dropped at Efogi North today delay in advance must result'.[81]

It was now obvious to Allen that his own personal position was becoming precarious. When on 13 October he received what he called a 'harassing message from NGF', he commented to his staff 'I am more afraid of the stab in the back than I am of the Japs'.[82] Later in the day he received a letter from Blamey which confirmed his suspicions. After pointing out to Allen that he had sufficient supplies to carry out his task, Blamey continued:

I am very delighted to know that you are fit and well. It is essential that you should retain your fitness. Having some knowledge of mountain conditions I know the great strain under which you are working, and this, added to the difficulties of a tropical rainy climate, make me concerned that you should not be submitted to any undue strain.
It was with a view to giving some relief to the officer in charge of pressing on with the advance that I arranged to have a second Major General brought up here, and I want you, if you feel the least need for a bit of a change or rest, to say so. Then you and Vasey can change over . . . My idea is that after you have done a fair tour, Vasey should go on and do his tour, and then you could replace him again . . . It is just as important to relieve the Commander and Staff in the forward area as it is to relieve the troops . . .

I have not mentioned this to Vasey, but will rely on you to keep in the forefront of your mind the absolute necessity of defeating the Japs.[83]

Blamey may not have told Vasey, but Hopkins certainly had, and Vasey wrote to his wife:

Hoppy told me the other day that Albert was considering very seriously sending me up to relieve Tubby. Very flattering no doubt but you can imagine the pretty scene that would have caused. Things were going too slowly. I have told Ned very plainly I don't want to get stuck in those hills. There are better jobs than that about.[84]

On the day that Blamey wrote to Allen, he also wrote to MacArthur, explaining that the operations were progressing satisfactorily and as speedily as the limitations imposed by conditions permitted: 'The advance over the mountains is at present going through its most difficult phase. The troops have literally to climb to meet the enemy'.[85] He reported that the 6th Independent Company and a battalion of the 128th U.S. Regiment were about to be airlifted to Wanigela, from where they were to advance along the coast towards Buna. This had been decided because the 17th Brigade had not yet arrived at Milne Bay. He also explained that Clowes was preparing to send a battalion to seize Goodenough Island. A battalion of the 126th U.S. Regiment was struggling overland towards Jaure and he hoped that it would reach there in about a week. However it was having some difficulties and, if Allen's advance on the Kokoda Trail was successful, then he hoped to press forward along this axis, fly supplies into Kokoda, and advance to Buna without waiting for the Americans.

If Blamey was cautiously optimistic about the outcome of the operations, General E. F. Harding, the commander of the 32nd U.S. Division, was excessively so. The march of the 2nd Battalion of the 126th Regiment was turning into 'one green hell',[86] but Harding now planned to fly the remainder of his troops across the mountains to a field known as Abels Field, and shortly afterwards a number of other landing fields were discovered.

On 14 October Harding wrote to Sutherland and explained that he hoped to concentrate the 2nd Battalion of the 126th Regiment at Jaure on 26 October.

When it gets there, my plan is to move it on Buna, if Headquarters New Guinea Force will permit me to do so. By that time, if the Aussies will let me I'll have all of my battalions north of the Owen Stanley Range converging on Buna from the South.

There are some big 'ifs' in the foregoing paragraph the biggest being the last one.

This was because he believed that General Herring was concerned over the possibility of a seaborne attack on Port Moresby and wanted to retain a reserve in that area. He continued:

My idea is that we should push towards Buna with all speed, while the Japs are heavily occupied with the Guadalcanal business . . . I think it quite possible that we might find it easy pickings with only a shell of sacrifice troops left to defend it and Kokoda. This may be a bum guess, but even if it proves to be incorrect I don't think it would be too much trouble to take Buna with the forces we can put against it.

He also requested that the 127 Regiment be sent to Port Moresby to provide a reserve, and because General 'Whitehead has proposed a plan for using it to take Lae as soon as we have polished off Buna. It is a feasible plan, and I'm all with him on it'.[87]

Meanwhile Blamey planned to supply the movement along the north-east coast of Papua with small craft, but in a letter to Mac-Arthur on 16 October he asked for larger ships to build up Buna after its capture in preparation for a move on Lae. He was now confident that the Japanese might be caught off balance by the force moving along the coast from Wanigela, but there was no mention of the move by the Americans across the mountains. Hopkins has written that he

did not notice any particular interest, or should I say proprietary interest on [Blamey's] part when the progress at Wanigela and the Rigo track were under discussion. It always looked to me like an American plan if only because it displayed a complete ignorance of the country being traversed.[88]

Harding certainly felt that Blamey was favouring the Australians, but the events of November later proved that Blamey was right about the American willingness to attempt schemes which had not been thought through. General Kenney noted that Blamey was not 'impressed with 32 Division staff work as shown by the way they continued to mess up the planning of the daily haul of troops and supplies across the "Hump" ', and added, 'I had to admit that Australian planning was much better'.[89]

While Blamey was struggling with these problems in Papua, events in another theatre were making themselves felt. For two months battles had raged on and around Guadalcanal in the Solomons, but as October wore on the situation began to take an unpleasant turn for the Americans. The Japanese, who had been preparing a full-scale counter offensive since August, had now completed their preparations and were ready to strike. Once Guadalcanal was taken they planned to turn their full efforts to capturing New Guinea.[90] The American forces depended on their navy for supplies and reinforcements, but a large number of ships had been lost. One historian has written that 'It is necessary to remember that as of October 10, 1942, there seemed a very good chance that we would lose [the war]'.[91]

On 13 and 14 October Japanese naval guns and bombers pounded Henderson Field and put it out of action. Then a Japanese convoy began to land troops in preparation for a ground offensive. On 16 October Admiral Ghormley warned Admiral Nimitz that the Japanese effort appeared to be 'all out' and that South Pacific forces were 'totally inadequate' and needed air reinforcements.[92] The same day Marshall warned MacArthur that the situation was 'most critical'.[93] MacArthur replied, indicating that he was giving air support to Ghormley and that his own operations in New Guinea were supported by only short range aircraft. He explained that his own supply difficulties were 'incredible' and were limiting the speed and size of his forces. 'Under severe pressure from this headquarters, much progress has been made beginning with the development of Port Moresby'. He concluded:

It is now necessary to prepare action that must be accomplished beforehand in preparation for possible disaster in the Solomons. If we are defeated in the Solomons, as we must be unless the Navy accepts successfully the challenge of the enemy surface fleet, the entire South West Pacific will be in gravest danger.

Information has already been derived from enemy sources that an attack on Milne Bay and possibly elsewhere in New Guinea is contemplated for mid-November. I urge that the entire resources of the United States be diverted temporarily to meet the critical situation; that shipping be made available from any source; that one corps be dispatched immediately; that all available heavy bombers be ferried here at once; that urgent action be taken to increase the air strength at least to the full complement allotted for this area; that immediate action be taken to prepare bases for Naval operations on the East coast of Australia; that the British Eastern fleet be moved to the West coast of Australia.[94]

This picture of desperation was a reflection of that which MacArthur had displayed at the end of August, and the underlying reasons were again the same. In fairness to MacArthur, it should be mentioned that his air force had done all that it could to help Ghormley, but again he was laying the groundwork for blaming any defeat on the shortsightedness of the Joint Chiefs of Staff. On 18 October he sent a personal message to the Secretary of War, H. L. Stimson, appealing for a complete review of Pacific strategy,[95] which explains why Stimson commented tartly that the recent cables were not 'as whole hearted as a less selfish man would send'.[96] General Arnold thought that MacArthur was battle weary.[97]

When Admiral Nimitz replaced Ghormley with Admiral Halsey on 18 October, the warning to MacArthur was clear.[98] He knew that he was not popular in Washington, and his great rival, General Eisenhower, was about to lead the invasion of North Africa. On 1 November Colonel G. H. Wilkinson, a British liaison officer, noted 'MacA thinks E [Eisenhower] will command the North African landings . . . and thinks (and possibly almost hopes?) that commanding fighting British officers will show up E's true proportions'.[99] He continued, 'if Roosevelt gains strength politically, it is quite possible that he will find some pretext to relieve MacA altogether of his command . . . and thinks that R might well pull it off on grounds of no confidence'.[1] The main reason, however, that MacArthur disliked the North African campaign was because it was drawing supplies and shipping from what he believed was the most important theatre.[2]

These pressures had two main effects on MacArthur. The first was to spur on the Australians on the Kokoda Trail to achieve an early victory, and the second was to ensure that there was a plan to withdraw the American forces in the event of a disaster in the Solomons.

The first reaction is shown in his signal to Blamey on 17 October: 'Press General Allen's advance. His extremely light casualties indicate no serious effort yet made to display enemy. It is essential that the Kokoda airfield be taken'.[3] As might be expected, Allen was not impressed when this message was relayed to him. His ADC noted that he 'was deeply hurt and visibly affected, not, as he said, for his own sake, but for the wonderful men who had been fighting'.[4] Allen replied immediately:

I respectfully submit that the success of this campaign cannot be judged by casualties alone . . . Respectfully suggest you defer judgment until you receive Minogue's [Lt.-Col. J. P. Minogue, a liaison officer from HQ NGF] report or until a more senior staff officer can come forward and discuss situation with me . . . .[5]

Allen said later:

General Blamey had two courses open to him on receipt of my signal [17 October] —
a. To have confidence in my judgment which, in view of my past experience, I claim he was justified in having.

b. Come forward himself or send General Herring or a senior staff officer forward to discuss the situation with me and appreciate the position on the spot personally.

It was not necessary to urge me or the troops under my command to capture Kokoda. We were more anxious to get there than he was. It was a considerable hardship living and fighting in that country. Had I pressed the troops harder than I was doing at this stage the operation could have resulted in failure to reach the objective and an unnecessary loss of life. I knew the capabilities of my brigade and battalion commanders and had confidence in them. Therefore I did not repeat this message to them.[6]

Allen's decision not to repeat Blamey's message is reminiscent of Rowell's decision in late August not to send forward the messages from LHQ to Clowes at Milne Bay. The result was that Rowell had to bear the brunt of the criticism from LHQ. Blamey was determined that he was not going to suffer the same fate as Rowell. To have followed the first course suggested by Allen would have meant that he would have had to defy MacArthur, and he did not feel that his position was strong enough to do this without being dismissed. More than anything else he was determined to maintain his position as Commander-in-Chief of the AMF.

Allen's second alternative was equally daunting. It was not until over a week later that the Americans managed to get an aircraft into Myola, so any senior officer would have to spend five days walking forward to Allen's headquarters. No doubt Blamey felt that he could not spare the ten days necessary for the round trip, nor is it certain that at the age of 58 he was physically capable of doing it. An alternative would have been to send Herring, who was eight years younger and who could probably have been spared from the headquarters. Yet this alternative held hidden dangers. The enmity between Herring and Allen would not have ensured an unbiased opinion, but the greatest danger to Blamey would be if Herring did agree with Allen. This would have placed Blamey in exactly the position which he was determined to avoid. His options would then have been either to dismiss both Herring *and* Allen or to face up to MacArthur, neither of which he would have found attractive.

The delicacy of Blamey's position, which was a result of the government's complete dependence on MacArthur, was revealed by his varied reactions to Allen's complaints. His letter to Curtin on 4 October and his letters to MacArthur of 5 and 13 October reveal his concern about the supply problem. Again on 18 October he wrote to MacArthur:

General Allen's progress has been slow. Prior to the receipt of your wire on the 17th October, I had already taken vigorous action to impress upon him the necessity of pressing the advance more vigorously . . . His difficulties, of course, are very great. In addition to the terrain and the constant rain, supply dropping grounds are very few and recoveries are not as great as one would hope. However, these will vanish when we are able to actually land forces on Kokoda drome. I have pointed out to him the advantages of pushing most vigorously while the enemy is gravely pre-occupied at Guadalcanal.[7]

In other words Blamey was content to make an 'implicit plea for understanding of Allen's problems'[8] but he was not willing to go the full distance and tell MacArthur unequivocally that with the current supply situation Allen could go no faster without taking great risks.

Blamey's attitude to Allen was equally ambivalent. He seems to have regarded Allen's claims about supply difficulties as merely excuses for his slowness. On 13 October he wrote to Allen: 'I have gone thoroughly into the question of provision of supply by air to you with the Staff here, and I am certain that every possible effort has been made to meet your demands'.[9] In the long run, of course, Blamey followed neither course suggested by Allen, but told him that his difficulties would be relieved by the capture of Kokoda and that he appreciated the severity of the conditions.[10]

While Blamey shared MacArthur's concern about Allen's slow progress, he still remained confident of capturing Buna quickly, and his interest now focused on the plan to land troops in the Markham Valley to capture Lae. Although the Americans were hoping to use their troops for this venture, Blamey planned to make it an Australian operation under the command of General Vasey.[11] Meanwhile he reported that all was going well in the advance of the 128th U.S. Regiment from Wanigela, and in their resupply by small ships.

In Brisbane, MacArthur continued to temper his view of the operations in New Guinea with the news of the situation in the Solomons. Faced with the prospect of an American defeat in the Solomons he now wrote to Blamey that the 'operations against the north coast of New Guinea must be approached with great caution'. He based his plans on two considerations. Firstly his force should be able to move rapidly on Buna if the situation was favourable, and secondly it should be readily extricable if the situation became unfavourable. With reference to a new airfield discovered by Harding's forces he wrote: 'Please initiate without delay the establishment at the new field of a supply level capable of supporting the successful withdrawal of the troops engaged on the trails giving access thereto. This should be at least a fifteen-days supply'. He then concluded his letter with yet another reference to Allen's advance on Kokoda: 'I feel it is essential that you take the action necessary to have the local commander employ his superior forces in concerted action with a view to the early capture of this important locality'.[12] Again the next day MacArthur signalled Blamey:

Operational reports show that progress on the trail is NOT, repeat NOT, satisfactory. The tactical handling of our troops in my opinion is faulty. With forces superior to the enemy we are bringing to bear in actual combat only a small fraction of available strength enabling the enemy at the point of actual combat to oppose us with apparently comparable forces.[13]

Blamey passed on this signal with his own comment:

You should consider acting with greater boldness and employment wide circling movement to destroy enemy in view of fact that complete infantry brigade in reserve is available to act against hostile counter-offensive.[14]

It is clear from Blamey's many messages to Allen that he believed that Allen could have moved his supplies forward if he had tried hard enough; but Blamey had no way of verifying this. If he was wrong, then indeed he was asking Allen to send his troops into battle with insufficient food and ammunition. He never made it clear to Allen that the situation was so urgent that such risks had to be taken. Had he directly ordered Allen to take these risks, which might have caused heavy casualties, there is no certainty that Allen would have obeyed, but Blamey shifted this awesome responsibility onto his division commander, who was less able to judge the urgency of the matter.

The urgency of the advance is in itself a matter for debate. It is true that with the Japanese occupied in the Solomons the time was ripe to strike, and MacArthur was ready to strike with American troops as soon as the Kokoda strip was captured. However on 16 October Blamey wrote to MacArthur that: 'So long as the enemy keeps sufficient strength . . . forward of Kokoda to delay Allen's advance, the movement against Buna from the South should obtain proportionately greater results'.[15]

This proposal did not appeal to MacArthur who insisted on a reserve of supplies for the troops of the 32nd U.S. Division. Whether Kokoda was captured or not made little difference to the rate of build up of the American supplies. The matter of supplies for the Americans will be discussed shortly, but it is obvious that MacArthur was determined to stick to his three-pronged advance, and that he was not willing to allow the Kokoda front to lag behind, even if it was occupying a major part of the Japanese force.

An alternative conclusion is that Blamey was determined that the 7th Australian Division should take part in the capture of Buna, and they could do this only if they captured Kokoda rapidly. There is little evidence for this point of view, and on 20 October MacArthur wrote to Blamey, 'It is imperative that we secure the Kokoda airfield in order to provide satisfactory supply and evacuation'.[16]

A plan of advance which relies on securing an administrative base after the advance has taken place faces the possibility of disaster.[17] Allen was unwilling to cut himself loose from Myola and make a dash for Kokoda, yet Major P. K. Parbury, a GSO2 on HQ NG Force observed that: 'Many serious administrative risks were of necessity taken by 7 Div at certain stages due to a lack of a secure L of C. [An example was] When 16 and 25 Bdes were forward of Eora Creek and Kokoda had not been captured'.[18] Colonel Kingsley Norris, Allen's ADMS, was another to realise the serious administrative risks and he wrote: 'I well know that disasters had occurred in past campaigns because of directing casualties forward with the advancing troops. Wolfe said war is an option of risks and I opted to evacuate stretchers and walkers forward down the mountain to Kokoda'.[19]

Allen's reaction to Blamey's message of 21 October suggesting a wide encircling movement was predictable, and he drafted a reply, 'If you think you can do any better come up here and bloody try'.[20] Colonel Spry persuaded him not to send it, but he did reply that he 'was singularly hurt' by MacArthur's signal.[21] He was also hurt by a message which he received on 23 October that Brigadier Potts had been relieved of command of the 21st Brigade and was to be replaced by Brigadier I. N. Dougherty. Both Allen and Rowell had been willing to keep Potts, whom they felt had learnt a lot from his experience.[22] Blamey has been blamed for the relief of Potts,[23] but Herring claims that he, rather than Blamey, pressed for the replacement. He did not know Potts but he felt that Potts had endured six weeks of withdrawing and had to be rested. Furthermore, Herring wanted Dougherty who had been one of his brigadiers in Darwin. In Herring's words, 'Blamey sent the message and got the kicks'.[24] There is no doubt that Herring did an injustice to Potts.[25]

Colonel Norris has written that 'Tubby and I were very close those days and I realised the strain when he showed me these signals'.[26] The news of Potts could not help but make Allen realise that his masters were capable of replacing commanders without adequately assessing their performances. Allen had served his country long and well in many campaigns. He was not afraid to take casualties where necessary, but he loved his soldiers. He was not willing to take unnecessary casualties now to gain a quick success and to stave off his replacement. Soon after he was relieved he wrote:

Reinforcements have been almost non-existent, and it has been necessary to advance so that casualties were reduced to a minimum. If this had not been followed and intense pressure had been maintained upon the enemy with consequent disregard for casualties, both the 16 and 25 Aust Inf Bdes would have found themselves in the same unhappy position as 21 Aust Inf Bde (where two bns, through total absence of reinfts being provided, were reduced, after five weeks fighting to a total combined strength of 240 all ranks).[27]

It was to Allen's credit that he brought his two under-strength brigades[28] across the Range against enemy resistance in a condition to fight the savage battle at Oivi and then to advance rapidly to Gona and Sanananda.

The battle of words between NGF and the 7th Division continued, but Blamey had already made up his mind, and he told a press correspondent: 'If it wasn't for the fact that it takes six days to send in a relief I'd sack the old bastard (Allen)'.[29] On the day that Allen sent his 'singularly hurt' message to Blamey, Vasey wrote to his wife: 'Tubby's stocks have slumped even in the highest quarters. I believe Albert said the other day that he was sorry he had [not] sent me along to replace him a week ago'.[30] Again on 26 October Blamey signalled Allen: 'essential that forward commanders should control situation and NOT allow situation to control them'.[31] Allen replied:

Present delay has and is also causing me considerable concern in view of its probable effect upon your general plan. Japanese however is most tenacious and fighting extremely well. His positions are excellent, well dug in and difficult to detect. I feel it will be necessary to dig him out present positions since his actions to date indicate that threat to his rear will not necessarily force him to retire . . . You may rest assured that I and my brigade commanders are doing everything possible to speed advance.[32]

Blamey had now manoeuvred himself into a situation from which there was only one escape. MacArthur continued to demand action. Unwilling to risk his own job and in an effort to placate MacArthur, Blamey decided to replace Allen. While it is now obvious that Blamey's motives were at least partly dominated by self-interest, it is unlikely that he saw the matter in this light. His biographer, John

Hetherington, wrote that operational tiredness 'was precisely the reason why he had relieved Allen'.[33] No doubt he convinced himself that Allen needed a rest and was not moving as quickly as he might. Later, writing to Forde, Blamey pointed out that:

The conditions under which operations are carried out lead to occasional changes in the distribution of personnel . . . This is the effect of the conditions of tropical warfare. For instance in New Guinea it became necessary to relieve General Allen by General Vasey . . . .[34]

This smacks of an attempt to reinforce the notion that Allen was replaced only because he was tired. Perhaps by that time Blamey really believed that that was why he had acted. Nevertheless both Herring[35] and Hopkins[36] have confirmed that they believed that Allen was moving too slowly, and even Rowell has said that he would probably have eventually relieved Allen.[37] On the other hand Rowell had no more experience of fighting in the mountains than Herring, Hopkins or Blamey. On 27 October Blamey wrote to MacArthur that he had pressed Allen very hard 'but he does not seem to be able to make progress. He has been operating on this front now since he captured Iorabaiwa on 27th September. The conditions are most trying in every possible way'.[38]

It is true that Allen was tired, but no more so than his troops, and they were fighting savagely in chilling rain at Eora Creek. A new commander would be able to do little more than Allen until some time after the handover, but a change of commanders would at least keep MacArthur quiet for a number of days. Just on dusk on 27 October Allen received the final blow: 'Consider that you have had sufficiently prolonged tour of duty in forward area. General Vasey will arrive Myola by air morning 28 Oct. On arrival you will hand over command to him and return to Port Moresby for tour of duty in this area'.[39] He handed the signal to Norris with the words, 'Well, that's that'.[40] There was little else that Allen could do, but he replied bitterly to Blamey:

It is regretted that it has been found necessary to relieve me at this juncture especially since situation is improving daily and I feel that worst is now behind us. I must add that I feel as fit as I did when I left Base Area and would have preferred to have remained here until my troops had also been relieved.[41]

Blamey's replacement of Allen was not caused through personal vindictiveness, for he delayed acting for a number of weeks despite pressure from MacArthur. To say it was caused through Blamey's self-interest is to over-simplify matters. The crux of the affair was not whether Allen had performed well or not, but rather whether Blamey should have replaced him when he was in no position to assess accurately how well he was performing. Few division commanders in history have been replaced by their army commander without having been visited by either the army or corps commander, or indeed by anyone above the rank of lieutenant-colonel. If it was possible to fly Vasey into Myola on 28 October, and Allen and Norris assert that it had been possible to use Myola from 22 October,[42] then surely it was possible for Herring to fly in to visit Allen on 28 October. Had he then decided to relieve Allen, Vasey could have flown in the following day.

The conclusion can only be that Blamey felt that he *had* to relieve Allen to placate MacArthur. In other words Blamey displayed a remarkable lack of loyalty to his subordinate. Herring was equally at fault for he was too ready to please his superior and not willing enough to speak up for a subordinate towards whom he, like Blamey, felt no attraction and whose loyalty he suspected. Loyalty cannot be expected if you do not give it and it must start at the top.

On 6 November Vasey wrote to his wife:

Poor Tubby, it was just beyond him, he simply has no idea what a div staff is for or can do. The following day [after he took over] I moved HQ forward and again the next day so as to get on the tail of the brigadiers and get them forward. One of the grouses against Tubby was that he let the situation control him instead of controlling it. I never believed in allowing that to occur and decided to take control quickly.[43]

This is less than charitable to Allen and indeed Norris has recorded that as he and Vasey walked back after saying farewell to Allen 'the silence was broken after a while. "Poor old Tubby. He really has done a grand job", [said Vasey]. George could be very gentle and generous'.[44] Furthermore it was all very well for Vasey to speak of moving his headquarters forward, but that was only possible because in the face of determined attacks the Japanese abandoned the whole Eora Creek position on the night of 28-29 October. Vasey assumed command on the morning of 29 October.

Soon after his relief Allen noted that his 'slow' advance could be attributed to five 'retarding factors':

a. Terrain.
b. Transport of supplies.
c. Strength of units.
d. Condition of troops.
e. Evacuation of wounded.

The first factor could not be blamed on anyone, but its effects were not understood at HQ NGF. The other factors could have been minimised by efforts from Port Moresby. Allen commented that: 'At no time throughout this op[eration] were the quantity of sup[plies] etc as promised by NG Force delivered'. The lack of adequate and varied food, 'the constant exposure plus high exertion and nervous strain inevitably tells'.

Allen claimed that he did not write the notes in a spirit of 'criticism of any HQ concerned but rather to explain the difficulties encountered'.[45] It is impossible now to determine in exactly what manner HQ NGF could have improved Allen's position, but it is certain that by his messages Blamey showed that he had no idea of Allen's difficulties:

You have been furnished with supplies as you required and ample appear to be available. (11 October)
Every possible effort has been made to meet your demands. (13 October)
You should consider acting with great boldness and employment [sic] wide encircling movement. (21 October)
Your difficulties are very great but enemy has similar.
In view of your superior strength, energy and force on the part of all commanders should overcome the enemy speedily. (26 October)[46]

Allen wrote that the receipt of these signals embarrassed him

considerably, particularly the ref[sic] that no serious effort was being made to dislodge the enemy. This was not only a serious reflection upon his own leadership but also upon his staff, bde comds, and tps. Those sigs did nothing to speed the adv because all steps possible had already been taken before their receipt. It is felt that had some system of liaison been implemented by higher authority early in Oct such disturbing sigs would not have been despatched.[47]

It cannot be determined whether Blamey deliberately limited liaison visits to Allen's headquarters so that he was protected from unpalatable truths, or whether he underestimated the necessity for such visits. Herring, who after all was the commander responsible, showed a remarkable lack of interest in determining the exact situation on the Range. Whatever the reason for the lack of knowledge at HQ NGF, it was a discreditable situation for which Blamey must bear full responsibility.

For his reluctance to accept Blamey's view that Allen was doing all he could, MacArthur showed an abysmal lack of trust in his subordinate, and an unwarranted interference in the tactical handling of troops some 1,500 miles from his headquarters. Had Blamey stood up to MacArthur, he would have won the respect of the Australian Army. As it was he did MacArthur's bidding and won the opprobrium of the troops. Kokoda was not captured any faster for his action.

Allen's relief had the desired effect. On 29 October Blamey signalled MacArthur: 'General Vasey relieved General Allen at 0800 hours 29th October. Latter rather strained. Am sending him south for short break. Have told him to call on you if you wish to see him'.[48] MacArthur replied immediately: 'Concur fully your action in placing Vasey in command at front. Feel sure he will take his column through without undue delay. Please give him my felicitations and tell him of my confidence'.[49] Allen would have appreciated such an expression of confidence.

When Blamey relieved Allen, he wrote to MacArthur that Allen would become responsible for the defence of Port Moresby. With this change in command the forces in New Guinea were now organised as follows:

(a) Forward Division — Major-General Vasey — 7th Australian Division. 16th and 25th Brigades and 3rd Battalion.

(b) Rearward area — Major-General Allen — 6th Division. 21st Brigade, 14th Brigade (less 3rd Battalion), 30th Brigade (two battalions) 7th Australian Divisional Cavalry Regiment, 2/1st and 2/6th Field Regiments RAA.

(c) Milne Bay area — Major-General Clowes — 17th Brigade, 18th Brigade with battalions at Wanigela, Goodenough Island and Milne Bay, 7th Brigade, 2/5th Field Regiment RAA.

(d) American forces — Major-General Harding — 128th U.S. Regiment with battalions at Wanigela, Mendaropu, near Pongani, and at Moresby awaiting transport by air to Mendaropu, 2/6th Independent Company, 126th U.S. Regiment with a battalion arriving at Jaure via the Jaure trail, and two battalions in the Moresby area.

(e) Kanga Force — Lt.-Col. Fleay — 2/5th and 2/7th Independent companies and troops of the NGVR.

It can be seen that few major units had arrived in New Guinea since Rowell's departure. The 2/7th Independent Company arrived in early October and the 17th Brigade in mid October. The 127th U.S. Regiment did not begin to arrive until 26 November. Blamey's problem was therefore one of deployment, and he explained to MacArthur that he thought he could push along the north-east coast of Papua with relative safety until the area of Oro Bay was reached, where he intended to wait until Kokoda was secured. Taking heed of MacArthur's warnings he concluded: 'The necessity for lines of withdrawal from dangerous areas and the precarious nature of the lines of supply will be carefully watched during the period of approach to the critical phase of the capture of Buna'.[50]

MacArthur was not yet convinced that it was safe to move the remainder of the American troops across the Range. Indeed on 31 October he issued the Petersburg Plan with details for the withdrawal of the troops should the Japanese take Guadalcanal and turn their full strength on New Guinea.[51] Nevertheless Harding was becoming anxious to move on and that day wrote to Sutherland: 'We are getting along very well with the Aussies. General Herring, with whom I do most of my business is especially fine to work with'. He did feel, however, that the instructions to establish a ration dump at Abels field was 'an unnecessary precaution', as he believed that the supplies could be flown in if necessary.[52]

Blamey pressed MacArthur to allow him to fly the remaining troops over the Range so that they could be in position for an early attack on Buna, but MacArthur hesitated. Meanwhile at Eora Creek the Japanese had been driven back. With characteristic enthusiasm Vasey urged his troops forward: 'The enemy is beaten. Give him no rest and we will annihilate him. It is only a matter of a day or two. Tighten your belts and push on'.[53]

On 2 November Vasey's leading troops entered Kokoda. That day also saw the end of a naval battle off Guadalcanal in which the Japanese suffered a severe defeat. MacArthur acted quickly and finally agreed to Blamey's request to land troops on the north side of the Range, although, still worried about supplies, he added that before the actual attack on Buna

At least ten days supply of food and appropriate amount of ammunition and medical supplies for the three units engaged should be placed behind each of the three columns. These supplies should be accumulated before the movement by air of remaining two battalions of 126 Infantry. Even a rough calculation shows a tremendous strain upon air transport involved. Can this be met?[54]

MacArthur now chose 15 November as the tentative date for the attack. His plan envisaged a three-pronged attack, with the Australians forming the left column, and the Americans the centre and right columns.[55] In accordance with this plan, on 3 November New Guinea Force ordered the 32nd Division to patrol forward to the line Oro Bay-Bofu-Wairopi.[56]

MacArthur meanwhile had become concerned about the command

arrangements in New Guinea. With the commitment of the 32nd U.S. Division to battle, Blamey would, in effect, be assuming his position as commander of the Allied Land Forces. On 19 October MacArthur had commented to Colonel Wilkinson that 'it would *not* do to leave Blamey in Supreme Command',[57] and now with victory apparently within his grasp, Blamey would be given full credit. It was important to MacArthur that he should be seen to be commanding the troops in New Guinea at their time of success, and therefore on 6 November, a little over a week before the attack was due to begin, he set up his own advanced headquarters in Port Moresby.

Thus ended Blamey's period of six weeks as an independent commander in New Guinea. Just as Blamey had arrived at Rowell's headquarters at a crucial time, now Blamey would have MacArthur looking over his shoulder. There were differences. MacArthur brought his own advanced headquarters and he did not journey to New Guinea as a result of a tactical reverse. Nevertheless Blamey must have been aware of the irony of the situation.

It was clear that the personalities of the commanders would still play a major part in the conduct of the campaign. With the capture of Kokoda Vasey was able to supply his troops, but while the 25th Brigade was preparing the airstrip he followed the plan which Allen had already explained to his brigadiers,[58] and pushed the 16th Brigade south of Kokoda towards the Kumusi River. On the afternoon of 3 November they struck the enemy before Oivi and by 5 November were up against the main defences. While this was taking place Herring and Hopkins flew in to Kokoda to confer with Vasey. Following the visit Vasey wrote to his wife: 'It appears that Albert has now decided that there are certain of his generals he can trust to do a real job and that we shall be sent to do those jobs, whilst others take over when the job is complete and things quieten down'.[59]

On the evening of 6 November Vasey decided 'to risk having no backstop on this front'[60] and ordered the 25th Brigade to swing south of the enemy's position and to cut his line of communication to Wairopi on the Kumusi. They contacted the enemy on 8 November and a heavy fight began which lasted for three days, but with the help of pressure from the 16th Brigade, they destroyed the Japanese force. Possibly 600 were killed in the area, and others were either drowned trying to cross the Kumusi, or were lost in the rugged country.[61] The 7th Division report noted that 'the defeat of the Japanese was decisive and this without doubt resulted in his subsequent withdrawal to the Gona-Soputa area'.[62] By the afternoon of the 13th the first troops of the 25th Brigade were on the Kumusi River.

This rapid advance brought immediate relief to Blamey and Herring in Port Moresby. Obviously Herring felt that he had to reassure Vasey that he was not being criticised in the same fashion as Allen, for after the successful Battle of Oivi he wrote to him: 'No one here considers *you* have been slow. Everyone realises that digging out and killing of the Jap is a slow process. Your handling of the battle has been appreciated and admired.[63]

The build-up for the campaign also contained indications of the tensions likely to be engendered by the difficulties of Allied co-operation. Herring stated his view of the approaching operations to Vasey: 'I am all for a joint attack by both Divs rather than letting 32 U.S. loose on its own. The joint show even if causing a day or two's delay at the outset may well produce the quickest results in the end'.[64] But Harding's Americans did not see things in the same light, and after the order of 3 November stipulating that ten days supplies were to be built up, one American observer noted:

Opinions were freely expressed by officers of all ranks . . . that the only reason for the order was a political one. GHQ was afraid to turn the Americans loose and let them capture Buna because it would be a blow to the prestige of the Australians who had fought the long hard battle all through the Owen Stanley Mountains and who therefore should be the ones to capture Buna.[65]

This was unfair criticism, for as we have seen, it was MacArthur's caution which had delayed the build-up of American forces. However, it was made in ignorance. It was an illustration of the kind of friction which exists in a multinational force.

The Allied forces which were about to attack what was thought to be the remnants of a defeated Japanese force had suffered greatly from their advance to the start line. Vasey's 7th Division was exhausted from its march over the mountains and its fight with the Japanese. Harding's inexperienced 32nd Division had not had to contend with the Japanese, but had suffered from exhaustion, lack of acclimatisation, sickness and disorganisation. Both divisions were under establishment, each lacking a brigade or regimental combat team, and their artillery, and both were at the ends of tenuous lines of communication. The Allies had not yet gained control of the sea, but they did hold local air superiority.

Despite his earlier caution MacArthur was boundlessly optimistic. Blamey, however, was aware that it would be vital for the sea route to be utilised for resupply. Nevertheless on 14 November he wrote en-

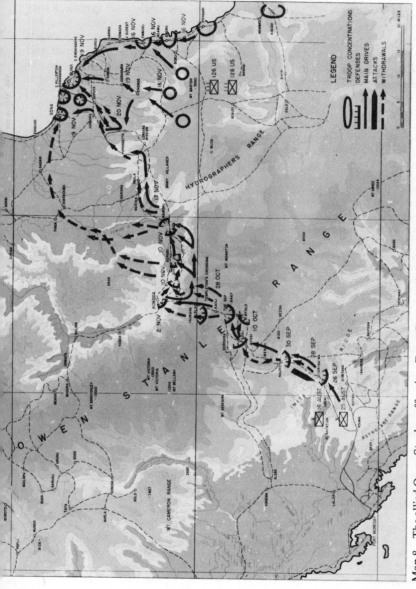

Map 8   The allied Owen Stanley offensive. From *Reports of General MacArthur*, Vol.1, p.77.

couragingly to Frederick Shedden, the Secretary of the Department of Defence: 'I think the very stiff fighting is over unless the Japanese succeed in landing forces in the next week. We expect to begin our advance on Monday morning [16 November] and in a few days to sweep through to Buna and Gona'.[66] On the eve of the attack on Buna and Gona Blamey spoke to press correspondents in Port Moresby and explained how air transport was used to move the Americans forward. He pointed out that the Japanese might reinforce their area by using small boats or submarines,

therefore it is incumbent upon us not to press the 128 U.S. Regt into trouble but to wait until the complete assembly of the forces that we could concentrate. I consider you would be the first people to criticise me if we pushed them on and they took a knock . . .

The American troops have been almost completely concentrated and today they have moved forward to their objective and they have gone on towards Buna. The 7 Aust Div is going to Gona and Sanananda, but to put just a lot of infantry there which is all we can do, is a very dangerous business in view of the Japs having their ships and troops, and therefore the most anxious period is the consolidation of the Buna area . . .

However, we believe that the Jap is not at Buna in strength and we would be foolish to believe that he cannot reinforce there. If we can get small boats up there so can he.[67]

It has been claimed that Blamey's handling of the operations covering the build-up for the battles of Buna and Gona has never been seriously questioned. This presupposes that Blamey was in a position to make decisions of great moment, and that he made the right decisions. Both assumptions are only partly correct.

The decision to fight back across the Kokoda Trail was made by Rowell in accordance with his initial instructions from MacArthur. The decision to send troops to Wanigela was made by MacArthur and it has already been related that in Rowell's opinion this was of little value. The decision to send the 2nd Battalion of the 126th Regiment across the Jaure Trail was made in MacArthur's headquarters and proved to be a foolish one. It was made, however, before aircraft were available to fly troops across the mountains. Lida Mayo has written about the fiasco of the Jaure Trail that it

. . . stemmed from impatience and ignorance. The report of the reconnaissance party that the track was practicable for marching was probably inspired by the urge — common in all armies — to tell generals what they wanted to hear. In turn, the generals had believed it because they wanted to believe it.[68]

Although Rowell opposed the expedition there is no evidence that Blamey expressed any grave doubts to MacArthur. The plan to fly U.S. troops to the newly discovered airfields south-east of Buna was hatched by the Americans in New Guinea. Initially Blamey opposed it because of inadequate reconnaissance. Finally he agreed and obtained MacArthur's approval but Blamey was still unable to prevent landings at a number of different localities.

It can be seen, therefore, that most of the major plans and decisions were not made by Blamey. A number of his suggestions were rejected by MacArthur and his plan, or perhaps the U.S. Air Force's plan, to land troops in the Markham Valley, was premature by about a year. All this is not, in itself, an indictment of Blamey, but there are other areas where his performance must be scrutinised.

The period of six weeks from the departure of Rowell to the attack on the beachheads held more problems for the administrator than for the tactician. In this respect the staff of New Guinea Force performed a great deal, both in building up reserves in Port Moresby and Milne Bay, and in the movement of four brigades to the Japanese beachhead. It is difficult to determine how much HQ NGF should be held responsible for the serious casualties from malaria, which became evident during this period.[69] They can, however, be held responsible for the fate of the battle casualties on the Kokoda Trail. Major-General Norris has recorded how:

the sick and wounded literally took up their beds and walked back those ten stages to Moresby, an odd procession, arms in plaster, legs in splints and one man with a fractured patella, the stem of a banana leaf binding each side of his leg.[70]

He and other medical officers were convinced that no serious effort was made to fly casualties out of Myola, but Brigadier W. W. S. Johnston, the DDMS at HQ NGF, felt that everything possible was done.[71] Lieutenant-Colonel Chenhall commanding the 2/6th Field Ambulance at Myola was bitterly critical of the medical administration:

He asserted that medical supplies were not only very short but bore little or no relation to the indents which he submitted; that, though air evacuation might not be possible, no proper alternative had been prepared for dealing with casualties; that no basic staff planning properly underlay the general medical situation.[72]

Two major lessons of the period were well learnt. The first was that jungle warfare required endurance and courage of the highest order,

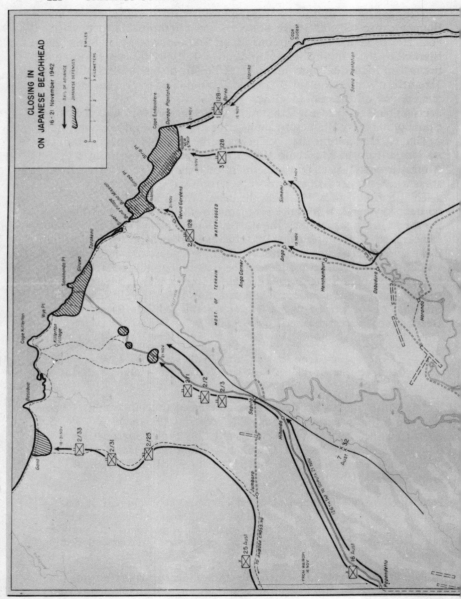

and the second was the importance of adequate supply. Through Blamey's reluctance to believe Allen's account of his difficulties against the Japanese, and the brilliance of Vasey's victory at Oivi, Blamey and MacArthur failed to take heed of another major lesson of the period. They did not understand the fierce determination of the Japanese in defence — his fanatical resistance and his willingness to die for the Emperor. This lack of understanding was behind the decision to send lightly armed troops against the Japanese defences at Buna, Gona and Sanananda.

The Allen incident underlines the fact that neither Blamey, Herring nor MacArthur had given thought in peacetime to the problems of tropical warfare in mountains, or to the difficulties of command in these areas. Both Wellington and Montgomery went to great pains to select the best officers to be their eyes, and to report to them from the corners of the battlefield that they had no opportunity or time to see for themselves. In view of their advanced age, neither Blamey (58) nor MacArthur (62) was capable of confirming what was reported to them if the reports indicated that the situation was not satisfactory.

Save for the Allen incident which was the inevitable progression from the Blamey-MacArthur command relationship — itself a result of the government's desperation in early 1942 — no reputations were made or broken in the period of the lead-up to the 'Battle of the Beachheads'. But decisions were made which directly affected the conduct of the coming battle. Few reputations were to remain untarnished.

10
Buna, Gona and Sanananda: First month, 16 November – 16 December 1942

The Allied offensive against the Japanese beachheads on 16 November began in an atmosphere of extreme optimism, tempered by last minute doubts and uncertainty. The commanders of the two Allied divisions, Major-Generals G. A. Vasey and E. F. Harding, expected quick success. Vasey's staff estimated the Japanese strength at between 1,500 and 2,000, Harding's thought that there was no more than a battalion at Buna, and even the GHQ intelligence staff believed that the enemy strength in the beachhead was no more than 4,000.[1] In fact there were soon 9,000 Japanese defenders across a front totalling some eleven miles, most of which was swamp.[2]

Two days earlier Blamey had expressed his confidence to Shedden,[3] but on the eve of the battle he pointed out to press correspondents that the Japanese might land reinforcements.[4] Now as the 16th and 25th Brigades crossed the Kumusi and set out, hungry and with tired feet, towards Sanananda and Gona, and as the Americans edged forward at Buna, an air of uncertainty hung over the enterprise. That day, Lieutenant-General E. F. Herring, who was commanding the attacking forces, received news that the great naval battle, which had raged in the Solomons since 12 November, had concluded. The results, which eventually favoured the Americans, were at this stage unknown.

On 16 November General Harding was moving along the coast in a small fleet of luggers with his artillery. The fleet was attacked by Japanese Zeroes and sunk, and Harding was forced to swim to shore. The experience had an unnerving effect on him at a time when he was to be sorely tested. Of greater importance, however, was the blow to his administrative arrangements, and the loss of valuable guns. There was a compensating factor, for it forced Harding to accelerate plans to prepare an airstrip at Dobodura, and after considerable effort this was completed on 21 November, but the break in the administrative chain caused his troops considerable misery and delayed his attack until 19 November.

On 17 November General Blamey wrote to Herring that the Japanese had suffered a severe defeat at sea off Guadalcanal, but that they were assembling aircraft to attack any sea movement south of Buna.

There are indications that [the enemy] is gathering transports and protective destroyers to land reinforcements at Buna.

It is imperative that our forces push forward at the greatest speed to seize the sea front in the Buna Area and destroy any enemy remaining in the region of operations as early as possible.[5]

Blamey's intelligence was correct, for that night the Japanese landed a battalion of 1,000 men at Buna. Another 1,000 were expected to land the following night. Meanwhile Harding was manoeuvring his force in preparation for an attack at Cape Endaiadere on 19 November. On his right flank he had the I and III battalions of the 128th Regiment and the I battalion of the 126th Regiment (I/126). Thrusting north from Dobodura towards Buna he had the II/128, and covering his left flank out towards the Girua River, he had Colonel Tomlinson's 126th Regiment less the I Battalion. Already Herring and his subordinates were being pressed, although perhaps with justification at this time, for quick results.

On 19 November fighting erupted on all fronts. The 128th Regiment at Cape Endaiadere was quickly halted, the 16th Brigade struck the enemy at Soputa, forcing them back, and the 25th Brigade met the Japanese at Gona, but was held up through lack of supplies. Herring saw the chance of attacking the Japanese concentrations west of the Girua River with maximum force and, overruling Harding's protests, he put Tomlinson's 126th Regiment under Vasey's command. The following day, with the 16th Brigade pushing forward towards Sanananda, Tomlinson arrived at Soputa.

When the Americans were repulsed severely on 19 November, MacArthur's early optimism changed to grave fears. The Japanese were attempting to reinforce their troops, and on 19 and 20 November heavy rains interrupted resupply to the Allies on the north coast. General Kenney has recorded that MacArthur's staff advised a 'withdrawal' and an early extrication from the whole show', but Kenney promised that he would be able to fly on the next day.[6] Another indication of MacArthur's concern was a message which he sent to

Blamey on 20 November that the forces must attack the next day and 'all columns will be driven through to objectives regardless of losses'.[7] This message was passed to Harding, who with promises of heavy air support prepared to attack. On the morning of 21 November MacArthur sent Harding a further message: 'Take Buna today at all costs. MacArthur'.[8]

When the attack went in at Cape Endaiadere, however, all was confusion. The aircraft bombed their own men and the attack was halted by the Japanese. MacArthur's message did not assist Harding in any way, but rather placed him under increased pressure. It revealed MacArthur's lack of appreciation of the tactical difficulties, and also of the necessity of preserving the chain of command. If Blamey objected, it is not recorded.

The command situation on the north coast was becoming dangerously muddled. Early in the campaign Herring had given Vasey one of Harding's regiments (126th) less one battalion. Then Vasey had returned one of the battalions to Harding. Harding now made readjustments to his command arrangements, which resulted in there being two intermediaries between himself and the commander of his right wing, called Warren Force. To make matters worse his force south of Buna, called Urbana Force,[9] now consisted of the II/128 and the II/126 Battalions, and each was commanded by a different Herbert Smith.[10] Vasey also had a minor command problem. He wrote later that Herring was not aware that Colonel Tomlinson's 126th Regiment was not complete when he asked Vasey to send a battalion back to Harding.[11] The result was that Herring thought Tomlinson still had two of his battalions whereas he now had only one.

These problems were caused partly because Herring had not yet been able to establish his headquarters over the Range. Originally he had intended to open his headquarters at Kokoda and move forward behind the advancing 7th Division, but owing to bad weather few landings were made at Kokoda.[12] The heavy rains of 19 and 20 November further delayed the move, and then the movement of the 21st Brigade took priority.

One week after the beginning of the offensive the Americans had been unsuccessful on all three fronts where they were operating. During 25 November General Herring visited Popondetta and was disturbed by what he saw. In the afternoon he returned to Port Moresby,[13] and he and Blamey arrived at Government House to discuss these repulses with MacArthur. It is not known whether Blamey had received, by the time of the conference, a letter from Vasey written that day, but if he had it would have strengthened his case. The letter read: 'The situation on the front of 126 U.S. Regt remains inactive and unsatisfactory. I saw Tomlinson this afternoon and he said he was "embarrassed" by the present situation. I said I was too'. Vasey continued that the U.S. companies had 'maintained a masterly inactivity'.[14]

This was the sort of information which Blamey used to give MacArthur back some of the medicine which he had been forced to swallow in August and September when the Australians were being driven back along the Kokoda Trail, and were in action at Milne Bay. General Eichelberger commented later that General Berryman told him in effect:

The jokes of the American officers in Australia, making fun of the Australian Army were told all over Australia . . . Therefore . . . when we've got the least thing on the American troops fighting in the Buna sector, our high command has gone to General MacArthur and rubbed salt in his wounds.[15]

He added that MacArthur, Kenney and Sutherland were 'not guiltless' among those who made disparaging remarks about the Australians. Blamey's behaviour was not dignified, but in view of MacArthur's strictures on the AIF, it can be understood. It had already been decided to reinforce the 7th Division with the understrength 21st Brigade,[16] and at the conference MacArthur suggested bringing the 41st U.S. Division up from Australia. Kenney, who was present, has written that,

Blamey frankly said he would rather put in more Australians, as he knew they would fight . . . I think it was a bitter pill for General MacArthur to swallow but he agreed that we would fly in the Australian 21st Brigade.[17]

Meanwhile on the Sanananda Track and at Warren Force the Americans had attacked without great success. A troop of Australian artillery was now supporting each division, but this was not sufficient. Blamey's efforts to find another way of seizing Buna illustrate the problems of co-operating with Allies and other services. On a number of occasions during November he had urged MacArthur to obtain the assistance of the Navy,[18] but without success, so on 26 November he wrote to MacArthur:

A liaison officer has just returned from 32nd U.S. Division. It appears that the Division is firmly held and is unable to advance against the enemy's prepared positions. We are not able to develop covering artillery fire sufficiently to overwhelm the enemy strong points.[19]

He suggested, therefore, that if one or two destroyers could be made available, he could land a small force of Australian troops from Milne Bay, presumably the 2/9th Battalion, on the beach near the Buna Mission on the night of the 27th. In co-operation with the U.S. forces less than a mile from the coast, they would then seize Buna. MacArthur replied immediately that his naval advisers had told him that they would be unable to navigate their ships through the tricky waters, and that the destroyers were not available. MacArthur continued that Blamey should study the best place to land troops, and concluded: 'Any penetration in rear of the hostile position should result in decisive flanking action against the remaining enemy elements'. Blamey noted in the margin: 'obviously written without studying position in detail'.[20]

Blamey was not to be dissuaded and again wrote to MacArthur pointing out that the Japanese appeared to have no hesitation about operating in the area: 'In view of our air superiority, the action of the Japanese Navy contrasts strongly with that of our own Navy'.[21] These were harsh words. Brigadier Hopkins later wrote that at Headquarters New Guinea Force they were:

more than displeased with our naval effort . . . It was not until I sailed in these waters myself in 1943 with 7th Amphibious Force that I realised what the Navy had been up against. Perhaps their only defect was a failure to communicate their problems to us.[22]

Blamey continued to MacArthur that the Japanese were bringing in supplies and reinforcements, and withdrawing sick and wounded, and he therefore requested action against the Japanese naval craft. He informed MacArthur that plans were in hand to capture Gona on the 29th (Dougherty's attack with 21st Brigade), and he again pressed for his seaborne assault.

MacArthur replied that he agreed with the soundness of Blamey's conception of a seaward attack, but again stressed that he had been unable to secure the support of the naval captains who would have to navigate in the waters.[23] With complete optimism he wrote that he was confident that the 7th Division and the battalion of the 126th Regiment would soon reach the coast and that Buna would then be 'enveloped'. The artillery would then be 'so emplaced as to enfilade the entire position, making it untenable to the enemy. I believe a breakthrough at practically any place will ensure the ultimate collapse of the hostile position'.[24]

This correspondence reveals a complete lack of appreciation of the

Japanese on the part of both commanders. Had Blamey landed a battalion at Buna it is far from likely that the Japanese would have ceased to fight. Indeed it is probable that they would have stayed in their bunkers and, whilst losing a number of their own men, have cut down the Australians.[25] Moreover there is no certainty that Urbana Force would have been able to fight forward to relieve them. General Clowes, with experience of Japanese tenacity at Milne Bay, added to his unpopularity with Blamey by objecting strongly to this plan.[26] It is fortunate that the navy opposed the plan, for MacArthur showed that he too misjudged Japanese tenacity. His two assumptions, that artillery would make the area untenable, and that a breakthrough would result in an enemy collapse, were soon proved unfounded.

Thus a week after the beginning of the offensive little had been achieved and problems of co-operation had appeared. But on the morning of 28 November Herring finally opened his advanced headquarters on the north coast at Popondetta. Brigadier R. N. L. Hopkins was with him as BGS, and Brigadier L. E. S. Barker was CCRA. Brigadier J. R. Broadbent, the DA & QMG, remained in Port Moresby and the DAQMG of the Corps (Major I. D. Hayward) became responsible for administration at Popondetta. At last Herring was in a position to take a firm grip on the operations, but he was faced with a number of very difficult problems. He had troops fighting in four separate areas and communications were difficult. Once the airfields at Dobodura were developed he moved his headquarters to that area, and therefore to attend a conference at HQ 7th Division at Soputa took most of the day, involving slow jeep travel along corduroy tracks, and then much foot slogging through deep mud.[27] For Herring, as for all other commanders, it was a very trying time. Brigadier Hopkins has described his commander during this period:

He had a keen analytical brain, welcomed discussion and was painstaking with everything he did . . . He . . . maintained the highest principles and had earned the respect of all who had served with him.

His tactical knowledge was sound but, of course, he was without the experience of many of his contemporaries who had held infantry commands through the Western Desert, Greece, Crete and Syria. After all, command of a supporting arm such as artillery does not carry responsibility for many tactical decisions. Gen Herring, I think, always showed sound sense and good decision once his mind was made up. It could be said that he tended to agree with plans rather than give them critical examination but, in the first New Guinea campaign, there were few occasions when the operations were on an infantry brigade scale; mostly, in essence, they were unit affairs with the brigade commander co-ordinating, reinforcing and effecting reliefs. If Gen

Vasey, for example, avoided interfering with his subordinate commander on the spot, how much more difficult would it be for General Herring who, in some ways was rather shy and diffident.[28]

With the arrival of Herring on the north coast it might have been assumed that the initial command problems would have been resolved. This was not to be the case.

One major problem to be tackled by Herring was that of co-operating with the Americans. He prided himself on his ability to get along with people, but Harding felt that he had been receiving less than his share of administrative support. In a letter to Herring on 28 November he made this clear: 'Everything had been going beautifully until November the 16th, the day they blitzed the four ships, all of which were loaded with supplies and ammunition'.[29] He asked for tanks and was told that Bren gun carriers were being sent forward. On 13 November Blamey had ordered Clowes at Milne Bay to send a troop of tanks forward, but when on 19 November a barge sank with a tank on board, Milne Force recommended that carriers be sent, and this was ordered by NGF on 21 November. They had not, however, arrived, although they had reached Porlock Harbour. Harding also asked for all or part of the 127th Regiment which had begun arriving in Port Moresby on 26 November, but Herring replied, 'I cannot see what it is needed for, as you seem to have ample reserves'.[30]

The inactivity of the Americans on Vasey's front was also causing some concern. It was now six days since they had moved forward and they had not yet achieved anything. Herring explained the situation to Blamey:

Tomlinson is willing George says but his companies have never got very far or where they were wanted to. So that we can't feel that 127 [Regiment] would help at this juncture. Their (Tomlinson's) casualties so far are under 8 per cent and if there is to be a relief of 25 Bde as I think there should, it shouldn't be 127.[31]

Herring then asked for the 30th Brigade to replace the 25th. Probably he meant the 16th Brigade, for the 30th was almost as exhausted as the 25th which was at that instant being relieved by the 21st at Gona. Nevertheless Blamey agreed immediately to this request and sent the 30th Brigade to replace the 16th.[32]

These and similar reports were already causing MacArthur to be greatly disturbed. In Kenney's words, he 'really began to be worried about the calibre of his infantry'.[33] When Colonel Larr, General

Chamberlin's deputy, returned from a visit to Harding's front, Mac-Arthur decided to send for Lieutenant-General R. L. Eichelberger, the commander of I U.S. Corps, who was in Rockhampton.

Herring continued to be worried by the Americans, and he told Blamey that he would 'try and contact Harding and see if I can stir him into doing something tomorrow, so as to show signs of activity at all points'.[34] Early on the morning of 30 November Herring flew across to Harding's headquarters at Dobudura. Harding complained that he had lost some of his troops to Vasey and again pressed for at least part of the 127th Regiment as he had no reserves. Harding later recalled:

I tried to give Herring the picture by letter, radio, and finally face to face, but he never seemed to get it. He was a gentleman . . . a scholar, and a pretty good guy withal, but his heart, I am sure, was with the Australians. He seemed to take an almost detached view of the trials and tribulations of my all-American contingent. I felt all along that he had very little scope for independent decision.[35]

Shortly afterwards Sutherland arrived and he supported Herring, pointing out that the 127th could not be supplied. Harding also requested that Colonel Tomlinson be returned, but that was likewise refused. Harding was upset at these refusals and considered that he had been given 'the brush-off'.[36]

After Herring departed Sutherland told Harding that MacArthur had called Eichelberger to Port Moresby and that he would probably be ordered to the front. On the surface, Harding appeared to have cause for complaint about his lack of reserves, but Eichelberger wrote later that the statements were 'those of an aggrieved man'.[37] Herring found that Harding cut a 'pathetic figure', was in a very bad state and that there was no point in arguing.[38] Furthermore Sutherland agreed with Herring. In other words, Harding had lost face with Herring, Blamey and MacArthur, and was in no position to make demands.[39] Herring thought that Harding had never overcome the shock of the first day of the campaign when the lugger he had been in off Oro Bay had been sunk by Zeroes, and he had had to swim to shore.[40]

Later in the afternoon back at Popondetta, Herring and Sutherland received a report from a senior Australian liaison officer, Lieutenant-Colonel W. T. Robertson, whom Herring had sent to inspect Harding's front. Robertson had been 'astonished and dismayed' at the American effort.[41] It was the observations made during his own visit and in this report which Sutherland now took back to MacArthur. It is likely, also, that he took Herring's letter to Blamey. Herring wrote:

I think it is fair to say that 32 U.S. Div has still not realised that the enemy will only be beaten by hard fighting, and that while bombing, straffing, mortars and artillery may soften his resistance to some extent, the men who are left will fight it out and will have to be taken out and killed in hard fighting. This I was at pains to explain to Harding this morning. He is anxious to have more men but still hasn't really made anything like full use of the men he has . . .

On the east side there does not seem to have been any really organised plan but just a lot of what Gen Vasey calls milling around. The organisation of HQ is worse than primitive.[42]

It is not known whether Blamey showed this letter to MacArthur, but even before Sutherland had returned MacArthur had determined his course of action. To Blamey he 'expressed his very serious disappointment with Harding' and he proposed to make the whole north coast area a corps command garrisoned solely by Americans with Eichelberger in command. The Australians were to be withdrawn to a separate command covering Milne Bay and Port Moresby. Blamey talked him out of that plan and MacArthur agreed finally to leave the Australian division, although he was determined that Eichelberger should command the corps with Australians on his staff. It was not clear whether Herring was to remain at Popondetta or to return to Port Moresby to command New Guinea Force from there.[43] It was yet another of MacArthur's flirtations with unsatisfactory command arrangements.[44] When Sutherland reported, MacArthur was further dismayed and Blamey wrote that MacArthur 'is now going to take very drastic action' and that he was going to send Eichelberger over with authority to relieve Harding, all his regimental commanders and several battalion commanders.[45]

The emotion-charged events which took place at Government House in Port Moresby in the late afternoon of 30 November have been described in detail in Eichelberger's *Jungle Road to Tokyo*, and in the official American history, *Victory in Papua* by Samuel Milner.[46] In essence, Sutherland's report and perhaps Herring's letter had caused MacArthur to accelerate his plan to send Eichelberger to Buna.

'Bob', said General MacArthur in a grim voice. 'I'm putting you in command at Buna. Relieve Harding. I am sending you in Bob, and I want you to remove all officers who won't fight. Relieve regimental and battalion commanders if necessary, put sergeants in charge of battalions and corporals in charge of companies — anyone who will fight. Time is of the essence; the Japs may land reinforcements any night . . . .
'I want you to take Buna, or not come back alive'.[47]

MacArthur was upset and said that he was humiliated by reports that American soldiers had dropped their weapons and run, but by the following morning he had calmed down and told Eichelberger that he was to take care of himself as he was 'no use to him dead'.[48] If Eichelberger was successful MacArthur promised to decorate him and to release his name to the press. Eichelberger was surprised by the outbursts, but later wrote: 'At the time I did not realise General MacArthur was being gloated over by the Australian High Command who had been criticised in turn by him previously'.[49] This was undoubtedly true but it stemmed from MacArthur's inability to see his command as a truly Allied one.

Later on the morning of 1 December Eichelberger and his corps staff arrived at Dobodura. Harding noted in his diary, 'I wasn't sure just where that left me, but I gathered MacArthur was much dissatisfied with [the] way things were going'.[50] Eichelberger, however, remembered differently. He was determined to try to save his West Point classmate and was willing to take a risk to do so. 'The minute I got off the airplane' wrote Eichelberger, 'I said to him, "Forrest, I have been ordered by General MacArthur to bust you, but stick by me and I'll try to keep you here" '.[51] The next day Eichelberger inspected the Urbana front which was being commanded by Harding's chief of staff, Colonel Mott. Hopkins, who visited Urbana Force on 1 December, felt that Mott was handling the situation intelligently, but Eichelberger, who impressed Hopkins by his energy, was not satisfied. Harding supported Mott and angry words were spoken. The following morning Eichelberger replaced Harding with the artillery commander, Brigadier-General A. W. Waldron, and he replaced Mott and Colonel Hale of Warren Force with two of his own staff officers, Colonels Martin and Grose.[52] Eichelberger also put the supply organisation under the command of his own supply officer, Colonel G. De Graaf.

Milner has explained all the problems faced by Harding and has created the impression that he was dogged by bad luck and the uncharitable attitude of the Australians. But there is no excuse for bad discipline amongst troops. Harding was too far to the rear and had no idea of the situation in the front line. The major reason he was replaced was that through his inability to cope with the situation he lost the confidence of his superiors, Herring and MacArthur. In other words the pressures became so great that he was unable to operate effectively. By his peremptory order, 'Take Buna today', MacArthur magnified that pressure. Eichelberger believed that the experience gained by Harding should not be lost and that he should be given another chance with a new division.[53]

On his arrival at Buna Eichelberger 'found units scrambled like eggs',[54] but he sought immediately to organise his force for a new attack by Warren and Urbana Forces to be co-ordinated with an attack by the III/126th on the Sanananda track. He asked Herring for Tomlinson and his headquarters to be returned and Herring now agreed.[55] Apparently he felt that he could deal more freely with Eichelberger. Tomlinson's last battalion with Vasey now came completely under the command of the 16th Brigade. Herring described Eichelberger's arrival as 'a very pure breath of fresh air', that 'blew away a great deal of the impurities that were stopping us getting on with the job'.[56] The tall, dignified, quietly-spoken American professional soldier gained the confidence of all with whom he came in contact. Hopkins found that: 'He had a transparent honesty, went straight to the heart of things and could be devastating if he encountered inefficiency'.[57] Although he had not served in France in World War I, he had been in Siberia from 1918 to 1920. He had a warm personality and was not averse to friendly publicity — a trait which did not endear him to MacArthur. Few could deny his effect on the troops at Buna. On 3 December Herring wrote to Blamey:

There is no doubt that Eichelberger's visit to see for himself exactly what the forward troops are doing, has had a great effect. He practically walked into Buna village. No one could deter him, tho' I gather a number of windy gentlemen tried to.[58]

Eichelberger's greatest contribution was that he brought a spirit of co-operation to the American forces, and he and Herring became firm friends.[59] Yet, for all his outstanding qualities, he could not bring about an instant change of heart, or increase the experience of his bewildered troops. Nor could he, any more than the Australians, provide a solution to the ever-deepening problem now facing the Allies.

The arrival of Eichelberger did not solve all the command problems. The frustrations of two weeks of fighting without success were now affecting the performances of the commanders in various ways. Brigadier Eather, whose 25th Brigade had been replaced on 3 December by the 21st Brigade, spent a few days at Herring's headquarters before flying back to Port Moresby. To his eyes the command situation was now a 'dog's breakfast'. Blamey was also worried about this matter and wrote to Herring: 'I am very worried over the mixture of tactical units which is continuing in the force. I think this is always a mistake . . . Once tactical unity is broken, it is very hard to re-

Above X Rowell with his BGS, Brigadier H. G. Rourke, and his DA & QMG, Brigadier J. R. Broadbent
Above XI Milne Bay on the road near Gilli Gilli
Below XII Forde,. MacArthur, Blamey and Kennedy, 2 October 1942

Left XIII MacArthur at Ower's Corner

Below XIV General Allen and Brigadier Eather discussing the attack on Ioribaiwa, 27 September 1942. On the right, Allen's ADC, Lt Fayle

establish'.[60] On the eve of battles on all fronts this was wise advice, for Blamey was not referring specifically to the Americans. Early in December Brigadier Porter, the commander of the 30th Brigade (39th, 49th and 55/53rd Battalions, all militia) had arrived at Soputa. Vasey decided to send the 39th Battalion to Gona, where with the 2/14 Battalion Dougherty was to push along the coast to Sanananda. This soon proved impracticable and next day Dougherty took over all of the Gona area. It was planned that after the attack by the III/126th on the 5 December, the remainder of the 30th Brigade would take over from the 16th Brigade. The official historian commented that 'There was more than a hint of bewildered desperation to these rapidly changing plans'.[61] Recent evidence reveals Vasey's attitude. He admitted to his wife that he had no idea that the Japanese 'could be as obstinate and stubborn as he has proved to be . . . the Jap is not playing to our rules'.[62] Some idea of Vasey's dilemma can be gauged from his reply to a battalion commander at Gona who complained of the heavy and unnecessary casualties. Vasey sent him a short note: 'Canberra must have news of a clean up and have it quick or we will both go by the boot'.[63]

Although units were disorganised, a new attack was imperative. On the morning of 2 December the Japanese landed between 400 and 500 men at the mouth of the Kumusi River, directly threatening the Gona area.[64] The Japanese had masses of reinforcements at Rabaul and if they could be landed at Buna and Sanananda the Allies would be in a very dangerous position.[65] With this in mind, on 4 December Vasey, Eichelberger, Herring and Willoughby from GHQ met at Brigadier Lloyd's 16th Brigade headquarters to discuss the attack of the III/126th.

Over at Warren Force Brigadier Hopkins and Colonel Martin were preparing for an attack using five Bren gun carriers. Their role was to gain positions from which flanking fire across the front of the advance would allow infantry to get close enough to assault. It was stressed that they were not to be used as tanks, yet to consider even using them at all was, wrote the official historian:

a prospect that could be justified only by a desperate need. That need was twofold: to adopt any expedient, however slender its chance of success, which might result in the prising of a hole through the Japanese casemates; to hearten the bewildered Americans whose first two weeks of warfare had been such a stunning shock to them.[66]

It was also a symptom of the need for haste. There was no time for consultation or suggestion from Advanced NGF to Blamey.[67] These Bren gun carriers had been sent to Buna on Blamey's orders. He had tried to send forward tanks and this had failed. He had attempted to persuade MacArthur to land a battalion in the Japanese midst and this had failed. The carriers were, therefore, a last resort.

Blamey was also faced with a rapidly dwindling reservoir of troops. He now had three Australian divisions in New Guinea (less one brigade).[68] Since July 1942 the army had been reduced by one division. With the drain of casualties and sickness in New Guinea, Blamey wrote to Curtin on 4 December that he now intended to reduce the army by a further division: one of those in Western Australia. As might have been expected his mind again turned to the return of the 9th Division from the Middle East. He wrote:

I had hoped that our strategical plans would have been crowned with complete and rapid success in the tactical field. It was completely successful strategically in as much as we brought an American Division on to Buna and an Australian Division on to Gona simultaneously. But in the tactical field after the magnificent advance through the most difficult area, the Owen Stanley Range, it is a very sorry story.

It has revealed the fact that the American troops cannot be classified as attack troops. They are definitely not equal to the Australian militia, and from the moment they met opposition sat down and have hardly gone forward a yard. The action, too, has revealed a very alarming state of weakness in their staff system and in their war psychology. General MacArthur has relieved the Divisional Commander and has called up General Eichelberger the Corps Commander, and sent him over to take charge. He informs me that he proposes to relieve both the regimental commanders, the equivalent of our brigade commanders, and five out of six of the battalion commanders; and this in the face of the enemy. I am afraid now that the bulk of the fighting will fall on our troops in spite of the greatly larger numbers of the 32nd U.S. Division.

The brigades that went over the mountain track are now so depleted that they are being withdrawn and I am utilising the only remaining AIF brigade in Port Moresby and a brigade of Militia, that has been intensively trained here, and I think we will pull it off all right.

The Americans say that the other division which they left in Australia is a much better one than the one they have here, but since they chose this as number one, I believe their view to be merely wishful thinking. I feel quite sure in my own mind that the American forces, which have been expanded even more rapidly than our own were in the first years of the war, will not attain any high standard of training or war spirit for very many months to come.

Blamey then went on to request the return of the 9th Division, and concluded:

The 6th and 7th Australian Divisions after the Buna operations are completed must have a prolonged rest out of action. They both have a very large number of reinforcements to absorb and a very large number of sick to return. This means that the defence of Papua will rest for a time mainly on Militia and American forces. My faith in the Militia is growing, but my faith in the Americans has sunk to zero. If the 9th Australian Division is not return-ed I fear very greatly that we will have to sit down for a very long time in this area in an endeavour to defend it mainly by keeping the Jap flotillas away by air action.[69]

This letter may have come as a considerable surprise to Curtin, for at the end of November he had written to MacArthur that 'as the campaign in New Guinea for recapture Gona and Buna now approaching successful conclusion, feel I should initiate action at once for recognition services outstanding officers to whom these results are due'.[70] This would have been an added spur to MacArthur — a reminder that others thought that he should have a rapid success.

On 5 December battle opened on three fronts. At Urbana, urged on personally by Eichelberger and Waldron, the troops edged forward. Waldron was wounded and Eichelberger made his own Chief of Staff, Brigadier-General C. E. Byers, the new commander of the 32nd Division. The battle continued, and eventually one platoon reached the sea. On the Sanananda track the Americans became disorganised. General Willoughby was there to observe and after the battle he interrogated an Australian observer who 'was very blunt regarding what he considered the Americans' lack of fighting qualities'.[71] At Warren Force disaster struck and all five carriers were destroyed. The infantry did not advance at all.

Herring's operation order for the 6 December emphasised the need to attack once more: 'The possibility of further landings cannot be excluded. The completion of operations must therefore be achieved with all speed consistent with the standard of training and endurance of troops'.[72] He stressed to Eichelberger, however, that after his efforts of the previous day he was not to run personal risks and that he was to keep his senior officers out of the front line.[73]

That day, Dougherty's force attacked at Gona, but without success. His troops west of Gona were becoming squeezed between the Japanese who were advancing from their landing at the mouth of the Kumusi, and the main defences at Gona. On the Sanananda front Porter's 30th Brigade began to relieve Lloyd's 16th, and on 7 December the 49th Battalion attacked, followed later by the 55/53rd. Both failed with heavy losses. Across the whole front there was now a temporary sense of bafflement. The militia of the 55/53rd Battalion had proved irresolute and the Americans, already exhausted, were not much better.[74] Herring decided to bring over the 36th Battalion, the last of the fresh militia battalions at Port Moresby, and the 2/7th Cavalry Regiment which had been trained in infantry tactics, but he was scraping the bottom of the barrel. Permission was finally given for the 127th Regiment to begin moving to Dobodura. Only the 2/1st Pioneer Battalion remained available in Port Moresby.

At Milne Bay, however, there were still considerable forces available. These consisted of the 7th and 17th Brigades, with the 18th Brigade divided between Goodenough Island, Wanigela and Milne Bay. MacArthur had already declared that he considered that at least two brigades should remain there in case the Japanese attempted another landing.[75] Blamey wished also to retain the 17th Brigade in reserve in case of a Japanese thrust towards Wau, or for use if it suddenly became possible to seize Lae or Salamaua. Inevitably Blamey's mind turned again to using the tested troops at Milne Bay. He was greatly concerned and upset by the destruction of the carriers at Buna.[76] Yet what more could he expect? Australian carriers had been similarly misused in Syria and had suffered a similar fate.[77] Again Blamey raised the question of naval co-operation. He wanted their aid to land troops east of Buna and to transport the tanks from Milne Bay to the battlefront. His frustration is shown in his letters to Herring and MacArthur on 8 December. To Herring he wrote: 'The Navy principle is now "Safety First" and they may not do it [land troops]. Can you imagine Nelson's reaction to a Navy that fears to go where the enemy goes regularly'.[78] Nevertheless Blamey decided to push on with his plan. This was to endeavour to land tanks in the rear of the 32nd Division to attack from the south, and to land a force by night east of Buna to operate in conjunction with the attack by the 32nd Division. He went ahead with preparations intending to use his small fleet of luggers and barges, but was able to move only 400 men — less than the full battalion which he felt was necessary. He wrote to MacArthur:

Unless the Navy is prepared to co-operate the risks are great owing to the reduced numbers that can be transported. It is somewhat difficult to understand the Navy attitude of non-co-operation because of risk. 'Safety First' as a Naval motto — Shades of Nelson![79]

While most of the front paused and the worried commanders cast around for another way of breaking the Japanese line, Dougherty at Gona was preparing for one final effort. His total force was now less than a full strength battalion. On 8 December he attacked and took heavy casualties, but the 39th Battalion fought into the centre of the Japanese position. The next day they attacked again and took the battered shell of a village. Early that morning Colonel Honner sent back his famous message, 'Gona's gone!'[80] The fighting was not yet over for it continued until 18 December against the Japanese who had landed at the mouth of the Kumusi on the night 1-2 December, and then against those who landed at the mouth of the Mambare River on 14 December, but the capture of Gona village was a significant boost to morale. MacArthur was delighted.

MacArthur's reactions must be measured against events not only within his own area, but also against events in the Solomons. On 30 November the Joint Chiefs of Staff had decided to send the 25th Division to Guadalcanal, and in early December the American Division began to relieve the 1st Marine Division. This build up of U.S. troops made it clear that they would soon have some success. The capture of Gona therefore gave MacArthur a victory, however slight, which he could use to let his masters know that he too was successful.

Blamey, too, was pleased with the capture of Gona, for to some degree it removed the danger to the Allied left flank, enabling the full Allied strength to be applied to the problems on the Buna front. This area was important not just because the Americans needed to be bolstered, but because the Japanese in the area posed a threat to the rapidly developing Allied airfield complex which was to be used as a springboard for later offensives and bombing attacks on Rabaul. The capture of Gona therefore eased the pressure on the commanders at all levels. It now remained for Blamey to maintain the initiative. If he could not do so little would have been achieved by the capture of Gona.

Unlike MacArthur, Blamey knew that exhortations to tired troops would not win the battle for Buna. Faced with the 'safety first' attitude of the navy, he was compelled to discard his plan to land troops on the hostile shore. The navy, however, agreed eventually to supply three corvettes to move the troops forward, and therefore on 9 December Blamey wrote to Herring:

These considerations have led me to the conclusion that if we are to attack with tanks from the South East, it must be a complete Australian operation and the proposals briefly are (i) to land the tanks somewhere near where the carriers were landed (ii) to bring the 2/9 Bn to the same area and to make a straight run through of it.[81]

Since this operation would be a combined operation with tanks and

Australian and American troops, Blamey realised that there should be one overall commander, and he decided that Brigadier Wootten should command it. He therefore asked Herring to secure Eichelberger's authority to place Warren Force under Wootten's command.

On 10 December Wootten flew to Popondetta to confer with Herring and then to Dobodura to see Eichelberger. Blamey made it quite clear to Herring that Wootten's force should be considered as a task force whose mission was to capture Buna.[82] In Herring's view the best method of achieving this was to employ Wootten's forces against the Buna mission as this was 'the vital ground'.[83] Blamey realised the importance of showing confidence in his subordinate, and told Herring that provided he kept Wootten's force together, the decision was up to him.[84]

Wootten and Hopkins, who was a former GSO1 of the 1st Armoured Division and a former Director of Armour, had by this time been able to carry out a reconnaissance of the Cape Endaiadere area, and they were convinced that this was the most suitable area to use tanks. On 12 December Herring informed Blamey that he had decided that the attack would be made in this area.[85] It was a sensible decision, for it would have been impossible to move the tanks through the swamps to the Urbana front. The command arrangements were also finalised, and it was agreed that Wootten should command Warren Force, which would consist of the 128th Regiment and his own 18th Brigade, and that he would be responsible to Eichelberger. Eichelberger's willingness to place his troops under Wootten's command indicates his determination to set aside national differences for the common good.

In the period since Eichelberger had assumed command, he had sought to instil fighting spirit into his soldiers, but he had also attempted to improve their physical comfort. This was now showing results, and Herring's confidence in them was rising. Hopkins visited Warren Force and spoke highly of its commander, Colonel Martin. On 10 December Herring wrote: 'Since [Eichelberger's] fellows have been cared for and properly fed, they have been a different show'.[86] The next day he wrote: 'I doubt whether any troops would do much better than they are doing at the moment. They are making a little progress each day, and are learning the tricks'.[87]

Blamey did not share Herring's confidence and his disappointment with the Americans continued. On 9 December he wrote to Shedden:

this [disappointment] has not abated although General Eichelberger has taken a real grip on the show there and with the relief of the 126 and 128 U.S. Regts by the 127 U.S. Regt, we will find a different spirit, I hope, if General Eichelberger can stay the distance.[88]

Two days later he wrote to Herring: 'I would be very sorry to do anything that would impair the good relations you have established with the Americans, but I doubt very much whether Buna will be captured if we rely on them to do it'.[89]

Perhaps Blamey was using the poor performance of the Americans as a weapon with which to counter MacArthur's constant, almost hysterical, demands for immediate success. Despite the continuing preparations for the attack with tanks, these demands did not abate. On 10 December Allied aircraft attacked a Japanese convoy approaching the north-west of New Guinea, forcing it to return to Rabaul. On 12 December the convoy set out again and the next day was spotted by Allied bombers before escaping in a thunderstorm. The effect on MacArthur was electric. He fired off a short one-paragraph letter to Eichelberger:

Time is fleeting and our dangers increase with its passage . . . remember that your mission is to take Buna. All other things are merely subsidiary to this . . . Hasten your preparations and when you are ready — strike, for as I have said, time is working desperately against us.[90]

MacArthur sent a copy of this letter to Blamey and pointed out that as the Allies were superior in numbers the infantry should be more active. In addition he was willing to provide a regiment of the 41st U.S. Division.[91]

The lack of activity across the Range was also worrying Blamey. On 11 December Herring had written to Blamey that he had directed his troops to 'go quietly, take out a post here and a post there each day if possible . . . maintaining pressure everywhere and break down [the enemy's] morale'.[92] Blamey had replied that he was afraid of this policy. 'We have a devilish determined enemy to deal with and delay is dangerous'.[93] Following MacArthur's letter of 13 December Blamey again tackled Herring on this question, for he saw no reason why Herring should not bypass the enemy and push on to the coast:

This is a question that General MacArthur has put to me this morning and on various occasions in the last few days, and I must admit that I can find no satisfactory answer. They were the tactics employed by Vasey most successfully in spite of the jungle and difficult country of the mountains.[94] It may be that General Vasey is over-wearied; he has had enough to cause this and if there is any sign of it you should let me know immediately. I am quite prepared to send up Allen again to replace him. Allen has had a spell and is quite fresh and fit. It would be a mistake to let Vasey wear himself out, there is still too much ahead of us.[95]

To the latter suggestion Herring felt that he 'preferred Vasey tired to Allen fresh'.[96]

MacArthur's urging of Eichelberger had an immediate effect. Troops of the 127th Regiment had begun to move into the Urbana area on 11 December, and on the 14th they attacked towards Buna village. Eichelberger and Byers were again with the forward troops and by nightfall the III/127th had captured the village. The government station and an area known as the 'Triangle' still remained in Japanese hands, but MacArthur's headquarters magnified this success into a decisive victory. The *New York Times* carried the headline, 'Allies Take Buna in New Guinea'.[97]

To the commanders in Port Moresby, however, the situation was still serious. That morning the Japanese landed some 800 men at the mouth of the Mambare River, between 30 and 50 miles north of Sanananda. Throughout December the intelligence summaries stressed the threat of Japanese landings.[98] The Allies were operating on a very limited supply system and were suffering considerable losses in men from both casualties and sickness, particularly malaria. Therefore, if the Japanese had been able to reinforce their area substantially, the situation might have become critical. Eichelberger later wrote to MacArthur:

As you know when I first went to the Urbana Force there were only two very thin battalions and about one company was all that could be prepared to canalise the coconut grove. If five hundred Japanese had come boiling out of that place they could have rolled up the American lines. I feel that our constant attacking deceived them concerning our real strength.[99]

In the month since the Allies had begun their final offensive to eliminate the Japanese in Papua, they had achieved two successes. At great cost they had captured the shattered villages of Gona and Buna. But the main Japanese defences remained secure. Four Australian Brigades and three American Regiments had been committed and all had suffered heavily.[1] The Allies could not afford to continue the advance at this slow rate. If Wootten's attack on 18 December proved expensive and, like so many others, achieved nothing, then MacArthur faced the unpalatable prospect that the Japanese might win this

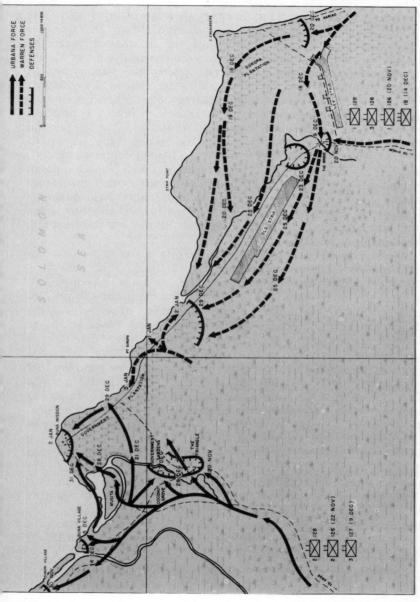

Map 10   The capture of Buna. From *Reports of General MacArthur*, Vol.1, p.94

battle of attrition, forcing him to either withdraw or throw in his last reserves. A great deal hinged on the attack by Wootten's 18th Brigade.

It is interesting to recall, at this stage, the difference between the commanders who were faced with purely military problems, and those who had to balance military worries against the interference of politicians and the insidious effects of public opinion, imagined or real. It is clear, from the voluminous correspondence between Blamey and Herring, that they were much more in each other's confidence than had been Blamey and Rowell in September. Blamey put the situation squarely to Herring, who understood fully what was required. They did not always agree. When Blamey expressed his continuing disappointment with the Americans his opinion was not based on personal observation, but it revealed the effect that the earlier taunts from the Americans had made on him. It also revealed the difficulty of achieving a balanced view of the tactical situation when other considerations are included. At least Blamey left the final tactical decisions to Herring.

Blamey's doubts were expressed to Herring in such a fashion that the latter could at least understand the friction at his superior's headquarters. MacArthur's reaction to the strain was less controlled. It is true that as he was in the highest position the strain was most intense but MacArthur did not display 'the quality of robustness, the ability to withstand the shocks of war', which Lord Wavell held to be 'the first essential of a general'.[2] Indeed, it is difficult to determine in what way he contributed positively to the campaign. His presence was necessary to co-ordinate the air and naval forces in the area, but that was only because he was unwilling to delegate that authority to a task force commander. Nevertheless, Rowell and Blamey had been able to work with the air and naval commanders before MacArthur arrived. Blamey would certainly have been in a difficult position in trying to relieve Harding, but since it was obvious that the 41st U.S. Division would eventually be sent to New Guinea, Eichelberger's Corps Headquarters would have been deployed and Eichelberger would have been in a position to either guide or relieve Harding. MacArthur allowed his decisions to be biased by his personal fears, thus placing his subordinates under increased strain. As will be expounded in the next chapter, the trials of battle were providing sufficient distress for the commanders over the Range without the additional burden of MacArthur's urging.

11
Victory at Buna, Gona and Sanananda, 16 December 1942 – 22 January 1943

The second month of the Buna-Gona-Sanananda campaign began well for the Allies. The commanders could be excused if they believed that the immense pressure imposed by the impatience of GHQ and the intractability of the tactical situation was now about to ease. The events of the first month had, however, made a deep impression on the psychological well-being of the commanders. All began to show signs of anxiety. It was a time for sympathy and tact, attributes displayed unexpectedly by Blamey, but not by MacArthur and his staff.

On 11 December, in preparation for a decisive attack, General Herring moved his Advanced Headquarters New Guinea Force from Popondetta to Dobodura where the airfields were rapidly developing. Eichelberger had just moved his own headquarters forward from Dobodura, and after General Byers was wounded on the 16th, Eichelberger assumed direct command of the 32nd Division. Shortly after he and his staff had arrived on the north coast, Eichelberger had placed the administration of the U.S. Division in the hands of his own corps supply officer, Colonel G. De Graaf. Then soon afterwards, recognising efficiency, and being without his own DA & QMG, Herring placed De Graaf in charge of the corps administration.[1] Eventually, Colonel S. F. Legge, who had been on the administrative staff of Landops and then of New Guinea Force since late November, arrived to assume duties as the senior AQ officer.[2] Following the establishment of Herring's headquarters at Dobodura, construction began on a road from Oro Bay to Dobodura, and, in anticipation of an early victory, the vast base which was to be the springboard for the Allied offensive began to be developed.

Meanwhile the preparations for Brigadier Wootten's attack continued. On 16 December the 2/9th Battalion and the tanks were ready, and the next day Wootten took over Warren Force. On 18 December both Urbana and Warren Forces, and the 30th Brigade on the Sanananda track, attacked with vigour. The Urbana attack failed with heavy casualties in a battle which continued until 20 December. Eichelberger was again with the attacking troops. Wootten's troops, although taking casualties, pushed on with significant success and by 22 December they had closed up to the Simeni Creek. Herring wrote to Blamey on the evening of 18 December that the 2/9th and the tanks had 'fought magnificently'.[3] The next day he again wrote to Blamey:

Wootten handled his force very well yesterday . . . The outstanding factors in the [operations] so far are I think three. The first is Wootten's leadership, the second the value of the tanks for which we have to thank you and the third the capacity of seasoned AIF troops.[4]

The achievements of the 18th Brigade compared most favourably with the faltering efforts by Vasey's troops on the Sanananda front, where the attack of the 49th Battalion brought some success, but the 55/53rd failed. On 19 December the 2/7th Cavalry Regiment attacked from an area known as Huggins Roadblock and formed yet another roadblock, but gained little else.[5] Brigadier Dougherty with the headquarters of the 21st Brigade now commanding the Americans, the 39th Battalion and the 2/7th Regiment in the roadblock area, was ordered not to attempt any further large-scale operations. In the 30th Brigade area the 36th Battalion attacked on 21 December but had little to show.

It is doubtful whether any other troops could have done much better in the circumstances, but the sensitivity of the commanders to implied criticism can be gauged from their reactions. Brigadier Porter was bitterly critical of the militia and these criticisms were reflected at all levels. The Commanding Officer of the 36th Battalion, Lieutenant-Colonel O. C. Isaachsen, wrote that a number of men had never thrown a grenade before going into action, and were therefore nervous of handling them.[6] Brigadier Porter wrote:

What success these units achieve or may achieve is due to a percentage of personnel who are brave in the extreme; and, is the result of unskilful aggression. Unfortunately, the latter personnel have almost been exterminated in 55/53 Bn and are likely to be exterminated in 36 Bn.[7]

Vasey's frustration can be gauged by his comments in a letter to his wife on 18 December:

I became browned off with Ned [Herring] the other day: but was sorry afterwards. He is very pleasant and means well: but just doesn't understand lots of what is going on and having Hoppy as offsider doesn't help. The trouble with them is they will keep on telling me *how* to do my job. If they would only give me the resources I know how to do it.[8]

The next day, 'without being alarmist', Vasey listed for Herring problems experienced in his division, indicating a deep concern for the well-being of his soldiers. His requests ranged from rations with the 'greatest possible variety' to mail, 'authentic world news', canteen stores and increased medical supplies.[9]

Vasey's major worry, however, was his lack of numbers and the poor training of the militia. On 24 December he wrote to Herring that in one battalion seven members were under arrest on charges of cowardice. He continued:

My experience of the past two months convinces me that for success in jungle warfare, such as is taking place in the Sanananda-Soputa area, the first requisites for success in either attack or defence are high morale, a high standard of training, both individual and collective, and, for successful offensive action, superiority of numbers is also necessary. I regret to have to report that none of these conditions is present in my command.[10]

The result of the failures on Vasey's front was that Herring asked Blamey for the 17th Brigade,[11] but Blamey was 'loathe to commit this'.[12] The request, however, probably convinced Blamey that when the first troops of the 41st U.S. Division became available, they should be sent to Vasey's area.

After his initial success Wootten paused, gathering his strength and preparing for a final blow. Already he had begun to feel the pressure for quick results which had affected his predecessors. He knew that MacArthur was urging Eichelberger forward and was anxious lest Blamey thought that with tanks and five battalions under his command he was going too slowly. His main worry, however, was that he did not believe that he could rely on the three American battalions for offensive action.[13] He need not have worried about Blamey's reaction, for although Blamey had expected an early victory at the beginning of the offensive,[14] he was at last taking a realistic view of the difficulty of the operations. In a letter to Shedden on 19 December, he indicated that he expected the campaign to absorb all available resources 'both Australian and American, for many months to come'.[15]

In Urbana Force Eichelberger continued to urge his troops, and they pushed their way between the Japanese defences, but by 24

December they had been held up. Caught between Wootten's successes and MacArthur's demands, Eichelberger was beginning to feel the burden of command. The next day he wrote to MacArthur: 'I think that the all time low of my life occurred yesterday. We had seven line companies available. I had given five of them to Grose to make the attack . . . [He] took counsel of his fears and . . . delayed the advance'.[16]

During the preceding month the pressure on all commanders had been extreme. The constant exhortations from MacArthur, who knew that his own career was balanced on a knife's edge, placed the division commanders in a position where they were forced to accept heavy casualties yet achieve little. Blamey also must have been feeling the frustration of the situation. His task was immense for he was now commanding a number of organisations. He continued as Commander-in-Chief of the AMF, and was therefore responsible for the Australian Army not only in New Guinea, but in Australia and the Middle East where Morshead's 9th Division had just fought a gruelling battle at El Alamein. He was also commander of the Allied Land Forces, as well as commander of New Guinea Force. He tried to maintain the facade that Herring was commander of New Guinea Force, but there is no doubt that MacArthur considered Blamey to be its commander.[17]

Blamey was worried by the necessity to return to Australia to help resolve the mounting administrative problems of the AMF. Indeed on 26 November the Signals Officer-in-Chief, Major-General C. H. Simpson, had written to Blamey asking him to return as 'your presence would be a most important factor in the control and the increasing enthusiasm of the force in Australia. I feel that your drive and personality is required to co-ordinate and stimulate the interest and enthusiasm of all HQ, both base and field'.[18] Yet with MacArthur in New Guinea it was quite impracticable for Blamey to return to Australia, especially since Herring at Dobodura was in no position to control all of New Guinea Force. To ease the burden on Blamey, however, on 11 December Major-General Frank Berryman, the DCGS from Landops in Brisbane, arrived in Port Moresby to assist the Commander-in-Chief.[19]

Blamey thrived on these increased demands, but Herring was finding the job increasingly tiring. He had not had any long period of leave since the beginning of the war and after returning from the Middle East he had gone immediately to Darwin. A quiet, sensitive man, he was faced daily with mounting casualties. His relations with Vasey were always amicable, but Vasey was a professional who believed that the amateur soldier did not grasp fully the magnitude of his problems. Referring to his letter to Herring of 24 December,[20] Vasey wrote to his wife that Herring 'professes to realise what I am saying: but whether he really does or not I am not sure. I am at least certain that those further back do not and it is his business to see that they do'.[21] The presence of Brigadier Hopkins did not help. In his own words, 'It was never easy to discuss detail with Gen Vasey'.[22] The feeling was mutual. On 10 December Vasey wrote to his wife: 'Ned is up this way now — he has been for some time and he has Hoppy with him unfortunately. I'm afraid I dislike him more than ever'.[23]

These, and a multitude of supply problems, were having an effect on Herring. Bad weather, either at Port Moresby, Dobodura, or more pertinently, over the Owen Stanley Range, cut supply deliveries. Brigadier J. R. Broadbent in Port Moresby was bearing the brunt of the supply problems and Hopkins thought that he was doing 'a marvellous job — solid as a rock',[24] but a couple of consecutive days of bad weather would place the force in a parlous position. Hopkins has written that 'for months after the campaign, my waking thought was, "will they fly today?" '[25]

On 24 December Broadbent visited Dobodura and on returning reported to Blamey that he thought Herring was becoming tired. It was decided, therefore, that Herring would return to Port Moresby for Christmas dinner the following day. After dinner Herring and Blamey talked, and late in the evening Blamey called in Berryman and said that he was very perturbed about Herring's mental state. Broadbent had not overstated it at all. Herring said that he was worried about Vasey, but when offered Allen as a replacement he would not hear of it.

As a result of this discussion it was decided that Berryman would accompany Herring when he returned to Dobodura the following morning, and that Hopkins would return to Port Moresby to act as Blamey's chief of staff.[26] It was agreed that Blamey would attempt to prevent MacArthur from sending orders directly to Eichelberger and that brigades would not be allowed to attack until they were completely ready. Vasey was delighted with this new arrangement and wrote happily to his wife:

I'm not sure that Hoppy has not met the fate he deserves. For some little time now friend Berry has been over this way with Albert: but yesterday he replaced H [Hopkins] with B [Berryman]. There can be no question of B replacing [Herring]: but this may forecast a change. If it does it is not before time.[27]

This move was more than just a matter of personalities to Blamey. He knew that the strain of command was showing amongst the senior officers over the Range. By sending over the capable and vital Berryman, he injected new life into the team without offending sensibilities and pride. More than most, Blamey was always aware of the nerve-stretching effect of command in war.[28]

Berryman's request to try to prevent MacArthur from short-circuiting the chain of command can be well understood. Despite reports from his staff officers, MacArthur had no concept of conditions around Buna. Later, after the fighting had concluded, MacArthur told Eichelberger, 'I could have led them into Buna, Bob'. Eichelberger had replied: 'You may have been able to lead them, General, but you must remember that in most instances not over half a dozen men could have seen you at the time in that dense jungle'. From this and other comments, Eichelberger concluded that MacArthur 'still visualised a two-mile American front instead of little isolated high-ground projections that led towards the Japanese lines and which limited the American advance to various narrow places and few of these'.[29]

MacArthur's lack of appreciation of conditions at the battlefront is epitomised in his letter to Eichelberger on Christmas Day, when he urged Eichelberger to attack in thousands, not hundreds: 'You have probably eight or nine times the strength of the enemy . . . I feel convinced that our time is strictly limited and that if results are not achieved shortly, the whole picture may radically change'.[30] Eichelberger replied that he was willing to lay down his own life to achieve a victory.[31] He also added a few notes on his relations with the Australians:

My relations with General Herring have been most happy and I am inclined to think that his criticisms of the American troops might not have been as strong as General Blamey might indicate . . . You have been very patient but I hope you will not let any Australian generals talk down their nose at you. When these [American] troops have been chased by the Japanese as often as the Australians they will be just as good and I think perhaps better.[32]

The next day he continued in the same vein, cautioning MacArthur not to let the Australians 'spring the numerical strength of my forces on you', as he had a long L of C and many men in hospital.[33]

This correspondence throws into relief the problem of the chain of command. MacArthur had asked Eichelberger to write frequent reports which were not to go through the Australian High Command. Eichelberger did this, but he informed Herring. However, when

Above XV On the road from Buna to Sanananda
Below XVI Blamey at Wanigela with Brigadier-General J. Hannaford MacNider, 32nd
US Division, Major N. Carlyon, MA to C-in-C and Lieut-General J. G. Dobbs, CO of
2/10th Battalion

Above XVII HQ 7th Australian Division, Soputa
Below XVIII Blamey and Lt-General R. L. Eichelberger at Buna. Blamey said that 'a miracle had been performed'

Eichelberger wrote directly to Kenney, for example to complain about U.S. planes bombing Americans, the letters were usually ignored.[34] The historian of the 32nd Division, E. T. Lauer, was particularly bitter about the problem of command, which he saw as threefold, the interference of senior commanders and sometimes their staff officers in the operations of units several echelons below them, the international character of the chain of command, and the mixing of combat units. He concluded that the factors causing this were:

The constant pressure of, first the situation as it existed, and second, of General MacArthur himself. When there was failure, these pressures resulted in senior officers jumping in directly in an attempt to get results. Similarly, expedience, rather than logical organisation for combat, dictated the assignment of units to tasks.[35]

Before returning to Dobodura on 26 December Herring called on MacArthur whom he found greatly disturbed. He told Herring: 'This situation is becoming very serious. If we can't clear this up quickly I'll be finished and so will your General Blamey'.[36] Herring replied that he was very pleased with the effort of the 18th Brigade, and MacArthur then informed him that he could expect that the first regiment of the 41st U.S. Division would be made available to General Vasey. Blamey was therefore very surprised when during the afternoon of 27 December General Sutherland told him that the first regiment of the 41st Division (163rd) was to be sent to Eichelberger's command. Perhaps MacArthur had taken notice of Eichelberger's caution not to let the Australians spring the 'numbers game' on him.

Blamey wrote immediately to MacArthur pointing out that Wootten had not yet committed all of his forces, but was expected to do so shortly and would be successful. Furthermore, the 127th Regiment on the Urbana front was relatively fresh and fighting in an area no wider than 500 yards. On the other hand one of Vasey's battalions had an effective strength of 55 (2/27th Battalion) and another 89 (2/16th), and both were having their second tour of duty in operations in New Guinea. Blamey obviously felt that this was a matter of principle and that he was now strong enough to stand up to MacArthur. He continued:

I regret still more that you should have personally taken control of a single phase of the action. I certainly agreed to General Sutherland going forward to assist General Eichelberger in planning action on his front, but I thought I made it clear that I did not concur in the command of the action being taken out of my hands as is being done if the details of units to be utilised is removed from my control . . . With the greatest respect I would urge for your consideration that this alteration of plan will profoundly disturb [Herring's] confidence and upset his arrangements. General Herring is responsible for the whole front and I regret exceedingly that he should be placed in the position of doubt and uncertainty as to the troops that will be available to him, and as to which authority he may exercise over them.

I do not for one moment question the right of the Commander-in-Chief to give such orders as he may think fit, but I believe that nothing is more contrary to sound principles of command than that the Commander-in-Chief or the Commander, Allied Land Forces, should take over the personal direction of portion of the battle. This can only result in disturbing the confidence of the inferior commanders.[37]

Just as Rowell had protected Clowes from interference from MacArthur, so now Blamey attempted to protect Herring. Yet when MacArthur had sent his strong signals from Brisbane criticising Allen on the Kokoda Trail, Blamey had not objected. This illustrates how closely a commander's performance is tied to what he perceives is the strength of his position, and indeed the strength of his rival's position.

MacArthur did not agree with Blamey. He felt that the Buna area was the most important and when it was cleared 'the Sanananda sector will present no difficulties and can be rapidly rolled up'. He believed that the Japanese force at Sanananda was less than that imagined by the local commanders.[38] He concluded:

I do not for a moment agree with your view that I am unduly interfering with the local details of the operation. I am in no way attempting to control tactical execution on the front but am merely strategically advising as to where I believe it would be wise to exert the main effort of the ground forces. I think you will realise from your own long experience that no Commander-in-Chief, present on the field of operations as I am, could have given greater latitude to you or expressed both by word and deed greater confidence in the commanders involved. Complete cordiality, understanding and goodwill have prevailed between us up to the present and I cannot but hope that this condition, so essential to success, will be maintained. You have mistaken my advice as an arbitrary order. Since my assumption of this command, and throughout its duration, any order that I issue has been and will be in written form. My verbal discussions are advisory only.[39]

It will be recalled that when Blamey had gone to Milne Bay on 25 September he had advised Clowes to send troops to Wanigela.[40] Blamey had been adamant that it had been advice only and not an order. He now found himself in the same position as Rowell. Nevertheless he chose to ignore the implied threats of MacArthur's letter, and accepted it at face value. He wrote and informed Herring that there had been 'a keen difference of opinion between' him and MacArthur. 'However, all ended well and Colonel Doe [Commander of the 163rd Regiment] will now go to you', for use in Vasey's area.[41] No more was heard from MacArthur on the subject. His comments to Herring two days before indicate he viewed his position as precarious. In the event he did not overrule Blamey.

Meanwhile, Eichelberger's forces continued the battle. By the evening of 27 December he 'was thoroughly alarmed',[42] and Sutherland said later that after the fiasco of the day's attack, Eichelberger was 'never closer to being relieved'.[43] The next day Eichelberger pressed his attack. Warren Force, which had trapped the enemy at Giropa Point, also attacked on 28 December, but was repulsed with heavy casualties. Wootten paused to bring up the 2/12th Battalion and Herring suggested to Eichelberger, who was upset that he was not to receive the 163rd Regiment which MacArthur had promised,[44] that he too should pause to reorganise. Eichelberger was 'surer than hell' that he was going to reorganise,[45] but since the suggestion had come from Herring he suspected that the Australians were trying to reach Buna before him.[46] Furthermore, he was aggrieved at not receiving the 163rd Regiment.[47] The result of this was that Eichelberger ordered another assault, which like the previous ones proved abortive.

Wootten's next assault was planned for 1 January 1943 and Eichelberger ordered a full-scale drive by Urbana Force to coincide with it. Both went in as planned, although Wootten's was more successful. By the evening of 2 January the enemy had been crushed. Thirteen hundred bodies were found and buried, while others lay undiscovered in the jungle, and a few Japanese escaped along the coast to Sanananda. Since 16 November, in the Buna area, the Allies had sustained 2,870 battle casualties, 913 of them Australian.[48]

The fighting on the beachhead was not, of course, over, but MacArthur hailed the capture of Buna as a great victory — he needed a great victory. To onlookers around the world it appeared as though the campaign was at an end. The U.S. Secretary of War, Stimson, wrote to MacArthur: ' . . . it is a tremendous satisfaction to feel that the American fortunes in SWPA are in such skilful hands'.[49] Curtin wrote a similar letter. MacArthur's true feelings were revealed in his reply to General Marshall's message of congratulations: 'However unwarranted it may be, the impression prevailed that this area's efforts were belittled and disparaged at home, and despite all my efforts to the contrary the effect was depressing'.[50] The capture of Buna was a

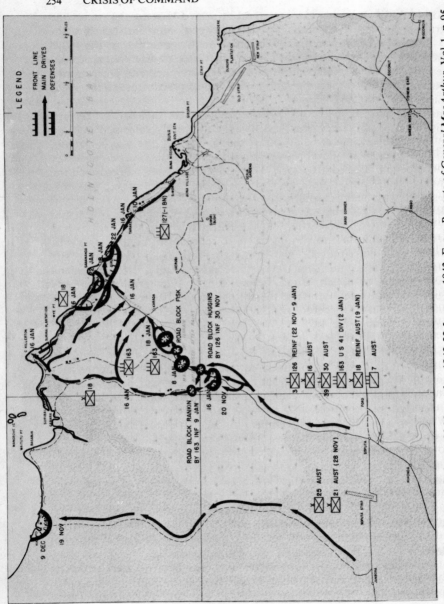

Map 11 The Sanananda front, 22 November 1942-22 January 1943. From *Reports of General MacArthur*, Vol.1, p.95.

considerable achievement and Blamey and Herring sent their congratulations to Eichelberger, but there was no word from MacArthur.

Blamey's decision to resist MacArthur's intention to send the 163rd Regiment to Buna was proved fully justified, but MacArthur's attempts to influence the battle cost valuable lives. Feeling that Sutherland was looking over his shoulder to report to MacArthur, Eichelberger had thrown his troops into ill-prepared attacks. In this instance the interruption to the chain of command did not prove disastrous, but for many soldiers it proved fatal.

The last Japanese bastion remained and the troops and commanders on the north coast were under no illusion as to the difficulty of the task. But in the planning for the new attack, the presence of Berryman at the Corps Headquarters was now being felt. He was a forceful, tough staff officer who was never at a loss for an idea. Juniors found him cold and sarcastic, but because of his decisiveness they always knew exactly what was required. Major T. Grahamslaw of ANGAU, who arrived at Advanced HQ NGF at Dobodura at this time was impressed by Berryman whom he found 'expected 100 per cent efficiency and saw to it that he got it. Officers who didn't measure up were summarily "bowler hatted" '.[51] At the end of December Berryman summed up the situation: 'We have air superiority, and are superior in numbers, guns, mortars and tanks. The problem is to use them to the best effect in the jungle'.[52]

Herring's plan was for Eichelberger's force to push along the coast towards Sanananda, while the 7th Division, consisting of the 14th, 18th and 30th Brigades and the 163rd Regiment, advanced along the Sanananda track towards Sanananda and Cape Killerton. On 4 January Herring conferred with Eichelberger, Vasey, Berryman and Wootten and issued his orders for the attack.[53] The details, however, were to take a number of days to work out. The 163rd Regiment had to relieve the HQ of the 21st Brigade, the 2/7 Regiment and the 39th and 49th Battalions in the roadblock area. The 2/7th, 39th and 49th had to relieve the 36th, 55/53rd, and I/126th to reform the 30th Brigade. The 36th and 55/53rd then became the 14th Brigade and moved to Gona to protect the left flank, while the I/126th, which had been almost wiped out, left the battle area. The 18th Brigade and the tanks were brought over from Buna, and these were to form the spearhead of the attack planned for 12 January. MacArthur impressed on Blamey that the attack had to be initiated swiftly because the air transport was 'rapidly deteriorating', and the Japanese were preventing the establishment of airfields at Dobodura,[54] but the major reorganisation took time and Herring was determined that the attack would be well conducted.

If the commanders on the north coast were worried about the approaching battles, those in Moresby now believed, or at least appeared to believe, that the fighting was almost over. On 3 January Blamey wrote to General Northcott and outlined his plans for the recuperation and training of the 6th and 7th Divisions on the Atherton Tableland. He concluded that he expected to return to Australia soon, and 'I do not think this will be very long delayed as we have narrowed the Jap down to a very small area on which we can concentrate our aerial bombing and our artillery fire'.[55] At this stage Blamey had not visited the battlefront, and it is not known whether he changed his opinion after doing so.

On 5 and 6 January Blamey visited the Buna and Sanananda battlefields. Eichelberger found him 'very cordial and full of praise for everything that was done',[56] and Blamey said that 'a miracle had been performed'.[57] Blamey's visit to the Sanananda area caused Vasey to have some worries about the C-in-C's safety.[58] There was no doubting Blamey's courage, but one wonders why he had not visited the forward area earlier. The reason was perhaps that he did not want to put MacArthur in an awkward position. Blamey's PA (Personal Assistant) Colonel D. H. Dwyer has written that Blamey regularly asked MacArthur to accompany him to Buna. 'For some reason which had nothing to do with MacArthur's unquestionable courage . . . he delayed visiting the Buna area'.[59]

MacArthur did not visit the battlefront at any time during the fighting, although in later years he attempted to create the impression that he had been there. Eichelberger was also disgruntled that General Kenney, whose aircraft had often bombed American troops, at no time got 'into one of his many airplanes' and flew the 40 minutes to Buna.[60] On the other hand Sutherland visited Eichelberger on a number of occasions. Eichelberger was bitter about the lack of visits from other senior officers and was very disappointed that MacArthur had not congratulated him on his victory — a victory which MacArthur was using with considerable propaganda effect. Finally, on 8 January, perhaps at the instigation of Blamey,[61] MacArthur wrote to Eichelberger:

I am returning to GHQ, Brisbane Saturday morning, the 9th, so will not see you until some later time. I have been wanting to personally congratulate you on the success that has been achieved. As soon as Fuller[62] takes hold, I want you to return to the mainland. There are many important things with reference to rehabilitation and training that will necessitate your immediate effort. The 32nd Division should be evacuated as soon as possible so that it can be rejuvenated.

I am so glad that you were not injured in the fighting. I always feared that your incessant exposure might result fatally.

With a hearty slap on the back.[63]

MacArthur's decision to return to Australia was motivated by a number of factors. His main headquarters remained in Brisbane and he wanted to supervise the preparation of plans for continuing the offensive. Furthermore, petty as it may seem, there were a number of senior staff officers on MacArthur's HQ who were anxious to return to Brisbane for personal reasons.[64] MacArthur was, however, keen to reorganise his command, and he asked that General Walter Krueger and the headquarters of an army be sent from America to take command of the American forces.[65] He was determined that in any further offensive American troops would not be commanded by an Australian. Another reason why MacArthur wanted to return to Australia was to demonstrate that the fighting was no longer a cause for concern, and to ensure that the Joint Chiefs of Staff realised that he had obtained his victory while the troops on Guadalcanal were still preparing for their final offensive.

Having decided to return to Australia, MacArthur told Blamey that he need not delay his return beyond what he considered necessary,[66] but it is probable that he expected Blamey to remain in New Guinea for some time.[67] As may be expected, however, Blamey had no intention of allowing MacArthur to confer with Curtin without being able to present his own point of view.[68] He had no desire to remain in command of New Guinea Force, and in view of the arrival of more American troops in Australia, abdicate as Commander, Allied Land Forces. Furthermore, there was a large number of policy matters concerning the Australian Army which had accumulated over the previous three or four months. The organisation of the Australian Army was also creating a number of problems. The 6th and 7th Divisions were now almost exhausted, and Blamey planned for them to rest and retrain on the Atherton Tableland in north Queensland. The 32nd Division would also be withdrawn and the 41st U.S. Division under Major-General H. H. Fuller would take over at Sanananda.

The Japanese defeats and the impending arrival of the 9th Australian Division in Australia from the Middle East meant that more militia brigades could be sent to New Guinea. General Milford and his 5th Division, consisting of the 7th and 29th Brigades, would therefore be responsible for Milne Bay.[69] On 8 January Blamey explained these changes to Herring and informed him that, 'You will continue in command of the whole of New Guinea Force'. Blamey attempted to maintain the charade that Herring had always been in command of the Force, but this was in line with his attempts to ensure that he maintained his position as Commander, Allied Land Forces. With the impending return of the HQ 6th Division to Australia, HQ Milne Force, now called 11th Division, moved to Port Moresby, and because of Clowes's continued absence, caused by malaria, Allen assumed command.[70] With the news that the Japanese were landing troops at Lae and Salamaua, perhaps with the idea of advancing on Wau, Blamey moved the 17th Brigade from Milne Bay to Port Moresby. He continued in his letter to Herring that:

If the enemy is not particularly aggressive and we don't decide immediately on the move to Wau, you might like to leave General Allen here for a while, while you take leave. On the other hand you might consider it desirable to remain for a month or so before you do. In that case I can quite easily arrange for your relief.
I feel rather disposed to leave Berryman with you, for a time at least, unless you prefer to retain Hopkins. But if Allen is to hold the fort while you take leave, I definitely prefer that Berryman should remain. He has worked well with Allen before and knows him well.[71]

The next day Blamey elaborated on these plans. He explained to Herring that he had decided to send the first battalion of Brigadier Moten's 17th Brigade to Wau and concluded:

I am now under urgent pressure to return to Australia and would like to do so as soon as you feel able to come back here. I suggest the possibility of handing over to Eichelberger, as Corps Commander, and leaving Berryman with him. You could then come back and take over control here with Brig Hopkins to help.[72]

While Herring agreed to these plans,[73] he objected strongly to MacArthur's statement that the situation on the Sanananda track was merely 'mopping up'. The GHQ communique of 8 January said: 'One of the primary objects of the campaign was the annihilation of the Japanese Papuan army . . . This can now be regarded as accomplished'.[74] Eichelberger wrote that Herring 'was furious and said that he and I were the goats'.[75] Nevertheless Herring was, no doubt, pleased to return to Port Moresby. He appeared unwell and was becoming very 'nervy', and estimated that it would take about four months to gain a victory over the Japanese.[76] Eichelberger wrote later that the Australian commanders at Sanananda were pessimistic about chances of an early victory and 'many of them foresaw, as a result of optimistic reports released to the press, the ruin of their own careers — and mine. Sanananda would not be easy'.[77]

Eichelberger's last prediction was soon proved correct, although his assumption of command of the corps was very smooth, and he wrote to MacArthur, 'I have no complaint concerning the Australians. They have seemed willing to extend the hand of friendship'.[78] Planning for Vasey's offensive had continued through this period, and on 12 January, the day that Herring returned to Port Moresby, the attack went in. Three tanks were knocked out and the attacking battalions took heavy casualties with nothing to show.[79] Vasey was bitterly disappointed, and in the afternoon discussed the situation with Wootten, whose troops had been repulsed. They decided that to attack again under the existing conditions would lead only to very heavy casualties, and Vasey directed Wootten to continue aggressive patrolling.[80]

That evening (2000 hours) Vasey rang Berryman and asked if Eichelberger could visit his HQ,[81] and at midday on 13 January Eichelberger and Berryman arrived at Vasey's HQ and discussed the situation. Vasey explained that his force consisted of the 18th Brigade and the 163rd Regiment which had no battle experience. The 30th Brigade consisted of two battalions, each of about 110 all ranks, and the 2/7 Cavalry had 210 all ranks and was sick and tired. Vasey concluded that: 'To attack [the enemy] with infantry using their own weapons is repeating the costly mistakes of 1915-17 and, in view of the limited resources which can be, at present, put into the field in this area, such attacks seem unlikely to succeed'. Vasey therefore wanted to by-pass the Japanese and push on to the coast, or to land additional troops on the coast, although he knew that he did not have the resources to carry out such a plan.[82] On the other hand Berryman wanted to blockade the Japanese, pound them with artillery and starve them out. Eichelberger tentatively accepted this plan, but ordered further reconnaissance and decided to wait until 15 January for the results of this.

That evening Eichelberger wrote to Herring (Blamey had returned to Australia that day), that Generals Vasey and Berryman and Brigadier Wootten agreed that further all-out attacks on the Japanese area would be abortive. He wrote that: 'The best plan would seem to be to surround the area and cut off all supplies, accompanied by plenty of mortar fire and constant harassing'.[83] On 14 January Vasey wrote to Herring with his assessment of the situation: 'Doubtless you have heard of the lack of success of the attack of 18 Aust Inf Bde on

12 Jan and also of my interview with Eichelberger and Berryman yesterday'. He went on to explain that he did not agree with Eichelberger's policy, but assured Herring that he would 'carry out these instructions to the best of my ability and there is no question of quibbling or querying orders'.[84]

Herring was upset at the news that the Japanese enclave was not to be attacked again, and he prepared to fly back across the Range to urge another attack.[85] In the meantime, he sent Eichelberger a signal to this effect. Eichelberger replied, 'Tomorrow I hope to have really good news for you because you certainly deserve a break'.[86] It is probable that by this time Eichelberger had received a telephone call from Vasey, for at 2 o'clock that afternoon Vasey rang with startling news — in his own words, 'the bugger's gone'.[87] Vasey's depression had left him, for a prisoner had reported that the Japanese were withdrawing, and Wootten's patrols were already confirming this.

The withdrawal was the result of a decision made in Tokyo on 4 January that the troops in Guadalcanal and Papua should be withdrawn and a new defence line established through Lae and Salamaua. On 13 January the local commander at Sanananda, General Yamagata, was ordered to move towards the mouths of the Kumusi and the Mambare and then towards Salamaua and Lae. Before receiving these orders, however, the Japanese had already begun to withdraw.

Vasey acted immediately, sending Wootten in pursuit, and ordering Doe's 163rd Regiment to attack. Wootten pushed his troops forward with great confidence and dash, but the 163rd found the Japanese very stubborn.[88] On 16 January Vasey wrote that he was 'not convinced that [the Americans] are quite as aggressive when it comes to close work as is necessary to finish the Japs'.[89] The next day they gained no ground, and on 18 January Vasey discussed the 'lack of offensive spirit' of the 163rd with Eichelberger,[90] but after inspecting Doe's troops in the forward pits, they agreed that Doe was acting aggressively.

The back of the Japanese defences had now been broken, and scattered groups, totalling possibly 1,000, made their way north along the coast and through the jungle towards Salamaua. Between 13 and 20 January about 1,200 sick and wounded escaped by barge. By midday 22 January the last Japanese resistance ceased.

The Buna-Gona-Sanananda campaign was dominated throughout by MacArthur's constant exhortations for more speed. This attitude was brought about by a number of factors. One of these was that MacArthur was under considerable personal pressure. In North Africa

Eisenhower was continuing his success,[91] and on Guadalcanal Halsey was slowly gaining control. If MacArthur were to suffer a defeat, then he could not expect to continue as Commander-in-Chief of the South-West Pacific Area, and indeed Sutherland told Kenney that 'if anything went wrong, General MacArthur would be sent home'.[92]

The events in the Owen Stanley Range had a detrimental effect on the shape of the operations on the north coast. The lesson of Eora Creek, that the Japanese were tenacious in defence, was not learnt by MacArthur. Rather he took a simple view of the battle; that the ponderous Allen had been replaced by the dashing Vasey and that this had brought immediate results.[93] Furthermore, Vasey's outstanding success at Oivi seemed to indicate three facts; that victory over the Japanese could be obtained using infantry alone, without great amounts of supporting arms, that the Japanese would leave their defences if their L of C were cut, and that outstanding leadership could make up for lack of support and supplies. Allen had vehemently denied the truth of these views, but he was conveniently disregarded.

When the offensive began on 16 November the Allies knew very little about the Japanese defences, but they were right in their appreciation that the Japanese would land reinforcements. There was, therefore, justification in pushing on rapidly in an attempt to clear the area of Japanese. When the attacks of 19 November were repulsed it became obvious that the Japanese were going to hang on grimly to their foothold in Papua. Surely this was the time for a reappraisal of the tactics to be employed in the area.

What was obvious from the beginning was that the offensive had been initiated with a very slender line of communication to each division. This was demonstrated when Harding's 'Lilliput' fleet was attacked by Zeroes on 16 November.[94] The result was that insufficient artillery and ammunition could be assembled to support adequately the assaults on all fronts. Furthermore the artillery was too light to damage the Japanese bunkers effectively.

MacArthur's reaction to the repulses was to urge his troops forward with orders like, 'Take Buna today at all cost'. The consequence was heavy casualties.[95] MacArthur's reason for such orders was that his forces were running out of time. The Allies were rapidly using their reserves of troops and the effects of casualties and sickness, particularly malaria, were reducing the numbers in the fighting area. Medical facilities were never adequate and troops were unprepared for tropical conditions.

The lack of numbers of troops could have been compensated for by using machines, but it proved extremely difficult to move light tanks along the coast from Milne Bay. To move the medium tanks, which would have been better suited to the task, was just not possible. Similarly it would have been difficult to move heavy artillery, whereas it was possible to fly in cut-down 25 pounders. There was scarcely enough ammunition for the few guns which were flown in. Furthermore there were mixed feelings about the value of artillery against the Japanese dug-in defences. Gunners found that they had to improvise delayed action fuses to obtain the best results.

A number of commanders in the forward areas believed that not enough was done to bring forward more artillery and ammunition. General Waldron suggested that a few 155s might have eliminated the need for tanks.[96] General Berryman believed that more artillery should have been used, and Colonel Doe of the 163rd U.S. Regiment later commented: 'I served under Bloody George [Vasey]. He was a gunner and you would have expected him to make more use of artillery'.[97] This comment was a little unfair to Vasey who could use only what he was given. While Doe was a highly capable commander with combat experience in both World Wars he could be a difficult subordinate.[98] His claim that 'what ammunition there was, was generally wasted on harassing fire, which was ineffective against bunker positions'[99] should be recognised as a general dissatisfaction with the artillery situation, rather than an indictment of individuals. In later years Herring wrote to Eichelberger:

One thing that annoys me as a gunner who was always most anxious to get as many guns into action as possible is the suggestion that someone, presumably at NGF, was not interested in increasing the number of guns on the front. As you will remember, it was ammunition that was our chief worry, and as our aeroplane could only carry a very limited amount of artillery ammunition, it just was not possible to get ammunition up until a securer route by sea had been established. The author of *Victory in Papua* does not seem to have realised to the full the calls that were made on the available aircraft, that an extra plane load of ammunition that the guns already there could have fired off in a few minutes left so much less food for the troops, as you will remember.[1]

General Kenney tried to convince MacArthur that aircraft could be an effective substitute for artillery, but throughout the campaign close air support proved most ineffective. Pilots were inexperienced and ground liaison was poor. Often Allied planes bombed their own troops. The Allied Air Force did, however, render valuable service in disrupting the Japanese supply lines. Had the Japanese not been prevented from heavily reinforcing and supplying their garrison, the

Allied victory might have been long delayed, or at best, the Japanese might have eventually extricated most of their forces as they did at Guadalcanal.

Despite these limited efforts to support the infantry, there was the attitude that one last push by the infantry would be sufficient to win the battle, and that there was no time to bring up heavy weapons. The American commanders rarely made this mistake again. The tenacity of the Japanese came as a surprise to the Allies. Eichelberger felt that if they had been opposed by Germans they would have surrendered at least two weeks before the end.[2] The determination of the Japanese, the parlous supply situation, the problems of jungle warfare and the particular difficulties of the Buna area were never really understood by MacArthur. He always thought in broad sweeping strategic terms and he had little knowledge of the minutiae of soldiering. Yet the strategic march of the Allied forces could stumble on a small tactical obstacle.

The final paradox of the campaign came after the fall of Buna, and when MacArthur returned to Australia. On one hand his communique said that losses were light because there was no hurry, and that the Japanese had been all but annihilated. On the other hand, there was his order to Blamey of 4 January for a swift attack on the Japanese because of the 'rapidly deteriorating' air transport. This order committed the Allied forces to more costly attacks to secure the developing Dobodura complex. Herring believed, and still believes, that there was no alternative to pursuing a victory to the bitter end.[3] Berryman still believes that the Japanese could have been sealed off and pounded with artillery. In the long run, as a result of the Japanese order of 4 January, the argument proved to be academic, but many good men were lost on 12 January in an attack which merely accelerated the Japanese plans to withdraw.

Few people can dispute the necessity for seizing the north coast of Papua. Here was the most suitable area for constructing airfields to enable the Fifth Air Force to continue to support the offensive, and to carry the fight to the Japanese in the Huon Gulf. Buna also became the supply base for the 9th Australian Division at Lae and Finschhafen. A year later, after these successful campaigns, Herring wrote to Eichelberger: 'Buna-Gona was the first real step towards driving the Jap out of New Guinea and New Britain. If we had failed, the edifice could never have been started . . . '.[4]

The Buna battles proved to be a test of command and leadership in every respect and at all levels. The performances of individual commanders have been indicated in the narrative, and the reputations of none of the senior commanders remain untarnished. Even the level headed Eichelberger sent his men on ill-prepared attacks at Buna in the closing days of December. Yet it should be stressed that the tactical errors were made because neither MacArthur nor Blamey visited the front early in the campaign. They lacked knowledge of the ground, the conditions, the state of their own troops and of the enemy. Furthermore it is not completely possible to divorce the tactical situation from a discussion of the pressures endured by the commanders.

Internal friction played a significant part in the campaign. The 'Battle of Brisbane' in late November 1942[5] was but a symptom of the irritation that had developed between the Australians and the Americans since the early battles on the Kokoda Trail. It was understandable that Blamey and MacArthur should look after the interests of their soldiers, but correspondence from Eichelberger to MacArthur and from Herring to Blamey does not reveal any great dissatisfaction with troops of their ally. It seems likely, therefore, that much of the antagonism was generated at Blamey's and MacArthur's headquarters. Vasey's complaints about Tomlinson and Doe should not necessarily be seen as an indictment of the Americans,[6] for he made similar complaints about his own militia units and their officers.

Undoubtedly the presence of Eichelberger helped Allied cooperation north of the Range, for he worked very well with Herring. Herring believed that his own main contribution to victory was in ensuring the smooth operation of the Australian and American elements of his command.[7] Between them, Herring and Eichelberger did much to ease the mistrust generated in Port Moresby.

Herring's experiences provide a good example of the manner in which pressures build up upon a commander as he finds himself squeezed between the demands from his superior and an almost insoluble tactical problem. He does not appear to have been helped by his BGS, the capable but difficult Brigadier Hopkins, nor by the mercurial Vasey, who, more than most, resented interference from superiors. Blamey handled these developments with unexpected sensitivity, thus eliminating another potential command crisis.

On the other hand MacArthur's handling of his subordinates was abysmal. Eichelberger was surely one of Wavell's 'robust' generals. He endured the humiliation of being ordered back to Australia by the jealous Sutherland.[8] He accepted the order to take Buna or not come back alive. He put up with Sutherland looking over his shoulder as he prepared his attacks. But he was distressed that neither MacArthur nor Kenney visited him and that the congratulations from MacArthur were belated and begrudgingly given. Unlike Blamey, MacArthur appeared to have no concept of the strain under which his subordinates laboured. Indeed he seemed unaware that by his actions he contributed to that strain.

Command remained a problem throughout the campaign. Hopkins believed that it was never more than a corps command. It is true that there were never more than two divisions in contact with the enemy, but the terrain necessitated a commander at Buna and another at Port Moresby. There was no need for the theatre commander to be located in Port Moresby also. The reason given by MacArthur was that his presence was required to co-ordinate the army, navy and air forces.[9] Consistently, throughout the war, he refused to place these forces under a task force commander except, as in the case at Milne Bay, when the force was threatened with attack. In north-west Europe in 1944 there may have been some necessity for Eisenhower to retain this power of co-ordination; after all, he had three army groups in action. But MacArthur had one understrength corps in action.

The result of MacArthur's command arrangements was a lack of cohesion. When Blamey wanted the assistance of the Navy for his advance along the north coast, he had to ask MacArthur. Similarly the troops at Buna had extreme difficulty co-operating with the Air Force over the close air support. The channel for communications was from the 32nd Division to Advanced HQ New Guinea Force, to New Guinea Force, to Advanced General Headquarters, and finally to the Advanced Headquarters of the Allied Air Forces. In this manner the presence of MacArthur and his headquarters in the battle zone hindered the conduct of the campaign.

No doubt MacArthur's reluctance to leave the campaign in Blamey's hands had its basis in his desire to ensure that he alone received publicity for any victory. His well-oiled public relations department ensured that. Furthermore, MacArthur was probably loath to leave Blamey in command of an Allied force as he did not want Americans to have to serve under an Australian. When MacArthur took the 32nd Division under his wing, he made it more difficult for Blamey and Herring to deal objectively with the Americans. MacArthur became unable to see the battle as a whole. His advice to Blamey to send the 163rd Regiment to Buna was a direct result of his proprietary interest in the performance of the Americans. Blamey and Herring could react in only one way; that was to ensure that the Australian interests were safeguarded.

MacArthur's presence caused more difficulties than merely those of co-operation. Despite his claims to the contrary, he interfered directly with Blamey's conduct of the campaign. His letters to Eichelberger are evidence of this interference, which was more reprehensible because it was not based on any detailed knowledge of conditions at the front. Not once did he visit the battlefield. At 62 perhaps he would have found such a visit too trying, but it was simply not MacArthur's method of command.[10] Later he visited battlefields, but these visits were probably for the benefit of his public relations department. The actual conditions of the fighting never seemed to interest him.

For a commander of his experience, Blamey's tardiness in visiting the front is inexplicable. His influence on the campaign was direct, if not always favourable. He made the disastrous decision to send the carriers to Buna and then the correct decision to send in Wootten's brigade with tanks. The movement of the 17th Brigade from Milne Bay to Port Moresby and then to Wau showed a keen awareness of the use of airpower and the wisdom of keeping the brigade in reserve.

Yet Blamey's handling of the battle was limited by his lack of knowledge of the terrain and conditions on the north coast. He did not visit the front until after the success of the 32nd Division and the 18th Brigade at Buna. When, on 30 November he wrote to Herring, suggesting that the Japanese pockets be bypassed 'to seize other enemy positions and destroy any formed bodies',[11] he did not realise that the swamps made the Japanese positions difficult to bypass, and made it almost impossible to reinforce or supply forward troops.

When Herring began to falter, Blamey did not go forward to see him, but rather called Herring back to Moresby. Admittedly Moresby was a more relaxing venue for the hard-pressed Herring, but the old adage that the commander in the rear has more time than the one at the front should be remembered. Probably Blamey did not want Herring to feel that he was looking over his shoulder, but all commanders expect, and often look forward to a visit from their superior. A year later in the Ramu Valley Vasey was to write to his wife: 'I can't say I am getting all the support, even if only moral, from the rear that I would like . . . although I have had a lot of visitors none of them are senior people from NGF'.[12] If Blamey's concern for the administration of the AMF meant that he did not have the time to visit the north coast, then this is yet a further indictment of the system whereby he held several separate commands.

Herring was never really required to demonstrate his ability as a corps commander. Essentially the battles remained in the hands of his brigade and battalion commanders. Like the other commanders at Buna and Gona, Herring was a victim of MacArthur's drive for speed. Whether this was controlled more by personal reasons than by strategic and tactical necessity is difficult to determine. Probably the issue became so confused in MacArthur's mind that he would have found it impossible to separate his motives. MacArthur's Chief of Intelligence, General Willoughby, has attempted to explain the necessity for speed: 'Buna was a head-on collision of the bloody, grinding type that MacArthur was henceforward to avoid, but it was necessary. The Allied world was starved for victory at the end of 1942, its morale was at its lowest ebb'. He continued that the Chinese were reported to be negotiating with the Japanese and the Germans were pushing towards the Volga in south-east Russia: 'The world needed a symbol of victory'.[13]

This facile explanation overlooks a number of facts. By December 1942 Montgomery had won the battle of El Alamein, and the Allies had landed in Morocco and Algeria. The Germans were already on the defensive at Stalingrad and on Guadalcanal the Americans were gaining the upper hand. Buna was not a battle that MacArthur had to fight to save Australia, although it was a battle which he had to fight if he was to prepare for an offensive against Rabaul (as plans were at that time). Furthermore Buna was a necessary battle for his troops to gain a moral ascendancy over the Japanese, but this did not necessarily mean more speed. In Burma, Slim achieved the aim of improving morale by allowing battalions to wipe out Japanese platoons in small actions.[14] Having postulated the theory that MacArthur fought at Buna because the world needed a symbolic victory, Willoughby then came back to earth with what he believed was the essence of the battle: 'It became a race between Eichelberger and the Marines under Admiral Halsey's command to see who would turn in the first important land victory of the Pacific War'.[15]

The fact that the war assumed such personal proportions for MacArthur has its roots partly in the command structure accepted readily by the Australian Government in March 1942, and also partly in MacArthur's personality. He was not like Mountbatten, the Supreme Commander of the South East Asia Allied Command, who allowed Slim to conduct his campaign in Burma much as he wished. Nor was he like Eisenhower at Normandy standing back and allowing Montgomery to fight the battle for the beachhead. Rather he was a theatre commander who, during the Buna campaign, interfered to the point of sending his division commanders such peremptory messages as: 'Take Buna today'.

Conclusion

Although Curtin was to wait a further five months before announcing to the public that Australia was secure, the Japanese defeats at Guadalcanal, Milne Bay, Kokoda and Buna had eliminated the threat of invasion. It is true that the Japanese maintained in New Guinea considerable forces which were to take many months to defeat, but with American help the Japanese were driven relentlessly from their conquests. The cessation of fighting in Papua in January 1943 also marked the end of the phase in which the command system had been established and tested. In many ways it was found wanting, and there were to be more command problems to be faced by the Australian generals in World War II. Nevertheless the campaign ended victoriously.

When Blamey returned to Australia in January 1943, the writing was already on the wall with regard to his position as commander of the Allied Land Forces. It was clear that MacArthur intended to act as his own commander of the land forces and control operations through task force commanders. To this end, in February 1943 Lieutenant-General Walter Krueger arrived to take command of the Sixth U.S. Army, and soon afterwards MacArthur formed Alamo Force to conduct the operations of the Sixth Army. There were not yet enough troops to form a U.S. Army in Australia, but Krueger, who also commanded Alamo Force, realised 'that this arrangement would obviate placing Sixth Army under the operational control of CG Allied Land Forces'.[1]

Throughout 1943 it became increasingly obvious that MacArthur had edged Blamey out of his position as commander of the land forces. This is not to suggest that MacArthur's new system was unworkable. However, his method of achieving the new system was, in the words of Gavin Long, 'by stealth and by the employment of sub-

terfuges that were undignified, and at times absurd'.[2] These subterfuges revealed a lack of consideration by MacArthur towards a
subordinate who had shown outstanding loyalty. Indeed, on 17 May
1943, MacArthur's Chief Public Relations Officer, Colonel L. A.
Diller, wrote to MacArthur from Melbourne: 'I found no question
from any source of General Blamey's loyalty and fidelity'.[3] F. M.
Forde commented later that Blamey 'worked very hard in order to
give satisfaction to General Douglas MacArthur and to render a maximum of assistance'.[4]

There is no evidence that, at this stage, Blamey lost any sleep over
MacArthur's machinations. Rather, he was concerned with completing the reorganisation of the army for the Pacific offensive. In
early 1943 the 9th Division arrived in Australia and Blamey grouped it
with the 6th and 7th Divisions on the Atherton Tableland to form I
Corps. This was to be his main striking force for the advance through
the islands. The commander of the corps was Lieutenant-General Sir
Leslie Morshead, who had commanded the 9th Division in the Middle
East.

The reduction in establishment, foreshadowed by Blamey in his letter to Curtin in early December, now began.[5] Reductions continued
throughout the war until, by July 1945, the army had six divisions in
action in the islands (3rd, 5th, 6th, 7th, 9th, 11th), but no other
divisions organised in Australia.[6] Blamey took the opportunity during
the reorganisation in early 1943 to establish finally the command
structure to which he had been gradually working. He still felt that
there were a number of senior officers who were either too old or
lacked the drive and ability required by the war. Furthermore, he felt
that it was important that commanders with recent experience of
battle should be given commands.

It will be recalled that in September 1942 it had been decided to convert the 1st and 2nd Motorised Divisions to Armoured Divisions, but
it was not until November that the 1st Motorised Division became
known as the 2nd Armoured Division. Then in February 1943 it was
decided not to proceed with the 3rd Armoured Division.[7] This left
Major-General W. A. B. Steele, who had been commander of the 1st
Motorised Division since April 1942, without a job. However, in late
1942 both Lavarack and Northcott had complained to Blamey about
Steele's performance.[8] Eventually the problem was solved when Steele
'asked for an opportunity to do a tour of service in the field and [was]
prepared to accept a reduction in rank to enable him to do so'.[9] Shortly afterwards Steele went to New Guinea as a brigadier to command
COSC.

At the same time as it was decided not to continue raising the 3rd Armoured Division, it was decided to disband the 2nd Armoured Division which was commanded by Major-General W. J. M. Locke who, like Steele, was a Staff Corps officer who had not served overseas during the war.[10] In the opinion of General Hopkins, Locke 'had energy and ability but a somewhat abrasive personality'.[11] He was reduced and became Brigadier IC Administration Northern Territory Force. On 7 June 1943 Vasey wrote to his wife:

I hear that Locke has at last received his due. You know, I think that he reverted (not of his own request) to Brigadier and I hear now he is being relegated to something quite insignificant if not out altogether. The latter will be to the good of the Staff Corps.[12]

Blamey had become increasingly dissatisfied with the performance of Stantke as Adjutant-General. It was felt that Stantke was obstructionist and was unwilling to visit the forward areas, or even to leave Melbourne.[13] General Durrant, the GOC of the Queensland L of C Area, was retired 'for medical reasons',[14] and Stantke replaced him in Brisbane. Brigadier C. E. M. Lloyd, the Director of Staff Duties, became the new Adjutant-General. Allen of the 6th Division changed places with Steevens of the Northern Territory Command,[15] and Brigadier Wootten, who had performed well at Milne Bay, Buna and Sanananda, was promoted to command the 9th Division.

In New Guinea Herring continued to show the strain of the two months of bitter fighting. In late January 1943 his Chief Medical Officer, Brigadier H. C. Disher, wrote to General Burston:

The GOC is looking a bit weary though better. I was a bit worried about him for a day or so and will be glad when he is able to get away on leave. I feel he won't go until sent for from LHQ. How about tackling the C-in-C about it?[16]

Soon afterwards Herring returned to Australia on leave and was replaced by Lieutenant-General Mackay of the Second Army. Thus Blamey streamlined and prepared the army for its coming battles.

Although the army could approach the battles of 1943 with confidence, the events of 1942 raise a number of questions about the Australian commanders and the planning for defence against the Japanese. It is worthwhile to reflect that to a significant extent the shortcomings in peace-time planning for the defence of Australia contributed to the crisis of command in 1942.

It should be noted that in the years before 1939 the Australian generals displayed a greater awareness of strategic possibilities than did the government and many members of the other services. But there were limitations to their thinking. Although the government had requested the army to plan for an expeditionary force valuable funds were spent on coastal fortifications. It can be argued that the money would have been better spent on preparations for an expeditionary force. Although the stated aim of this force might have been to reinforce an Imperial army, it could also have been used to strengthen New Guinea or indeed threatened areas of Australia. It is true, however, that the army was operating in a strategic straight-jacket. Troops could only be sent to New Guinea or remote areas of Australia if the lines of communication could be secured by naval forces, and if they were supported by the airforce. Neither support could be guaranteed.

Australia's peace-time planners were faced with a difficult problem of deciding the priorities of spending a moderately sized defence vote. In 1937 Lavarack saw the priorities as:

a. Rearmanent of the outdated defences of Sydney, Newcastle, Brisbane and Fremantle;
b. Acquiring new equipment; and
c. The maintenance and improvement of the efficiency of the permanent staff and the militia leaders.

There was some justification for this expenditure, but Gavin Long felt that 'the years of parsimony had produced a distrust of politicians' so that the army leaders gave 'priority to guns and concrete rather than men and training'; if the defence vote was reduced 'the guns and concrete would remain'.[17]

The efficacy of the planning is worthy of further study, but it is clear that it had a detrimental effect on Australia's war effort. During 1940 and 1941 most of the military effort was directed towards supporting the AIF and at the end of 1941 the nation's defences, little improved since 1939, were in a weak condition.

The army also faced problems of organisation. With the exception of the small Darwin Mobile Force, before September 1939 there was no balanced full-time unit that could be relied upon for action at short notice. Australia's military defences were chained to the militia system which, considering the country's vastness and transport weakness, meant that the militiamen would be deployed initially near their homes. Furthermore the military district system was ill-suited to prepare for the defence of the country as a whole. The Command system, introduced by Squires in October 1939, did something towards improving the situation, but the Command headquarters were still not organised to control units in the field. Rowell was to find this to be a considerable problem in 1942 when he took over the headquarters of Southern Command and converted it into the headquarters of I Corps.

It was not until the appointment of a GOC-in-C Home Forces in September 1941 that something was done about the problem of co-ordinating the defence of Australia. Even then Mackay's powers were limited and in fact the headquarters consisted of little more than Mackay and his chief of staff (first Brigadier Combes and then General Vasey). Initially orders had to be issued through Army Headquarters. It takes a while for a new headquarters to be raised and trained, and it is surprising that General White had opposed appointing a GOC-in-C Home Forces a year earlier. Efforts made by respective GOC of Commands were not co-ordinated and their plans were based on the militia in their areas. The Military Board seemed preoccupied with raising and training the AIF, purchase of munitions, and training the militia. General Mackay had much work to do.

Planning and training was hindered by the age and capabilities of the Australian generals. The retiring age for officers was too advanced and the small size of the army meant that men of ability and drive languished in the lower ranks. At the outbreak of war the senior RMC graduate was a lieutenant-colonel, yet many graduates had had war experience at up to battalion and regimental command level, they had held senior staff appointments and had attended overseas staff colleges. It is true that after the outbreak of war a number of senior officers were retired, but it seems strange to read that they were in many cases replaced by colonels who were often of about the same age. This second echelon of commanders included such men as Northcott, Smart, Wynter and Sturdee, but it also included men about whom Archduke Albert's comments of minds 'worn out by attention to trifles' seem to hold true. Furthermore, the turnover of militia officers in the first year of war was less marked than with the permanent officers. The more capable permanent and militia officers soon found their way to the AIF in the Middle East. Men of lesser ability, or those who were either too old or not fit, were left to run the army in Australia.

This did not mean that Sturdee was unaware of these shortcomings, and it was at his instigation that senior officers like Mackay and Rowell were brought back from the Middle East in late 1941. After the entry of Japan into the war this movement was accelerated and the officers who took over the major Australian units in January 1942 made an immediate impact. In essence Blamey's reorganisation of March-April 1942 was a continuation of that begun by Sturdee some months earlier.

The new generals came to their commands with distinct advantages over their predecessors. They were younger and they had recent combat experience. They had spent over two years in an army which was operating on a war-time footing. When they had not been fighting in the Middle East they had been training for war. They knew what was required in modern warfare. The strengths of the new Australian generals were therefore their youth and experience — a fine combination.

The conduct of the early battles in New Guinea proved the mettle of these officers, and they demonstrated professional competence and leadership of a high order. They were confident and they transmitted this confidence to soldiers who, early in the campaign, could have been excused for losing it.

Generally speaking the senior officers could be divided into two categories, militia and regular. Of particular note was the ability of many of the militia officers. Most had served as young officers in World War I, and they had honed their organisational and leadership skills in the hard school of commerce and industry. The events in the Middle East enabled them to build on their already considerable military knowledge. On the other hand a number of regular officers, although knowledgeable and well-trained, lacked the ability to command troops. Their lack of opportunity to practise leadership stemmed from the days when they had become staff officers in World War I and had continued through the period between the wars. But by 1942 most of these officers had been identified and they filled important staff postings. Their comrades who proved to be natural leaders lost nothing beside the militia officers. Nevertheless as the army expanded and became more complex the expertise required of the senior commanders increased. In many cases the only officers with the knowledge to fill these positions were regular officers who, by temperament, may not have made ideal commanders.

Amongst the regular officers the rise of the Duntroon graduate to high positions was significant. In March 1943 the only regular major-generals who had not been commissioned from Duntroon were Morris, the GOC of ANGAU, Stantke, The GOC of the Queensland L of C Area, and Plant, the GOC of the Victorian L of C Area.[18]

One of the great strengths of the Australian officer corps was also to prove to be its weakness. Most of the senior regular officers had been cadets together at Duntroon, and the small size of the army between the wars meant that they all knew each other well. Even the militia officers were well known, both to each other and to the regular officers. They attended exercises together and soon found themselves together again in the Middle East. They knew each other's capabilities and susceptibilities. It is quite understandable that Rowell and Vasey would have complete confidence in their old RMC classmate Cyril Clowes at Milne Bay.

But this close knowledge of each other caused unseemly and often destructive internal wrangling amongst the senior commanders. The more capable officers were dismayed to see their less talented comrades promoted simply because they had 'hung around' throughout the lean years. Moreover those who remained in Australia in 1940 were often promoteg ahead of those in the Middle East. There was, however, more to it than that, for there was the jealousy between the amateur and the professional compounded by the selection of Blamey. The jockeying for Blamey's position in March 1942 was but a symptom of the underlying tension endemic in a small army where command opportunities are limited. This small army was again another result of the shortsightedness of the past.

This tension did not have just an historical or organisational basis. A commander can only perform his duties whilst his prestige remains high. Commanders are jealous of their reputations and resentful of denigration. Often they risk all — disgrace or success. They are willing to take their chances with the enemy and the elements, but when the other imponderables, such as the loyalty of subordinates and seniors, politics, public opinion and personal antagonism must be taken into account, the strain becomes intense. This is the friction of war, just as much as the more obvious frustrations such as rations being dropped into the jungle, rain preventing aircraft flying or trucks becoming bogged in mud. As Clausewitz wrote: 'Friction is the only conception . . . which distinguishes real War from War on paper'.[19]

Although the events before 1942 provided all the elements for a command crisis to develop in the emergency of early 1942, the most enduring criticism has occurred around the role played by General Blamey after he returned to this already turbulent situation in March of that year. It raises important questions about command relations.

It has been indicated how MacArthur manoeuvred Blamey out of his position as commander of the land forces. It may be presumed from this that it was an unwise decision to make him both C-in-C of the Australian Army as well as Commander of the Allied Land Forces, but Gavin Long was of the opinion that in the crisis of March

1942 there was no alternative. Indeed he suggested that Blamey could see that there would be eventually a majority of U.S. troops, and in that circumstance he would have to revert to commanding just the Australian component of MacArthur's force.[20] It is not possible to determine the validity of Long's assertion, but it is true that that was how it worked out. Blamey's fight during the lattter part of 1942 to maintain his position as Commander of the Allied Land Forces does not negate Long's argument, for at that time the majority of the land forces were Australian, and Blamey would have felt a responsibility to maintain his position.

It can also be argued that it was necessary for Blamey to fill the two positions of Commander of the Allied Land Forces and commander of the Australian operational forces during 1942. However, Blamey had another responsibility. As Commander-in-Chief of the AMF, he was also responsible for the administration of the Australian Army. Colonel E. G. Keogh has discussed this situation at some length. He used the example of the United Kingdom to suggest that Australia should have retained the Military Board and appointed a Commander-in-Chief of the Home Forces.[21] He overlooked the fact that the UK Army Council remained responsible for a number of overseas theatres as well as for the home theatre, while by March 1942, with the exception of the 9th Division in the Middle East, all of Australia's forces were concentrated for the defence of Australia alone. Keogh concluded that:

Even if the prevailing conditions in Australia rendered necessary the replacement of the Military Board with a Commander-in-Chief AMF, it would have been far better if our Government had followed the British example and avoided getting the strings of responsibility crossed by allowing the same officer to undertake the duties of operational commander as well.[22]

Despite the very fine work of Sturdee and Rowell in the first months after Japan entered the war, in the opinion of General Berryman, there was no alternative to the appointment of a C-in-C in the emergency of March 1942. Blamey's signals with the prefix 'Z' ensured immediate action. Indeed, the expansion and training of the Australian Army in mid 1942 was an impressive feat, facilitated by the rapid decisions from Land Headquarters. Furthermore, it was necessary for Blamey to be C-in-C to check the almost complete power of MacArthur. It is doubtful whether another man, or another organisation, could have done so much in achieving that.

The arrangement worked smoothly until GHQ moved to Brisbane, forcing Blamey to follow suit and open Landops in Brisbane. Blamey then found himself in the position of having to fly between his operational headquarters in Brisbane and his administrative headquarters in Melbourne. Nevertheless, he was determined to make the system work. Lavarack was responsible for the defence of the east coast of Australia, and Rowell was given command of all the forces in New Guinea. Vasey, in his letters, has testified that there was not really a great deal of day-to-day work at Landops. Yet he was often placed in the invidious position, in Blamey's absence, of having to argue the Australian cause to MacArthur's staff.

A good case could have been made for changing the command structure completely in 1944 or 1945. For example, Gavin Long has suggested that there should have been three land forces — the Australian Army Group under Blamey, and the Sixth and Eighth U.S. Armies.[23] A number of Australian generals, for example Rowell and Berryman, believed that command could have reverted to a Military Board system with a separate commander of the operational forces. Whether Blamey would have filled the CGS or C-in-C position is open to conjecture.

In early 1945 this matter was discussed at length; on 19 February 1945 Blamey wrote to Shedden and referred to the formation of Krueger's Sixth Army:

At no stage was I given any information as to the proposals for their arrival or the development of the organisation. In fact, General MacArthur took upon himself the function of Commander, Allied Land Forces, and my functions were limited to command of the Australian Military Forces.[24]

Shedden then wrote to MacArthur and summed up the whole problem:

I recall having originally discussed with you in Brisbane in October 1942, General Blamey's dual position as Commander of the Allied Land Forces and Commander-in-Chief of the Australian Military Forces. The view that you then expressed was that, sooner or later, General Blamey had to make a decision as to whether he was going forward in command of the advance forces in the offensive operations or was remaining in Australia in connection with the administration of the Australian Military Forces. We reverted to the subject on subsequent occasions, when you expressed the opinion that General Blamey should remain in Australia as Commander-in-Chief of the Home Forces and Lieut. General Morshead should be appointed Commander of the Australian Divisions in an Expeditionary Force which would be placed at your disposal . . .

2. At a recent conference between the Prime Minister, the Minister for the Army, General Blamey and myself, which is the basis of the Prime Minister's letter to you, I asked General Blamey whether, as Commander-in-Chief of the Australian Military Forces, he contemplated controlling the forces on the mainland, those in New Guinea, New Britain, in the Solomons, and the 7th and 9th Divisions, operating in your offensive campaign. He replied that such was his idea.

3. There is, of course, not only your own aspect, as Commander-in-Chief of the South West Pacific Area, but also that of the Australian Government in regard to the current problems of administration of the Australian Army, on which General Blamey is the Government's adviser.

4. My own private and personal opinion, for what it is worth, is that it has to be seriously considered whether the responsibilities for the higher direction of the Australian Military Forces should be divided into two major spheres as follows:

(i)   Responsibility for the command and administration of the forces on the mainland and the provision of supplies and reinforcements for the forces serving outside Australia, subject to responsibility to the Commander-in-Chief, South West Pacific Area, for the operational control of the forces on the mainland which, in view of the removal of the threat of attack, would largely be nominal.

(ii)   Responsibility for the command, operational control and administration of the forces serving outside Australia, subject to:

    (a) Responsibility to the Australian authorities on certain major questions, such as appointments to the command of the higher formations.

    (b) Responsibility to the Commander-in-Chief, South West Pacific Area, for the operational control of the Australian forces outside Australia.

If you considered a change on these lines should be made, insofar as operational control is concerned, and the Government agreed from its point of view, I don't know which command, if any, would be acceptable to General Blamey. In (i), he would remain the Chief Military Adviser to the Government, but would not have an active operational command. In (ii), he would be subordinate to the authority in (i), as he was when in the Middle East. Having been Commander-in-Chief of the whole show, this might not be acceptable to him.[25]

MacArthur's reply was quite frank. He explained that his method of operation was to use task forces with a commander of rank appropriate to the size of the task force. He considered that:

the assignment of the Australian commander should be a matter for determination by the Australian Government. It is considered to be impossible, however, from an operational viewpoint for the officer so designated to be concerned with command of Australian troops in New Guinea and Australia. It is essential that the Task Force Commander remain in the field with his troops and that he have no other duties of any kind.[26]

Blamey's position as Commander of the Allied Land Forces was not mentioned at all in MacArthur's three-page letter.

In August 1942 the situation was entirely different. Until Blamey was ordered to New Guinea in September, it was possible for him to fill his dual role as C-in-C AMF, and Commander, Allied Land Forces. Only after he arrived in Port Moresby was it clear that he could not adequately perform his many tasks. It is surprising that he did not make this completely clear to Curtin, who was obviously confused about Blamey's role. On the other hand, Blamey may have been unwilling to raise a question which, once asked, would have to be answered. The solution would have been either to make Blamey the operational commander, which would have stripped him of his administrative authority in Australia, or to select a new operational commander, which would have removed him from a position of influence with MacArthur. Blamey would have seen the latter as being detrimental to Australia's position. Furthermore, it would have meant that the new operational commander, probably Lavarack, would have supplanted Blamey, or at least equalled him, as Australia's most influential soldier. Blamey held on grimly to personal power.

Obviously Blamey realised the difficulty of his position, for the day after he arrived in Port Moresby (24 September), he recommended to Curtin that Northcott should be made Deputy C-in-C as well as CGS, so that he could take over some of the administrative responsibility.[27] The government was unwilling to take this step as it felt that Morshead would make a suitable Deputy C-in-C. Blamey was adamant that the Deputy C-in-C should be the same person as the CGS, otherwise 'such an appointment is like placing a fifth wheel on the coach'.[28] Blamey had already been a 'fifth wheel' in the Middle East, so this was not just theorising. The matter was not resolved and Blamey asked eventually that the question be put off until he returned to Australia.[29] Blamey was probably pleased to be able to use his presence in New Guinea as an excuse for delaying discussion of his position. Nevertheless, he must have been worried by reports that the War Cabinet was examining proposals to revive the Military Board.[30] General Wynter wrote later that he was having trouble with 'what Wardell [DQMG (Plans) LGA Branch LHQ] calls the "bastardry" of the Civil Staff. They take any and every opportunity to oppose the C-in-C. This has been their attitude virtually since November 1942 when

Sinclair [Secretary of the Department of Army] first started his intrigue for replacing the C-in-C by an Army Council'.[31]

The matter of the command structure and Blamey's ambivalent position has been discussed to point out the manner in which it placed the various commanders under considerable pressure. It has been shown how it led directly to the relief of Rowell, and how it was a backdrop to the relief of Allen.

Yet Blamey's difficult command position was but one of the many variables affecting the conduct of the campaign. Almost as important was the attitude and personality of MacArthur. He influenced the campaign and placed his subordinates in difficult positions in a number of ways — through his inaccurate strategic assessments in July and August 1942, through his determination to edge Blamey out and take over as commander of the land forces, through his interference in the tactical conduct of the campaign, through his influence over the Australian Government and through his fears that an apparent military reverse might lead to his dismissal. He placed his commanders under unnecessary, and at times dangerous, strain. Clowes at Milne Bay, Allen at Eora Creek, and Eichelberger at Buna, all felt the burden of his exhortations. In this respect Allen had the last word — 'Well, that's not the way to urge Australians'.[32]

It appears from this study that the area of greatest discontent lay somewhere between the theatre and the division commanders. This is not to say that the theatre commander, MacArthur, was not under great pressure; he was, although in some cases it may have been a figment of his imagination. But MacArthur was also in a position of great strength and he could manipulate events and people to help alleviate the pressure. For example he used his communiques to convince the people in America that he was winning great victories, thus building himself up to be a hero who would be difficult to replace. When it appeared likely that Port Moresby might fall, he sent Blamey there so that, if there were a disaster, he could claim that he had done everything possible to avert it.

At the other end of the scale the division commanders tended to be insulated from this pressure by their corps commanders. Thus Rowell refused to pass on some messages to Clowes and never blamed Allen for the catastrophe on the Kokoda Trail. Yet Allen at Eora Creek was not protected in the same way. At Buna, both Harding and Eichelberger received messages directly from MacArthur. There is no evidence that Blamey or Herring made vigorous efforts to protect their American subordinates from MacArthur's interference.[33]

Each commander handled the impact of these influences as he saw fit. As Field Marshal Montgomery has written, 'the crucible of war will determine the fine metal of which a general is made'.[34] Sturdee threatened the government with resignation if it did not recall the AIF to Australia, but after the anxious days of early 1942 he clearly found his new job in the United States a welcome relief. Rowell too preferred to stand firm as a matter of principle. Herring bent like a willow before the storm, maintained his position, and carried out his task. Towards the end the strain began to show, as it had with Rowell, but it did not have the same consequences. Blamey's position was the most precarious. He walked a tightrope between maintaining his own position and protecting the Australian commanders, between risking his own replacement and risking the distrust of his subordinates. He pursued ruthlessly the course of survival — a course he saw as one synonymous with the best interests of the Australian Army and nation.

Blamey's contribution to the Australian military achievement in World War II has not yet been assessed properly but the admiration in which he is held by a score of senior officers thirty years after the war is an indication of the value of his work. Yet Blamey's detractors seem to believe that, as A. J. Sweeting noted, 'by some mysterious power the senior officers still dance to the beat of the dead field marshal's baton'.[35] Likewise, the contribution of the other senior officers should not be overlooked. They all made mistakes and their conduct was not always as pure as it might have been, but generally speaking Australia was well served by her generals in 1942.

The intangibles, and their interaction with the personalities of the commanders, have been studied too little in Australian military history. This is not because Bean and Long were unaware of them, but probably because neither saw this aspect as part of his charter. Furthermore it involves personal assessments which may be inappropriate in an official history, and which are possible only a number of years after the event. Nevertheless the official histories are remiss in not making an attempt to indicate the pressures on commanders and the influences which helped them formulate their plans. In Gavin Long's volume, *To Benghazi*, General Mackay and his headquarters are shadowy figures: imagine *Hamlet* with the Prince speaking always from off-stage, but rarely seen!

This book has attempted to show the commanders at work in a number of critical situations. We have seen Mackay, Sturdee and Rowell producing appreciation after appreciation for a confused government. There was MacArthur and Blamey's plan for the defence of Australia. There was the successful prosecution of the campaign in

Papua, and there were the command crises. But there has not been the opportunity to analyse that end of the spectrum where Vasey had command of the 7th Division, nor has there been the opportunity to delve into the relationship between MacArthur and Curtin, and the unpublicised role of Frederick Shedden. Perhaps Shedden's long hidden and government subsidised manuscript holds the answer to the command relationships at the political military interface.

The personalities of a number of generals have been examined to determine how they interacted with one another, and how they shaped the operations. There has been little opportunity to demonstrate the impact that these personalities made on the troops themselves. When Allen was replaced by Vasey the troops were greatly upset.[36] Yet Vasey quickly impressed his personality on the division. This was a fine performance and of equal importance to any tactical decision he might have made. But a discussion of this achievement is beyond the realm of the work.[37]

The events in Australia and New Guinea in 1942 and 1943 show that command structures which are improvised and unrehearsed are usually extremely difficult to operate properly, and may well do so only at the expense of some talented but unfortunately placed general such as Rowell. Furthermore, not only must the generals prepare their contingency plans, but politicians must be schooled into understanding the plans and making the sort of decisions which, as representatives of the people, only they can make. It may be true that no war will ever be exactly like the last one, for the weapons, equipment and conditions will almost certainly change. One of the lessons of history, it has been said, is that people never learn from history. Consequently, generals will still be expected to fight their battles with imperfect tools and in unpropitious circumstances. At the same time, they will also be subject to the sorts of pressures endured by Blamey, Rowell and Herring in 1942. As Liddell Hart put it:

Human nature . . . changes but slowly, if at all and human nature under stress of danger, not at all.[38]

Appendixes

RMC Graduates of General Rank, 1941-1943

July 1942

Maj.-Gen. E. J. Milford, MGO (1 Jan. 41), then GOC 5 Aust Div (6 Apr. 42), graduated 1915.

Maj.-Gen. S. F. Rowell, DCGS (1 Sept. 41), promoted to Lieut.-Gen. GOC 1 Aust Corps (6 Apr. 42), graduated 1914.

Maj.-Gen. G. A. Vasey, MGGS, Home Forces (5 Jan. 42), DCGS (6 Apr. 42), graduated 1915.

Maj.-Gen. H. C. H. Robertson, GOC, 1 Aust Cav Div (5 Jan. 42), GOC, 1 Aust Armd Div (6 Apr. 42), graduated 1914.

Maj.-Gen. W. A. B. Steele, Base Commander 3 MD (5 Jan. 42), GOC, 1 Aust Mot Div (6 Apr. 42), graduated 1914.

Maj.-Gen. W. J. M. Locke, GOC, 2 Aust Cav Div (5 Jan. 42), graduated 1914.

Maj.-Gen. C. A. Clowes, GOC, 1 Aust Div (7 Jan. 42), graduated 1914.

Maj.-Gen. A. J. Boase, GOC, AIF (Ceylon) (18 March 42), graduated 1914.

Maj.-Gen. L. E. Beavis, MGO, LHQ (6 Apr. 42), graduated 1915.

Maj.-Gen. F. H. Berryman, MGGS, HQ 1st Army (6 Apr. 42), graduated 1915.

Maj.-Gen. W. Bridgeford, DA & QMG, HQ 1st Army (6 Apr. 42), graduated 1915.

Promoted by July 1943

Maj.-Gen. J. A. Chapman, DA & QMG, Adv LHQ (7 Aug. 42), graduated 1915.

Maj.-Gen. J. S. Whitelaw, MGRA, LHQ (27 Aug. 42), graduated 1914.

Maj.-Gen. C. E. M. Lloyd, AG, LHQ (9 Feb. 43). He had been a Maj.-Gen. from 28 Jan. 42 to 1 Mar. 42 as Deputy Intendant-General on Wavell's ABDACOM HQ, graduated 1918.

Maj.-Gen. G. F. Wootten, GOC, 9 Aust Div (15 Mar. 43), graduated 1914.

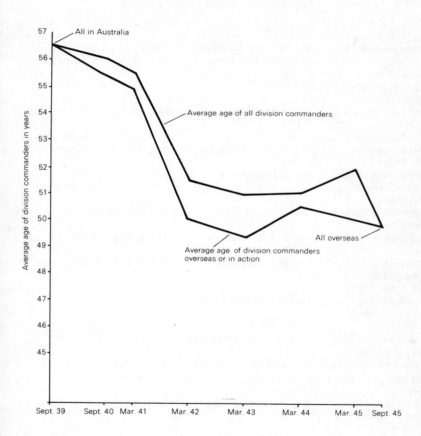

Appendix 3

Senior Command and Staff Appointments
September-December 1939

Posting	September	December
Inspector-General	Lt.-Gen. E. K. Squires (57)	—
Chief of the General Staff	Maj.-Gen. J. D. Lavarack (54)	Lt.-Gen. E. K. Squires (57)
Deputy Chief of the General Staff	—	Maj.-Gen. J. Northcott (49)
Adjutant-General	Maj.-Gen. Sir Carl Jess (55)	Maj.-Gen. C. G. N. Miles (55)
Quartermaster-General	Maj.-Gen. O. F. Phillips (57)	Maj.-Gen. E. K. Smart (48)
Master-General of the Ordnance		Maj.-Gen. T. R. Williams (55)
Director of Military Operations and Intelligence	Col. J. Northcott (49)	Col. B. Combes (47)
Director of Military Training	Col. E. C. P. Plant (49)	Col. E. L. Vowles (46)
Director of Staff Duties	Col. V. A. H. Sturdee (49)	Col. L. E. Beavis (44)
Director of Organization and Personnel Services	Col. R. E. Jackson (53)	Col. R. G. Prisk (45)
Deputy Master-General of the Ordnance	Col. T. R. Williams (55)	—
Director of Supply and Transport	Lt.-Col. B. M. Morris (51)	Col. R. T. A. McDonald (54)
Director of Artillery	Lt.-Col. E. J. Milford (44)	Col. G. P. W. Meredith (52)
Director of Ordnance Services	Col. G. E. Manchester (54)	Col. W. W. Whittle (47)
Commandant of Royal Military College	Brigadier C. G. N. Miles (55)	Brigadier E. C. P. Plant (49)
Chief Instructor of the Command and Staff School	Brigadier H. W. Wynter (53)	Col. A. J. Boase (45)

All these were permanent army officers. Ages in years are given after each name. It can be seen that in most cases the appointments of December 1939 were filled by younger men than those of September 1939.

Unit Commanded	September	December
1 MD	*Brig. E. M. Williams, 54 (1/1/36)	Northern Command *Maj.-Gen. H. D. Wynter, 53 (18/10/39)
1 Cav Bde	Brig. R. M. Stodart	
7 Inf Bde	Brig. J. Hill, 51 (1/8/35)	as for Sept.
11 Inf Bde	Brig. J. Craven, 45 (1/8/35)	
2 MD	*Maj.-Gen. J. L. Hardie, 57 (1/6/35)	Eastern Command *Lt.-Gen. V. A. H. Sturdee, 49 (13/10/39)
1 Cav Div	Maj.-Gen. J. D. Richardson, 59 (1/7/37)	
2 Cav Bde	Col. J. L. G. Johnstone, 58 (20/7/36)	as for Sept.
4 Cav Bde	Brig. F. B. Hinton, 47 (1/9/37)	
1 Div	*Maj.-Gen. J. L. Hardie, 57 (1/6/35)	*Maj.-Gen. R. E. Jackson, 53 (6/11/39)
1 Bde	Brig. F. P. M. Solling, 47 (1/5/38)	
3 Bde	Brig. M. B. B. Keating, 52 (15/5/38)	as for Sept.
Arty	Brig. S. G. Friend, 43 (15/5/38)	
2 Div	Maj.-Gen. I. G. Mackay, 57 (1/7/37)	as for Sept.
5 Bde	Brig. L. J. Morshead, 50 (1/1/37)	Brig. H. B. Taylor, 49 (23/10/39)
9 Bde	Brig. J. J. Murray, 47 (1/5/38)	as for Sept.
14 Bde	Brig. A. S. Allen, 45 (1/5/38)	Brig. W. E. Smith, 44 (23/10/39)
Arty	Brig. H. C. deLow, 47 (18/10/35)	as for Sept.
3 MD	*Maj.-Gen. J. L. Whitham, 58 (1/7/37)	Southern Command *Lt.-Gen. J. D. Lavarack, 54 (13/10/39)
2 Cav Div	Maj.-Gen. G. J. Rankin, 52 (1/7/37)	
3 Cav Bde	Brig. F. H. Christison, 48 (1/2/39)	as for Sept.
3 Div	Maj.-Gen. E. A. Drake-Brockman, 55 (1/6/37)	
4 Bde	Brig. E. F. Lind, 51 (1/5/37)	
10 Bde	Brig. S. G. Savige, 49 (1/6/35)	Brig. R. W. Tovell, 49 (14/10/39)
15 Bde	Brig. A. Jackson, 52 (1/2/37)	as for Sept.
Arty	Col. E. F. Herring, 47 (1/8/39)	Brig. D. O. L. Kitto, 44 (20/11/39)

4 Div	*Maj.-Gen. J. L. Whitham, 58 (1/7/37)	} as for Sept.
2 Bde	Brig. F. P. Derham, 54 (24/11/33)	
6 Bde	Brig. C. H. Simpson, 45 (1/5/39)	Brig. J. A. Clareborough, 44 (15/11/39)
Arty	Col. A. M. Ramsay, 44 (1/8/39)	Brig. V. H. Gatliff, 50 (20/11/39)
4 MD	*Brig. A. M. Martyn, 58 (1/1/36)	*Brig. M. C. Bundock, 53 (11/12/39)
6 Cav Bde	Brig. A. R. Wendt, 47 (10/8/37)	} as for Sept.
3 Inf Bde	Brig. A. R. Allen, 41 (13/12/36)	

Western Command
*Maj.-Gen. J. M. A. Durrant, 54 (13/10/39)

5 MD	*Brig. J. M. A. Durrant, 54 (4/9/39)	
13 Inf Bde	Brig. A. R. Baxter-Cox, 41 (1/5/39)	—
6MD	*Col. C. A. Clowes, 47 (29/8/39)	*Brig. C. A. Clowes, 47 (13/10/39)
7MD	*Col. H. C. H. Robertson, 45 (13/3/39)	*Col. H. C. H. Robertson, 45 (13/10/39)

6th Division Second AIF
GOC: Maj.-Gen. T. A. Blamey, 55
*GSO1: Col. S. F. Rowell, 44
*AA&QMG: Col. G. A. Vasey, 44
16 Bde: Brig. A. S. Allen, 45
17 Bde: Brig. S. G. Savige, 49
18 Bde: Brig. L. J. Morshead, 50
CRA: Brig. E. F. Herring, 47

* Permanent army officer.

It is obvious that whilst there were considerable changes amongst the permanent officers, except where they were transferred to the AIF, the militia officers remained in their original appointments.

Dates in brackets are the dates of appointment.

Appendix 4

First Curtin Ministry: 7 October 1941 to 21 September 1943

Rt Hon. John Curtin	Prime Minister; Minister for Defence Co-ordination to 14 Apr. 1942; from 14 Apr. 1942 Minister for Defence.
Hon. Francis Michael Forde	Minister for the Army.
Hon. Joseph Benedict Chifley	Treasurer; from 22 Dec. 1942 Minister for Postwar Reconstruction.
Rt Hon. Herbert Vere Evatt, K.C.	Attorney-General and Minister for External Affairs
Hon. John Albert Beasley	Minister for Supply and Development to 17 Oct. 1942; from 17 Oct. 1942 Minister for Supply and Shipping.
Senator the Hon. Joseph Silver Collings	Minister for the Interior.
Hon. Norman John Oswald Makin	Minister for the Navy and Minister for Munitions.
Hon. Edward James Holloway	Minister for Social Services and Minister for Health; from 21 Feb. 1942 Minister assisting the Minister for Munitions.
Senator the Hon. Richard Valentine Keane	Minister for Trade and Customs and Vice-President of the Executive Council.
Hon. Arthur Samuel Drakeford	Minister for Air and Minister for Civil Aviation.
Hon. William James Scully	Minister for Commerce to 22 Dec. 1942; from 22 Dec. 1942 Minister for Commerce and Agriculture.
Senator the Hon. William Patrick Ashley	Postmaster-General and Minister for Information.
Hon. Edward John Ward	Minister for Labour and National Service.
Hon. Charles William Frost	Minister for Repatriation and Minister in charge of War Service Homes.
Hon. James Johnstone Dedman	Minister for War Organisation of Industry and Minister in charge of Council for Scientific and Industrial Research.
Hon. Hubert Peter Lazzarini	Minister for Home Security and Minister assisting the Treasurer.
Senator the Hon. James Mackintosh Fraser	Minister for External Territories; Minister assisting the Minister for Commerce to

	17 Oct. 1942; from 21 Feb. 1942 assisting the Minister for the Army; from 17 Oct. 1942 assisting the Minister for Supply and Shipping.
Senator the Hon. Donald Cameron	Minister for Aircraft Production; Minister assisting the Minister for Munitions to 21 Feb. 1942.
Hon. George Lawson	Minister for Transport and Minister assisting the Postmaster-General.

War Cabinet: From 7 October 1941

Rt Hon. John Curtin, Hon. Francis Michael Forde, Hon. Joseph Benedict Chifley, Rt Hon. Herbert Vere Evatt, K.C., Hon. John Albert Beasley, Hon. Norman John Oswald Makin, Hon. Arthur Samuel Drakeford; from 11 Dec. 1941 Hon. John Johnstone Dedman.

Production Executive
(Established 6 November 1941)

Hon. John Albert Beasley, Hon. Norman John Oswald Makin, Hon. Edward John Ward, Hon. John Johnstone Dedman; from 12 Dec. 1941 Hon. Joseph Benedict Chifley and Senator the Hon. Donald Cameron also members; from 29 Jan. 1942 Senator the Hon. Richard Valentine Keane; from 26 Feb. 1942 Hon. William James Scully, Hon. Edward James Holloway.

Appendix 5

Senior Command and Staff Appointments
1 September 1941

AHQ

CGS	*Lt.-Gen. V. A. H. Sturdee	30/8/40	
DCGS	*Maj.-Gen. S. F. Rowell	1/9/41	
AG	*Maj.-Gen. V. P. H. Stantke	1/8/40	
MGO	*Maj-Gen. E. J. Milford	1/1/41	
QMG	Maj.-Gen. J. H. Cannan	24/10/40	From 2 Div, previously Unattached List
RMC	*Brig. E. F. Harrison	1/8/40	From Retired List
C&SS	Lt.-Col. J. L. Ord, R. A.	26/4/41	From British Army

GOC in Chief Home Forces	Lt.-Gen. I. G. Mackay	1/9/41	
N.Comd	*Maj.-Gen. J. M. A. Durrant	13/7/41	
E.Comd.	*Lt.-Gen. C. G. N. Miles	30/8/40	
1 Cav Div	Maj.-Gen. J. D. Richardson	16/1/36	
1 Div	Maj.-Gen. A. C. Fewtrell	1/7/40	From Unattached List
2 Div	Maj.-Gen. H. W. Lloyd	24/10/40	From Reserve
S. Comd	*Lt.-Gen. E. K. Smart	24/10/40	
2 Cav Div	Maj.-Gen. G. J. Rankin	15/10/36	
3 Div	Maj.-Gen. E. A. Drake-Brockman	1/6/37	
4 Div	Maj.-Gen. F. P. Derham	1/5/40	
4 MD	*Brig. H. C. Bundock	11/12/39	
6 MD	*Brig. G. E. Manchester	29/4/40	
W. Comd	*Maj.-Gen. R. E. Jackson	14/7/41	
Darwin (7 MD)	*Brig. D. V. J. Blake	1/9/41	
New Guinea (8 MD)	*Brig. B. M. Morris	19/5/41	

* Permanent army officers.

The only officers holding the same postings as in December 1939 are Richardson, Rankin, Drake-Brockman and Bundock.

AIF Senior Command and Staff Appointments — 1 September 1941

GOC-AIF (Middle East)	Gen. T. A. Blamey	10/12/40	*

AIF Rfct Depot	Brig. H. C. H. Robertson	13/3/41		*
HQ AIF Base	Brig. J. A. Chapman	14/8/41		*
DOS HQ AIF	Brig. L. E. Beavis	8/2/41		*
DAG HQ AIF	Brig. C. E. Prior	10/5/41		
1 Aust Corps	Lt.-Gen. J. D. Lavarack	18/6/41		*
BGS	Brig. F. H. Berryman	3/8/41		*
CRA	Brig. C. A. Clowes	4/10/40		*
DA & QMG	Brig. W. Bridgeford	14/11/40		*
CE	Brig. C. S. Steele	4/4/40	M	*
CSO	Col. C. H. Simpson	4/4/40	M	*
Comd AA Bde	Brig. H. B. Sewell	20/4/41		
6 Aust Div	Maj.-Gen. E. F. Herring	14/8/41	M	*
GSO1	Col. R. B. Sutherland	13/3/41		
AA & QMG	Col. R. Bierwirth	3/6/41		
16 Bde	Brig. A. J. Boase	14/8/41		*
17 Bde	Brig. S. G. Savige	13/10/39	M	*
19 Bde	Brig. G. A. Vasey	13/3/41		*
CRA	Brig. H. W. Strutt	3/8/41	M	
7 Aust Div	Maj.-Gen. A. S. Allen	14/3/41	M	*
GSO1	Col. H. F. H. Durrant	18/8/41		
AA & QMG	Col. V. C. Secombe	7/5/41		
18 Bde	Brig. G. F. Wootten	1/12/40	M	*
21 Bde	Brig. J. E. Stevens	4/4/40	M	*
25 Bde	Brig. E. C. P. Plant	23/6/41		*
CRA	Brig. H. G. Rourke	14/8/41		
9 Aust Div	Maj.-Gen. L. J. Morshead	6/2/41	M	*
GSO1	Col. C. E. M. Lloyd	24/12/40		*
AA & QMG	Col. B. W. Pulver	14/6/41		
20 Bde	Brig. J. J. Murray	4/4/40	M	*
24 Bde	Brig. A. H. L. Godfrey	13/3/41	M	
26 Bde	Brig. R. W. Tovell	1/7/40	M	
CRA	Brig. A. H. Ramsay	17/10/40	M	*
GOC AIF (Malaya) — also Comd 8 Div				
	Maj.-Gen. H. G. Bennett	24/9/40	M	*
GSO1	Col. J. M. Thyer	22/7/41		
AA & QMG	Col. J. R. Broadbent	1/7/40	M	
27 Bde	Brig. D. S. Maxwell	1/7/41	M	
22 Bde	Brig. H. B. Taylor	1/7/40	M	
23 Bde	Brig. E. F. Lind	1/7/40(not in Malaya)	M	
CRA	Brig. C. A. Callaghan	1/7/40	M	*
1 Armd Div (Aust)	Maj.-Gen. J. Northcott	1/9/41		*
GSO1	Col. R. N. L. Hopkins	1/5/41		

AA & QMG	Col. W. M. Anderson	1/7/41	
1 Armd Bde	Brig. F. B. Hinton	19/6/41	M
2 Armd Bde	Brig. J. A. Clareborough	1/7/41	M

*   Officers who had reached general rank by December 1943
M Militia officers at the outbreak of war

Appendix 6

Senior Command and Staff Appointments, 1 February 1942

AHQ

CGS	Lt.-Gen. V. A. H. Sturdee	30/8/40	*
DCGS	Maj.-Gen. S. F. Rowell	1/9/41	* †
AG	Maj.-Gen. V. P. H. Stantke	1/8/40	*
MGO	Maj.-Gen. E. J. Milford	1/1/41	* †
QMG	Maj.-Gen. J. H. Cannan	24/10/40	
RMC & C & SS	Brig. B. Combes	15/1/42	*

GOC-in-Chief Home Forces

	Lt.-Gen. Sir Iven Mackay	1/9/41	†
MGGS	Maj.-Gen. G. A. Vasey	5/1/42	* †
1 Armd Div	Maj.-Gen. J. Northcott	1/9/41	*
N. Comd	Maj.-Gen. J. M. A. Durrant	13/7/41	*
E. Comd	Lt.-Gen. H. D. Wynter	19/12/41	* †
Base Comdt	Maj.-Gen. A. C. Fewtrell	7/1/42	
1 Cav Div	Maj.-Gen. H. C. H. Robertson	5/1/42	* †
1 Div	Maj.-Gen. C. A. Clowes	7/1/42	* †
2 Div	Maj.-Gen. H. W. Lloyd	24/10/40	
Newcastle Covering Force	Maj.-Gen. J. J. Murray	7/1/42	†
S. Comd	Lt.-Gen. E. K. Smart	24/10/40	*
Base Comdt	Maj.-Gen. W. A. B. Steele	5/1/42	*
2 Cav Div	Maj.-Gen. W. J. M. Locke	5/1/42	*
3 Div	Maj.-Gen. S. G. Savige	7/1/42	†
4 Div	Maj.-Gen. F. P. Derham	1/5/40	
4 MD	Brig. H. C. Bundock	11/12/39	*
6 MD	Brig. E. L. Vowles	6/1/42	*
W. Comd	Maj.-Gen. E. C. P. Plant	6/1/42	* †
7 Mil Dist (Darwin)	Maj.-Gen. D. V. J. Blake	1/9/41	*
8 Mil Dist (Pt Moresby)	Maj.-Gen. B. M. Morris	19/5/41	*

* Permanent army officers
† Service in Middle East

Officers placed on the Retired List
Staff Corps   Maj.-Gen. R. E. Jackson, aged 56, GOC W.Comd
Brig. G. E. Manchester, aged 56, Commander 6 MD
Brig. E. F. Harrison, aged 61, Comdt RMC

CMF   Maj.-Gen. J. D. Richardson, aged 61, GOC 1 Cav Div
Maj.-Gen. G. J. Rankin, aged 54, GOC 2 Cav Div
Maj.-Gen. E. A. Drake-Brockman, aged 57, GOC 3 Div

Appendix 7

Directive to MacArthur

30 March 1942

Directive to the Supreme Commander in the
Southwest Pacific Area
(CCS 57/1)

By agreement among the governments of Australia, New Zealand, United Kingdom, and the United States.

1.   The SOUTHWEST PACIFIC AREA has been constituted as defined in Annex One. Definitions of other areas of the PACIFIC Theater are as shown therein.

2.   You are designated as the Supreme Commander of the SOUTHWEST PACIFIC Area, and of all armed forces which the governments concerned have assigned, or may assign to this area.

3.   As Supreme Commander you are not eligible to command directly any national force.

4.   In consonance with the basic strategic policy of the governments concerned your operations will be designed to accomplish the following:

a.   Hold the key military regions of Australia as bases for future offensive action against Japan, and in order to check the Japanese conquest of the SOUTHWEST PACIFIC AREA.

b.   Check the enemy advance toward Australia and its essential lines of communication by the destruction of enemy combatant, troop, and supply ships, aircraft, and bases in Eastern Malaysia and the New Guinea-Bismarck-Solomon Islands Region.

c.   Exert economic pressure on the enemy by destroying vessels transporting raw materials from the recently conquered territories to Japan.

d.   Maintain our position in the Philippine Islands.

e.   Protect land, sea, and air communications within the SOUTHWEST PACIFIC Area, and its close approaches.

f.   Route shipping in the SOUTHWEST PACIFIC Area.

g.   Support the operations of the friendly forces in the PACIFIC OCEAN Area and in the INDIAN Theater.

h.   Prepare to take the offensive.

5.   You will not be responsible for the internal administration of the respective forces under your command, but you are authorized to direct and coordinate the creation and development of administrative facilities and the broad allocation of war materials.

6.   You are authorized to control the issue of all communiques concerning the forces under your command.

7.   When task forces of your command operate outside the SOUTHWEST PACIFIC Area, coordination with forces assigned to the

areas in which operating will be effected by the Joint Chiefs of Staff, or the Combined Chiefs of Staff, as appropriate.

8.   Commanders of all armed forces within your Area will be immediately informed by their respective governments that, from a date to be notified, all orders and instructions issued by you in conformity with this directive will be considered by such commanders as emanating from their respective governments.

9.   Your staff will include officers assigned by the respective governments concerned, based upon requests made directly to the national commanders of the various forces in your Area.

10.   The governments concerned will exercise direction of operations in the SOUTHWEST PACIFIC Area as follows:

a.   The Combined Chiefs of Staff will exercise general jurisdiction over grand strategic policy and over such related factors as are necessary for proper implementation, including the allocation of forces and war materials.

b.   The Joint U.S. Chiefs of Staff will exercise jurisdiction over all matters pertaining to operational strategy. The Chief of Staff, U.S. Army will act as the Executive Agency for the Joint U.S. Chiefs of Staff. All instructions to you will be issued by or through him.

ANNEX ONE

DIVIDING LINE BETWEEN INDIAN THEATER AND PACIFIC THEATER

From CAPE KAMI in the LUICHOW PENINSULA around the coast of the TONKIN GULF, INDO-CHINA, THAILAND, and MALAYA to SINGAPORE: from SINGAPORE south to the north coast of SUMATRA, thence around the east coast of SUMATRA (leaving the SUNDRA STRAIT to the eastward of the line) to a point on the coast of SUMATRA at Longitude 104½ East, thence south to Latitude 08½ South, thence southeasterly towards ONSLOW, AUSTRALIA, and on reaching longitude 110° East, due south along that meridian. The PACIFIC THEATER extends eastward of this dividing line to the continents of NORTH and SOUTH AMERICA.

DEFINITION OF SOUTHWEST PACIFIC AREA

The westerly boundary of the SOUTHWEST PACIFIC Area is the westerly boundary of the PACIFIC Theater, the Area including necessary naval and air operational areas off the West Coast of Australia. The north and east boundaries of the SOUTHWEST PACIFIC Area run as follows: From CAPE KAMI (LUICHOW PENINSULA) south to Latitude 20½

North; thence east to Longitude 130½ East; thence south to the Equator; thence east to Longitude 165½ East; south to Latitude 10½ South; southwesterly to Latitude 17½ South, Longitude 160½ East; thence south.

DEFINITION OF SOUTHEAST PACIFIC AREA

From the MEXICAN-GUATEMALA western boundary southwesterly to Latitude 11½ North, Longitude 110½ West; thence south.

DEFINITION OF THE PACIFIC OCEAN AREA

The PACIFIC OCEAN Area includes all of the PACIFIC Theater not included in the SOUTHWEST and SOUTHEAST PACIFIC Areas, and is sub-divided into the:

NORTH PACIFIC AREA, North of Latitude 42½ North;
CENTRAL PACIFIC AREA, between the Equator and Latitude 42½ North;
SOUTH PACIFIC AREA, South of the Equator.

From: Morton, op.cit., pp. 614-16.

Senior Command and Staff Appointments, 1 May 1942

LHQ

C-in-C	General Sir Thomas Blamey	
CGS	Lt-Gen. V. A. H. Sturdee	30/8/40
DCGS	Maj.-Gen. G. A. Vasey	6/4/42
LGA	Lt-Gen. H. D. Wynter	6/4/42
AG	Maj.-Gen. V. P. H. Stantke	1/8/40
MGO	Maj.-Gen. L. E. Beavis	6/4/42
QMG	Maj.-Gen. J. H. Cannan	24/10/40
E-in-C	Maj.-Gen. C. S. Steele	6/4/42
SO-in-C	Maj.-Gen. C. H. Simpson	6/4/42

First Army

GOC	Lt-Gen. Sir John Lavarack	6/4/42
MGGS	Maj.-Gen. F. H. Berryman	6/4/42
DA & QMG	Maj.-Gen. W. Bridgeford	6/4/42

I Corps

GOC	Lt-Gen. S. F. Rowell	6/4/42
3 Div	Maj.-Gen. S. G. Savige	7/1/42
7 Div	Maj.-Gen. A. S. Allen	18/6/41

II Corps

GOC	Lt-Gen. J. Northcott	6/4/42
1 Div	Maj.-Gen. C. A. Clowes	7/1/42
2 Div	Maj.-Gen. H. W. Lloyd	24/10/40
10 Div	Maj.-Gen. J. J. Murray	7/1/42

5 Div

GOC	Maj.-Gen. E. J. Milford	6/4/42

1 Mot Div

GOC	Maj.-Gen. W. A. B. Steele	6/4/42

Second Army

GOC	Lt-Gen. Sir Iven Mackay	6/4/42
2 Mot Div	Maj.-Gen. W. J. M. Locke	14/3/42
41 US Div	Maj.-Gen. H. H. Fuller	
32 US Div	Maj.-Gen. E. F. Harding	
12 Bde Gp	Brig. P. C. Thompson	

III Corps

GOC	Lt-Gen. H. G. Bennett	6/4/42
4 Div	Maj.-Gen. J. E. S. Stevens	6/4/42

NT Force

GOC	Maj.-Gen. E. F. Herring	28/3/42

NG Force
GOC   Maj.-Gen. B. M. Morris   15/4/42

LHQ Reserve
1 Armd Div   Maj.-Gen. H. C. H. Robertson   6/4/42
19 Bde Gp   Brig. J. E. G. Martin   27/12/41

L of C Areas (Formerly District Bases)
Qld L of C Area   Maj.-Gen. J. M. A. Durrant   3/7/41
NSW L of C Area   Maj.-Gen. A. C. Fewtrell   7/1/42
Vic L of C Area   Maj.-Gen. E. C. P. Plant   6/4/42
SA L of C Area   Brig. H. C. Bundock   11/12/39
WA L of C Area   Brig. O. V. Hoad   1/5/40
Tas L of C Area   Brig. E. L. Vowles   6/1/42
NT L of C Area   Maj.-Gen. D. V. J. Blake   6/4/42
8 MD (Absorbed   Maj.-Gen. B. M. Morris   19/5/41
by HQ NGF)

Note: the date for General Blamey's appointment has been left blank because although he was appointed in March 1942 he was not gazetted as C-in-C until 27 November 1942.

Appendix 9

Machinery for Higher Direction in its Relation to Australian Government Machinery

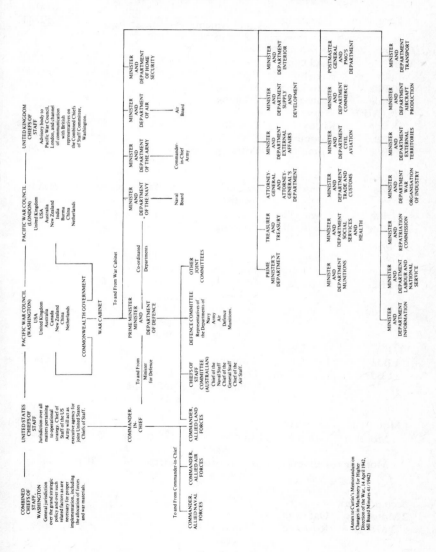

Combat Efficiency of Army Units, 19 July 1942

Formation	Location	Present Employment	Combat Efficiency		
			Training*	Equipment	Vehicles
I Corps	Toowoomba				
3 Div	MacLean				
4 Bde	Eagleby	Training	C	81%	50%
10 Bde	Jimboomba	Training	D	70%	
15 Bde	Casino	Training	D	61%	
7 Div (AIF)	Woodford				
18 Bde	Kilcoy	Training	A	82%	Complete
21 Bde	Woombye	Training	A	78%	
25 Bde	Caboolture	Training	A	84%	
5 Div	Townsville				
7 Bde	Milne Bay	Preparing for ops	D	84%	75%
11 Bde	Townsville	Training	E	84%	
29 Bde	Townsville	Training	E	77%	
II Corps	Burwood		D		
1 Div					
9 Bde	Thornleigh	Training	(Contains	77%	62%
28 Bde	Mt Keira	Defence in Sydney-	one Garrison	65%	
31 Bde	Lugarno	Kembla Area	Bn which is not mobile)	65%	
10 Div	New Lambton				
1 Bde	Tomago	Training	F	70%	52%
32 Bde	Vale's Point	Defence in Kembla Area	F(only 2 units, one is Garrison Bn)	70%	
1 Motor Div	Rutherford				
1 Mot Bde	Gympie	In process of conversion	F(reorg in progress)	58%	55%
2 Mot Bde	Dungog	In process of conversion	F(reorg in progress)	53%	44%
Second Army					
2 Motor Div	Oakleigh				
3 Mot Bde	Rowville	Training. In process of conversion	D	40%	46%

6 Armd Bde Tasmania Force	Kardinia Hobart	Training	F	40%	50%
12 Bde	Brighton	Training	E	77%	40%
32 US Div	Adelaide, moving to Brisbane	Movement in progress	C	84%	81%
41 US Div	Seymour, moving to Rockhampton	Movement in progress	F	Complete	90%
III Corps	Perth				
4 Div	Guilford				
2 Bde	Moora	Corps Reserve Training	E	85%	87%
6 Bde	Geraldton	Mobile defence Geraldton area	E	85%	
13 Bde	Bellevue	Training	D	85%	
2 Div	Chidlow				
5 Bde	Melville	In process	C	72%	81%
8 Bde	Chidlow	of moving	C	78%	
Northern Territory					
Force	Darwin				
3 Bde	Darwin	Training	E	74%	75%
23 Bde	Darwin	Preparation	E	74%	
19 Bde	Darwin	for Operations	A, except one bn which is E	74%	
N.G. Force	Port Moresby	Training and			
30 Bde		Preparation	F	Complete	Complete
14 Bde		for Operations	E		
LHQ Reserves					
1 Armd Div	Minimbah	Equipping Tank	E	80%	79% Tanks
1 Armd Bde		Gunnery Tp			100% MT
2 Armd Bde		and Sqn Training			
Support Group		Training			
3 Army Tank Bde	Largs	In process of Conversion	F re-organizing	50%	56% Tanks 40% MT

*CLASSIFICATION OF COMBAT EFFICIENCY

A   Efficient and experienced for mobile offensive operations.

B   Efficient as a formation for mobile offensive operations but not experienced.

C   Individual brigades are efficient for mobile offensive operations, but higher training has not been completed.

D   Individual brigades are efficient in a static role. Additional brigade and higher training is required.

E   Units have completed training. A considerable amount of brigade and higher training is required.

F   Unit training is not yet complete.

(Data from Operations Report for Australian Army, 19 July 1942, File 42/401/142, MP 729/6.)

Directive of 2 July 1942

JOINT DIRECTIVE FOR OFFENSIVE OPERATIONS IN THE SOUTHWEST PACIFIC AREA AGREED UPON BY THE UNITED STATES CHIEFS OF STAFF, 2 JULY, 1942

1. OBJECTIVE: Offensive operations will be conducted with the ultimate objective of seizure and occupation of the NEW BRITAIN-NEW IRELAND-NEW GUINEA Area.

2. PURPOSE: To deny the area to JAPAN.

3. TASKS:

    a. TASK ONE. Seizure and occupation of SANTA CRUZ ISLANDS, TULAGI, and adjacent positions.

    b. TASK TWO. Seizure and occupation of the remainder of the SOLOMON ISLANDS, of LAE, SALAMAUA, and Northeast Coast of NEW GUINEA.

    c. TASK THREE. Seizure and occupation of RABAUL and adjacent positions in the NEW GUINEA-NEW IRELAND Area.

4. GENERAL INSTRUCTIONS:

    a. The composition of the forces to be used, the timing of the tasks, and the passage of command will be determined by the U.S. Chiefs of Staff.

    b. For planning purposes a target date for TASK ONE is tentatively set as August 1, 1942.

    c. Direct command of the tactical operations of the amphibious forces will remain with the Naval task force commander throughout the conduct of all three tasks.

    d. The withdrawal of the naval attached units of the U.S. Fleet may be ordered by the U.S. Chiefs of Staff upon the completion of any particular phase of the operation in the event that:

        (1) conditions develop which unduly jeopardize the aircraft carriers:

        (2) an emergency arises in other Pacific areas which dictates such withdrawal.

    e. The eastern and western boundaries of the SOUTHWEST PACIFIC AREA and of the SOUTH PACIFIC AREA respectively will, as of August 1, 1942, be longitude one hundred fifty-nine degrees east from the equator southward.

5. FORCES

    a. Ground, air, and naval forces now under the command of the Supreme Commander, Southwest Pacific Area.

    b. At least two aircraft carriers with accompanying cruisers and destroyers, and the South Pacific Amphibious Force, with necessary transport divisions.

    c. Marine air squadrons and available land-based air support in South Pacific Area.

d.   Army occupational forces now in the South Pacific Area to be utilized to garrison TULAGI and adjacent island positions; troops from AUSTRALIA to provide other garrisons required.

6.   COMMAND

a.   TASK ONE. Seizure and occupation of SANTA CRUZ ISLANDS, TULAGI, and adjacent positions.

(1)   Task Force Commander will be designated by the Commander in Chief, U.S. Pacific Fleet.

(2)   Necessary Naval reinforcements and land-based air support will be attached by the Supreme Commander, Southwest Pacific Area, who will also provide for interdiction of enemy air and naval activities westward of the operating area.

b.   TASK TWO. Seizure and occupation of the remainder of the SOLOMON ISLANDS and of LAE, SALAMAUA, and Northeast Coast of NEW GUINEA. The task forces engaged in this operation will be under the direction of the Supreme Commander, Southwest Pacific Area.

c.   TASK THREE. Seizure and occupation of RABAUL and adjacent positions in the NEW GUINEA-NEW IRELAND Area. The task forces engaged in this operation will be under the direction of the Supreme Commander, Southwest Pacific Area.

From Morton, op.cit., Appendix E.

Appendix 12

Appreciation by Colonel K. A. Wills, 20 July 1942

Secret

EASTERN NEW GUINEA, SOLOMONS, NEW BRITAIN AREA
MGGS.
1.   Enemy forces estimated on 29 Jul 42 as follows:—

LAE	2500
SALAMAUA	1000
BUNA	2000
	5500

2.   Six ships including one possible MLC carrier sighted BUNA area on 29 Jul 42. These could have increased BUNA force by from 3000 to 6000 troops. No report of tonnage so say 4500 average.
3.   It is reasonable to assume that there are now some 10,000 Japanese troops on the NE coast of NEW GUINEA in the LAE, SALAMAUA, BUNA areas.
4.   Shipping sighted at RABAUL on 29 Jul 42 consisted of 19 vessels incl 15 tpts.
5.   In the last few days after a quiescent period, air raids have taken place on DARWIN, TOWNSVILLE, and HORN ISLAND in addition to the usual raids on PORT MORESBY.
6.   There have been numerous sightings of enemy warships incl cruisers. These are seldom used to escort supply ships but they are invariably used in escorting troop ships and for assisting at landings.
7.   Japanese air strength shows a slight increase.
8.   He has air landing grounds at LAE and SALAMAUA. On disembarkation in the BUNA area, he wasted no time in constructing aerodromes, but boldly and rapidly pushed on to KOKODA in a manner which indicates more than mere defensive precautions for his new base.
9.   It may be recalled that just prior to the CORAL SEA Battle when he had collected his tpts at DEBOYNE I. about half these tpts had commenced to move on a bearing which indicated a direct attack on MORESBY, whilst the remainder were moving off in a direction which might well have implied a landing near BUNA.
      It appears to me worth while remembering his method of capturing BANDJERMASIN — after our success in the MACASSAR STS, he abandoned his direct seaborne attack and advanced overland across most difficult terrain from BALIKPAPAN. He did not make seaborne landing at BANDJERMASIN until his overland force had almost reached their objective.
10. From the facts outlined above, I am of the opinion that the enemy is

beginning an offensive operation and is not merely seeking to establish defensive bases in NE NEW GUINEA. Whether this is part of a more ambitious plan it is hard to say, but I am convinced that his immediate objective is the capture of Moresby, and that he intends to attack overland, probably in conjunction with a seaborne attack.

K.A.W.
Col.
GS

30 Jul 42

Photostat from Brigadier Sir Kenneth Wills.

Appendix 13

Chain of Command, August 1942

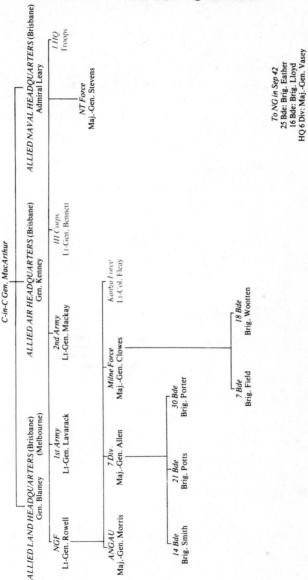

GHQ (Brisbane)
C-in-C Gen. MacArthur

ALLIED LAND HEADQUARTERS (Brisbane)
Gen. Blamey   (Melbourne)

ALLIED AIR HEADQUARTERS (Brisbane)
Gen. Kenney

ALLIED NAVAL HEADQUARTERS (Brisbane)
Admiral Leary

1st Army
Lt-Gen. Lavarack

2nd Army
Lt-Gen. Mackay

III Corps
Lt-Gen. Bennett

LHQ
Troops

NT Force
Maj.-Gen. Stevens

NGF
Lt-Gen. Rowell

ANGAU
Maj.-Gen. Morris

7 Div.
Maj.-Gen. Allen

Milne Force
Maj.-Gen. Clowes

Kanbai Force
Lt-Col. Fleay

14 Bde
Brig. Smith

21 Bde
Brig. Potts

30 Bde
Brig. Porter

7 Bde
Brig. Field

18 Bde
Brig. Wootten

To NG in Sep 42
25 Bde: Brig. Eather
16 Bde: Brig. Lloyd
HQ 6 Div: Maj.-Gen. Vasey

Headquarters and Staffs, August 1942

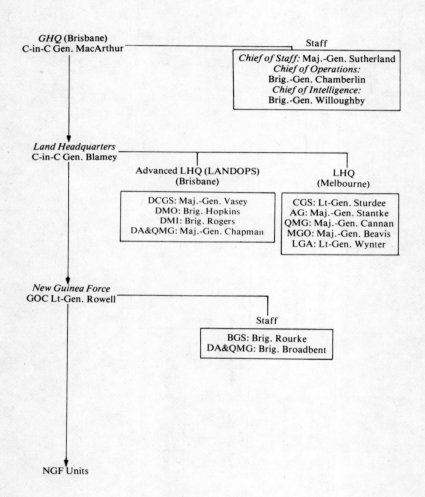

GHQ (Brisbane)
C-in-C Gen. MacArthur

Staff

Chief of Staff: Maj.-Gen. Sutherland
Chief of Operations:
Brig.-Gen. Chamberlin
Chief of Intelligence:
Brig.-Gen. Willoughby

Land Headquarters
C-in-C Gen. Blamey

Advanced LHQ (LANDOPS)
(Brisbane)

DCGS: Maj.-Gen. Vasey
DMO: Brig. Hopkins
DMI: Brig. Rogers
DA&QMG: Maj.-Gen. Chapman

LHQ
(Melbourne)

CGS: Lt-Gen. Sturdee
AG: Maj.-Gen. Stantke
QMG: Maj.-Gen. Cannan
MGO: Maj.-Gen. Beavis
LGA: Lt-Gen. Wynter

New Guinea Force
GOC Lt-Gen. Rowell

Staff

BGS: Brig. Rourke
DA&QMG: Brig. Broadbent

NGF Units

Appendix 15

Future Operations N.G. Force

1.   The main reasons for the success of the Japanese in forcing the Owen Stanley Range and advancing on Moresby are as follows:—
   (a)   Superior enemy strength at the decisive time and place.
   (b)   More simple administrative needs of the Japanese soldier and his better clothing and equipment particularly in respect of camouflage.
   (c)   Lack of reinforcing troops to restore a situation where the enemy was gaining superiority e.g. at Isurava and Efogi.
   (d)   Higher standard of training of enemy in jungle warfare. Our men have been bewildered and are still dominated by their environment.
2.   A stage has now been reached where there is every prospect, owing to the enemy administrative difficulties and to the very considerable reinforcements arriving for us here, that any further deep penetration, other than by small patrols, can be stopped. The problem now to be solved is what is to be the future role of New Guinea Force in the Moresby area.
3.   The primary task, as I see it, is the retention of Moresby as an Air Operational Base. This now demands adequate protection against seaborne attack as well as defence against further enemy inroads, either by the direct route into Moresby or by side-tracks and trails such as those down the Goldie and Brown Rivers.
4.   Until recently, the only form of defence considered here was that against seaborne attack, but the needs of the situation to the north have forced me to draw away more and more troops until today there is only one battalion [53rd] of indifferent fighting quality available for direct defence, and that is employed entirely on unloading ships. There are, in addition, certain beach defence guns and MMGs in more or less permanent locations. This stage of affairs should not be permitted to persist and I consider that a garrison of not less than one division with a complement of tanks should be located here for this role alone.
5.   The defence of Moresby from the north can be best achieved by operations which will force the enemy further and further back. The projected move of 126 U.S. Infantry Regt may conceivably help to achieve this, but it will take some little time to stage and its effect will not be felt immediately. It may, of course, merely have the effect of forcing the enemy to reinforce the Buna area to meet the threat, a move for which he presumably has adequate troops at Rabaul. It is not proposed to allow 126 U.S. Regt to commence its move from Moresby until the local situation is stabilised. Present plans are based on its moving via Rigo, but I consider that base should be moved to Abau, subject to satisfactory results of recce [reconnaissance] by the Engineer in Chief at GHQ.
6.   Operations astride the Myola-Kokoda track will be costly, both in combat troops and administrative effort. I consider the best results are likely to be obtained by applying steady pressure on the main track as far to the

north as possible, and relying on exploitation by side-tracks to cut into the enemy L of C and so force him to withdraw. Possibilities in this regard are, up the Goldie River into Ioribaiwa, and from Itiki through Jawarere to Nauro.

7.   The limiting factor in these proposals is always administrative. Lack of pack transport and continual decrease in availability of native porters will restrict the size of flanking forces which can be employed. Improvement of tracks and arrival of pack transport companies will, however, increase the probable scope of such moves.

8.   Defensive requirements to the north, together with provision of adequate troops for offensive operations, will call for a division. This does not need to be organised on standard lines — in fact, such an organisation is wasteful here. For example artillery is not necessary, but infantry units should have a very much larger number of personnel in rifle companies.

9.   In this regard there are two important factors to be stressed:
   (a) Wastage of manpower in jungle and mountain warfare.
   (b) Training in this type of warfare.
   (a) MANPOWER
        The wastage of personnel from battle casualties and physical exhaustion is extremely high. This demands greater infantry W/Es [War Establishments] as well as reserves of fresh units to replace those temporarily depleted in numbers or otherwise battle weary.
   (b) TRAINING
        Training as known in Queensland bears no relation to jungle conditions. The Port Moresby area itself is just as bad a training ground. It is essential that troops get into actual jungle and learn to master its difficulties of tactics, movement and control.

10.   These two factors, taken together, postulate the need for a second division of the special type that can be always available for active operations, and the other for re-fitting and training. There would accordingly always be the equivalent of a division available here, specially organised and trained for operations outside the Moresby area, if and when the occasion arises.

11.   The question of personnel replacement requires urgent attention. All except one of the AIF Bdes, are now in, or en route to New Guinea, and they all need reinforcements to a greater or lesser degree. If personnel are not available these formations will merely waste away, and there are not unlimited troops (U.S.) to take their place.

Rowell to Adv LHQ, 20 September 1942, AWM 577/3/1.

Appendix 16

Correspondence Relevant to the Dismissal of Rowell

A
Minute Lt-Gen. S. F. Rowell to Gen. Blamey 26 Sep 42

1.   By the terms of para 3 LHQ Operation Instruction No 30 dated 9 Aug 42, GOC 1 Aust Corps, which appointment I was holding at the time, was designated Commander 'New Guinea Force'.

2.   Para 4 of the same instruction authorised me to exercise operational control over all military forces constituting New Guinea Force at that time and such other troops as may have been subsequently assigned thereto.

3.   Your arrival at Moresby to operate as Commander-in-Chief from here will inevitably vary my authority and it is submitted that the position needs to be defined so that all concerned will know what variation is contemplated. This applies particularly to Allied formation commanders now exercising command under my orders as well as the joint service aspects of Navy, Army and Air cooperation. In this connection I instance your verbal orders to Commander Milne Force at Milne Bay on 25 Sep 42 regarding the despatch of a detachment to Wanigela.

4.   The question of the exercise of powers of the Authorised Person under National Security (Emergency Control) Regulations will also need to be determined. By the terms of Para 18 of LHQ Operation Instruction No 30, the powers of the Authorised Person are vested in me. The wording of the regulation is as follows:

'The Senior Officer of the Military Forces for the time being present and having the operational command of the Military Forces serving in that part'.

It would now appear that this authority should pass to you and that fresh delegations be made to replace those already issued to me.

[sgd.] S. F. Rowell

AWM 33/1/4

B
Letter Gen. Blamey to Lt-Gen. Rowell 26 September 1942
1.   I have been directed by the Prime Minister and the Commander-in-Chief, South-West Pacific Area, to take control of the forces in the New Guinea area.

2.   For the present it does not appear necessary or desirable to set up an additional headquarters staff. Therefore I propose to exercise command through yourself and the present Staff.

3.   I will be glad if you will direct that arrangements are made to furnish me promptly with all tactical and other information and alterations in the functions, allocations, dispositions and location of troops.

4.   I will be glad if you will ensure that all messages and information for Headquarters Allied Land Forces, or Headquarters Australian Military Forces are submitted to me, including Situation Reports, before despatch.

In the event of my absence from Headquarters, where it is apparent that such absence would cause undue delay in furnishing such information, you will forward it direct, at the same time taking such action as is necessary to ensure that I am kept fully informed.

The above applies also to matters of Administration of any importance.

5.   You will also be good enough to ensure that I am kept fully informed on the administrative situation, on arrivals of personnel, equipment and supplies.

6.   Please ensure that I am kept fully informed on matters affecting sea and air forces that reach this Headquarters through Staff channels.

7.   Control of field censorship, accredited war correspondents, army publicity, in accordance with Standing Orders for Accredited War Correspondents and Field Press Censors, will be exercised by Lieut-Colonel J. H. Rasmussen, Deputy Director of Public Relations.

[Sgd.] T. A. Blamey

AWM 33/1/4

C
Letter Lt-Gen. Rowell to BGS and DA & QMG 26 September 1942
The attached copy of a letter from C-in-C dated 26 Sep 42 gives the proposed layout. I refer below to paras as shown in his letter:—

Para 2. C-in-C does not intend to deal normally direct with BGS and DA & QMG. That is to say, orders will either be given in writing or to me verbally, or, in my absence, to one of you. He may consult you on matters of general information.

Para 3. BGS to see that C-in-C is on distribution list for normal intelligence information and Op Instructions. Ask C.O.I.C. for an extra copy of their report.

Para 4. *Situation Reports* — GOC or BGS will show C-in-C a *typed* copy before despatch.

All messages — this does not refer to routine stuff which normally C-in-C would not be shown at LANDOPS.

What he wants to avoid is to have signals sent from here to LANDOPS or LANDFORCES referred back to him here.

I suggested, and he agreed, that any such matters be put up to him either verbally or in writing and he would deal with them on the spot. If he agreed, he would then issue the necessary order to LANDOPS or LANDFORCES.

You will both need to see that your juniors do NOT dash off messages without reference to you.

Para 5. DA & QMG to give daily or periodical story to P.A. to C-in-C.

Para 6. BGS and DA & QMG to arrange.

Para 7. FENTON to hand over to RASMUSSEN. When latter sufficiently in picture, former to go back to AUSTRALIA.

[Sgd.] S. F. Rowell

AWM 33/1/4

D

Letter from General Blamey to Lt-General Rowell 28 September 1942

Following upon our conversation this morning I regret that I feel it my duty to relieve you of the Command of the New Guinea Force.

You will please arrange to return to Australia at your early convenience and report to the Chief of the General Staff at Melbourne.

A copy of the message sent to the Prime Minister, and the Commander in Chief, SWPA, dealing with the matter is available for your perusal at my office. I would be glad if you would please call there and peruse and initial it.

I have directed the Staff to ensure that all possible facilities for your departure and comfort are provided.

[Sgd.] T. A. Blamey

AWM 33/1/4

E

Most Secret signal from General Blamey to Prime Minister and General MacArthur 28 September 1942

Part A. 1. On arrival here I informed General Rowell of my instructions from the Prime Minister and C-in-C SWPA. He proved most difficult and recalcitrant, considering himself very unjustly used. I permitted him to state his case with great frankness. It was mainly a statement of grievances primarily against myself because he had received only one decoration for war services in the Middle East where certain other officers had received two. He charged me with having failed to safeguard his interests, and said he felt he was being made to eat dirt. All my persuasion could not make him see matters realistically. On the second evening I asked General Burston as an old friend of Rowell to endeavour to induce a proper frame of mind, but Burston met with no success. Instead of setting out full information for me here, I have had to search out details and feel a definite atmosphere of obstruction.

Part 2. Urge that Herring be sent immediately by air as successor of Rowell. If Herring not approved, Mackay second choice, but Herring much younger, this important in this climate.

Re disposal of Rowell if you decide to continue his services he could replace Herring in comd 2 Corps but events here make me doubtful of wisdom of allocating disgruntled officer to this appointment.

In this connection Morshead now cables that he would be glad to accept Stevens as second in command AIF ME. If you concur Darwin Command will be vacant. Rowell competent to fill Darwin which is a Maj-General's Command. Second Corps Command could be operated by senior divisional commander temporarily or by General Eichelberger with mixed American and Australian staff.

Part B.   I was forced to give Rowell written orders defining the position. Atmosphere now completely strained. Although I have exercised great patience, it is quite obvious that, as Rowell has taken my coming here as personal against himself, he would be seriously disruptive influence if retained here. More especially am not satisfied that necessary energy, foresight, and drive is being put into certain activities. Rowell is competent, but of a temperament that harbours grievances. He has had very limited experience of command. Essential to have commander of cheerful temperament and who is prepared to co-operate to the limit. In view of circumstances I have relieved him of command and directed him to return to Australia and report to CGS.

`Copy of this wire has been shown to General Rowell.

RG4, Box 1A, MacArthur Memorial

F
Signal from General MacArthur to Prime Minister, 28 September 1942

In view of General Blamey's action relieving General Rowell from New Guinea Command and the necessity of immediate replacement I request authority to despatch General Herring by air to report at once to General Blamey at Port Moresby.

AWM 33/1/4; also
RG4, Box 1A, MacArthur Memorial.

G
Telegram to Blamey from PM 29 September 1942; also to MacArthur
Secret and personal. I approve of appointment of Lt Gen Herring to replace Lt Gen Rowell as Commander NG Force. C-in-C SWPA and CGS informed. I shall discuss with Minister for Army and CGS your recommendation regarding future use of services of General Rowell.

AWM 33/1/4, RG4, Box 1A, MacArthur Memorial

H

Letter Gen. Blamey to Prime Minister 1 October 1942

1.   I would like to say that the personal animus displayed towards me was most unexpected. . .

2.   In regard to his [Rowell's] . . . claim that I had failed to safeguard his interests in accepting the direction of yourself and the C-in-C, SWPA, I informed him perfectly frankly of the exact incidence of events which led me to come to New Guinea, and there appears to be no ground for any resentment or objections on his part. It seemed to me when I received your directions and those of the C-in-C, SWPA, that it behoved me to carry out those instructions, and there can be no doubt that when the consequent instructions were given to General Rowell, it was his duty also to carry them out without question, cheerfully and co-operatively.

1 endeavoured to induce him to see this point of view, but his resentment was too deep.

3.   I informed him that I did not propose to make any alteration in the method of command, and I would do nothing that would derogate from his authority. He asserted his intention of refusing to accept the situation, and remain in New Guinea. I pointed out that such an attitude would be unacceptable to any Government and that it would certainly mean his retirement from the Forces. He asked me if this was a threat and I assured him it was not, but I was endeavouring to make him realise the inevitable result to any officer of a refusal to obey the direction of the head of the Government in such a matter. He replied that only lack of private means would prevent him doing so.

This was the substance of my interview with him on the day of my arrival on 23 September . . . [Para 4 not sighted].

5.   His attitude remained completely non-cooperative and he asserted that it would be impossible to operate my proposals except by the establishment of a special Staff. This was, of course, quite unnecessary. In fact similar conditions have arisen more than once in the Middle East when the C-in-C has temporarily taken over the general direction of operations in given operational areas from Army Commanders.

In fact such a demand could not be admitted in any organisation, e.g., it would be equivalent to a branch manager of a business telling the Managing Director who came to look into affairs that he would not agree to him utilising the ordinary existing machinery.

6.   General Rowell's resentment appeared to increase until the position became very strained.

It was obvious that he would not co-operate on the lines I had laid down and that this attitude would soon react adversely on the working of the Staff and the operations of the Force.

Matters reached a stage when I deemed it essential to direct him to return to Australia.

7.   With reference to the statement in my message that I was not satisfied

that necessary energy, foresight and drive had been shown, the following items are cited —

    (i) The capacity to drive the Japanese from New Guinea depends on our capacity to place sufficient forces in suitable tactical positions to do so.

        The present line of advance via Kokoda is so difficult that it will be months before a force of 2,000 men could be supplied by this route. There is no hope of achieving victory along this route alone.

        I had urged on my previous visit, a fortnight earlier, that the route north from Abau should be examined energetically. No action was taken by General Rowell to do so. It was left to GHQ SWPA to direct their Chief Engineer, General Casey, to make such an investigation.

        I took immediate action to energize this effort.

   (ii) A second instance is the lack of effort to take advantage of our success at Milne Bay.

        Details of an operation about to take place for this are contained in another communication.

        General Rowell's attitude to this operation was expressed in his own words in the presence of myself and another officer — 'If we take it on it will only lead to the Japs sending more in.' He said, however, he was prepared to direct General Clowes to carry out the operation.

        It was clearly a case that demanded vigorous action by the Commander of the Force. I took such action and went to Milne Bay with the American Air Force Commander, and, in consultation with General Clowes, outline of the operation was decided.

        General Rowell, however, held that I had taken the command out of his hands.

  (iii) In connection with (i) above, I found that the Intelligence Section of the General Staff at this Headquarters was very deficient in energy, initiative and enterprise in collecting and seeking information.

        I had the greatest difficulty in obtaining information from the Intelligence Section. It operates as though we were at peace.

        An independent Commander must ensure a high degree of efficiency in this section and this must have been neglected.

        I intend to effect considerable changes in this branch on General Herring's arrival.

8.   On the other side, I would like to say that the effort that has been put into this locality has produced most striking results and that General Rowell has cooperated in the development of this area with the Air Force splendidly.

9.   Apart from his insubordinate attitude, my principal criticism is a lack of appreciation of the need for seeking out energetically the possibilities of

developing aggressive action. This, I think, is due mainly to limited experience of command.

10. I regret extremely that I should have felt obliged in the interests of this force to take the action I did, particularly as much against my will, the matter was given a strong personal note.

For this reason I refrained from making any recommendation on the matter, but confined myself to suggesting avenues of employment for General Rowell should you decide to continue his services.

[Sgd.] T. A. Blamey

(This letter is held in AWM 33/1/4, but much of it is still closed. Parts which are still closed can be read in McCarthy, op.cit., pp. 237-39, and in Hetherington, op.cit., pp. 250, 257. Other parts remain completely closed.)

I
Letter from Lt-Gen. S. F. Rowell to HQ AMF (for CGS)
14 October 1942

1. I desire to record the circumstances under which I was relieved of the command of NEW GUINEA Force.

2. I was appointed to this Command by the terms of LHQ Operation Instruction No 30, dated 9 Aug 42, and retained the appointment until relieved by the C-in-C at MORESBY at 0900 hrs 28 Sep 42. The C-in-C's order of the day dated 28 Sep 42 does not reconcile with the date of my relief since it states that General Blamey assumed command of the forces in NEW GUINEA on 24 Sep 42. It is submitted that a correction is necessary if only for the purpose of accurate record.

3. On 21 Sep 42 I received a semi-official letter from the C-in-C advising that he was proceeding to MORESBY on 23 Sep 42 to operate from there.

I met the C-in-C at the aerodrome at 1700 hrs on 23 Sep 42. During the evening of that day, and once on each of the two days following, we had a full and frank discussion of the position of the G.O.C. NEW GUINEA Force in view of the C-in-C's arrival. At times the discussion was acrimonious as I then believed, and still do believe, that the C-in-C's confidence in me, expressed in broadcast of 16 Sep 42, no longer existed.

4. The main theme of these discussions, apart from the question of loss of confidence, was an endeavour to find a working arrangement suited to the circumstances. The fact that General Blamey had no staff with him made it inevitable that my own staff would, sooner or later, be called on to serve two masters and that I would gradually become a figure-head.

The C-in-C suggested that I should become a deputy to him but I demurred at this as it would have merely made me a staff officer with all vestige of command authority removed.

I submitted a proposal, which was not acceptable to the C-in-C, that the size of the force either in NEW GUINEA or under orders to move warranted the establishment of an Army Headquarters under which myself and my staff would have been responsible for the defence of MORESBY and for operations in the OWEN STANLEY Range. The superior Headquarters would then have had general responsibility for the whole area, as well as the detailed control of MILNE BAY and Commando units at WAU.

5. On the morning of 26 Sep 42 I addressed a memorandum to the C-in-C (attached at 'A') in which I sought to have some definition of our respective powers. This was necessary:

(a) In view of the terms of LHQ Operation Instruction No 30 which was still in force and which assigned me the command of all troops in NEW GUINEA.

(b) In order to make the position clear to my divisional commanders, since the C-in-C had visited MILNE BAY on 25 Sep and had given GOC MILNE Force direct verbal orders without reference to me.

6. No reply was received to this memo, but a directive was issued to me by the C-in-C at 1800 hrs 26 Sep setting out the position and directing certain procedure (attached at 'B'). This was discussed with C-in-C the same evening, as a result of which I issued an instruction to my senior staff officers defining the details (attached at 'C').

The arrangement decided on between myself and the C-in-C was that matters of major policy, which I would normally have referred to BRISBANE or MELBOURNE for decision, would be discussed daily at 0900 hrs. This was done on 27 Sep 42.

7. When I visited the C-in-C's tent for the morning conference at 0900 hrs 28 Sep he informed me that he had decided to relieve me of my command and that he had sent what he somewhat guardedly called an adverse report on me to the PM and to Gen. MacArthur.

I asked for a letter of instructions as to my disposal and for the right to see and initial the report mentioned above.

8. I received a confirmatory letter at 1630 hrs 28 Sep (attached at 'D') and saw the C-in-C immediately afterwards to read and initial the report. This is not an appropriate occasion on which to comment on this report, other than to regret that two statements, made in the heat of the moment, should have been divorced from their context and made to appear as the only points raised in three very big discussions. I respectfully request that I should be supplied with a copy of this report for future reference.

9. It is to be emphasized that I had no written instructions as to procedure for three days after the C-in-C's arrival. Once these instructions were received, I was determined to do my best to make the arrangement work. My instructions to my staff, noted in para 6 above, are adequate proof of this.

[Sgd.] S. F. Rowell

Headquarters and Staffs, 18 December 1942

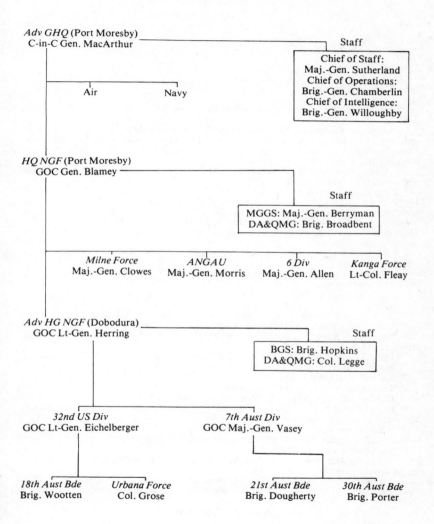

Adv GHQ (Port Moresby)
C-in-C Gen. MacArthur — Staff

Chief of Staff:
Maj.-Gen. Sutherland
Chief of Operations:
Brig.-Gen. Chamberlin
Chief of Intelligence:
Brig.-Gen. Willoughby

Air   Navy

HQ NGF (Port Moresby)
GOC Gen. Blamey —

Staff

MGGS: Maj.-Gen. Berryman
DA&QMG: Brig. Broadbent

Milne Force   *ANGAU*   *6 Div*   *Kanga Force*
Maj.-Gen. Clowes   Maj.-Gen. Morris   Maj.-Gen. Allen   Lt-Col. Fleay

Adv HG NGF (Dobodura)
GOC Lt-Gen. Herring — Staff

BGS: Brig. Hopkins
DA&QMG: Col. Legge

32nd US Div   *7th Aust Div*
GOC Lt-Gen. Eichelberger   GOC Maj.-Gen. Vasey

18th Aust Bde   *Urbana Force*   *21st Aust Bde*   *30th Aust Bde*
Brig. Wootten   Col. Grose   Brig. Dougherty   Brig. Porter

Endnotes

Introduction pp. xv-xxii

[1] Quoted in J. F. C. Fuller, *Generalship, Its Diseases and their Cure* (London, 1933), p. 5.

[2] Colonel E. G. Keogh, *South West Pacific 1941-45* (Melbourne, 1965), assesses some aspects of Blamey's performance. R. A. Paull, *Retreat from Kokoda* (Melbourne, 1958), contains a vitriolic attack on Blamey during the command crisis, but there is no balanced assessment.

[3] S. Encel, The Study of Militarism in Australia in J. Van Doorn (ed.), *Armed Forces and Society* (The Hague, 1968), p. 134.

[4] When the official history of World War II was being discussed by War Cabinet in 1943, 'It was considered that the history of Defence Policy should be dealt with in a separate volume', but the commencement of such a volume was deferred (War Cabinet Minute 10 June 1943, Agendum No. 154/1943, Military Board Minutes Misc 149/1942). Gavin Long eventually tried to incorporate defence policy into the civil and service volumes.

[5] B. H. Liddell Hart, *Thoughts on War* (London, 1943), p. 219.

[6] See Appendix 1.

[7] See *Committee of Inquiry into the Citizen Military Forces Report March 1974* (Dr T. B. Millar, Chairman).

[8] Quoted in G. de S. Barrow, *The Fire of Life* (London, 1941), p. 199.

[9] Ibid.

[10] Sir Archibald Wavell, *Generals and Generalship* (London, 1941), p. 2.

[11] B. L. Montgomery, *A History of Warfare* (London, 1968), p. 23.

[12] Napoleon's Maxims, quoted in T. R. Phillips (ed.), *Roots of Strategy* (London, 1943), p. 235.

[13] J. F. C. Fuller, *The Foundations of the Science of War* (London, 1925), p. 126.

[14] Francis Tuker, *Approach to Battle* (London, 1963), p. 391.

[15] J. Connell, *Auchinleck* (London, 1959), p. 237.

[16] The ranks are those held at the time.

[17] Quoted in S. L. A. Marshall, *Men Against Fire* (New York, 1947), p. 103.

[18] From Pierron, *Les Méthodes de la Guerre* (1889-1895), quoted in Fuller, *Generalship, Its Diseases and their Cure*, p. 30.

[19] Fuller, *Generalship, Its Diseases and Their Cure*, p. 32.

[20] J. Hetherington, *Blamey, Controversial Soldier* (Canberra, 1973), p. 212.

[21] See Appendix 2.

[22] The Australian Army reached its peak strength in 1943, but by July 1942 the number of divisions had begun to decline.

[23] For example the Canadian Corps Commander, Lt-Gen. Guy Simonds, was 42 in 1944. Maj-Gen. J. Cassells, the commander of the 51st Highland Division, was 38 in 1945.

[24] Fuller, *Generalship, Its Diseases and Their Cure*, pp. 87, 88.

[25] Liddell Hart, op. cit., p. 222.

[26] General Carl von Clausewitz, *On War* Vol. 1 (London, 1968), p. 68.

[27] Liddell Hart, op. cit., p. 218.

Chapter 1 pp. 1-7

[1] P. Hasluck, *The Government and the People* (Canberra, 1952), Vol. I, p. 42.

[2] W. Perry, Lieutenant General Henry Douglas Wynter, *Victorian Historical Magazine*, Vol. 43, No. 2, May 1972.

[3] W. Perry, Lieutenant General Sir John Dudley Lavarack, *Victorian Historical Magazine*, Vol. 46, No. 2, May 1975.

[4] J. M. McCarthy, Singapore and Australian Defence 1921-1942, *Australian Outlook*, Vol. XXV, No. 2, August 1974.

[5] Ibid.

[6] J. M. McCarthy, Australia and Imperial Defence: Co-Operation and Conflict 1918-1939, *Australian Journal of Politics and History*, Vol. XVII, No. 1, April 1971.

[7] Perry, Lieutenant General Henry Douglas Wynter.

[8] In 1935 Lavarack was junior to the following officers: Brigadier J. T. McCall, seniority, October 1923, born 19 April 1878; Brevet Colonel E. M. Williams, 1 October 1923, born 12 February 1885; Brigadier E. M. Ralph, 1 October 1926, born 7 April 1876; Honorary Brigadier-General C. M. Jess, 9 April 1926, born 16 February 1884; Honorary Brigadier-General O. F. Phillips, 1 May 1926, born 9 June 1882; Lavarack became a Brevet Colonel on 1 August 1926. He was born 19 December 1885.

[9] S. F. Rowell, *Full Circle* (Melbourne, 1974), pp. 30-1.

[10] This description of Lavarack's personality is drawn from the author's interviews with Gen. Sir John Wilton, 15 November 1974; Lt-Gen. Sir Frank Berryman, 1 May 1974 and 22 July 1974; Lt-Gen. Sir Sydney Rowell, 26 June 1974; Lt-Gen. Sir Edmund Herring, 25 June 1974; Brig. Sir Charles Spry, 8 August 1974; Brig. J. D. Rogers, 25 June 1974; Maj-Gen. Sir Kingsley Norris, 27 June 1974; Col. E. Mander-Jones, 12 August 1974; Maj-Gen. Sir Victor Windeyer, 2 May 1974; Col. D. H. Dwyer, 21 February 1975. All those interviewed gave different examples of Lavarack's temper and unpredictability. See also F. K. Norris, *No Memory for Pain* (Melbourne, 1970), pp. 105, 109, and P. Spender, *Politics and a Man* (Sydney, 1972) p. 83. Norris related to the author that if the padre beat Lavarack at chess it was a terrible night for the whole mess.

[11] For a discussion of Wynter's views see Perry, Lieutenant General Henry Douglas Wynter.

[12] For an outline of the Beavis affair see Hasluck, op. cit., Vol. I, p. 454, and D. P. Mellor, *The Role of Science and Industry* (Canberra, 1958), pp. 28, 29.

[13] Lt-Gen. Sir Sydney Rowell, General Sturdee and the Australian Army, *Australian Army Journal*, August 1966. In fact Rowell was referring to the atmosphere a little later than this period, but the comments still hold true.

[14] Perry, Lieutenant General Sir John Dudley Lavarack.

[15] First Report by Lieutenant-General E. K. Squires, 16 December 1938, AWM 243/6/58.

[16] G. Long, *To Benghazi* (Canberra, 1952), p. 45.

[17] Brigadier A. R. Allen should not be confused with the famous A. S. (Tubby) Allen who was also a brigadier at the time.

[18] Long, *To Benghazi*, p. 9.

[19] W. B. Russell, *There Goes a Man* (Melbourne, 1959), p. 189.

[20] F. Legg, *The Gordon Bennett Story* (Sydney, 1965), p. 151.

[21] A considerable number of retired senior officers, both citizen and permanent soldiers, to whom I have spoken, declare that there was no animosity between the militia and the Staff Corps. Yet those in higher positions before the war believe that there was, so it seems likely that the animosity was at the higher levels and in localised areas.

[22] J. Hetherington, *Blamey, Controversial Soldier* (Canberra, 1973), pp. 83, 84.

[23] Rowell, *Full Circle*, p. 39.

[24] J. M. McCarthy, Australia and Imperial Defence.

[25] D. Cowie, Australia's New Army, *Army Quarterly*, Vol. XXXIX, No. 1, October 1939.

[26] J. J. Dedman, Defence Policy Decisions before Pearl Harbour, *Australian Jour-*

nal of Politics and History, Vol. XIII, No. 3, December 1967, p. 333.

[27] See Appendix 3 for list of major units in September 1939.

[28] See Rowell, *Full Circle*, p. 41, for a description of Squires's disappointment with the government. In August 1939 Menzies announced that the government had decided not to increase the regular army by 1,571 men as had been announced in March of that year. One reason given for this was that he did not want to alarm the people, and if there was no war there would be difficulty returning the men to the work force. E. M. Andrews, The Australian Government and Appeasement in W. J. Hudson (ed.), *Towards a Foreign Policy, 1914-1941* (Melbourne, 1967), p. 84.

[29] A very brief outline of Shedden's career is found in E. W. O. Perry, Sir Frederick Shedden, 1893-1971, An Appreciation, *Victorian Historical Magazine*, Vol. 42, No. 3, August 1971.

[30] Rowell, *Full Circle*, p. 194.

[31] N. Gow, The Australian War Cabinet, 1939, unpublished paper (RMC, 1974).

[32] Hasluck, op. cit., Vol. I, p. 443. In fact during the period when Fadden was Prime Minister, R. G. Menzies remained the Minister for Defence Co-ordination.

[33] Also known at the time as Chief of the Australian Section of the Imperial General Staff.

[34] Responsibilities of the CGS and DCGS, 18 March 1940, File 2/401/11 MP 729/6, Australian Archives (Melbourne).

[35] He had been QMG since July 1934.

[36] Maj-Gen. R. N. L. Hopkins to author, 12 August 1974; Brig. Sir Charles Spry to author, 8 August 1974; Rowell, *Full Circle*, p. 38.

[37] G. Long, *The Six Years War* (Canberra, 1973), p. 15.

[38] Long, *To Benghazi*, p. 39.

[39] Menzies's admiration for Blamey stemmed from the time when he was the Victorian Attorney General. One incident in this relationship was when a demonstration in Bourke Street looked like developing into violence. Menzies had been impressed with Blamey's handling of the incident. D. H. Dwyer, Interlude with Blamey (unpublished manuscript, 1970).

[40] Hetherington, op. cit., p. 80.

[41] Maj-Gen. L. E. Beavis in a review of G. Long, *The Final Campaign* in *Stand-To*, Vol. 9, No. 1, January-February 1964.

[42] Long, *The Six Years War*, p. 22.

[43] This enmity stems from the period when Lavarack was GSO1 of the 4th Australian Division in France and Blamey was BGGS of the Australian Corps. The animosity between the two continued between the wars and during World War II. It was in Lavarack's nature that he showed it more than Blamey.

[44] Long, *To Benghazi*, p. 44.

[45] Ibid., p. 46.

[46] Brig. S. G. Friend, CRA 1st Division, was 43; Col. A. H. Ramsay, CRA 4th Division, was 44; Brig. H. C. de Low, CRA 2nd Division was 47.

[47] Air Chief Marshal Sir Charles Burnett, the new CAS, wrote to Air Marshal Drummond: 'I am a Scotsman as you are an Australian, but I am an Imperialist first and foremost'. J. M. McCarthy, Air Power and Australian Defence: A Study in Imperial Relations 1923-1954, Ph.D. Thesis, ANU, 1971, p. 243.

[48] Legg in his book on Gordon Bennett (p. 162) claims that a 'Senior Administrative Officer of the Staff Corps' opposed Bennett's appointment. This may be so, yet on 9 May 1940, while GOC Eastern Command, Sturdee wrote to Major-General C. G. N. Miles, the Adjutant-General, that Bennett 'is probably the most efficient senior militia officer in the Commonwealth. . . . He is looked up to as an excellent leader and organiser and one who maintains the dignity of a senior officer . . . like all energetic public spirited men, he has some critics, especially amongst the less efficient' (Military Board Proceedings, p. 65/40). Bennett's papers in the Mitchell Library indicate that the opposition to his appointment may have come from the new Adjutant-General, Major-General V. P. H. Stantke.

[49] See G. H. Johnston, *Australia At War* (Sydney, 1942), Chapter XXII.

Chapter 2 pp. 15-24

1 Rowell, 'General Sturdee and the Australian Army', p. 6.

2 Wilton to author, 15 November 1974.

3 Hopkins to author, 12 August 1974.

4 Lecture on the plan of Concentration by Lieutenant-Colonel V. A. H. Sturdee, Senior Officers' Course 1933, AWM 243/6/150.

5 Long, *The Six Years War*, p. 37.

6 For example, J. M. McCarthy, Singapore and Australia Defence, 1921-1942; I. Hamill, The Imperial Commitment, The Singapore Strategy in the Defence of Australia and New Zealand, 1939-1941, MA Thesis, ANU, September 1974.

7 See N. Gow, Australian Army Planning, 1919-1939, a paper presented to the History of Australian Defence and Foreign Policy Conference, August 1975.

8 Appreciation of Australia's Position in Case of War in the Pacific, March 1930, revised to 23 March 1932, AWM 910/2/4.

9 Concentration of the Australian land Forces in Time of War, 6 January 1932, AWM 243/6/6.

10 Hasluck, op. cit., Vol. I, pp. 173-4.

11 Keogh, op. cit., pp. 62-3.

12 Dedman, Defence Policy Decisions before Pearl Harbour, p. 339.

13 Hamill, op. cit., pp. 134, 135.

14 Hasluck, op. cit., Vol. I, p. 222.

15 Memorandum on the Employment of the AMF for the Defence of Australia, 29 April 1940, AWM 243/6/160.

16 Appreciation (HJP/3) re possible Japanese major attack on coast of NSW, 7 December 1940, AWM 243/6/135.

17 Ibid.

18 Appreciation by GOC E. comd, Sydney, 26 June 1940, AWM 243/6/71.

19 Appendix B to a letter written by Major-General R. E. Jackson in November 1948, forming a representation about his pension. Jackson is wrong with his dates as White was killed on 13 August 1940.

20 Combined Far Eastern Appreciation of Australian Chiefs of Staff, February 1941, CRS A2671, War Cabinet Agendum No. 64/1941.

21 L. Wigmore, *The Japanese Thrust* (Canberra, 1957), p. 59.

22 Hamill, op. cit., p. 147.

23 War Cabinet Minute No. 802, CRS A2671, War Cabinet Agendum No. 64/1941.

24 AHQ Operation Instruction No. 12, 24 February 1941, AWM 243/6/42.

25 Dedman, Defence Policy Decisions before Pearl Harbour, p. 338.

26 Hasluck, op. cit., Vol. I, p. 566.

27 See Appendix 4 for the Curtin Ministry.

28 Spender, op. cit., p. 146.

29 D. Kahn, *The Code-Breakers: The Story of Secret Writing* (New York, 1967). See also R. W. Clark, *The Man who Broke Purple* (London, 1977).

30 See F. W. Winterbotham, *The Ultra Secret* (London, 1974) for an account of the British machine. For the exchange of machines, see S. E. Morison, *The Two-Ocean War* (Boston, 1963), p. 71; also Roberta Wohlstetter, *Pearl Harbour, Warning and Decision* (Stanford, California, 1962), p. 173. For top-level intelligence co-operation between Britain and USA see William Stevenson, *A Man Called Intrepid* (London, 1976).

31 Kahn, op. cit., p. 486.

32 See Ladislas Farago, *The Broken Seal, The Story of Operation Magic and the Pearl Harbour Disaster* (London 1967); Wohlstetter, op. cit., and Kahn, op. cit.

33 Dedman, Defence Policy Decisions before Pearl Harbour, p. 346.

34 COIC Weekly Intelligence Summary, December 1941, AWM 423/11/2.

35 Farago, op. cit., p. 350.

36 E. R. Thorpe, *East Wind, Rain* (Boston, 1969), p. 51.

37 Farago, op. cit., p. 351.

38 Lt-Gen. Sir Sydney Rowell to author, 26 June 1974, also Rowell, *Full Circle*, p. 100.

Chapter 2 pp. 24-30

[39] Rowell to author, 26 June 1974.

[40] Military Board Agendum 92/1935 and Army War Book, July 1939, with revisions to September 1939, both in AWM 577/7/33.

[41] File Appointment of Commander-in-Chief Australia, 1941-1943, C-in-C AMF, Div. Commander AMF, Supplement No. 4, Appointment of GOC-in-C, Home Forces, CRS A2671/KR, Item 146/1941, Australian Archives (Canberra).

[42] War Cabinet Agendum, 146/1941, File 2/401/40, MP 729/6, Australian Archives (Melbourne).

[43] Supplement No. 1 to Agendum 146/41, May 41, loc. cit.

[44] War Cabinet Minute No. 1146, 10 June 41, loc. cit.

[45] Lt-Gen. Sir Sydney Rowell to author, 26 June 1974. This is confirmed by a circular from Army Headquarters to Commands dated 5 September 1941 which states: 'There is now to be a GOC Home Forces as in Great Britain. The Military Board exercises the same functions as the Army Council and AHQ as the War Office'. (AWM 199/2/5).

[46] For a short while Sturdee had considered General Gordon Bennett for the appointment, Wigmore, op. cit., p. 97.

[47] For a short biography of Mackay see A. W. Bazley and G. Long, Iven Giffard Mackay: Citizen Soldier, *Australian Army Journal*, June 1967. For a full length biography, see Ivan Chapman, *Iven G. Mackay, Citizen and Soldier* (Melbourne, 1975).

[48] Copy of leading article from *Daily Telegraph* (Sydney), in File 2/401/40 MP 729/6.

[49] Ibid., CGS's comments.

[50] Instructions for GOC-in-C, Home Forces in ibid.

[51] Plans for Mobilisation, Mil. Board Minutes, misc., 105/41.

[52] Durant assumed duty on 17 July 1941.

[53] Appendix B to a letter written by Maj-Gen. R. E. Jackson in November 1948.

[54] Appreciation of the Situation by GOC N. Comd. at Brisbane, 24 September 41, AWM 422/7/8.

[55] See E. Spratt, *Eddie Ward, Firebrand of East Sydney* (Adelaide, 1965), for a description of Ward's claims.

[56] John Dedman agrees that 'it was highly improbable that either the Menzies or the Fadden Governments ever had under consideration plans for the military defence of the mainland of Australia against invasion'. J. J. Dedman, The Brisbane Line, *Australian Outlook*, Vol. XXII, No. 2, August 1968.

[57] Combined Planning Committee Eastern Command, Appreciation No. 1, 19 September 1941, AWM 243/6/69.

[58] That is, 1st and 2nd Cavalry Divisions, the 1st, 2nd, 3rd and 4th Infantry Divisions with components of a fifth division, corps troops and coastal defences.

[59] In addition to the militia, at the end of August 1941 the Permanent Military Forces in Australia numbered 5,025; there were 12,915 in garrison battalions and 43,720 in the VDC. On 13 August the formation of the Australian Women's Army Service was approved. D. McCarthy, *South West Pacific Area: First Year* (Canberra, 1959), p. 2.

[60] War Cabinet Agenda 192/1940, File 2/401/30, MP 729/6.

[61] Appointment of Commander-in-Chief Australia, etc. CRS A2671/XR, Item 146/1941.

[62] Higher Army Administration, Supplement No. 1 to War Cabinet Agendum No. 197/1940, File No. 2/401/30, MP 729/6.

[63] Vasey to his wife, 24 June 1941, Vasey Papers 2/5.

[64] Louch to Vasey, 19 October 1941, Vasey Papers 2/5.

[65] Appointment of Commander-in-Chief Australia, etc. CRS A2671/XR, Item 146/1941.

[66] G. Drake-Brockman, *The Turning Wheel* (Perth, 1960), p. 253. Drake-Brockman was Director of Engineer Services in the Branch of the Quartermaster-General for most of the war.

[67] Ibid., p. 291.

[68] General Cannan, in a letter to the author dated 1 October 1974, described his ap-

Chapter 2 pp. 30-1

pointment as follows: The 'Menzies Government was smarting under severe criticism of Army control. This resulted in the Menzies Government deciding that as 95 per cent of troops were not permanent forces, an officer from Citizen Forces [sic] should take a seat on the Military Board. This displeased Sturdee. He said "never in the history of the British Empire had there been such an appointment to become a principal staff officer". Menzies replied to Sturdee, "Well this could be the first time so please make your recommendations for Cabinet approval". Sturdee approached me per telephone from Melbourne. I said I would like 48 hours to consider the proposal. I suggested Gordon Bennett. Sturdee said Bennett was one officer he would never agree to as Bennett was an unfair critic of A and I staff and also of Duntroon officers. Sturdee said the matter was urgent and would ring me next day for a reply. I conferred with my wife and her reply was encouraging. She said Gen. Sturdee would not give me the offer unless he thought I was capable and qualified. So when he rang next day I said yes. So off I went to Melbourne to become QMG and to sit on the Military Board; Sturdee, CGS, Stantke AG, Williams MGO and myself'.

69 Rowell, General Sturdee and the Australian Army, p. 7.
70 Vasey to his wife, 16 July 1961, Vasey Papers 2/5.
71 Rowell to Vasey, 19 May 1941, Vasey Papers 2/5.
72 Hetherington, op. cit., p. 188.
73 Vasey to his wife, 24 July 1941, Vasey Papers 2/5.
74 See Appendix 5.
75 See Appendix 6.

Chapter 3 pp. 32-8

1 Hasluck, op. cit., Vol. I, p. 558.
2 Hasluck, op. cit., Vol II, p. 56.
3 Defence of Australia and Adjacent Areas — Appreciation by Chiefs of Staff, 11 December 1941, CRS A2671, Item 14/301/227.
4 War Cabinet Agendum No. 418/1941, 12 December 1941, CRS A2671, Item 14/301/227.
5 Chiefs of Staff Appreciation, 15 December 1941, War Cabinet Agendum No. 418/1941, 18 December 1941, CRS A2671, Item 14/301/227.
6 Memo Brig-Gen. Raymond E. Lee for AC/S, WPD, 9 January 1942. Quoted in U.S. Official History, Draft Chapter I, AWM 492/4/38.
7 Chiefs of Staff Appreciation, 15 December 1941, War Cabinet Agendum No. 418/1941, 18 December 1941, CRS A2671, Item 14/301/227.
8 Keogh, op. cit., p. 109.
9 Rowell to author, 26 June 1974.
10 Major H. V. Howe, Secretary to the Minister for the Army, to Gavin Long, 16 March 1944. G. Long Notebook 46, p. 54.
11 Wigmore, op. cit., Ch. 19.
12 Rowell to author, 26 June 1974.
13 Wigmore, op. cit. p. 424.
14 See Hamill, op. cit., and J. M. McCarthy, Singapore and Australian Defence.
15 Hamill, op. cit., p. 289.
16 Defence of Australia and Adjacent areas — Appreciation by Chiefs of Staff. 11 December 1941, CRS A2671, Item 14/301/227.
17 M. Matloff and C. M. Snell, Strategic Planning for Coalition Warfare, 1941-1942 (Washington, 1953), p. 87.
18 Wigmore, op. cit., p. 182.
19 For a discussion of ABDACOM, see ibid., pp. 182-4, 206, 255-6.
20 UK appreciation and Aust. Chiefs of Staff Report attached to War Cabinet Agendum No. 455/1941, CRS A2671/XR, Item 445/1941.

Chapter 3 pp. 38-45

[21] This was originally named U.S. Forces in Australia (USFIA) but was renamed USAFIA on 5 January 1942.

[22] Rowell has left an interesting account of the first meeting of the Joint Planning Committee. Rowell, *Full Circle*, p. 101.

[23] Account of conference taken from Notes on Conference on 3 January 1942, War Cabinet Agendum No. 6/1942, CRS A2670, and also J. R. Barnes, Report on Organisation and Activities U.S. Forces in Australia 7 December 1941-30 June 1942, held in CMH, Washington.

[24] War Cabinet Agendum No. 32/1942, CRS A2670, Item 32/1942.

[25] Chiefs of Staff Paper No. 3 — Defence of Australia, 16 January 1942, attached to ibid.

[26] G. Hermon Gill, *Royal Australian Navy 1939-1942* (Canberra, 1957), p. 508.

[27] A. Chandler Jr (ed.), *The Papers of Dwight David Eisenhower, The War Years* (Baltimore, 1970), p. 77.

[28] Defence of Australia, 4 February 1942, CRS A2684, Item 905.

[29] Appendix II to War Cabinet Agendum 96/1942, CRS A2684, Item 905.

[30] See Appendix 6 for the army order of battle, 1 February 1942.

[31] Plant to G. Long, 1 October 1943, G. Long Notes, AWM 577/7/32.

[32] Appendix III to War Cabinet Agendum 76/1942, CRS A2684, Item 905.

[33] AHQ Operation Instruction No. 26, 13 December 1941, AWM 243/6/42.

[34] Appendix I to War Cabinet Agendum 96/1942, CRS A2684, Item 905.

[35] War Cabinet Agendum 96/1942, loc. cit.

[36] War Cabinet Agendum 96/1942, 18 February 1942, CBS A2670, Item 96/1942.

[37] Wills's Appreciation, 2 February 1942, Personal Records of Major-General C. S. Steele, Part I, AWM.

[38] Lavarack to Sturdee, 6 February 1942, AWM 54/1/4.

[39] Lloyd to Gavin Long, G. Long Notebook No. 1, p. 27.

[40] Lloyd to Rowell, 8 February 1942, AWM 541/1/4.

[41] Wigmore, op. cit., p. 444.

[42] L. Morton, *Strategy and Command: The First Two Years* (Washington, 1962), p. 203; also Matloff and Snell, op. cit., p. 128.

[43] Paper by the Chief of the General Staff on Future Employment of AIF, 15 February 1942, AWM 541/1/4.

[44] Wigmore, op. cit., pp. 445-6.

[45] *Sydney Morning Herald*, 24 February, 1942.

[46] Colonel J. P. Buckley to author, 20 August 1974. Buckley is Sturdee's son-in-law and was in the Department of Defence until he retired recently. Rowell has written that this was 'the most fateful recommendation [Sturdee] had to make in his service'. Rowell, 'General Sturdee and the Australian Army', p. 9.

[47] This episode is covered in Wigmore, op. cit., pp. 442-52; W. S. Churchill, *The Second World War*, Vol. IV (London, 1951); J. J. Dedman, 'The Return of the AIF from the Middle East', *Australian Outlook*, Vol. 21, No. 2, August 1967, and J. Marsh, 'Churchill versus Curtin, February 1942', *Australian Army Journal*, January 1971.

[48] Comments on U.S. War History, Vol. I, Chapter I, by Lt-Gen. V. A. H. Sturdee and Lt-Gen. S. Rowell, early February 1948.

[49] The most complete account of this attack is found in D. Lockwood, *Australia's Pearl Harbour, Darwin 1942* (Melbourne, 1966).

[50] Appreciation by Chiefs of Staff, 27 February 1942, CRS A2670, Item 96/1942.

[51] Appreciation by Chiefs of Staff, 11 December 1942, CRS A2671, Item 14/301/227.

[52] General Gordon Bennett has written: 'During early March 1942 the Minister for the Army, Frank Forde, asked my opinion on this matter, expressing Cabinet's doubts of the wisdom of the recommendation. Unhesitantly I told him that the Japanese must be fought to the death in New Guinea and must not be permitted to set foot on Australian soil. He expressed great relief at hearing this opinion which, he said would be

Chapter 3 pp. 45-50

welcome news for the Cabinet which was greatly worried'. Memoirs, misc. draft, Item 3, p. 42, Bennett Papers, MS 307/22, Mitchell Library.

[53] War Cabinet Agendum No. 96/1942, 5 March 1942, CRS A2670, Item 96/1942.

[54] Curtin to Secretary of State for Dominion Affairs, 1 March 1942, RG4 Box 1A, MacArthur Memorial.

[55] Curtin to Secretary of State for Dominion Affairs, 4 March 1942, CRS A816, Item 14.301.223A.

[56] Ibid.

[57] S. Milner, *Victory in Papua* (Washington, 1957), p. 12.

[58] Probable Immediate Japanese Moves in the Proposed New Anzac Area, 5 March 1942, CRS A2684, Item 905. Also RG4, Box 1A, MacArthur Memorial.

[59] Milner, op. cit., p. 13.

[60] This issue is dealt with in the following places: M. Fuchida and M. Okumiya, *Midway, The Battle that Doomed Japan* (Ballantine, New York, 1955), pp. 60, 63; N. Ike (ed.), *Japan's Decision for War — Records of the 1941 Policy Conference* (Stanford, California, 1967); D. Bergamini, *Japan's Imperial Conspiracy* (London, 1971); Morton, op. cit., p. 214 and Appendix B; T. Hattori, *Complete History of the Greater East Asian War* (Tokyo, 1953), microfilm copy in AWM; D. C. S. Sissons, Australia and New Guinea in Japanese Post-Mortems of the Pacific War, *Australian Army Journal*, September 1957; L. C. F. Turner, The Crisis of Japanese Strategy, January-June 1942, *RMC Historical Journal*, Vol. I; C. A. Willoughby, *et al.* (comp.), *Reports of General MacArthur*, Vol. II, *Japanese Operations in the Southwest Pacific Area*, Part I (Washington 1966). Compiled from Japanese Demobilization Bureaux Records. Hereafter cited as *Reports of General MacArthur*, Vol. II.

[61] Brett to AG, War Department, Washington, 4 March 1942, AWM 423/11/202.

[62] J. R. Barnes, Report of Organisation and Activities, U.S. Forces in Australia, December 7 1941-June 30 1942, held CMH, Washington.

[63] Morton, op. cit., p. 188.

[64] Brig-Gen. P. J. Hurley to Marshall, 21 February 1942, OPD 381, SWPA, RG165, Nat. Archives (Wash.).

[65] Appreciation of Situation in Far East submitted to HM Government in the United Kingdom by their Military Advisers. War Cabinet Agendum, Supplement No. 1 to Agenda No. 146/1942, CRS A2684, Item 904.

[66] War Cabinet Agendum, loc. cit.

[67] Ibid., Supplement No. 2.

[68] Maj-Gen. Rowell (DCGS) attended this meeting as Sturdee was ill. He recorded that with three King's Counsels, in Menzies, Spender and Hughes, to contend with 'it wasn't roses all the way'. Rowell, *Full Circle*, p. 104.

[69] Advisory War Council Minute No. 842, 18 March 1942, CRS A2670, Item 96/1942.

[70] Mackay to Vasey, 3 June 1943, Vasey Papers 3/3.

[71] Mackay to Gavin Long, 4 June 1943, G. Long Notes, AWM 577/7/32.

[72] Vasey to U.S. General, 20 March 1942, AWM 243/6/60.

[73] Notes on immediate Strategic Problems in the Defence of Australia. Document from 7 Fleet History File, 1942 A3, endorsement G3, FSC. Filed with other documents on the defence of Australia, early or mid March 1942. GHQ, SWPA Communiques 1945 for G3 Journal Part 3, AWM 423/11/202. On the other hand, on 13 March 1942, in a paper entitled Possible Japanese Action Against Australia and New Zealand, the U.S. Chiefs of Staff estimated that it was unlikely that the Japanese would attack the Australian mainland. (G. P. Hayes, Pearl Harbour Through Trident, Vol. I, USA Joint Chiefs of Staff, Historical Section, 1953, unpublished, held at U.S. National Archives, Military Section, Washington, p. 173.)

[74] Supplement No. 2 to War Cabinet Agendum No. 146/1942, CRS A2684, Item 904.

[75] GHQ, SWPA Report on Organisation and Activities, USAFIA, 7 December 1941-June 30, 1942, AWM 16/3/5. As late as 20 March 1942 Brett believed that the main

Chapter 3 p. 50

threat was in the Darwin-Broome area. (Agendum for Consideration by Chiefs of Staff, the Commander of the Anzac Force and the CG USAFIA, 20 March 1942, AWM 243/6/119.)

76 Probable Immediate Japanese Moves in the Proposed new Anzac Area, 5 March 1942, CRS 2684, Item 905.

77 Impression gained by Brigadier J. D. Rogers, who returned from the Middle East in February 1942 to become Mackay's Chief Intelligence Officer [to author, 25 June 1974]. Herring had the same impression and thought Curtin was very frightened [to author, 25 June 1974]. Sir Kingsley Norris did not have the impression that the despondency was widespread, although he felt the government was frightened [to author, 27 June 1974]. Brig-Gen. Hurley reported to America: 'The people do not appear to be aware of the critical situation confronting them. The newspapers the day after the raid [on Darwin], and on Saturday, had much more news concerning horse racing than they did concerning the raid on Darwin. This is not a criticism of Australia. They give about as much space in their newspapers to racing as we do to glamor, sex appeal and the figures of almost naked beautiful women. The point I am trying to convey is that the serious situation confronting this great continent of Australia has not fully aroused the populace and the military establishments seem to be too complacent and self assured'. (Hurley to Marshall, 21 February 1942, OPD 381 SWPA, RG 165, Nat. Archives (Wash.).)

78 The *Bulletin*, 11 March 1942.

79 The *Bulletin*, 18 March 1942.

80 R. E. Sherwood, *The White House Papers of Harry L. Hopkins*, Vol. I (London, 1948), p. 440.

81 For an account of the Japanese propaganda war see L. D. Meo, *Japan's Radio War on Australia* (Melbourne, 1968).

82 N. Command Intelligence Summaries, 1942, No. 2, 3 March 1942, AWM 423/11/165.

83 Report on Civilian Morale in North Queensland, 1 February 1943, by Dr R. D. Wright and Dr I. Hogbin, Hasluck Papers, AWM.

Chapter 4 pp. 51-2

1 Advisory War Council Minute No. 812, 5 March 1942, CRS A2682, Vol. IV.

2 He was the first RMC graduate to reach general rank.

3 Col. D. H. Dwyer, who was Miles's ADC for a while during the early part of the war, found him a 'typical staff officer of the old school. Not a commander to set the world on fire, although he had served with distinction in the first World War, but a mild mannered competent and pleasant man who fulfilled very ably his post as General Officer Commanding Eastern Command' (Dwyer op. cit.).

4 After the Syrian campaign Plant told Berryman that commanding a brigade in action was for a younger man. For a very short biography of Plant see We Will Remember Them, an anonymous article, probably written by A. W. Bazley, in *Stand-To*, Vol. 1, No. 6, July 1950.

5 *Sydney Morning Herald*, 2 January 1942.

6 Hetherington, op. cit., pp. 193, 194. Savige was to become Director of Recruiting and Propaganda. (Lt-Gen. S. G. Savige, Personal Records — Greece, Crete and Syria, Notes, Sunday 14 December 1941, AWM 253/4/2.)

7 Savige had commanded the 17th Brigade in Libya, Greece and Syria, Murray the 20th Brigade at Tobruk. The diary of Mrs G. A. Vasey for Monday 20 November 1944 contains an interesting sidelight on these appointments. 'A long ago story — Frankie Forde — talking to GAV — asked effusively, "Well George, how does it feel to be a general?" GAV with his naughty boy laugh and shy shrug, "No bloody good — in this company!" F. F. "Oh Yes I quite understand that. We know Savige and Murray were not successes in the ME. We'll watch them but the Cabinet thought it would give the public confidence if we said we have brought these men back from the ME" '. Mrs Vasey's Diary, Vasey Papers, Box 7.

Chapter 4 pp. 52-8

[8] Although the promotion for these two officers was backdated to 1 January 1942, it was not approved by War Cabinet until 21 January 1942 following a submission by the CGS stressing the strategic importance of their areas, their isolation and their responsibilities. War Cabinet Agendum 5/1942 and Minute 1725, CRS A2670, Item 5/1942.

[9] For new appointments and officers retired see Appendix 6.

[10] *Sydney Morning Herald*, 3 January 1942.

[11] The *Bulletin*, 7 January 1942.

[12] *Sydney Morning Herald*, 9 January 1942, p. 9.

[13] *Sydney Morning Herald*, 13 March 1942, p. 4.

[14] *Sydney Morning Herald*, 31 March 1942, p. 4.

[15] Comments by Lt-Gen. S. G. Savige on the *Official History*, Savige Papers, AWM.

[16] Advisory War Council Minute No. 812, 5 March 1942, CRS A2682, Vol. IV.

[17] Report to the Honourable the Minister for the Army from the GOC-in-C Home Forces, 22 December 1941, AWM 199/1/4. Also Headquarters Home Forces, Operation Instruction No. 1, 22 December 1941, AWM 243/6/17.

[18] Cutting from Dept of Army File 2/401/40, MP 729/6.

[19] From an article titled Unity of Command — Australia's Most Vital Need — What is Obstructing it? *Sydney Morning Herald*, 15 January 1942, p. 6.

[20] The *Bulletin*, 14 January 1942.

[21] *Sydney Morning Herald*, 23 February 1942.

[22] Statement by the Government on the System of the Higher Command of the AMF in the event of War in Australia, Dept of Army File 12/402/1, MP 729/6.

[23] Hetherington, op. cit., p. 199.

[24] Advisory War Council Minute No. 812, CRS A2682, Vol. IV.

[25] Advisory War Council Minute No. 831, CRS A2682, Vol. IV.

[26] G. Long Diary No. 3, p. 27.

[27] Memorandum, Redesignation of Formations, Sturdee to Minister, Dept of Army File 19/401/151, MP 729/6.

[28] War Cabinet Agendum, 16 March 1942. Not presented to Cabinet, Dept of Army File 2/401/79, MP 729/6.

[29] War Cabinet Minute No. 1931, CRS A2673, Vol. II.

[30] Col. E. Mander-Jones to author, 12 August 1974. Mander-Jones said that he had 'personal direct evidence with my own eyes'.

[31] Forde to Blamey, 21 March 1942, Blamey Papers 23.8.

[32] Hetherington, p. 210, says Herring left Adelaide for Melbourne on Sunday 15 March 1942, and on p. 213 states that he was ordered to Darwin two days later. However D. McCarthy, pp. 72-3, says Herring was ordered to Darwin on 24 March and left Adelaide for Darwin on 27 March, 'little more than a week after they arrived back from the Middle East'. McCarthy should know as he was with Herring's party. It seems, therefore, that Hetherington has made a mistake and that Herring left Adelaide for Melbourne on Sunday 22 March. If that is the case, then Herring, Vasey and Steele already knew of MacArthur's arrival in Australia (17 March in Darwin, 21 March in Melbourne), although they probably did not know that Blamey was due to arrive in Perth on 23 March. This incident is dealt with in detail in Hetherington, op. cit., pp. 210-14. See also Rowell, *Full Circle*, p. 105.

[33] Hetherington, op. cit., p. 213. Also transcript of interview with F. M. Forde, 4 March 1971, TRC 121/8, NLA.

[34] He had assumed duty as acting C-in-C on 20 March 1942. The Military Board continued to function under his direction. Military Board Minutes, misc. 32/1942.

[35] Rowell had been BGS of I Aust. Corps during the Syrian Campaign when Lavarack had commanded the Corps.

[36] Berryman had been GI of the 6th Division at Bardia, CRA of the 7th Division and then commander of the I Corps Artillery in Syria where for a short while he had commanded a brigade-sized unit called Berryforce. Stevens had commanded the 21st Brigade in bitter fighting in Syria.

Chapter 4 pp. 58-64

37 Bridgeford was AA & QMG of I Corps, Sewell was the CCRA and Secombe the DDST. Dougherty, who had commanded a battalion in Libya, Greece and Crete, was just about to be sent to Darwin to replace Lind as commander of the 23rd Brigade. He was promoted on 24 March 1942.

38 Rowell, *Full Circle*, p. 105.

39 Lavarack to Forde, 23 March 1942, AWM 33/1/4.

40 See p. 57.

41 See next chapter for an account of Herring's problems in Northern Territory.

42 The need for a high ranking Australian Officer in Washington was demonstrated by a comment from R. G. Casey, the Australian Minister there, in a cable to Curtin on 31 January 1942: 'The Naval Attache assists me where practicable on all service matters. . . . His rank however precludes him from access to American Chiefs of Staff whom he sees only on comparatively rare occasions. This is not peculiar to the Australian Naval Attache but is common to all Service attaches here' (Casey to Curtin, 31 January 1942, CRS A1608, Item A41/1/5, Part 4). On 1 April 1942, Evatt in Washington cabled Curtin: 'I think that the time has now come to despatch a military officer to Washington. He should be of very high rank and if possible had active service in the present war. Above all he should be able to state Australia's cause at all times'. Curtin replied on 8 April that Smart would be sent. (CRS A816, 14-301-223A.) On 26 May 1942 was the first meeting of the committee known as the Military Representatives of the Associated Powers (MRP). (Hayes, op. cit., Vol. I, p. 232.)

43 Blamey to Forde, 31 March 1942 CRS A2670, Item 186/1942, and War Cabinet Agendum No. 186/1942, 31 March, CRS A2673, Vol. II.

44 See Appendix 8 for details of new organisation.

45 *Sydney Morning Herald*, 2 April 1942.

46 Transcript of Interview with F. M. Forde, 4 March 1971, TRC 121/8, NLA.

47 *Sydney Morning Herald*, 18 March 1942.

48 D. McCarthy, op. cit., p. 17.

49 Memorandum, Colonel Wilson to Secretary, Dept of Defence Co-ordination, 1550 hours, 17 March 1942, CRS A816, Item 14.301.223A.

50 War Cabinet Minute 2021, 17 March 1942, CRS A2673, Vol. II.

51 *Courier-Mail*, 19 March 1942.

52 The *Bulletin*, 25 March 1942.

53 Chandler, op. cit., p. 190.

54 L. Mayo, *Bloody Buna* (New York, 1974), p. 4.

55 C. Lee and R. Henschel, *Douglas MacArthur* (New York, 1952), p. 161.

56 Transcript of Interview with F. M. Forde, 4 March 1971, TRC 121/8, NLA.

57 G. H. Brett, 'The MacArthur I Knew', *True*, October 1947, quoted in D. McCarthy, op. cit., p. 20. Eichelberger commented on this: 'I doubt that Mac's religion was more than words'. (From Eichelberger's copy of McCarthy in possession of Professor J. Luvaas.)

58 F. C. Pogue, *George C. Marshall: Ordeal and Hope 1939-1942* (New York, 1966), p. 375.

59 Thorpe, *East Wind, Rain*, p. 117.

60 Extract from G. Long Diary after interview 8 June 1944, AWM 577/7/32.

61 Article by C. Thorne in *Australian*, 6 June 1974.

62 Forde interview with E. D. and A. Potts, St Lucia, 19 December 1973, copy in MacArthur Memorial. For further biographical details of MacArthur see F. Hunt, *The Untold Story of Douglas MacArthur* (London, 1954); D. C. James, *The Years of MacArthur*, Vol. I (London, 1970); Vol. II (Boston, 1975); G. C. Kenney, *The MacArthur I Know* (New York, 1951); Lee and Henschel, op. cit.; G. Long, *MacArthur as Military Commander* (London, 1969); D. MacArthur, *Reminiscences* (London, 1964); R. H. Rovere and A. Schlesinger, *The MacArthur Controversy and American Foreign Policy* (New York, 1965); C. A. Willoughby and J. Chamberlain, *MacArthur 1941-1951* (Melbourne, 1956). In all, over sixty books on MacArthur have been produced.

Chapter 4 pp. 64-7

[63] Advisory War Council Minute 869, 26 March 1942, CRS A2684, Minute No. 967.

[64] MacArthur to D. Menzies, Secretary Defence Committee, Dept of Defence Co-ordination, 1 April 1942, RG4, Box 1A, MacArthur Memorial.

[65] Directive dated 30 March 1942 from Morton, op. cit., p. 614. See Appendix 7. Cable Marshall to MacArthur containing directive, 3 April 1942, Chandler, op. cit., p. 222.

[66] Lee and Henschel, op. cit., p. 166.

[67] W. Frye, *Marshall, Citizen Soldier* (New York, 1947), p. 307.

[68] Marshall to MacArthur, 9 April 1942, in Chandler, op. cit., p. 232.

[69] Milner, op. cit., p. 23.

[70] Kenney wrote that MacArthur said to Sutherland, 'The trouble with you, Dick, I am afraid, is you are a natural born autocrat'. G. C. Kenney, *General Kenney Reports* (New York, 1949), p. 152. Years later Kenney commented about Sutherland: 'He was an arrogant, opinionated, and very ambitious guy . . . I don't think Sutherland was ever loyal to MacArthur. He pretended that he was and I think MacArthur thought he was, but I wouldn't trust him'. (Interview quoted in James, op. cit., Vol. II, p. 201.)

[71] J. Miller Jr, *Cartwheel: The Reduction of Rabaul* (Washington, 1959), p. 20.

[72] Willoughby and Chamberlain, op. cit., p. 35.

[73] J. Luvaas (ed.), *Dear Miss Em, General Eichelberger's War in the Pacific, 1942-1945* (Westport, Conn. 1972), p. 99.

[74] Eichelberger Dictations, Book 2, p. 11-14. On the other hand Brigadier L. C. Lucas, the Australian Deputy Engineer-in-Chief, found that he got on reasonably well with Sutherland, but his appears to have been an exceptional case. (Lucas to author, 25 February 1975.)

[75] Shortly afterwards MacArthur requested that his title should be Commander-in-Chief, South-West Pacific Area.

[76] *Sydney Morning Herald*, 16 April 1942.

[77] Sturdee to Supreme HQ, SWP, 4 April 1942, Blamey Papers 23.72. Weekly report to PM by CGS for week ending 11 April 1942, CRS A2670. Agenda No. 201/192. AHQ Operation Instruction No. 50, 9 April 1942, signed by Major-General G. A. Vasey, Deputy CGS, Blamey Papers 12. See Appendix 8 for details of reorganisation.

[78] Gen. Plant, GOC in Western Australia, later commented that the State Ministers had been very indignant and had accused the army of lack of preparedness. They were very perturbed at the prospect of an invasion and they managed to persuade Federal Ministers to have the two brigades sent to Western Australia and to have the 2/11th Battalion detached from the 19th Brigade and sent to its home state. Plant had told the State Ministers that they had never done anything to help the army and that they were partly responsible for the situation. (Plant to Gavin Long, 7 October 1943, G. Long Notes, AWM 577/7/32.)

[79] It was later announced that all persons subject to military law serving in the Commonwealth were on active service as from 14 April 1942. RO II Corps, 27 April 1942, Northcott Papers 1431/29-66, Mitchell Library.

[80] Curtin to MacArthur, 17 April 1942, loc. cit.

[81] Milner, op. cit., p. 21.

[82] MacArthur's staff was as follows: Chief of Staff, Maj-Gen. R. K. Sutherland; Deputy Chief of Staff, Brig-Gen. R. J. Marshall; Assistant Chief of Staff (G-1), Col. C. P. Stivers; Assistant Chief of Staff (G-2), Col. C. A. Willoughby; Assistant Chief of Staff (G-3), Brig-Gen. S. J. Chamberlin; Assistant Chief of Staff (G-4), Col. L. J. Whitlock; Chief Signal Officer, Brig-Gen. S. B. Akin; Anti-Aircraft Officer, Brig-Gen. W. F. Marquat; Chief Engineer, Brig.-Gen. H. J. Casey; Adjutant-General, Col. B. M. Fitch; Public Relations Officer, Col. L. A. Diller. Only Chamberlin, Whitlock and Fitch were not of 'the Bataan Gang'. *Reports of General MacArthur*, Vol. I, *The Campaigns of MacArthur in the Pacific* (Washington, 1966), pp. 31, 33, hereafter cited as *Reports of General MacArthur*, Vol. I.

[83] Memorandum by Curtin, 14 April 1942, Mil. Board Minutes misc. 41/1942. See Appendix 9 for diagram of machinery for higher direction.

Chapter 4

84 Shedden to Blamey, 23 April 1942, loc. cit.
85 Curtin to Blamey, 25 April 1942, loc. cit., also Blamey Papers 23.7.

Chapter 5 pp. 68-76

1 For example see Morton, op. cit., and Turner, op. cit. Many other sources listed in the bibliography cover this topic.
2 See Lockwood, op. cit., for an account of the raid.
3 D. McCarthy, op. cit., p. 68.
4 Report on Visit of GOC-in-C, Home Forces, to Darwin and Townsville, March 1942, 21 March 1942, Vasey Papers 6/4.
5 War Diary HQ 6 Division, G Branch, January-March 1942, AWM 1/5/12.
6 GHQ Operation Instruction No. 4, 30 April 1942 AWM 243/6/121. Later, on 8 July 1942, this order was amended so that Herring was given command of all forces from that date.
7 Major, later Brigadier, G. H. O'Brien.
8 Lt-Gen. S. G. Savige, Notes on *Official History*, Savige Papers; Savige was critical of Herring in his report, and noted later: 'That section of my report did not pay dividends'.
9 Vasey to his wife, 12 September 1941, Vasey Papers 2/5.
10 Vasey to his wife, 15 August 1941, Vasey Papers 2/5.
11 Vasey to his wife, 29 August 1941, Vasey Papers 2/5.
12 Vasey to his wife, 12 September 1941, Vasey Papers 2/5.
13 Vasey's letters to his wife in 1943, Savige's comments in the Savige Papers, and General Burston to Brig. Disher, 7 June 1943, War Diary DDMS, HQ NGF 1943, Confidential Messages Brig. H. C. Disher, AWM 11/1/47.
14 War Diary HQ 6 Division, G. Branch, January-March 1942, AWM 1/5/12.
15 D. Gillison, *Royal Australian Air Force 1939-1942* (Canberra, 1962), p. 554.
16 Owen Griffiths, *Darwin Drama* (Sydney, c.1944), p. 109.
17 Maj. D. R. Robertson to Gavin Long, 24 July 1944, G. Long Notes, AWM 577/7/32.
18 D. McCarthy, op. cit., p. 75.
19 Maj. D. R. Robertson to Gavin Long. Notes, AWM 577/7/32.
20 Gillison, op. cit., p. 555.
21 War Diary, HQ 6 Division G Branch, January-March 1942, AWM 1/5/12.
22 Weekly progress reports by Chief of Staff, Report ending 23 March 1942, CRS A2670, Agenda No. 248/1942.
23 Herring to GHQ, 30 May 1942, File 42/401/142, MP 729/6.
24 Advisory War Council Minute No. 869, 26 March 1942, CRS A2684, Minute No. 967.
25 The Joint Planning Staff consisted of Barnes (U.S. Army) as Chairman, Brig-Gen. Clark (U.S. Army), Commander Kelly (USN), Col. Eubank (USAF), Commander Nichols (RAN), Gp-Capt. Hancock (RAAF), Col. Hopkins (DMO, LHQ) and Lt-Col. Booker (DD Plans, LHQ).
26 Second Report of Joint Planning Staff, 28 March 1942, AWM 243/6/119.
27 Milner, op. cit., p. 25.
28 Appreciation by Chiefs of Staff, February 1942, CRS A2670, Item 96/1942.
29 For example, D. McCarthy, op. cit., p. 112, n.2; Milner, op. cit. pp. 24, 25.
30 See p. 59.
31 Milner, op. cit., p. 26.
32 GHQ (Australia) Operation Instruction No. 1 to GOC First Army, 10 April 1942, Blamey Papers 12; also AWM 243/6/121.
33 See p. 47.
34 Australian High Commissioner to Curtin, 4 April 1942, CRS A2670, Item 96/1942.

Chapter 5 pp. 76-81

[35] Churchill to Curtin, 6 April 1942, CRS A2684, Item 904.

[36] Advisory War Council Minute No. 905, 16 April 1942, CRS A2670, Item 96/1942.

[37] J. J. Dedman, The Brisbane Line, *Australian Outlook*, Vol. XXII, No. 2, August 1968, p. 154.

[38] For an account of the SIS, see G. R. Thompson and D. R. Harris, *The Signal Corps: The Outcome* (Washington, 1966), p. 328.

[39] Kahn, op. cit., pp. 586, 587.

[40] R. S. Cline, *Washington Command Post: The Operations Division* (Washington, 1951), pp. 82, 83.

[41] Maj.-Gen. C. A. Willoughby in an affidavit dated 8 May 1945, quoted in Roberta Wohlstetter, *Pearl Harbor, Warning and Decision* (Stanford, California, 1962), p. 181, n.24.

[42] Sutherland to CG, U.S. Army Air Force, 16 April 1942, GHQ, SWPA, Communiqués from G3 Journal, AWM 423/11/202.

[43] Sutherland to Commanders AAF, ALF, ANF, USAFIA, 22 April 1942, loc. cit.

[44] Appreciation of the Position in the South West Pacific as at 22 April 1942. In 7th Fleet History 1942 file, probably a Joint Staff Appreciation, loc. cit., part 3.

[45] MacArthur to Patch, 25 April 1942, loc. cit.

[46] Marshall to MacArthur, 30 April 1942, loc. cit.

[47] MacArthur to Marshall, 1 May 1942, loc. cit.

[48] GHQ Operation Instruction No. 2, 25 April 1942, Blamey Papers 12.

[49] Copy of extracts from G3 Journal, 25 April 1942, AWM 243/6/61.

[50] Plan A, 24 April 1942, Blamey Papers, 43.5, Part 1.

[51] First Army Operation Instruction No. 6, 4 May 1942, AWM 243/6/133.

[52] Milner, op. cit., p. 25.

[53] Ibid., p. 27.

[54] D. McCarthy, op. cit., p. 86 quotes MacArthur as suggesting a 'limited offensive'. The author possesses a photostat of the carbon copy of the letter stating 'limited initiative', from RG4, Box 1B, MacArthur Memorial.

[55] D. McCarthy, op. cit., p. 86. General Vasey's visit may have been as a result of an earlier visit by Lt.-Col. D. W. Small, a signals liaison officer from GHQ (Australia). On 12 April 1942 Small wrote in his report: 'It would appear that very little is known at GHQ of the 8th Military District. The only officers to visit the District from AHQ since Japan entered the war were —
(i)   The Inspector General of Medical Services
(ii)   Lt. Col. Dixon of the E.S.B.
(iii) Myself.
I believe that no officer from either operations or intelligence has been in the district for a considerable period of time'. [Blamey Papers, 30.4.]

[56] It is not the purpose of this work to examine the argument over matters of higher strategy or the reason for Australia's repeated requests for additional forces, including the return of the 9th division. See Milner, op. cit., pp. 27-32; Hasluck, op. cit., Vol. II, Ch. 3; Morton, op. cit., Ch. 9; J. J. Dedman, The Return of the AIF from the Middle East, *Australian Outlook*, Vol. XXI, No. 2, August 1967.

[57] MacArthur to Blamey, 1 May 1942, RG4, Box 1B, MacArthur Memorial.

[58] *Sydney Morning Herald*, 2 May 1942.

[59] MacArthur to Blamey, 1 May 1942, loc. cit.

[60] S. E. Morison, *Coral Sea, Midway and Submarine Actions May 1942-August 1942* (Boston, 1967), Chapters II, III, IV, especially p. 63. On 17 June MacArthur said, quite erroneously, that Coral Sea 'was a great tactical victory which threw the enemy back on their haunches'. (Advisory War Council Minute No. 967, 17 June 1942, CRS A2682, Item Vol. 5.)

[61] D. McCarthy, op. cit., p. 82.

[62] Extracts from diaries and letters from Port Moresby, 1941-1944, Maj. Gen. B. M. Morris, AWM 419/73/10.

Chapter 5 pp. 81-6

[63] Extracts from Diary No. 2 — Gavin Long's visit to the Atherton Tableland, July 1943, G. Long Notes, AWM 577/7/32.

[64] D. McCarthy, op. cit., p. 65. Also Tom Grahamslaw, When Undisciplined, Poorly Led Troops Looted Port Moresby, *Pacific Islands Monthly*, Vol. 42, March 1971, p. 77.

[65] Gillison, op. cit., pp. 447, 448.

[66] Commander R. B. A. Hunt to author, 12 February 1975. R. A. Paull, *Retreat from Kokoda* (Melbourne, 1958), p. 25 claims that Porter, the new commander of 30th Brigade, ordered the enemy to be held on the beaches, but he is a little unclear as to the exact tactical plan. Porter told Gavin Long on 4 July 1942 that the army had retreated to the hills during the battle of the Coral Sea. (G. Long Diary, No. 8, p. 35.)

[67] For a short biography of Morris see an anonymous article, 'Basil Moorhouse Morris' in *Stand To*, Vol. 6, No. 5, September 1957-October 1958.

[68] Peter Ryan, The Australian New Guinea Administrative Unit (unpublished paper, 3 June 1968), AWM 80/1/3.

[69] Paull, op. cit., p. 20; Sir Kingsley Norris to author, 27 June 1974.

[70] Morris to author, 3 September 1974.

[71] Norris to author, 27 June 1974.

[72] Vasey to his wife, 27 July 1943, Vasey Papers 3/2.

[73] On 12 January 1943 Blamey wrote to Herring: 'I am not sure that a wise plot was made when Morris was made Commander, ANGAU. It is open to consideration as to whether a real live wire as a Brigadier Administration, ANGAU, would not be a better arrangement', Blamey Papers, 170.2.

[74] Although Morris was vehemently criticised for the lack of order in Port Moresby in February, Blamey was to judge later: 'General Morris set about his impossible task with courage and determination. The responsibility lies less with the commander on the spot than with those responsible for providing him with inadequate and incompetent forces'. D. McCarthy, op. cit., p. 65, n.6.

[75] Brigadier L. C. Lucas to author, 20 February 1975.

[76] MacArthur to Curtin, 12 May 1942, RG4, Box 1B, MacArthur Memorial.

[77] Advisory War Council Minute No. 938, 13 May 1942, CRS A2670, Agenda No. 228/1942.

[78] MacArthur to Curtin, 18 May 1942, RG4, Box 1B, MacArthur Memorial.

[79] Advisory War Council Minute No. 943, 19 May 1942, CRS A2670, Agenda No. 232/1942.

[80] Advisory War Council Minute No. 938, 13 May 1942, CRS A2673, Agenda No. 228/1942.

[81] Blamey to CGS and LGA, 21 May 1942, MP 729/6, File 58/402/466.

[82] S. and L. Brigg, *The 36th Australian Infantry Battalion 1939-1945* (Sydney, 1967), pp. 16, 17. War Diary, NGF, June 1942, AWM 1/5/51.

[83] Rowell to author, 26 June 1974.

[84] G. Long Diary No. 8, Sydney, 1 August 1942, p. 76.

[85] His appointment was criticised by Sturdee, GOC Eastern Command, in a despatch to General Miles. Sturdee to Miles, 9 May 1940, Mil. Board Minutes, P & S 65/40.

[86] Hetherington to author, 24 June 1974.

[87] Hopkins to author, 12 August 1974.

[88] Rowell to author, 26 June 1974.

[89] Ibid and Rowell, *Full Circle*, p. 117. Rowell said Blamey visited Greta in June but by June the brigade was arriving in Port Moresby. Rowell wrote that the commander of one of the battalions, who had commanded a pioneer battalion in the Middle East (Lt.-Col. A. Brown, 2/1st Pioneer and 36th Battalion), told him that his AIF Battalion at Ingleburn in 1940 on its first day was better than his new CMF command which was about to embark for the battle area (ibid.).

[90] Vasey to First Army, Second Army, 3rd Corps, 6 Div. (NT), NGF, 13 April 1942, MP 729/6, File 42/401/142.

[91] Hopkins to same addressees, 29 April 1942, loc. cit.

Chapter 5 pp. 86-91

[92] Blamey's headquarters was known as GHQ (Australia) to distinguish it from MacArthur's headquarters, GHQ. In late May GHQ (Australia) became Land Headquarters, LHQ. War Cabinet Agendum 251/1942, A2670, 251/1942.

[93] Provisional Operations Report for Australian Army, c. 1 May 1942, MP 7/29/6, File 42/401/142.

[94] Operations Report First Australian Army, 2 June 1942, loc. cit.

[95] NGF to GHQ (Australia), 4 June 1942, loc. cit.

[96] Australian Army Report, c. 1 June 1942, loc. cit.

[97] Operations Report of the Australian Army, 19 July 1942, loc. cit.

[98] See Appendix 10 for details of classifications in July 1942.

[99] Advisory War Council Minute No. 943, 19 May 1942, CRS A2670, Agendum No. 232/1942.

[1] On 8 August 1943 Blamey wrote to Forde proposing that Lloyd should command 1st Division. He added that Lloyd 'has shown an unusual capacity for training young soldiers and developing their morale. The 1st Division to which all young soldiers in Eastern Australia are drafted' was the best position for him. [Blamey Papers, 85.12.]

[2] Advisory War Council Minute No. 938, 13 May 1942, A2670, Agendum No. 228/1942.

[3] Blamey to CGS and LGA, 21 May 1942, MP 729/6, File 58/402/466.

[4] Advisory War Council Meeting, 1 July 1942, CRS A2670, Item 278/1942.

[5] Extracts from G. Long Diary No. 2, Visit to Atherton Tableland, July 1943, G. Long Notes, AWM 577/7/32.

[6] Sturdee to Lavarack, 18 May 1942, War Diary LHQ, operations general AQM 1/1/1.

[7] Herring to author, 25 June 1974; Rogers to author, 25 June 1974.

[8] See Hasluck, op. cit., Vol. II, Chapter 6.

[9] Lt. Gen. S. G. Savige, Notes on Volume V, Chapter 2 of *Official History*, Savige Papers, AWM. Savige was often biased, but this fact has been verified by studying AMF Gradation Lists.

[10] J. Field to Gavin Long, 14 February 1945, G. Long Notes, AWM 577/7/32.

[11] Hetherington, op. cit. p. 216.

[12] For example at the outbreak of war F. Hosking and B. J. O'Loughlin were both majors in the 29th Battalion and were both aged 35. O'Loughlin served with the 6th Division in Libya and Greece and with HQ I Corps in Syria and Java. Yet when he returned to Australia in 1942 and was promoted to Lt.-Col. he found that Hosking, who had remained behind, was a brigadier. On the other hand, after commanding the 15th Bde at Salamaua, Hosking reverted to Lt.-Col. in August 1943 and was given a battalion command.

[13] Mil. Board Minutes 72/42.

[14] Russell, op. cit., p. 251.

[15] Rowell to author, 26 June 1974.

[16] Performed well: 29th Bn of 30th Bde, 3rd Bn of 14th Bde. Performed adequately: 3 battalions of 7th Bde at Milne Bay. Performed poorly: 53rd and 49th Bns of 30th Bde, 55/53rd and 36th Bns of 14th Bde.

[17] Rowell, *Full Circle*, p. 109.

[18] G. Long Notes, Capt. W. L. Speight (ex 2/1st Bn), June 1942, AWM 517/7/32.

[19] Brig. T. S. Louch to Vasey, 21 August 1942, Vasey Papers 2/9.

[20] D. McCarthy, op. cit., p. 31.

[21] Herring to author, 25 June 1974.

[22] Brigadier J. Field to Gavin Long, 14 February 1945, G. Long Notes, AWM 577/7/32. For more of Porter's experiences see Paull, op. cit., pp. 18-26.

[23] MacArthur to Blamey, 20 May 1942, quoted in Milner, op. cit., p. 39.

[24] D. McCarthy, op. cit., p. 111. Brigadier Field of the 7th Brigade claimed that GHQ wanted to send a battalion to Milne Bay but that LHQ told MacArthur and Sutherland that they had 'sent enough penny packets into the Islands and it was a time

Chapter 5 pp. 91-7

for a self contained fight-force, so a brigade was sent. Later I persuaded them to send over an AIF brigade too and Milne Force came into being'. (Brigadier J. Field to Gavin Long, G. Long Notes AWM 577/7/32.) Indeed an LHQ memorandum dated 24 May 1942 quoted from a GHQ instruction that detailed the garrison at Boston [Milne Bay] to consist mainly of anti-aircraft units and one company of infantry. (AWM 243/6/121.)

[25] Ibid.

[26] Milner, op. cit., pp. 40, 41.

[27] Lavarack to Blamey, 19 May 1942, Blamey Papers, 43, 51. Blamey wrote on Lavarack's letter requesting an armoured brigade that there would be 'no further action at present'.

[28] Despatch from Norman Stockton, 18 May 1942, Townsville, AWM 723/4/61.

[29] Lavarack to Blamey, 21 May 1942, Blamey Papers, 43.51.

[30] Lavarack to Blamey, 22 May 1942, loc. cit.

[31] Brigadier J. Field to Gavin Long, G. Long Notes, AWM 577/7/32.

[32] For example Advisory War Council, 18 February 1942, Agendum headed 'Scorched Earth Policy' (Agendum 182/1942, CRS A2670) or Advisory War Council, 24 March 1942, 'House Security Measures, Evacuation'. (CRS A2680, Item 1033.)

[33] War Cabinet Minute 1850, 4 February 1942, CRS A2680, Item 1073.

[34] Extract from Hansard 'pull', House of Representatives, 27 March 1942, CRS A2680, Item 1073.

[35] War Cabinet Agendum No. 182/1942, CRS A2670, Item 182/1942.

[36] Blamey to Bennett, 19 May 1942, Blamey Papers, 170.4. Also Bennett Papers, 807/3.

[37] Comments by Blamey, Royle and Jones and a telegram from Evatt, 1 June 1942, Blamey Papers, 1.2.

[38] Hermon Gill, op. cit., p. 107.

[39] D. McCarthy, op. cit., p. 606.

[40] Advisory War Council Meeting, 11 June 1942, A2682, Vol. V. Also Curtin to Evatt, 12 June, RG4, Box 1A, MacArthur Memorial.

[41] Advisory War Council Minute No. 967, 17 June 1942, CRS A2632, Item Vol. 5.

[42] Col. G. G. Wilkinson's Journal, quoted in C. Thorne, 'MacArthur, Australia and the British, 1942-1943: The Secret Journal of MacArthur's British Liaison Officer (Part 1)', *Australian Outlook*, Vol. 29, No. 1, April 1975.

[43] *Sydney Morning Herald*, 12 June 1942.

[44] Hasluck, op. cit., Vol. II, p. 168.

[45] Ibid., p. 173.

[46] Matloff and Snell, op. cit., p. 259.

[47] Morton, op. cit., pp. 297, 298.

[48] James, op. cit., Vol. II, p. 188.

[49] NGF to LHQ, 23 June 1942, War Diary NGF, June 1942, AWM 1/5/51.

[50] LHQ to NGF, 24 June 1942, loc. cit.

[51] Morton, op. cit., p. 188.

[52] Ibid., p. 619. This directive is reproduced in Appendix 11.

[53] Present for the whole of the conference were: C-in-C AMF, CGS, DCGS, DQMG(P), CFO, AG, QMG, MGO, Commanders First and Second Armies, MGGS First Army, Commanders I, II, III Corps and Commanders Qld, NSW and Vic L of Cs. The LGA was present for 6 July ohly and the MGRA, E-in-C and SO-in-C for Item 1 on 6 July only.

[54] Record of Conference of Commanders held at Melbourne, 6/7 July by C-in-C AMF Mil. Board Minutes, misc. 49/42.

[55] D. McCarthy, op. cit., p. 120.

[56] Colonel Willoughby, MacArthur's Chief of Intelligence, had been promoted to Brigadier-General at the end of June.

[57] James, op. cit., p. 192.

[58] Milner, op. cit., p. 61.

[59] J. Toland, *The Rising Sun* (London, 1970), p. 348.

Chapter 5 pp. 97-101

[60] F. T. Smith Reports, 1/7/42 MS 4675, NLA.

[61] COIC Weekly Intelligence Summary, No. 2, 18 June 1942, AWM 423/11/2.

[62] Blamey to Curtin, 29 June 1942, CRS A2670, Item 231/1942. Also Mil. Board Minutes, misc. 45/1942.

[63] War Cabinet Agendum No. 281/1942, 30 June 1942, CRS A2670, Item 281/1942.

[64] Record of a Conference of Commanders held at Melbourne, 6/7 July, by C-in-C AMF. Mil. Board Minutes, misc. 49/1942.

[65] Memo, Order of Battle — Allied Land Forces — Reorganisation within the Army, 10 July 1942, signed by Brig. R. N. L. Hopkins, from Maj.-Gen. Hopkins.

[66] For details of changes in armoured units see R. N. L. Hopkins, *The Royal Australian Armoured Corps. 1927-1972*, soon to be published by the AWM.

[67] The 41st U.S. Division was to complete its move to Rockhampton on 31 July 1942 and the 32nd U.S. Division was to complete its move to Logan Village (south of Brisbane) by 3 August 1942. (First Army Operation Instruction No. 17, 17 July 1942, AWM 243/6/133.)

[68] These were: 3rd Divison (2 bdes), Brisbane area, 5th Division (2 bdes), Townsville, 7th Division (3 bdes), Woodford, north of Brisbane, 32nd U.S. Division (3 regts), Brisbane area, 41st U.S. Division (3 regts), Rockhampton.

[69] LHQ Operation Instruction No. 25, AWM 243/6/121.

[70] Coffey, a relatively junior ordnance specialist, had held the position off and on from early 1941, but he realised that a more senior representative was needed. See further, Long, *To Benghazi*, p. 93.

[71] Transcript of interview with F. M. Forde, 4 March 1971, TRC 121/8, NLA.

[72] General Sir John Wilton to author, 15 November 1974. Wilton was a senior staff officer on Sturdee's Washington staff.

[73] Rowell, General Sturdee and the Australian Army.

[74] Major-General R. N. L. Hopkins to author, 13 July 1974.

[75] In essence this promise was kept. His term as head of the Australian Military Mission in Washington was from 10 September 1942 to 29 February 1944. He then became GOC First Australian Army.

[76] Brig. L. C. Lucas to author, 20 February 1975.

[77] Luvaas, op. cit., p. 30.

[78] Shedden to Secretary, Dept of Army, A2676/538.

[79] B. Maughan, *Tobruk and Alamein* (Canberra, 1966), p. 8.

[80] Hopkins to author, 12 August 1974. Also Colonel E. Mander-Jones to author, 12 August 1974.

[81] Hopkins to author, 12 August 1974. Hopkins says that he checked this with Rowell and Berryman.

[82] MacArthur-Onslow to Gavin Long, 5 October 1942, G. Long Diary No. 9, p. 34.

[83] See Northcott Papers, Mitchell Library.

[84] Sturdee to Blamey, 25 September 1945, Blamey Papers, 170.

[85] L. E. Beavis, General Northcott: A Wartime Chief of Staff, *Australian Army Journal*, April 1967, p. 10.

[86] Blamey to Forde, 12 July 1942, Blamey Papers, 85.12.

[87] Blamey to Forde, 25 July 1942, loc. cit.

Chapter 6 pp. 102-3

[1] MacArthur, op. cit., p. 154. He did not move his HQ to Port Moresby until 6 November 1942. Willoughby and Chamberlain's *MacArthur: 1941-51* makes the same error of implication.

[2] A. J. Sweeting, Review of MacArthur, *Reminiscences* in *Stand To*, Vol. 10, No. 2, March-December 1965.

[3] A/Chief of Air Staff Intelligence and Historical Division, *Air Action in the Papuan Campaign 21 July 1942 to 23 January 1943* (August 1944), p. 17.

Chapter 6 pp. 103-8

4 Landops Melbourne to Milcomd Moresby, 12 June 1942, AWM 977/6/4.

5 PIB — Papuan Infantry Battalion, native troops with Australian officers.

6 Morris to author, 3 September 1974.

7 NGF to LQH (Melbourne), 17 July 1942, AWM 977/6/3.

8 Reports of F. T. Smith of Confidential Press Conferences given by Curtin 1942-1945, Report No. 15, 23 July 1942, MS No. 4675, NLA, hereafter F. T. Smith Reports.

9 LHQ to NGF, 28 July 1942, War Diary, NGF, July 1942, AWM 1/5/51.

10 G. Long Notes, N27/31, 32.

11 Wills had already shown himself remarkably adept at forecasting Japanese intentions; for example his appreciation for Lavarack on 2 February 1942 when they were on Java. [Wigmore, op. cit., p. 443.]

12 Appreciation of Situation in Eastern New Guinea, Solomons New Britain area, 30 July 1942. In possession of Brigadier Sir Kenneth Wills. See Appendix 12.

13 GHQ Intelligence Summary 29/30 August 1942, RG407, Records of GHQ, SWPA, G-3 Journal, August 1942, National Archives (Suitland, Maryland, USA). The Gap was a seven mile wide stretch of the main Owen Stanley Range with no high peaks. On clear days aircraft could fly through it at altitudes of from 8,000 to 10,000 feet. It was certainly not the narrow, easily-defended pass imagined by military planners in Australia.

14 Wills to author, 9 August 1974.

15 The *Bulletin*, 29 July 1942.

16 Advisory War Council Minute No. 1013, CRS A2682, Item Vol. 5.

17 Ibid.

18 LHQ Operation Instruction No. 29, 29 July 1942, RG407, G3 Journal, August 1942, Nat. Archives (Suitland).

19 Hopkins to author, 25 April 1974.

20 D. H. Dwyer, Interlude with Blamey, unpublished MS.

21 Blamey to Forde, 28 July 1942, Blamey Papers, 106.

22 F. T. Smith Reports, No. 27, 29 September 1942.

23 Milner, op. cit., p. 72.

24 On 29 July the 39th Battalion was driven out of Kokoda.

25 Rowell, *Full Circle*, p. 110.

26 The Inspection Organisation was set up soon after Blamey returned to Australia to eliminate waste in the army by inspection of administration. The Chief Inspector of Administration was Brigadier E. Gorman [Blamey to Shedden, 20 March 1942, Blamey Papers, 106]. The Inspector Army was Gorman's deputy and was located at Advanced Land Headquarters. Since both positions were held by old friends of Blamey, it enabled the latter to keep himself informed of events throughout the army. In the opinion of Brigadier Wills, Gorman had a 'destructive mind' and lacked administrative experience — either military or civilian. [Wills to Gavin Long, 29 October 1942, G. Long Diary No. 9, p. 38.]

27 Rowell to author, 14 February 1974.

28 War Diary, Adv LHQ, G Br, August 1942, AWM 1/2/1.

29 War Diary, HQ II Corps, G Br, July-August 1942, AWM 1/4/48.

30 Brigadier R. N. L. Hopkins, DMO, Colonel S. F. Legge, Colonel Admin., Q Branch, Landops, Colonel T. W. White, Colonel GS (SD & Trg) Landops.

31 Rowell to author, 14 February 1975.

32 Allen's GSO, Colonel C. M. L. Elliott, was absent with a leg injury.

33 War Diary, 7 Div., August 1942, AWM 1/5/14.

34 New Guinea Command and Administration, 30 July 1942, File 37/401/1168, MP 729/6.

35 On 25 July 1942 Blamey had written to Curtin: 'It is apparent that more active land operations will soon develop in the territory [New Guinea] and it is considered that a senior commander should be appointed whose sole responsibility will be the operational control of the Field Forces'. (Blamey Papers 85.2.)

36 Rowell, *Full Circle*, p. 111.

Chapter 6 pp. 108-14

[37] I Corps to 7 Div., 5 August 1942, War Diary, 7 Div., August 1942, AWM 1/5/14.

[38] Long, *To Benghazi*, p. 47.

[39] Rowell to author, 26 June 1974. The picture of Allen is drawn from conversations with Sir Charles Spry, 7 August 1974; Sir Frederick Chilton, 3 May 1974; Sir Kingsley Norris, 27 June 1974; Maj.-Gen. K. W. Eather, 29 April 1974 and Sir Kenneth Wills, 9 August 1974.

[40] Report on Ops 7 Aust. Div., AWM 577/7/34.

[41] These were issued at 2400 hours, War Diary 7 Aust. Div., August 1942, AWM 1/5/14.

[42] Dr Hartwell Woolford, ex RMO 2/6 Fd Regt, to Gavin Long, G. Long Notes AWM 577/7/52.

[43] Allen Papers, File 5, AWM 419/3/9.

[44] Hopkins to author, 12 August 1974. In May 1943 Col. L. A. Diller, MacArthur's Chief Public Relations Officer, wrote: 'Melbourne seethes with intrigue. A great deal of misinformation is openly discussed in the lounge of the Menzies Hotel and certain people in Melbourne seem to have almost immediate information about happenings at headquarters . . . Vicious, scandalous gossip is prevalent in Melbourne'. [Diller to MacArthur, 17 May 1943, RG4, Box 1B, MacArthur Memorial.]

[45] Vasey to his wife, 4 August 1942, Vasey Papers 2/7, MS No. 3782, NLA.

[46] Rowell, *Full Circle*, p. 111; Chilton to author, 3 May 1974. He was GSO1 in Port Moresby in July and early August 1942.

[47] NGF to Landops, 3 August 1942, AWM 579/6/2.

[48] Landops to NGF, 4 August 1942, AWM 579/6/2.

[49] D. McCarthy, op. cit., p. 140.

[50] Ibid., p. 121.

[51] Milner, op. cit., pp. 72, 73.

[52] C-in-C Conference with Press at L of C Brisbane, 4 August 1942, Blamey Papers, 139.3.

[53] Kenney, *General Kenney Reports*, p. 50.

[54] He was promoted to Brigadier on 1 September 1942.

[55] Adv HQ, Allied Land Forces Weekly Intelligence Summary No. 1, 31 July-7 August 1942, AWM 423/11/63.

[56] Eichelberger Dictations, Book 1, p. 127. On 21 September 1942 Col. W. L. Ritchie from the War Dept was visiting the SWPA and sent the following message to Marshall: 'I should like to reiterate the impromptu estimate I gave you of Japanese Siberia intentions with particular emphasis on the air indications. My purely personal estimate is by October tenth'. (RG 165, OPD Exec 10, Item 23b, Nat. Archives [Wash.].)

[57] The *Bulletin*, 12 August 1942.

[58] GHQ Op. Instr. No. 15, 6 August 1942, RG 407, G3 Journal, August 1942, Nat. Archives (Suitland).

[59] Morton, op. cit., p. 327.

[60] Of this 8,000 only 4,500 were infantry.

[61] Thorpe, op. cit., p. 91.

[62] Rowell, *Full Circle*, p. 101.

[63] MacArthur to Marshall, 9 July 1942, RG 165, OPD Exec. 10, Item 23a, Nat. Archives (Wash.). James, op. cit., Vol. II, p. 175, says jbarnes proved 'incompatible' with Sutherland and others at GHU.

[64] Gen. Eisenhower to Richardson, 16 May 1942, RG 165, OPD Exec. 333, Item 17, Nat. Archives (Wash.).

[65] James, op. cit., Vol. II, p. 183.

[66] Memorandum for AC of S from Arnold, 22 July 1942, RG 165, OPD 381, Australia 5.23.42, Nat. Archives (Wash.).

[67] Memorandum for C of S from Handy, 3 August 1942, RG 168, OPD Exec. 2, Item 1, Nat. Archives (Wash.).

68 Eichelberger Dictations, Book 4, p. VIII-36. Eichelberger said MacArthur told him that Richardson had agreed to become the corps commander, but when he had asked to go on to the U.S. from Noumea he had known that he would never return.

69 Richardson to WD, 8 July 1942, RG 165, OPD Exec. 10, Item 16, Nat. Archives (Wash.).

70 Memorandum for C of S by Richardson, 28 July 1942, RG 165, OPD 333, Item 17, Nat. Archives (Wash.).

71 Minutes of Conference 26 July 1942, RG 165, OPD 333, Item 17, Nat. Archives (Wash.).

72 The AAF in Australia to the Summer of 1942, typescript dated July 1944, compiled by Assistant Chief of Staff, Intelligence Historical Division, AWM.

73 G. Long, *The Final Campaigns* (Canberra, 1963), p. 599, says MacArthur changed the organisation by 'stealth' and 'subterfuges'. See also Willoughby and Chamberlain, op. cit., p. 124; W. Krueger, *From Down Under to Nippon* (Washington, 1953), p. 10; Long, *MacArthur as Military Commander*, p. 122; Keogh, op. cit., p. 473.

74 Minutes of Conference 26 July 1942, RG 165, OPD 333, Item 17, Nat. Archives (Wash.).

75 Eichelberger Dictations, Book 4, pp. VIII-35, VIII-36. In addition, Eichelberger recalled (p. VIII-37) that: 'In this connection, I must say that I found Gen. Blamey a very fair commander and I would have taken his judgment at any time far above the three characters who were behind me in the command chain — I refer to MacArthur, Krueger and Sutherland'.

76 Ibid., p. VIII-37.

77 Ibid., p. VIII-4.

78 Ibid., p. VIII-39. Richardson was an old friend of MacArthur. (James, op. cit., Vol. II, p. 183.)

79 Richardson later told MacArthur that he had wanted the corps command but that Marshall had concluded that he was prejudiced after commenting on the 'unsoundness' of the March directive to MacArthur (James, op. cit., Vol. II, p. 184). Richardson's signal to Marshall and Eichelberger's Dictations suggest that Richardson did not want the command. In June 1945 MacArthur offered Richardson an army command which he refused (Luvaas, op. cit., p. 281).

80 Eichelberger Dictations Book 2, p. II-31.

81 MacArthur to Marshall, 30 June 1942, Nat. Archives (Wash.) Lieutenant-General Sir Henry Pownall, who had been with Brett in ABDACOM, found him 'very agreeable and easy to work with. One can treat him as an Englishman — almost. He's a bit volatile and apt to go off the deep end from first impressions. But if one steadies him up his *second* thoughts are good ones'. (B. Bond [ed.], *Chief of Staff, The Diaries of Lieutenant-General Sir Henry Pownall*, Vol. 2 [London, 1974], p. 81.)

82 The AAF in Australia to the Summer of 1942, p. 34.

83 Kenney, op. cit., p. 63.

84 Kenney, op. cit., p. 31.

85 Rowell to Vasey, 1 September 1942, AWM 225/2/5.

86 On the other hand Kenney claims that he would visit MacArthur in his hotel and would talk long into the night about operational matters. (Interview related in James, op. cit., Vol. II, p. 247.)

87 MacArthur, op. cit., p. 157.

88 James, op. cit., Vol. II, p. 199.

89 Advisory War Council Minute No. 1030, CRS A2682, Item Vol. 5.

90 MacArthur to Curtin, 2 July 1942, CRS A2684, Item 1080, part 1.

91 Advisory War Council Minute No. 993, CRS A2684, Item 1080, Part 1.

92 Advisory War Council Minute No. 1051, CRS A2684.

93 MacArthur to Curtin, 6 September 1942, RG4 Box 1A, MacArthur Memorial (Norfolk, Virginia). In fact Carpender did not prove as amenable as hoped and was replaced by Kinkaid on 26 November 1943.

94 Rovere and Schlesinger, op. cit., p. 52.

95 Pogue, op. cit., p. 390.

[96] Vasey to his wife, 20 August 1942, Vasey Papers 2/8.
[97] For Chain of Command, see Appendix 13. For the Headquarters and Staffs in August 1942, see Appendix 14.
[98] He had commanded a LH troop and later a squadron for short periods on Gallipoli.
[99] Vasey to his wife, 7 August 1942, Vasey Papers 2/8.

[1] Vasey to his wife, 9 August 1942, loc. cit.
[2] Vasey to his wife, 25 August 1942, loc. cit.
[3] Allen Papers, File No. 5, AWM 419/3/9.
[4] Rowell to Vasey, 13 August 1942, AWM 225/2/5.
[5] Rowell to Blamey, 21 August 1942, Rowell Papers.
[6] Rowell to Vasey, 13 August 1942, AWM 225/2/5.
[7] At the request of Morris, his G1, Lt.-Col. Hatton, had been promoted to command 30th Bde. His GSO2, Maj. Pitt, had been promoted to G1, and he had asked for and received Maj. Serisier as AA & QMG. Rowell as DCGS had signed the approval (Mil. Board Minutes, P & S Committee No. 497/41).
[8] Rowell to Vasey, 13 August 1942, AWM 225/2/5.
[9] Norris, op. cit., p. 144.
[10] Rowell, *Full Circle*, p. 116.
[11] Paull, op. cit., p. 105; Observations on the New Guinea Campaign, August 26-September 26, 1942 by Chester Wilmot, ABC Archives.
[12] Rowell, *Full Circle*, p. 113.
[13] O. White, *Green Armour* (Melbourne, 1972), p. 186.
[14] W. F. Craven and J. L. Cate, *The Army Air Forces in World War II*, Vol. 4 (Chicago, 1950), p. 94.
[15] War Diary, Adv LHQ, G Br, August 1942, AWM 1/2/1.
[16] Daily Intsum 11/12 August 1942, RG407, G3 Journal, Nat. Archives (Suitland).
[17] Lt.-Col. L. K. Shave to author, 23 July 1974.
[18] Article by Tom Foley in the *Sunday Mail* (Brisbane), 20 February 1955.
[19] W. Craig, *The Fall of Japan* (London and Geneva, 1967), p. 241.
[20] Under his guidance the following organisations were set up: The Allied Translator and Interpreter Section, The Allied Intelligence Bureau, The Allied Geographical Section and The Central Bureau.
[21] Eichelberger Dictations, Book 2, p. II-23.
[22] Thorpe, op. cit., p. 95.
[23] Wills to author, 9 August 1974. Brig. L. C. Lucas agrees with this assessment (Lucas to author, 20 February 1975). A very senior Australian general called Willoughby the 'world's greatest liar'.
[24] HQ I Aust Corps Weekly Int Summary No. 11, 29 July-5 August 1942, AWM 423/11/132.
[25] The *Bulletin*, 5 August 1942, p. 22.
[26] White, op. cit., p. 181.
[27] Sutherland to Commander NGF, 13 August 1942, Blamey Papers 43.631.
[28] NGF to Landops, 6 September 1942, Rowell Papers.
[29] Vasey to Blamey, 7 September 1942, Vasey Papers 2/9.
[30] Rowell to Landops, 22 August 1942, Blamey Papers 43.631.
[31] Vasey to his wife, 18 August 1942, Vasey Papers 2/8.
[32] Blamey to Rowell, 17 August 1942, Rowell Papers.
[33] Intsum 17/18 August 1942, RG407, G3 Journal, Nat. Archives (Suitland).
[34] By 'stripped' it is meant that the battalions were lightly equipped and that they had left behind some administrative and heavy weapons elements.
[35] Rowell to Blamey, 21 August 1942, Rowell Papers.
[36] Seventh Division Report on Operations, 13 August-2 December 1942, AWM 577/7/3/4.

Chapter 6 pp. 128-34

[37] Rowell to Blamey, 21 August 1942, Rowell Papers.

[38] Notes for War Diary, 9 September 1942, Allen Papers, File No. 1, AWM 419/3/9.

[39] Rowell to Vasey, 13 August 1942, AWM 225/2/5.

[40] Vasey to Rowell, 21 August 1942, Rowell Papers.

[41] Report on operations, Owen Stanley Range, 21st Australian Infantry Brigade, 15 August-20 September 1942, by Brigadier A. W. Potts, AWM 577/7/3.

[42] Rowell to Vasey, 27 August 1942, AWM 225/2/5.

[43] Rowell, *Full Circle*, p. 115.

[44] Comments by Lt. Fayle, 22 August 1942, Allen Papers, File 1, AWM 419/3/9.

[45] Comments by General Allen, 24 August 1942, loc. cit.

[46] Memorandum for File, 1 September 1942, G3 Journal, RG407, Nat. Archives (Suitland).

[47] Rowell to Blamey, 23 August 1942, Rowell Papers.

[48] Rowell to Vasey, 27 August 1942, AWM 225/2/5.

[49] These did not arrive as promised. Vasey to Rowell, 28 August 1942, Rowell Papers.

[50] MacArthur to Blamey, 24 August 1942, G3 Journal, RG407, Nat. Archives (Suitland).

[51] Milner, op. cit., p. 71.

[52] NGF to Landops, 25 August 1942, Vasey Papers.

[53] Chilton to author, 3 May 1974. See G. Long, *Greece, Crete and Syria* (Canberra 1953), pp. 95-7. For a short biography of Chilton see Brigadier F. O. Chilton, DSO, an anonymous article in *Stand To*, Vol. 1, No. 9, December 1950.

[54] Prof. H. W. Piper to author, 30 April 1974.

[55] Chilton to author, 3 May 1974. Also D. McCarthy, op. cit., p. 166.

[56] Rowell to author, 26 June 1974.

[57] The picture of Clowes was obtained from conversations with the following: Lt.-Gen. Sir Frank Berryman, 22 July 1974; Lt.-Gen. Sir Sydney Rowell, 26 June 1974; Maj.-Gen. R. N. L. Hopkins, who visited Milne Bay just before the fighting, 12 August 1974; Brig. J. D. Rogers, war-time DMI, 25 June 1974; Brig. Sir Frederick Chilton, 3 May 1974; Prof. H. W. Piper, Wootten's Intelligence Officer, 30 April 1974. Their opinions were in unanimous agreement.

[58] Intsum 14/15 August 1942, RG407, G3 Journal, Nat. Archives (Suitland).

[59] Adv LHQ Weekly Int Summary No. 3, 14-21 August 1942, AWM 423/11/63.

[60] Seizo Okada, *Lost Troops*, p. 9, AWM 118-31. General Kengaro Tanaka, who had been a major in the Japanese attacking force, wrote in 1973 that neither Horii nor his Chief of Staff were confident of success. (A. D. Robertson, Problems of Supply Encountered by the Australian and Japanese forces on the Kokoda Trail, and the Question of Morale, B. A. (Hons.) thesis, University of Melbourne, 1973, p. 4.) A good account of the campaign from the Japanese point of view is the *Reports of General MacArthur*, Vol. 2, which was written from interviews with Japanese officers and captured documents.

Chapter 7 pp. 135-6

[1] R. L. Eichelberger, *Jungle Road to Tokyo* (London, 1951), p. 29.

[2] MacArthur, op. cit., p. 157. James, op. cit., Vol. II, p. 182, says Chamberlin was 'probably the most competent' of the GHQ staff section heads.

[3] Eichelberger to his wife, 6 August 1945. Eichelberger Papers, copies on loan to author from Prof. J. Luvaas.

[4] G3 Journal, August 1942, AWM 579/6/41.

[5] Landops to NGF, 26 August 1942, AWM 579/6/2.

[6] NGF to Milne Force, 26 August 1942, AWM 579/7/9.

[7] On 21 August MacArthur had written: 'To make something out of nothing seems to be my military fate in the twilight of my service. I have led one lost cause and am trying not to have it two'. (James, op. cit., Vol. II, p. 193.)

8 Advisory War Council Meeting, 27 August 1942, Minute No. 1044, CRS A2682, Item Vol. 5.

9 Vasey to Blamey, 26 August 1942, Vasey Papers 2/9.

10 Vasey to Rowell, 28 August 1942, Rowell Papers.

11 Clowes to Rowell, 26 August 1942, War Diary, NGF, August 1942, AWM 1/5/51.

12 Rowell to Vasey, 27 August 1942, AWM 225/2/5.

13 Hermon Gill, op. cit., Vol. II, p. 167.

14 Sutherland to Blamey, 28 August 1942, AWM 225/1/5.

15 Clowes replied immediately: 'Realise this action necessary but submit it must be accepted that troops required for such operation will render area indefensible against strong further landing in Bay other than North Shore'. Milne Force to NGF 2359 hrs 28 August, War Diary HQ 11 Div. G Branch, August 1942, AWM 1/5/25.

16 NGF to Milne Force, 28 August 1942, War Diary, NGF, August 1942, AWM 1/5/51.

17 Vasey to Rowell, AM 28 August 1942, Rowell Papers.

18 Landops Brisbane to Land Forces Melbourne, 1235 hrs, 28 August 1942, War Diary, Adv LHQ, G Br, August 1942, AWM 1/2/1.

19 Vasey to Rowell, evening 28 August 1942, Rowell Papers.

20 Landops to NGF, 29 August 1942, AWM 579/6/2.

21 Vasey to Rowell, evening 28 August 1942, Rowell Papers.

22 MacArthur to Marshall, 30 August 1942, RG165, OPD Exec. 10, Item 23a, Nat. Archives (Wash.).

23 In the words of General Arnold, the U.S. Air Chief, both he and Marshall had to be determined not to 'vacillate with every new demand made upon us from every point in the compass'. W. F. Craven and J. L. Cate (eds.), *The Army Air Forces in World War II*, Vol. 4 (Chicago, 1950), p. 92.

24 HMAS *Arunta*, which at that time was busy sinking a Japanese submarine just out of Port Moresby, was also ordered to Milne Bay (Hermon Gill, op. cit., Vol. II, p. 168).

25 H. L. Stimson, the Secretary of War, found MacArthur to be 'a constant bone of contention'. He admitted that MacArthur was extraordinarily brilliant, but lacked tact. He found the navy's 'astonishing bitterness against him . . . childish'. H. L. Stimson and McG. Bundy, *On Active Service in Peace and War* (New York, 1948), p. 507.

26 NGF to Landops, 29 August 1942, Rowell Papers.

27 That day Capt. G. H. Vernon lunched with Rowell and Broadbent, and recorded: 'I asked the General how things were going and he said, "Oh, we have our ups and downs" and at that time that seemed a very satisfactory answer'. War Diary of Capt. G. H. Vernon, p. 42, AWM 253/5/8.

28 Report by Capt. Wilson, War Diary Adv LHQ, G Br., September 1942, AWM 1/2/1.

29 NGF to Landops 2235, 29 August 1942, War Diary Adv LHQ, loc. cit.

30 Rowell to Vasey, 30 August 1942, AWM 225/2/5.

31 Ibid.

32 In a letter to Rowell on 28 August, Vasey offered to send a bottle of whisky to New Guinea, adding, 'I guess you need some the way you are being harried by the enemy at LHQ' (Rowell Papers). On 8 September Vasey wrote again, 'As John Rogers will have explained to you, we have the Brisbane front as well as others' (Rowell Papers).

33 Rowell to Vasey, 30 August 1942, AWM 225/2/5.

34 Wilton to author, New York, 15 November 1974.

35 Communique, RG165, OPD Exec. 10, Item 23a, Nat. Archives (Wash.).

36 Blamey to Rowell, 1 September 1942, Rowell Papers.

37 Vasey to Rowell, 1 September 1942, Rowell Papers.

38 MacArthur to NGF, 1 September 1942, War Diary, NGF, August 1942, AWM 1/5/51.

39 Chilton to author, 3 August 1974.

40 It is interesting to note the history of MacArthur's signal. At 1835 GHQ sent the signal direct to Milne Bay. At 1845 Brigadier Hopkins of Landops was given the signal

by GHQ and requested to send it to Milne Force. Colonel Rogers of Landops then returned to GHQ to get additional information, indicating that Blamey was not willing to send the message until further verification. (G3 Journal entry 1 September, RG407, Nat. Archives [Suitland].)

41 Rowell, *Full Circle*, p. 119.

42 Rowell to Blamey, 3 September 1942, Rowell Papers; also Blamey Papers 170.6.

43 Chilton to author, 3 May 1974; also Rourke to Vasey, 1 September 1942, Vasey Papers 2/9.

44 Communique, RG165, OPD Exec. 10, Item 23a, Nat. Archives (Wash.); also *Bulletin*, 2 September 1942.

45 Broadcasts by C-in-C, Blamey Papers 136-61.

46 Milne Force to NGF, 30 August 1942, War Diary HQ 11 Div G Br, August 1942, AWM 1/5/25.

47 NGF to Landops, 31 August 1942, Vasey Papers 2/9.

48 NGF to Landops, 6 September 1942, Vasey Papers 2/9.

49 Vasey to Rowell, 8 September 1942, Rowell Papers.

50 Vasey to Rowell, 10 September 1942, Vasey Papers 2/9.

51 Dunstan to Rowell, 29 September 1942, Rowell Papers.

52 MacArthur's use of communiques and his public relations techniques are discussed in a forthcoming book by Robert Sherrod of Washington. D.C. Sherrod was a correspondent with MacArthur during the war, and later became editor of the *Saturday Evening Post*.

53 NGF to Landops, 1 September 1942, Rowell Papers.

54 Report of NGF, 11 August-28 September 1942, AWM 58/7/35.

55 Landops to NGF, 31 August 1942, AWM 579/6/2.

56 Rowell to Vasey, 1 September 1942, AWM 225/2/5.

57 Ibid.

58 Rowell to Vasey, 27 August 1942, AWM 225/2/5.

59 Rowell to Vasey, 30 August 1942, AWM 225/2/5.

60 Rourke to Vasey, 1 September 1942, Vasey Papers 2/9.

61 Rowell to Vasey, 27 August 1942, AWM 225/2/5.

62 GHQ recognised that the Japanese advance against Kanga Force was probably only a reconnaissance and harassment, but noted that Kanga had 'stirred up a hornet's nest'. (GHQ Intsum 28/29 August 1942, RG407, G3 Journal, Nat. Archives [Suitland].) Willoughby later described it as a 'primitive reaction to . . . a local harassing force (Kanga)'. He continued that operations against the flanks and rear of an enemy was 'no Japanese copyright, but an echo of standard Napoleonic methods of manoeuvers; it was brilliantly demonstrated by Robert E. Lee, at Chancellorsville'. (Intsum 6-7 September 1942, loc. cit.)

63 Ibid.

64 Hopkins to Rowell, 3 September 1942, Rowell Papers.

65 The 16th and 17th Brigades of the 6th Australian Division had formed part of the garrison of Ceylon after service in the Middle East in 1940 and 1941. They arrived in Melbourne between 4 and 8 August.

66 Pogue, op. cit., p. 386.

67 *Reports of General MacArthur*, Vol. 1, p. 72.

68 Ibid., p. 74.

69 MacArthur to Marshall, 6 September 1942, RG165, OPD Exec. 10, Item 239, Nat. Archives (Wash.).

70 Ibid.

71 Milner, op. cit., p. 105.

72 R. Honner, The 39th Battalion at Isurava, *Australian Army Journal*, July 1967.

73 C. Wilmot, Observations on the New Guinea Campaign, 26 August-26 September 1942, from ABC Archives.

74 He was in Sydney taking the salute at the 16th Brigade march through the city (G. Long Diary No. 91, 5 September 1942, p. 22).

Chapter 7 pp. 150-6

[75] G3 Journal, September 1942, AWM 557/7/17.
[76] Landops to NGF, 7 September 1942, Vasey Papers 2/9.
[77] War Diary Adv LHQ, G Br September 1942, AWM 1/2/1.
[78] Vasey to Boase, 7 September 1942, Vasey Papers 2/9.
[79] NGF to Landops, AM 8 September 1942, Rowell Papers.
[80] Vasey to Rowell, 8 September 1942, Vasey Papers 2/9.
[81] NGF to Landops, PM 8 September 1942, Rowell Papers.
[82] Notes for War Diary, 8 September 1942, Allen Papers, File 1, AWM 419/3/9.
[83] Lt.-Gen. S. G. Savige, Comments on *Official History*, Savige Papers. Savige thought that Potts would have been most successful at Waterloo!
[84] Norris to author, 27 June 1974.
[85] Notes for War Diary, 8 September 1942, Allen Papers, File 1, AWM 419/3/9.
[86] Spry to author, 8 August 1974. Spry still believes that it would have been the best solution.
[87] Rowell to Vasey, 8 September 1942, AWM 225/2/5.
[88] Report on Operations New Guinea Force, AWM 58/7/35.
[89] Rowell, *Full Circle*, p. 53.
[90] Lucas to author, 20 February 1975.
[91] Vasey's letters to his wife, 25 September and 25 October 1942, Vasey Papers. Also a number of other reliable sources.
[92] Gen. Willoughby's Dispositions, GHQ File, written possibly 25 September 1942, AWM 923/1/7.
[93] Rowell, *Full Circle*, p. 174.
[94] Rowell to Vasey, 28 August 1942, AWM 225/2/5.
[95] Rowell to Vasey, 8 September 1942, AWM 225/2/5. In late September 1942 Chester Wilmot wrote: 'In the last three weeks of August only one air attack was made on the enemy supply lines. In the last three weeks of September 39 attacks were made on this area. Even in the first week of September when our troops were falling back under heavy pressure there were only seven attacks. The difficulty appears to have been that it took some time to convince the Air Force of the value of strafing. It was only after the RAAF at Milne Bay had shown what could be done by the Air Force by air attack that the Air Corps provided support on the scale needed. In August there were aircraft available in Moresby for strafing but they were not used in spite of frequent requests from the Army' (Observations on the New Guinea Campaign, August 26-September 26 1942, ABC Archives).
[96] U.S. Strategic Bombing Survey (Pacific), *The Campaign of the Pacific War* (New York, 1964), p. 183.
[97] Notes for War Diary, 11 September 1942, Allen Papers, AWM 419/3/9.
[98] Rogers visited New Guinea on 9 September 1942 (War Diary NGF, September 1942, AWM 1/5/51) and also accompanied Blamey on his visit from 12-14 September 1942. On 15 September 1942 Rogers told correspondents: 'I remember the fighting at Gallipoli and Passchendaele in the last war and in Greece and Crete in this war, but I have never before seen soldiers so fatigued, so grizzled, and so hammered as these men back from the Kokoda front. They have been through hell, and no tribute is too great for what they have done'. (*Argus*, 16 September 1942.)
[99] Denial of Resources to the Enemy. War Diary, NGF, 9 September 1942, AWM 1/5/51.
[1] Rowell to Vasey, 8 September 1942, AWM 225/2/5.
[2] GHQ Intsum, 8/9 September 1942, RG407, G3 Journal, Nat. Archives (Suitland).
[3] MacArthur to Blamey, 11 September 1942, RG407, G3 Journal, Nat. Archives (Suitland).
[4] The thinking of GHQ is revealed in LHQ Operation Instruction No. 34 of September 1942. This declared that: 'the rapid advance of the Japanese from Kokoda towards Moresby is endangering operations of the AAF in the Moresby area. It is considered that 25 and 16 Inf Bdes should provide sufficient troops in the Moresby area to

prevent further Japanese progress and allow us to regain the initiative . . . The Japanese are extremely tenacious in holding ground. Progress of a direct attack along the track Moresby-Kokoda is therefore likely to be slow. In order to force a withdrawal of enemy forces from the Kokoda area a wide turning movement is desirable'. (War Diary Adv LHQ, G Br, September 1942, AWM 1/2/1.)

⁵ Extract from G3 Journal, AWM 243/6/62.

⁶ Kenney, op. cit., p. 93. Also letter from Kenney's secretary, Mrs B. Daley, to author, 6 June 1974. Colonel W. L. Ritchie from the SWP Theatre section of the War Department was visiting the SWPA and radioed to Marshall on 21 September, 'An additional Regiment will reach Moresby by boat September twenty sixth. This outfit, while not tops, is tough and eager and knows why it is going in . . . The effect on the Australian soldier of aggressive action by even a small American Unit should be of enormous value' (RG165, OPD Exec. 10, Item 23b, Nat. Archives [Wash.]). General Eichelberger claims MacArthur said to him: 'Our men are in good physical trim and of high morale. There is no reason why they can't go over there and lick those Japs'. (Eichelberger Dictations, Book 1, p. 42.)

⁷ Talk to Press Correspondents -/11/42, Blamey Papers 139.3.

⁸ That day the GHQ communique described the Australians as 'fighting tenaciously and gallantly under conditions of extraordinary hardships and difficulty', *Reports of General MacArthur*, Vol. 1, p. 70.

⁹ Rowell wrote, 'I think I persuaded him that there were great difficulties and that we were not absolute tyros. My general impression now is that unless he is crooked, he will have confidence in our capacity to do the job as well as anyone else'. (Rowell to Vasey, 3 September 1942, AWM 225/2/5.)

¹⁰ F. T. Smith Reports, No. 23, 11 September 1942.

¹¹ MacArthur to Blamey, 11 September 1942, RG407, G3 Journal, Nat. Archives (Suitland).

¹² Minute No. 1052, Advisory War Council Meeting, 9 September 1942, CRS A2682, Item Vol. 5.

¹³ Minute No. 1053, loc. cit., September 1942.

¹⁴ Blamey to Forde, 11 September 1942, Blamey Papers. Forde's letter to Blamey dated 9 September 1942 is quoted in Hetherington, op. cit., p. 237. It read: 'The progress of the Japanese through the pass of the Owen Stanley Ranges in the vicinity of Kokoda is seriously viewed by members of the War Council and there is some apprehension whether the army is doing everything possible to prevent this progress. The view was expressed today by several members of the War Council that it was advisable for you to make a special visit to Moresby to confer with General Rowell and ensure that everything is being done to render it impossible for the Japanese to make further progress across country to Port Moresby.

I discussed the position with the Prime Minister afterwards, and he left the matter with me to contact you with a view to your giving your immediate consideration to a flight to Moresby to enable you to confer with General Rowell as to the strategy and report to the next meeting of the War Cabinet.'

¹⁵ Note for War Diary, 13 September 1942, Allen Papers, File 1, AWM 410/3/9.

¹⁶ Notes from Conference C-in-C GOC NGF, 13 September 1942, War Diary, Adv LHQ G Br, September 1942, AWM 1/2/1.

¹⁷ Rowell to Clowes, 14 September 1942, Rowell Papers.

¹⁸ G. H. Johnston, *New Guinea Diary* (Sydney, 1943), p. 156.

¹⁹ Wilmot, Observations on the New Guinea Campaign, Allen Papers, File 5, AWM 419/3/9.

²⁰ F. T. Smith Reports, No. 26, 21 September 1942.

²¹ Comments by Allen on Wilmot, op. cit.

²² Kenney in his book *General Kenney Reports* claims that he met and spoke to Rowell. Rowell in his book and to the author disclaims this. In his letters to Vasey he mentions meeting Sutherland, but not Kenney. Rowell's ADC, Capt. Gordon Darling, wrote that he has no record of a meeting between Rowell and Kenney until 24 Sep-

Chapter 7 pp. 159-61

tember. His diary for 12 September reads: 'We visited General Whitehead's Headquarters 1100 hours'. (Letter L. G. Darling to author, 7 August 1974.) Lt-Col. Vial, Rowell's GSO1 (Int) confirms this as does his late brother, who was an Air Force LO in Moresby at the time. (Letter R. R. Vial to author, 25 August 1974.) This evidence makes it difficult to believe Kenney's account of the pessimism at Port Moresby.

23 Kenney, op. cit., p. 94. Rowell's letters indicate that he was far from defeatist. This attitude has been confirmed from conversations with Brigadier Sir Charles Spry, G1 of 7 Div., Brigadier J. D. Rogers, who as DMI visited Rowell, and Capt. R. E. Porter, who as Blamey's ADC visited New Guinea on 20 September and then accompanied Blamey on 23 September. Vasey's letters to his wife indicate that Rourke was pessimistic, but not Rowell. Rowell's ADC Capt. Darling, and his GSO1 (Int) Lt.-Col. Vial, in letters to the author deny that their Commander was defeatist.

24 Eichelberger Dictations, Book 4, p. viii, GCM24.

25 Marshall to MacArthur, 12 September 1942. RG165, Exec. 10, Item 76, Nat. Archives (Wash.).

26 Luvaas, op. cit., pp. 27, 31. Also Eichelberger Dictations, Book 1, pp. 66, 88, 157 and Book 2, p. 59.

27 G. Long Notes N/74/18, 10 March 1945, Lae, and G. Long Notes N22/50.

28 Boase to Gavin Long, Lae, 16 July 1944, G. Long Notes, 40/24/25, AWM 577/7/32. Boase met Blamey in Sydney on 8 September 1942 and was told that both of his brigades would be moving to New Guinea fairly soon and that he was to have all arrangements and deficiencies in equipment made good as quickly as possible. The next day Boase obtained permission from the Second Army Commander (Mackay) to visit Brisbane, and on 10 September he received a signal from Vasey at Landops requesting him to visit Brisbane. He was in Brisbane on 11, 12, 13 September and saw the 16th Brigade stores loaded. On 14 September Boase met Vasey in Sydney and it was confirmed that Vasey was to command the Division. (War Diary, HQ 6 Div. G Br, August-September 1942, AWM 1/5/15.)

29 Vasey to his wife, 13 September 1942, Vasey Papers 2/7.

30 Rowell claimed to the author on 26 June 1974, that he had not expressed strong feelings on the matter, but on 25 September 1942 Vasey wrote to his wife that Rowell 'informed me that Albert [Blamey] had asked him whether he would prefer Buck [Boase] or me and had replied me'. Furthermore, the order for Vasey to move to New Guinea was sent by Blamey to Landops whilst he was in Moresby. Blamey's decision was strengthened when Colonel T. W. White, the Col. GS (SD & Trg) at Landops, who had been a battalion commander in Ceylon, informed Blamey that they had done no valuable jungle training whilst there (Rowell to author 26 June 1974). This was not true (McCarthy, op. cit., p. 74). In July 1944 Gavin Long questioned Boase about the training of 16 Bde. Boase told him that everyone in 16 Bde had told him that the training in Ceylon had stood them in good stead. There was nothing to unlearn. 'I take no credit for it', he said, 'A pamphlet on Jap tactics in Malaya had just arrived when we reached Ceylon and I adopted it. We based our training on that. It was published in Australia afterwards with an added chapter' (Gen. A. J. Boase to Gavin Long, Lae 16 July 1944; G. Long Notes 40/24/25, AWM 577/7/32). This confidence in the training of the 6th Division has been confirmed by other observers, for example Colonel J. C. Hay, who was OC of the 2/8th Fd Coy in Ceylon.

Chapter 8 p. 162

1 Broadcasts by C-in-C, Blamey Papers 136.31. Reports of this broadcast appeared in the daily papers on 16 September, which also carried reports of an interview with Blamey. The Argus, 16 September, said Blamey 'had been impressed with the confidence of the troops in their leader, Lt.-Gen. Rowell'.

2 Pogue, op. cit., p. 388. When Arnold arrived in Brisbane on 25 September MacArthur told him that the Australians 'were not good in the field, they were not good in the

Chapter 8 pp. 162-8

jungle, and they came from the slums of the cities of Australia and they had no fighting spirit'. (Article by C. Thorne in *Sydney Morning Herald*, 31 May 1974.) However, the Air Chief declared that he was certain that MacArthur would not make the same statement six months later, and should therefore be ignored. (Pogue, op. cit., p. 389.) James, op. cit., Vol. II, pp. 210-12, quotes from Arnold's papers. MacArthur told Arnold that the Australians were 'not even good militia'. He said that the Japanese could take New Guinea at will. Then they could take Fiji, after which they would control the Pacific for 100 years. At the end of the diary entry Arnold wrote: 'Thinking it over, MacArthur's two hour talk gives me the impression of a brilliant mind — obsessed by a plan he can't carry out — frustrated — dramatic to the extreme — much more nervous than when I formerly knew him. Hands twitch and tremble — shell shocked'.

[3] D. McCarthy, op. cit., p. 235.

[4] The Sydney *Sun* of the previous night had carried a story that E. J. Harrison, UAP, NSW, had asked the government whether it had considered sending Lt.-Gen. Gordon Bennett to New Guinea. On 17 September Harrison asked the question in the House of Representatives and Forde replied, 'We have a corps commander in New Guinea who is one of the outstanding military officers in Australia'. (The *Age*, 17 September 1942.)

[5] Rowell to Blamey, 1605 hours, 16 September 1942, Rowell Papers, also Blamey Papers.

[6] Minute No. 1067, Advisory War Council meeting, Canberra, 17 September 1942, CRS A2682, Item Vol. 5.

[7] F. T. Smith Reports, No. 25, 17 September 1942.

[8] Minute No. 1067, loc. cit.

[9] Ibid.

[10] Colonel W. L. Ritchie to Marshall, 21 September 1942, RG165, OPD, Exec. 10, Item 236, Nat. Archives (Wash.).

[11] D. McCarthy, op. cit., p. 235.

[12] Minute No. 1067, loc. cit.

[13] Kenney, op. cit., p. 99.

[14] D. McCarthy, op. cit. p. 235.

[15] Paull, op. cit., p. 247.

[16] Aust. Legation to government, 16 September 1942, AWM 577/7/52.

[17] Hetherington, op. cit. p. 240, also Rowell to author, 26 June 1974.

[18] F. T. Smith Reports, No. 25, 17 September 1942.

[19] Record of interview of Rt Hon. F. M. Forde with E. D. and A. Potts, St Lucia, 19 December 1973. Copies held in MacArthur Memorial, Norfolk, Va.

[20] J. J. Dedman, The Brisbane Line, *Australian Outlook*, Vol. XXII, No. 2, August 1968, p. 160.

[21] F. T. Smith Reports, No. 25, 17 September 1942.

[22] Publicity C-in-C, Blamey Papers 136.1.

[23] Paull, op. cit., p. 222.

[24] Paull, loc. cit., records that Allen said to Eather: 'There won't be any withdrawal from the Imita position, Ken. You'll die there if necessary. You understand that?' Major-General K. W. Eather in an interview on 29 April 1974 said that he could not recall Allen saying anything like that, although the line was 'weak and spluttering'. My account is from the 7th Div. War Diary, September 1942, AWM 1/5/14.

[25] NGF to 7 Div, 16 September 1942, War Diary 7 Div, September 1942, AWM 1/5/14.

[26] Consisting of the 36th and 55th Battalions.

[27] Capt. L. G. Darling, Rowell's ADC, to author, 7 August 1974.

[28] Rowell to Clowes, 14 September 1942, Rowell Papers.

[29] Seizo Okada, Lost Troops, p. 14. Typed manuscript, AWM.

[30] White, op. cit., p. 210.

[31] Okada, op. cit., p. 17.

[32] Milner, op. cit., p. 99.

[33] Rowell to Clowes, 14 September 1942, Rowell Papers.

Chapter 8 pp. 168-77

[34] Vasey to his wife, 25 September 1942, Vasey Papers 2/8.
[35] Rowell to Clowes, 27 September 1942, Rowell Papers.
[36] Rowell to Clowes, 22 September 1942, Rowell Papers.
[37] Rowell to Clowes, 27 September 1942, Rowell Papers.
[38] Vasey to his wife, 4 October 1942, Vasey Papers 2/8.
[39] Rowell to Blamey, 19 September 1942, Rowell Papers.
[40] War Diary, HQ 6 Div, August-September 1942, AWM 1/5/12.
[41] See Appendix 15 for Rowell's memorandum, Future Operations N.G. Force.
[42] MacNider to General Whitlock, 17 September 1942. Extract from AG, GHQ File, AWM 423/11/209.
[43] C-in-C's Press Conference, Perth, 9 July 1945, Blamey Papers 138.3.
[44] Hetherington, op. cit., p. 239, 241, 242.
[45] Rowell to author, 26 June 1974. Also Rowell to Clowes, 22 September 1942 and Rowell to W. Dunstan, 24 September 1942, Rowell Papers.
[46] Chester Wilmot to Molesworth, 23 January 1943, Long Correspondence, AWM.
[47] Dunstan to Rowell, 29 September 1942, Rowell Papers.
[48] Cannan to author, 1 October 1974.
[49] Hopkins to author, 12 August 1974.
[50] Rowell to Clowes, 22 September 1942, Rowell Papers.
[51] Rowell, *Full Circle*, p. 127.
[52] Extract from AG GHQ File No. 384, SWPA, AWM 423/11/209.
[53] On 24 September 1942 Rowell wrote to Dunstan: 'The Yanks feel it so keenly that they've all sent messages to MacArthur about it and that sort of thing speaks for itself'. (Rowell Papers.) Evidence of other messages to MacArthur has not been discovered.
[54] War Diary, NGF, September 1942, AWM 1/5/51.
[55] Notes on War Diary, 20 September 1942, Allen Papers, AWM 419/3/9.
[56] See Appendix 16 for copies of all correspondence relevant to the incident.
[57] Hetherington, op. cit., p. 245.
[58] Blamey to Curtin, 8 October 1942, Blamey Papers 23.81.
[59] Rowell, *Full Circle*, p. 128.
[60] Rowell to Clowes, 14 September 1942, Rowell Papers.
[61] Morton, op. cit., p. 337.
[62] MacArthur to Marshall, 22 September 1942, RG165, OPD Exec. 10, Item 236, Nat. Archives (Wash.).
[63] If MacArthur had gone to Noumea, he would have been about 300 miles closer to Brisbane than Blamey in Port Moresby. Sutherland would have been left to supervise the functioning of GHQ. It is inconceivable that Blamey would, in those circumstances, attempt to act as C-in-C of the SWPA in MacArthur's absence. Yet in The AAF in Australia to the summer of 1942, a typescript history prepared by the Assistant Chief of Air Staff, Intelligence, Historical Division, July 1944, p. 67, it was noted that Blamey was 'second in command of the SWPA, by virtue of his rank'.
[64] Keogh, op. cit., p. 225.
[65] *Reports of General MacArthur*, Vol. I, p. 74.
[66] To take the theory one step further, that is, that MacArthur wanted Blamey to lead an offensive in New Guinea and therefore manufactured his fears for Moresby to get Curtin to send Blamey, is almost beyond belief. Yet the fact remains that since July MacArthur had planned an offensive, and by late September he expected Blamey to conduct it. What is more, against his own wishes, Blamey did so.
[67] Landops to NGF, 20 September 1942, War Diary, Adv LHQ, September 1942, AWM 1/2/1. On 18 September Sutherland had sent a memorandum to Blamey suggesting that instructions should be sent to the Commander NGF 'To proceed with the performance of the mission of operating along the North East coast of New Guinea from the Milne Bay area with an immediate objective of securing the Wanigela Mission Area with a force not less than one company of infantry reinforced with the necessary automatic arms' (Sutherland to Blamey, 18 September 1942, AWM 225/1/5). There is

no evidence to show why this message was not sent to NGF until 20 September, although Blamey could have been waiting for the results of his conference with MacArthur on 19 September.

68   Milne Force to NGF, 21 September 1942, AWM 579/3/2.

69   MacArthur to Blamey, 20 October 1942, Blamey Papers 43.631.

70   MacArthur to Blamey, 25 January 1943, AWM 75/2/5.

71   Rowell, *Full Circle*, p. 136.

72   Kenney, op. cit., p. 118, my emphasis.

73   Rowell has described this incident. He said that he was sitting in his tent taking off his boots when Blamey bounced in and told him about the decision concerning Wanigela. Rowell said that he nearly ended all his troubles then and there: he had almost thrown the boot at Blamey. (Rowell to author, 26 June 1974.)

74   Rowell to Clowes, 27 September 1942, Rowell Papers. Clowes replied to Rowell: 'Am going ahead with the WAN affair, little as I like letting people out of here — and I note, in his memo to you, no reference was made to my objection from that aspect . . . As I've already indicated I *would* like an outline instn of sorts as to the purpose or role of the mission' (Clowes to Rowell, 29 September 1942, Rowell Papers. This letter was not sent as Clowes learnt of Rowell's return to Australia before he could send it to Port Moresby.)

75   Blamey to MacArthur, 25 September 1942, Blamey Papers 43.631, also AWM 577/3/1.

76   Rowell to author, 26 June 1974.

77   Report on N.G. Operations 23 September 1942-22 January 1943, by Blamey, AWM 519/6/58.

78   Hopkins to author, 13 July 1974.

79   Rowell to Clowes, 14 September 1942, Rowell Papers.

80   MacArthur to Blamey, 27 September 1942, Blamey Papers 43.631.

81   Milner, op. cit., p. 105.

82   On the evening of 27 September MacArthur signalled Marshall: 'Indications show that the enemy intends to throw large ground reinforcements into New Guinea from the North by means of numerous small increments using marine infiltration technique. By not anticipating the enemy through clearing the coast as far as Buna by trained amphibious combat teams operating in conjunction with projected enveloping movement by Infantry over the trails of the Owen Stanley Mountains, a golden opportunity is being lost. Earnestly request reconsideration of previous decision not to make available such forces until later development'. (MacArthur to Marshall, 1900 hrs, 27 September 1942, RG165, OPD Exec. II, Item 1, Nat. Archives [Wash.].)

83   Vasey to his wife, 25 September 1942, Vasey Papers 2/8.

84   Vasey to his wife, 28 September 1942, loc. cit.

85   See Appendix 16.

86   Rowell, *Full Circle*, p. 137.

87   Ibid., p. 138.

88   Dunstan to Rowell, 29 September 1942, Rowell Papers. Rowell, *Full Circle*, p. 138 mentions that when he saw Curtin on returning from New Guinea, Curtin 'read me a list of possible successors, myself included, which had been put forward from various sources'.

89   MacArthur-Onslow to Gavin Long, 5 October 1942, G. Long Diary No. 9, pp. 34, 35.

90   D. McCarthy, op. cit., p. 237.

91   D. McCarthy to author, 23 February 1974.

92   Rowell to Clowes, 22 September 1942, Rowell Papers.

93   Rowell to Vial, 28 September 1942. Photostat sent by Vial with letter to author, 25 August 1974.

94   Rowell to Allen, 28 September 1942, Allen Papers, File 7, AWM 419/3/9. On 30 September 1942 Allen wrote to Brigadier Wootten at Milne Bay: 'As you've probably heard Syd has returned to Australia and T.A.B. has assumed command. We're all very

Chapter 8 pp. 185-7

upset about Syd and feel a great sense of personal loss. He did all that was possible with the lousy resources that were afforded him. I judge Syd refused to be a "yes man" '. (Allen Papers, File No. 4, AWM 419/3/9.)

[95] Rowell to Clowes, 27 September 1942, Rowell Papers.

[96] McCarthy to author, 23 February 1974.

[97] See Chapter 2.

[98] Willoughby to Gavin Long, Brisbane 16 June 1944, G. Long Notes, AWM 577/7/32. 'Crete' should read 'Greece'.

[99] Hopkins to author, March 1973.

[1] Allen to Gavin Long, Sydney, 27 December 1944, G. Long Notes, AWM 577/7/32.

[2] Rowell to Dunstan, 24 September 1942, Rowell Papers. On 27 September Rowell wrote to Clowes: 'Hope to get down in a couple of days and stay overnight. Will let you know details. But I don't like to abandon my staff to his tender mercies'. Clowes replied: 'Hope you *will* be able to get down here soon *and* stay the night. We can have a *good* "grouse" party then'. (Rowell Papers.)

[3] Blamey to Shedden, 10 August 1943, Blamey Papers 163.1.

[4] Vasey to his wife, 8 October 1942, Vasey Papers 2/8.

Chapter 9 pp. 188-92

[1] On 24 July 1942 Lt.-Gen. Gordon Bennett, GOC III Corps, wrote to Blamey: 'During your visit, you discussed Lloyd's capacity as a Corps Commander, but at that time I had not an opportunity of seeing the result of his efforts'. Bennett Papers, MSS 807/3, Mitchell Library.

[2] Herring to author, 28 June 1974.

[3] Vasey to his wife, 4 October 1942, Vasey Papers 2/8.

[4] Allen felt that Herring was over-critical of his withdrawal through Larisa. After Libya Vasey had written to his wife that 'Tubby and his fellows did excellently', [6 January 1941] but after Greece he wrote that, 'Between ourselves questions are being asked about some of his actions in Greece'. (10 July 1941, Vasey Papers 2/5.)

[5] Vasey to his wife, 4 October 1942, Vasey Papers 2/8.

[6] Allen to Gavin Long, 10 November 1942, G. Long Diary, No. 9, pp. 64, 65.

[7] Hetherington, op. cit., p. 264.

[8] Comments on War Diary, 1 October 1942, Allen Papers, File No. 1, AWM 419/3/9.

[9] War Cabinet Minute No. 2427, Meeting, Canberra, 6 October 1942, CRS A2673, Vol. XII.

[10] Report by Minister for the Army on his visit to the New Guinea Theatre of Operations, October 1942, Blamey Papers Drawer 8.

[11] Ibid.

[12] Blamey to Forde, 10 November 1942, loc. cit.

[13] Ibid.

[14] Brig. Sir Frederick Chilton to author, 3 May 1974. An article in the Melbourne *Herald* on 1 June 1943 described Clowes: 'A quiet man, and it is said that few get under his skin. As a young officer in the previous war, he had a record of extraordinary gallantry, and shows a high sense of duty in command on the spot'.

[15] Report by Comd Milne Force on Operations between 25 August and 7 September 1942, AWM 579/7/17.

[16] Rowell to Allied Land Headquarters, 22 September 1942. Original held by Mr Bill Chapman, Chapman's Pharmacy, Boroko, Port Moresby.

[17] MacArthur to Blamey, 24 October 1942, RG4, Box 1B, MacArthur Memorial.

[18] Kenney, op. cit., p. 118.

[19] Chilton to author, 3 May 1974.

[20] The correspondence between Rowell and Clowes (Rowell Papers) indicates that Clowes shared Rowell's feelings towards Blamey.

Chapter 9 pp. 192-5

[21] Professor H. W. Piper, formerly IO of 18th Brigade, to author, 30 April 1974. Piper says that when Blamey was flying to Milne Bay, Milne Force received a signal from NGF, 'Turn out the band, Favourite song: My baby don't care for Clowes'.

[22] Comd 18 Bde to G2 Milne Force, 1150 hours, 27 August 1942. War Diary HQ 18 Inf Bde, Box 1731, AWM 8/12/18. Brigadier Field of the 7th Brigade was critical of the 2/10th Battalion (Field to Gavin Long, 14 February 1945, G. Long Notes, AWM 577/7/32).

[23] Colonel J. C. Hay to author, 20 February 1975.

[24] Vasey to his wife, 29 August 1941, Vasey Papers 2/5.

[25] War Diary NGF, October 1942, AWM 1/5/51.

[26] War Diary NGF, October 1942, Box 3, AWM 1/5/51.

[27] Blamey to Curtin, 8 October 1942, Blamey Papers 23.81.

[28] MacArthur to Curtin, 10 October 1942, RG4, Box 1B, MacArthur Memorial.

[29] It has earlier been postulated that MacArthur and Blamey had previously discussed this plan in Brisbane. See previous chapter.

[30] Draft signal, not sent, undated but about 27 September 1942, MacArthur to Blamey, Nat. Archives (Suitland), RG407, G3 Journal, September 1942.

[31] Eichelberger Dictations, Book 1, p. 14. Later, after Buna, MacArthur said to Eichelberger, 'Bob, stay away from the Australians'.

[32] Memorandum Eichelberger to MacArthur, 29 September 1942, Nat. Archives (Suitland), RG407, G3 Journal, September 1942.

[33] Eichelberger Dictations, Book 1, p. 7.

[34] Long, *MacArthur as Military Commander*, gives a scrupulously factual account of MacArthur's campaigns and he recognises MacArthur's faults: 'The setbacks in Papua had been largely the result of the failure of MacArthur and Blamey to send some of their best troops to the threatened area soon enough and promptly to organise air supply on a maximum scale' (p. 110). Yet his first mention of an offensive is the order of 1 October. This does not mean that Long was unaware of earlier planning, but by not mentioning it he implies that MacArthur decided that the situation was ready for an offensive. The truth is that the situation was ready for an Instruction: the offensive had already begun.

[35] Blamey to MacArthur, 29 September 1942, AWM 577/3/1.

[36] D. McCarthy, op. cit., p. 260.

[37] 7 Div. War Diary, October 1942, AWM 1/5/14.

[38] There is an interesting story concerning Forde's visit to New Guinea. He flew up with Brigadier C. E. M. Lloyd, the DSD, and during the flight Forde said to Lloyd: 'Gaffer, you don't think they'll get to Moresby do you?' 'No', said Lloyd. A bit later 'Are you really confident', 'Yes', 'You don't know what would happen if the Japs got to Moresby!' 'Don't I', said Lloyd. 'No', said Forde, 'I'd lose my seat in Capricornia'. (Maj.-Gen. Sir Kingsley Norris to author, 27 June 1974.) This incident is alluded to in a statement by Brig. Rasmussen, Blamey Papers 136-1.

[39] F. T. Smith Reports, No. 28, 3 October 1942.

[40] Kenney in *General Kenney Reports*, pp. 101-8 claims that he flew MacArthur to New Guinea on 18 September and returned on 21 September. This is not true and is a mistake. The most complete description of MacArthur's short visit to New Guinea is found in Mayo, op. cit., pp. 67-70.

[41] Colonel D. H. Dwyer, Blamey: personal memoir in *SMH*, 6 December 1972, also Dwyer to author, 21 February 1975.

[42] D. McCarthy, op. cit., p. 280. H. G. McCammon and C. H. Hodge, The Kokoda Trail, in A. J. Marshall (ed.), *Nulli Secundus Log* (Sydney, 1946), pp. 82, 83. McCammon was adjutant of the 2/2 Battalion. McCarthy probably used this account.

[43] Allen's comments on War Diary, 3 October 1942, Allen Papers, File No. 1, AWM 419/3/9. Allen's ADC added his own remarks. He thought that 'MacArthur impressed everyone as a very fine figure of a man. Very impressive — extremely friendly and considerate and very much a leader', but he found Forde 'a washout'. Lt. Fayle's comments, loc. cit.

Chapter 9 pp. 195-201

44 Review by Minister for the Army in War Cabinet Minute No. 2427, CRS A2673, Vol. XII.

45 The *Bulletin*, 7 October 1942, p. 22.

46 Blamey to Curtin, 4 October 1942, Blamey Papers 43.631.

47 This figure appears to be incorrect. It is considerably in excess of the 25th Brigade Group's strength, but may have referred to both the 25th and 16th Brigades.

48 Blamey to MacArthur, 5 October 1942, Blamey Papers 43.631.

49 Allen's comments on War Diary, 30 September 1942, Allen Papers File No. 1, AWM 449/3/9.

50 Blamey to MacArthur, 5 October 1942, Blamey Papers 43.631.

51 Annex E to Report on New Guinea Operations, 23 September 1942-23 January 1943, AWM 519/6/58.

52 Report on Operations in New Guinea by Brig. Gen. D. F. Johns, 25 February 1943, AWM 721/1/43. See also J. A. Huston, *The Sinews of War: Army Logistics 1775-1953* (Washington, 1966), p. 544; K. C. Dod, *The Corps of Engineers: The War Against Japan* (Washington, 1966).

53 The *Reports of General MacArthur*, Vol. I, p. 75.

54 Blamey to MacArthur, 7 October 1942, Blamey Papers 43.631.

55 Weekly Intelligence Summary No. 10, 2-9 October 1942, Adv HQ Allied Land Forces, AWM 423/11/63.

56 Weekly Intelligence Summary No. 11, 9-16 October 1942, loc. cit.

57 Rowell to Allen, 11 October 1942, Allen Papers, File No. 7, AWM 419/3/9.

58 Allen to Herring, 6 October 1942, Allen Papers, File No. 1, AWM 419/3/9.

59 Blamey to Allen, 11 October 1942, AWM 425/6/7.

60 Brigadier Sir Charles Spry to author, 8 August 1974. Also in Hetherington, op. cit. p. 265.

61 Lt.-Gen. Sir Edmund Herring to author, 25 June 1974.

62 Maj.-Gen. Sir Kingsley Norris to author, 27 June 1974.

63 Vasey to his wife, 6 November 1942, Vasey Papers 2/6.

64 Maj.-Gen. K. W. Eather to author, 29 April 1974.

65 Spry to author, 8 August 1974. Spry was wounded at Sanananda and replaced by Colonel R. G. Pollard. Spry did not return to the 7th Division. Vasey said later that Spry was 'overrated — too young [he was 32] and intolerant'. He found Colonel Canet, the AA & QMG, to be 'excellent'. [Vasey to Gavin Long, 23 March 1943, G. Long Diary No. 1, p. 35.]

66 Norris to author, 27 June 1974.

67 G. Long Notes, interview with A. S. Allen, Sydney, 27 December 1944, AWM 571/7/32.

68 Burston to Johnston, 9 November 1942. War Diary, DDMS, HQ NGF, 1943, Confidential Messages, Brig. H. C. Disher, AWM 11/1/49.

69 Herring to author, 25 June 1974.

70 Hopkins to author, 18 May 1974.

71 War Diary Adv LHQ Ops Sect, November 1942, AWM 1/2/3.

72 The staff officers included Colonels Legge, Robertson, Shave and Harrison.

73 Rowell to author, 26 June 1974. For a short biography of Hopkins see an anonymous article, Duntroon's New Commandant, in *Stand To*, Vol. 2, No. 1, January-March 1951.

74 Vasey to his wife, 22 October 1942, Vasey Papers 2/8.

75 Rowell to author, 26 June 1974.

76 Hopkins to author, 19 May 1974.

77 Vasey to his wife, 4 October 1942, Vasey Papers 2/8. In Libya Berryman was GSO1 and Vasey AA & QMG of the 6th Division. Berryman did not tell Vasey the plans for the attack on Bardia until the last minute, making his task very difficult. (Rowell to author, 26 June 1974.)

78 War Diary, DDMS, HQ NGF, November 1942, Notes on Medical Services NGF HQ mid August to mid December 1942, AWM 11/1/49.

Chapter 9 pp. 202-10

[79] Comments on War Diary 9, 11 October 1942, Allen Papers, File 1, AWM 419/3/9.

[80] Allen to NG Force, 12 October 1942, Blamey Papers 43.631.

[81] Ibid.

[82] Comments by Lt. Fayle on War Diary, 13 October 1942, Allen Papers, File 1, AWM 419/3/9.

[83] Blamey to Allen, 13 October 1942, Blamey Papers 43.631.

[84] Vasey to his wife, 16 October 1942, Vasey Papers 2/8.

[85] Blamey to MacArthur, 13 October 1942, Blamey Papers 43.631.

[86] Quoted in Milner, op. cit., p. 114.

[87] Harding to Sutherland, 12, 14 October 1942, AWM 581/3/5.

[88] Hopkins to author, 13 July 1974.

[89] Kenney, op. cit., p. 137.

[90] J. Miller, *Guadalcanal: The First Offensive* (Washington, 1949), p. 147.

[91] Fletcher Pratt, *The Marines War* (1948), p. 78, quoted in D. McCarthy, op. cit., p. 255.

[92] Miller, op. cit., p. 152.

[93] D. McCarthy, op. cit., p. 259.

[94] MacArthur to Marshall, 17 October 1942, RG165, OPD Exec. 10, Item 23a, Nat. Archives (Wash.).

[95] Morton, op. cit., p. 342.

[96] Pogue, op. cit., p. 392.

[97] Ibid.

[98] Roosevelt's Chief of Staff, Admiral Leahy, noted in his diary on 20 October 1942: 'Congressman Mel Maas of Minnesota called. He had just returned from a visit to the Pacific area which he said was in a sad condition of inefficiency because of the lack of unified command, inefficiency of the individuals in high command, and failure of Washington to provide essential material. Mr Maas said Douglas MacArthur had no independent authority over the Australian troops and that in addition MacArthur was N.G. [presumably No Good] — Mr Maas, who is well known to me, is very free of speech but, in my opinion, thoroughly honest'. (W. D. Leahy, *I Was There* [New York, 1950], p. 100.)

[99] Article by C. Thorne in *Australian*, 3 June 1974.

[1] Ibid., 4 June 1974.

[2] Eichelberger Dictations, Book 1, p. 4.

[3] MacArthur to Blamey, 17 October 1942, Blamey Papers 43.631.

[4] Comments by Lt. Fayle on War Diary, 21 October 1942, Allen Papers, File No. 2, AWM 419/3/9.

[5] Allen to Blamey, 17 October 1942, Blamey Papers 43.631.

[6] D. McCarthy, op. cit., p. 275, n.1.

[7] Blamey to MacArthur, Blamey Papers 43.631.

[8] Hetherington, op. cit., p. 268.

[9] Blamey to Allen, 13 October 1942, Blamey Papers 43.631.

[10] Blamey to Allen, 18 October 1942, 43.631.

[11] Blamey to MacArthur, 18 October 1942, Blamey Papers 43.631.

[12] MacArthur to Blamey, 20 October 1942, RG4, Box 1B, MacArthur Memorial, also Blamey Papers 43.631.

[13] MacArthur to Blamey, 21 October 1942, Blamey Papers 43.631.

[14] Blamey to Allen, 21 October 1942, AWM 425/6/7.

[15] Blamey to MacArthur, 16 October 1942, Blamey Papers 43.631.

[16] MacArthur to Blamey, 20 October 1942, Blamey Papers 43.631.

[17] Air support now makes this principle more flexible. During the Battle of Csesiphon in the Mesopotamian Campaign in World War I, casualties were evacuated forward expecting to arrive at the Tigris where barges could carry them back to the base. This did not happen and the advancing force, hindered by this policy, was defeated, and eventually captured.

Chapter 9 pp. 210-16

[18] Notes on Ops 7 Aust Div — Kokoda to Soputa — prepared by Maj. P. K. Parbury from observations, 13 January 1943, AWM 577/7/29.

[19] Norris, op. cit., p. 173. In fact Wolfe said 'War is an option of difficulties'.

[20] Hetherington, op. cit., p. 267. Placed in context by reference to Norris, p. 169. Norris records that Allen wrote, 'Come up yourself and fight the bloody battle with what I have, and see if you can do any better'.

[21] Allen to Blamey, 22 October 1942, Blamey Papers 43.631.

[22] Paull, op. cit., p. 256.

[23] Ibid., p. 257.

[24] Herring to author, 25 June 1974.

[25] D. McCarthy, op. cit., p. 247. In Norris's opinion Potts handled his brigade magnificently and never lost heart. Norris to author, 27 June 1974.

[26] Norris, op. cit., p. 169.

[27] Allen's Notes on the Operations of the 7th Division, AWM 577/7/10.

[28] When the brigades started for the forward areas the battalions averaged 580 all ranks.

[29] Blamey to Noel Monk, G. Long Diary No. 9, Sydney, 9 November 1942, interview with Chester Wilmot.

[30] Vasey to his wife, 22 October 1942, Vasey Papers 2/8.

[31] Blamey to Allen, 26 October 1942, Blamey Papers 43.631.

[32] Allen to Blamey, 26 October 1942, Blamey Papers 43.631.

[33] Hetherington, op. cit., p. 289.

[34] Blamey to Forde, 23 February 1943, Blamey Papers 85.12.

[35] Hopkins to author, 19 May 1974 and Herring to Firkins in P. Firkins, *Australians in Nine Wars* (Adelaide, 1971), p. 340. (This is not a reliable book.) Herring claimed to this author on 25 June 1974 that if it had been his decision he would have carried Allen.

[36] Hopkins to author, 12 August 1974. Hopkins wrote: 'We really moved heaven and earth to get him moving in pursuit of the Jap over the Range'. Hopkins to author, 19 May 1974.

[37] Rowell to author, 26 June 1974.

[38] Blamey to MacArthur, 27 October 1942, Blamey Papers 43.631.

[39] Blamey to Allen, 27 October 1942, Blamey Papers 43.631.

[40] Norris, op. cit., p. 169.

[41] Allen to Blamey, 27 October 1942, Blamey Papers 43.631. When Gavin Long and Chester Wilmot saw Allen in Sydney on 10 November 1942, they thought that he looked very fit. (G. Long Diary No. 9, Sydney, 10 November 1942.)

[42] Allen's Notes on the Operations of the 7th Division, AWM 577/7/10, and Norris, op. cit., p. 167.

[43] Vasey to his wife, 6 November 1942, Vasey Papers 2/6.

[44] Norris, op. cit., p. 170.

[45] Allen's Notes on the Operations of the 7th Division, AWM 577/7/10.

[46] Blamey to Allen, 26 October 1942, Blamey Papers 43.631.

[47] Allen's Notes, op. cit.

[48] Blamey to MacArthur, 29 October 1942, Blamey Papers 43.631. 'Later, in Australia [Allen] had the opportunity of speaking to General MacArthur to explain the conditions and he told MacArthur how much his signals had distressed him. In real or assumed surprise MacArthur said: "But I've nothing but praise for you and your men. I was only urging you on". Allen replied drily: "Well that's not the way to urge Australians".' (D. McCarthy, op. cit., p. 307; also Allen to Gavin Long, 10 November 1942, G. Long Diary No. 9, p. 65.)

[49] MacArthur to Blamey, 29 October 1942, Blamey Papers 43.631.

[50] Blamey to MacArthur, 27 October 1942, Blamey Papers 43.631.

[51] Milner, op. cit., p. 117.

[52] Harding to Sutherland, 31 October 1942, AWM 581/3/5.

[53] Adv HQ 7 Div to 16, 25 Bdes, 1 November 1942, Vasey Papers 2/8.

Chapter 9 pp. 216-23

[54] MacArthur to Blamey, 2 November 1942, Blamey Papers 43.631.
[55] *Reports of General MacArthur*, Vol. I, p. 85.
[56] Milner, op. cit., p. 119.
[57] Article by C. Thorne in the *Australian*, 5 June 1974.
[58] Eather to author, 27 April 1974.
[59] Vasey to his wife, 6 November 1942, Vasey Papers 2/6.
[60] D. McCarthy, op. cit., p. 321.
[61] Ibid., p. 331.
[62] 7 Div. Report on Operations 13 August-2 December 1942, AWM 577/7/34.
[63] Herring to Vasey, 11 November 1942, Vasey Papers 2/9.
[64] Ibid.
[65] Quoted in Milner, op. cit., p. 138.
[66] Blamey to Shedden, 14 November 1942, Blamey Papers 136.1.
[67] Talk to Press Correspondents by C-in-C on -/11/42, Blamey Papers 139.3.
[68] Mayo, op. cit., p. 75.
[69] A full account of the malarial problem is given in A. S. Walker, *Clinical Problems of the War* (Canberra, 1952), Chapter 7.
[70] Norris, op. cit., p. 173.
[71] D. McCarthy, op. cit., p. 317.
[72] Ibid., p. 309. See also A. S. Walker, *The Island Campaigns* (Canberra, 1957).

Chapter 10 pp. 224-8

[1] Milner, op. cit., pp. 138, 139.
[2] Long, *The Six Years War,* p. 235. Kane Yoshiwara, Southern Cross, AWM 423/4/154, p. 12, puts the strength of the garrison at 11,000 army and 880 navy. The *Reports of General MacArthur,* Vol. 2, p. 188, put the Japanese losses in the Buna-Gona area at between 7,000 and 8,000. About 2,200 escaped by various means (so by this account the strength would have been between 9,200 and 10,200).
[3] Blamey to Shedden, 14 November 1942, Blamey Papers 136.1.
[4] Talk to Press Correspondents by C-in-C on -/11/42, Blamey Papers 139.3.
[5] Blamey to Herring, 17 November 1942, Blamey Papers 43.631.
[6] Kenney, op. cit., p. 145.
[7] McCarthy, op. cit., p. 359.
[8] Mayo, op. cit., p. 102. HQ NGF received this order at 0240 hours, 21 November 1942. [War Diary HQ NGF, G(Air) Branch, November 1942, AWM 1/5/51.]
[9] This force was not actually called Urbana Force until after General Eichelberger's arrival.
[10] To avoid confusion in radio messages, General Harding designated Colonel Smith (II/128) as White Smith, and Major Smith (II/126) as Red Smith, Milner, op. cit., p. 183.
[11] Vasey — Notes on Operations in NG, War Diary 7 Div, G Branch, June 1943, AWM 1/5/14.
[12] NGF Weekly Information Letter, 20 November 1942, AWM 423/11/126.
[13] War Diary NGF, October 1942, Box 3, AWM 1/5/1.
[14] Vasey to Blamey, 25 November 1942, Blamey Papers 171.2.
[15] Eichelberger Dictations, Book 2, pp. VII-122, VII-123.
[16] NGF Weekly Information Letter, 20 November 1942, AWM 423/11/126.
[17] Kenney, op. cit., p. 151.
[18] For example, Blamey to MacArthur, 19 November 1942, Blamey Papers 43.631, and Blamey to MacArthur, 7 November 1942, GHQ, SWPA, Communiques 1945 from G3 Journal, part 2, AWM 423/11/202.
[19] Blamey to MacArthur, 26 November 1942, RG4, Box 1B, MacArthur Memorial.
[20] MacArthur to Blamey, 26 November 1942, Blamey Papers 43.631.
[21] Blamey to MacArthur, 27 November 1942, loc. cit.

Chapter 10 pp. 228-33

22 Hopkins to author, 18 May 1974. From 23 February 1943 to 19 September 1944 Hopkins was on the staff of Admiral Barbey, Commander of the 7th Amphibious Force. For an account of this force see D. E. Barbey, *MacArthur's Amphibious Fleet* (Annapolis, 1969).

23 Morison notes that "up to May 1943 every merchant ship of over 2,000 tons which ventured around East Cape got bombed, and many were sunk". S. E. Morison, *Breaking the Bismarcks Barrier 22 July 1942-1 May 1944* (Boston, 1953), p. 32.

24 MacArthur to Blamey, 27 November 1942, RG4, Box 1B, MacArthur Memorial.

25 James claims that Blamey's amphibious attack would probably have broken the siege more quickly as the principal Japanese defences were positioned on the inland side of the beachhead. He overlooks the fact that after the initial landing it would have been extremely difficult to resupply the Australians. The Allies did not have complete air superiority. James, op. cit., Vol. II, p. 283.

26 Chilton to author, 3 May 1974.

27 Personnel could be transported by air from Popondetta to Dobodura, but only one at a time, in the rear gunner's seat of a Wirraway — with the gun cocked in case of being jumped by a Zero. (Hopkins to author 18 May 1974).

28 Ibid.

29 Milner, op. cit., p. 199.

30 Ibid., p. 201.

31 Herring to Blamey, 28 November 1942, Blamey Papers 170.2.

32 Blamey to Herring, 28 November 1942, loc. cit.

33 Kenney, op. cit., p. 156.

34 Herring to Blamey, 28 November 1942, Blamey Papers 170.2.

35 Milner, op. cit., p. 201.

36 Ibid.

37 Eichelberger Dictations, Book 2, p. V-52.

38 Herring to author, 25 June 1974.

39 James, op. cit., Vol. II, p. 264.

40 This air attack is described in J. W. O'Brien, *Guns and Gunners* (Sydney, 1950), p. 171.

41 McCarthy, op. cit., p. 372.

42 Herring to Blamey, 1530 hrs, 30 November 1942, Blamey Papers 170.2. On 3 December 1942 Vasey's ADC Lt W. Riggall wrote to Mrs Vasey and probably expressed Vasey's views: 'The Americans across the river plod along their weary way and mil [sic] around in the jungle loosing off a shot or two now and again into the blue' (Riggall to Mrs Vasey, 3 December 1942, Vasey Papers 2/8:).

43 Blamey to Herring, 1400 hrs, 30 November 1942, Blamey Papers 170.2.

44 Unsatisfactory because it would have added another link to an already over-extended chain of command. To command what would have been five understrength divisions in New Guinea, two only of which would have been in action, there would have been a Corps Commander (Eichelberger), an Army Commander (Herring), the Commander of the Allied Land Forces (Blamey), and the theatre commander (MacArthur).

45 Blamey to Herring, 2030 hrs, 30 November 1942, Blamey Papers 170.2.

46 Eichelberger, op. cit., pp. 42, 43; Milner, op. cit., pp. 203, 204.

47 Eichelberger, op. cit., p. 42. It would be interesting to know what else MacArthur said to Eichelberger. Eichelberger has written: 'I tried not to quote General MacArthur's statements at full length in *Jungle Road* because I realised that he [MacArthur] was under great stress and because General Harding was my classmate.' (Eichelberger Dictations, Book 1, p. 7).

48 Milner, op. cit., p. 205 n. 35.

49 Luvaas, op. cit., p. 33.

50 Milner, op. cit., p. 205.

51 Eichelberger Dictations, Book 2, p. V-52.

Chapter 10 pp. 233-9

[52] There is disagreement about the actual time that Eichelberger relieved Harding. Milner (p. 212) quotes Harding's diary which gives the time as the evening of 2 December. Eichelberger in his dictations, Book 2, p. V-52, says that he relieved Harding after breakfast on the morning of 3 December. He wrote that Mott and Harding again lost their tempers. 'At that time I said to this effect, "All right, John, over the mountains for you", and when Harding lost his temper at that remark, then I said, "and that applies to you too, Forrest". That is why one wonders why one gets such categorical statements and why I feel sorry for the historian.'

[53] MacArthur to Marshall, 9 and 19 February 1943, RG 165, OPD Exec 10, Item 23b, Nat. Archives (Wash.).

[54] Luvaas, op. cit., p. 45; Eichelberger to Herring, 6 December 1942, Blamey Papers 170.2.

[55] Eichelberger asked for the HQ 126 Regt on 2 December and this was approved on 3 December. (War Diary HQ NGF G(Air) Branch, December 1942, AWM 1/5/51.)

[56] Luvaas, op. cit., p. 16.

[57] Hopkins to author, 18 May 1974.

[58] Herring to Blamey, 3 December 1942, Blamey Papers 170.2.

[59] Herring to author, 25 June 1974; Eichelberger Papers, *passim*.

[60] Blamey to Herring, 4 December 1942, Blamey Papers 170.2. Blamey must have remembered the landing and the following days at Gallipoli when tactical unity had been totally destroyed by the confusion of the tows and the difficult ground. See Hetherington, op. cit., pp. 35ff for Blamey at Anzac.

[61] D. MacCarthy, op. cit., p. 434.

[62] Vasey to his wife, 30 November 1942, Vasey Papers 2/6.

[63] J. Burns, *The Brown and Blue Diamond at War* (Adelaide, 1960), p. 147.

[64] About this time Blamey is said to have received a message from MacArthur one night: 'Gona will be captured at dawn'. (Hetherington op. cit., p. 286. No other evidence of this message has been discovered by the author:)

[65] Herring to author, 25 June 1974.

[66] D. McCarthy, op. cit., p. 376.

[67] Hopkins to author, 18 May 1974.

[68] 7th Division (18, 21, 25 Bdes), 6th Division (17, 16 Bdes), 11th Division (7, 14, 30 Bdes), commanded by Clowes as Commander Milne Force. In actual fact the 7th Division had under command the 21, 25, 16, 30 Bdes. 6th Division had 14 Bde and 2/7 Cav Regt and Milne Force had 7th, 16th and 18th Bdes.

[69] Blamey to Curtin, 4 December 1942, Blamey Papers 12.

[70] Quoted in a signal from Chamberlin to Sutherland, 27 November 1942, RG4, Box 1A, MacArthur Memorial. The original letter has not been located.

[71] D. McCarthy, op. cit., p. 404.

[72] NGF Operation Instruction No. 43, 6 December 1942, NGF War Diary, December 1942, AWM 1/5/1.

[73] Herring to Blamey, 6 December 1942, Blamey Papers 170-2.

[74] If Herring, like Vasey, was disappointed with the Americans, he was impressed by Eichelberger, and Herring wrote to Blamey, 'I would be glad if you would let General MacArthur know how much General Eichelberger has achieved in the short time he has been here . . . Gen Eichelberger is definitely an inspiring commander' (Herring to Blamey, 7 December 1942, Blamey Papers 170.2).

[75] MacArthur to Blamey, 20 October 1942, Blamey Papers 43.631.

[76] Blamey to Herring, 8 and 9 December 1942, Blamey Papers 170.2.

[77] G. Long, *Greece, Crete and Syria* (Canberra, 1953), pp. 370, 371.

[78] Blamey to Herring, 8 December 1942, Blamey Papers 170.2.

[79] Blamey to MacArthur, 8 December 1942, RG4, Box 1B, MacArthur Memorial, also GHQ, SWPA, Communiques 1945 from G3 Journal, Part 2, AWM 423/11/202.

[80] D. McCarthy, op. cit., p. 442. Also Vasey Papers 2/8.

[81] Blamey to Herring, 9 December 1942, Blamey Papers 170.2.

Chapter 10 pp. 240-4

82 Blamey to Herring, 10 December 1942, loc. cit.
83 Herring to Blamey, a.m. 11 December 1942, loc. cit.
84 Blamey to Herring, 11 December 1942, loc. cit.
85 Herring to Blamey, 12 December 1942, loc. cit.
86 Herring to Blamey, 10 December 1942, loc. cit.
87 Herring to Blamey, 11 December 1942, loc. cit.
88 Blamey to Shedden, 9 December 1942, Blamey Papers 43.631. Eichelberger was 56 years of age, two years younger than Blamey.
89 Blamey to Herring, 11 December 1942, Blamey Papers 170.2.
90 MacArthur to Eichelberger, 13 December 1942, RG4, Box 1B, MacArthur Memorial.
91 MacArthur to Blamey, 13 December 1942, Blamey Papers 170.2.
92 Herring to Blamey, 11 December 1942, loc. cit.
93 Blamey to Herring, 11 December 1942, loc. cit.
94 This was not true. These tactics had not been successful in the mountains. Vasey's tactics at Oivi were possible because of the relatively flat nature of the country. In the areas around Buna and Sanananda, mountains had been replaced by swamps in which soldiers were often submerged up to their necks. The Japanese occupied the firm ground.
95 Blamey to Herring, 13 December 1942, loc. cit.
96 Hetherington, op. cit., pp. 269-70.
97 Mayo, op. cit., p. 145.
98 Advanced HQ Allied Land Forces Weekly Intelligence Summaries, Nos. 18, 19, 20, AWM 423/11/63.
99 Eichelberger to MacArthur, 9 January 1943, Eichelberger Papers.
1 The Australian brigades used to this date had been the 16th, 21st, 25th and 30th. The American regiments had been the 126th, 127th and 128th.
2 Wavell, *Generals and Generalship,* p. 2.

Chapter 11 pp. 245-7

1 Eichelberger, op. cit., p. 56.
2 War Diary, NGF, December 1942, AWM 1/5/51.
3 Herring to Blamey, 18 December 1942, Blamey Papers 170.2.
4 Herring to Blamey, 19 December 1942, ibid. Eichelberger shared Herring's high opinion of 18 Bde. Later he wrote: 'One cannot compare the Australians who made the frontal attack at Cape Endaiadere with their American comrades two miles away fighting the water before Buna Mission. The Australians were fresh; they were veterans, they were not sick; they were well fed and well clothed. They fought with courage and tenacity and won a brilliant victory taking tremendous losses' (Eichelberger Dictations, Book 2, p. V-70). He also wrote of 18 Bde, 'I would say no finer soldiers ever fought on a desperate field' (Dictations, Book 2, p. III-54). Of Wootten he wrote, ' He was always one of the best'. (Dictations, Book 2, p. V-61).
5 For an account of the 2/7th Cav Regt at Sanananda see F. J. Hartley, *Sanananda Interlude* (Melbourne, 1949).
6 Memorandum by Isaachsen, 25 December 1942, Vasey Papers 6/4.
7 Memorandum by Porter, 22 December 1942, Vasey Papers 6/4.
8 Vasey to his wife, 18 December 1942, Vasey Papers 2/8.
9 7 Div to NGF, 19 December 1942, AWM 577/7/12.
10 Vasey to NGF, 24 December 1942, Vasey Papers 6/4.
11 Herring to Blamey, 20 December 1942, Blamey Papers 170.2.
12 Blamey to Herring, 20 December 1942, ibid.
13 Herring to Blamey, 22 December 1942, ibid.
14 Blamey to Maj.-Gen. C. H. Simpson, 3 December 1942, Blamey Papers 171.4.
15 D. McCarthy, op. cit., p. 620; also Blamey Papers.

Chapter 11 pp. 248-52

16 Eichelberger to MacArthur, 25 December 1942, Eichelberger Papers.

17 *Reports of General MacArthur,* Vol. 1, pp. 91, 92.

18 Simpson to Blamey, 26 November 1942, Blamey Papers 171.4.

19 On 9 December Lt-Gen. Northcott arrived at Landops to stand in for Berryman. He returned to Melbourne on 16 December leaving Brig. R. G. H. Irving in charge (War Diary, Adv LHQ Ops Sect, December 1942, AWM 1/2/3). In a letter to Blamey on 6 December, Northcott said that he was sending Berryman to New Guinea to discuss staff requirements, and to inform Blamey of the continuing discussion between the government and the CGS about whether the CGS should become Deputy C-in-C (Blamey Papers 23.81) On 10 December Blamey wrote to Herring: 'Tom White [Col. T. W. White, BGS, HQ NGF] has not been very well and I have sent down for Berryman. Tom has done exceptionally good work and I am very pleased with him indeed. He has been driving himself very hard and is really a very high class staff officer.' (Blamey Papers 170.2.)

20 See p. 247.

21 Vasey to his wife, 26 December 1942, Vasey Papers 2/6.

22 Hopkins to author, 18 May 1974.

23 Vasey to his wife, 10 December 1942, Vasey Papers 2/6.

24 Hopkins to author, 12 August 1974.

25 Hopkins to author, 18 May 1974.

26 Herring claims that Hopkins returned to Port Moresby because he was tired (to author 25 June 1974) but when Hopkins arrived in Port Moresby he continued as Blamey's Chief of Staff — not the role for a tired man. On 23 January 1943, the day after the conclusion of the fighting, Blamey wrote to Herring that he wanted Hopkins to return to Landops 'where he is very much missed' (Blamey to Herring, 23 January 1943, Blamey Papers 170.2).

27 Vasey to his wife, 27 December 1942, Vasey Papers 2/6. I have interposed 'Berryman' for 'Herring' to correct what was possibly a slip of the pen by Vasey. My version makes more sense of the letter.

28 Col. E. Mander-Jones to author, 12 August 1974.

29 Eichelberger Dictations, Book 1, p. 158.

30 MacArthur to Eichelberger, 25 December 1942, Eichelberger Papers.

31 Eichelberger's attitude towards this period changed later after he found out what had been happening in Port Moresby. He wrote: 'I remember George Kenney's book (which is full of errors) as he tells of the wonderful Christmas party at Port Moresby on Christmas 1942. Read of that wonderful party and of the girls who came from Australia to attend, and then read of what the historian has to say about what happened on that same day in a place only 40 minutes away by air'. (Eichelberger Dictations, Book 2, p. II-11.)

32 Eichelberger to MacArthur, 25 December 1942, Eichelberger Papers.

33 Eichelberger to MacArthur, 26 December 1942, ibid.

34 Eichelberger Dictations, Book 1, p. 158.

35 E. T. Lauer, *32nd Infantry Division World War II* (Madison, Wisconsin, *c.* 1956), p. 126.

36 Herring to author, 25 June 1974. Eichelberger wrote that Herring told him that when he was at MacArthur's HQ, MacArthur said to him, 'Young man, if this Buna fight continues another week I am ruined, and that applies to you, also young man.' (Eichelberger Dictations, Book 1, p. 9.) Another account reported MacArthur saying, 'Well, we're not getting on very fast, are we? . . . If we do not clear this position up quickly, I will be finished and so will your General Blamey, and what will happen to you young man, I just don't like to think.' (James, op. cit., Vol. II, pp. 269, 270.) The first hand account is probably more correct.

37 Blamey to MacArthur, 27 December 1942, Blamey Papers 43.631.

38 In this he was wrong. The Japanese forces in the beachhead probably numbered over 8,000. Of these there were about 2,500 in the Cape Endaiadere-Buna area (D. McCarthy, op. cit., p. 485). If we assume that there were 1,000 troops in the Gona area

Chapter 11 pp. 252-7

(Milner, p. 145, says 800) that leaves some 4,500 for the whole Sanananda area. There would have been at least 2,000 Japanese in the defences facing Vasey's troops. See Chapter 10, Footnote 2.

[39] MacArthur to Blamey, 28 December 1942, Blamey Papers, 43.631, also RG4, Box 1B, MacArthur Memorial.

[40] See Chapter 8.

[41] Blamey to Herring, 28 December 1942, Blamey Papers 170.2.

[42] Eichelberger, op. cit., p. 67.

[43] Quoted in Mayo, op. cit., p. 160.

[44] Ibid., pp. 161, 162.

[45] Eichelberger to Sutherland, 30 December 1942, Eichelberger Papers.

[46] Herring cannot remember telling Eichelberger to rest his troops but Eichelberger was convinced that he did, and that the Australians wanted to reach Buna. (Eichelberger Dictations p. V/II-123.)

[47] On 30 December 1942 Eichelberger wrote to Sutherland, "Vasey's getting a grand officer and a good regiment when he gets the 163rd. I hope he stops yapping about the tools which have been given him with which to do his job.' (Eichelberger to Sutherland, 30 December 1942, Eichelberger Papers.)

[48] D. McCarthy, op. cit., p. 495.

[49] Reports of General MacArthur, Vol I, p. 96.

[50] Milner, op. cit., p. 322.

[51] Tom Grahamslaw, 'Grim Retribution for Papuans who Backed the Losing Side', Pacific Islands Monthly, Vol. 42, May 1971, p. 43.

[52] D. McCarthy, op. cit., p. 510.

[53] War Diary HQ 7 Div G Br, January 1943, AWM 1/5/14.

[54] MacArthur to Blamey, 4 January 1943, RG4, Box 1B, MacArthur Memorial.

[55] Blamey to Northcott, 3 January 1943, Blamey Papers 23.72.

[56] Eichelberger to Sutherland, 6 January 1943, Eichelberger Papers.

[57] Luvaas, op. cit., p. 54.

[58] Hetherington, op. cit., p. 284. Brigadier Dougherty remembered seeing Blamey well forward on the Sanananda Track. There had been some disagreement about the use of tanks and Blamey had said 'let's go and see.' (Maj.-Gen. Sir Ivan Dougherty to author, 23 July 1974.)

[59] D. H. Dwyer, Interlude with Blamey, unpublished MS. Hetherington, op. cit., p. 284, claims that Blamey visited Gona in early December 1942, but a study of the War Diaries of NGF, Adv NGF, and 7 Div reveals no evidence of this, nor is it mentioned in Herring's letters to Blamey or in Vasey's letters to his wife.

[60] Eichelberger Dictations, Book 2, p. V-79.

[61] Luvaas, op. cit., p. 61. On 8 January Blamey wrote to Herring; 'I mentioned the matter of a letter to Eichelberger to General MacArthur, but did not receive the response that I had anticipated. I think he is still somewhat misinformed on the matter. However I will seek another opportunity of getting his mind right.' (Blamey Papers 176.3.)

[62] Major-General H. H. Fuller, the commander of the 41st US Division, which was moving to the Buna area.

[63] MacArthur to Eichelberger, 8 January 1943, Eichelberger Papers.

[64] When a party was held by Blamey at Landops in Brisbane in August 1942, a number of very senior American officers on MacArthur's staff declined to attend because they could not bring their drivers and secretaries. Col. D. H. Dwyer has written, 'They never seemed to be completely happy off duty unless they were accompanied by women.' (D. H. Dwyer, Interlude with Blamey. See also James, op. cit., Vol. II, p. 256.)

[65] Eichelberger claims that the week after MacArthur returned to Australia was spent by MacArthur in obtaining Krueger. (Luvaas, op. cit., p. 67.)

[66] Blamey to Herring, 8 January 1943, Blamey Papers 170.2.

[67] MacArthur told Shedden, 'I left him to take the final bow and here he has come back to Australia!' (Hetherington, op. cit., p. 287.)

Chapter 11 pp. 257-61

68 After returning to Australia on 13 January, Blamey saw Curtin on 15 January, (F. T. Smith Reports, No. 46, 15/1/43.)

69 War Diary, NGF February 1943, AWM 1/5/41. Milford arrived on 12 January with his HQ and elements of the 29th Brigade.

70 Ibid. Advanced HQ 11 Div arrived in Port Moresby on 16 January.

71 Blamey to Herring, 8 January 1943, Blamey Papers 170.2.

72 Blamey to Herring, 9 January 1943, ibid.

73 Herring to Blamey, 10 January 1943, ibid.

74 *Reports of General MacArthur*, Vol. 1, p. 98. Eichelberger wrote that on returning to Australia MacArthur told reporters to the effect: 'The losses at Buna among the American and Australian troops were small *because there was no hurry.*' Press men later told Eichelberger that some tried to refuse to send this communique as they felt it was not true but MacArthur's Public Relations Officer told them that 'they would send it or else be relieved from theatre.' (Eichelberger Dictations, Book 1, p. 10.) The communique did indeed imply that in battle casualties were low because there was no need to hurry — 'the time element was in this case of little importance.' (Milner, op. cit., p. 369.)

75 Luvaas, op. cit., p. 64.

76 Eichelberger to H. J. Manning, 13 March 1961, Vasey Papers 1/6.

77 Eichelberger, op. cit., pp. 76, 77. Eichelberger also wrote: 'The inference of course is that when the Sanananda campaign is conducted it was of such unimportance that the high command did not need to give it its personal attention, whereas if it fails I have been in command of an unsuccessful venture and will remain under a cloud.' (Luvaas, op. cit., p. 62.)

78 Eichelberger to MacArthur, 18 January 1943, Eichelberger Papers.

79 Eichelberger (*Jungle Road,* p. 78) says that on the night of 11 January he and his staff heard on the radio from San Francisco that Wootten would attack the next day. There is no other evidence of this, or whether, if it is true, the Japanese heard it.

80 Vasey's account of 7 Div operations, AWM 519/6/146.

81 War Diary HQ 7 Div, G Br, January 1943, AWM 1/5/14.

82 War Diary NGF, February 1943, AWM 1/5/51.

83 Eichelberger to Herring, 13 January 1943, Eichelberger Papers.

84 Vasey to Herring, 14 January 1943, War Diary HQ 7 Div, G Br, January 1943, AWM 1/5/14.

85 Herring to author, 25 June 1974. In a letter to Eichelberger on 15 January he wrote that he intended to come over 'to talk things out.' (Eichelberger Papers.)

86 Eichelberger to Herring, 14 January 1943, Eichelberger Papers.

87 On 15 January Eichelberger wrote to Sutherland, 'Vasey, from pessimism has changed 100%'. (Eichelberger Papers.)

88 For an account of the 163rd Regiment, see W. F. McCartney, *The Jungleers, A History of the 41st Infantry Division* (Washington, 1948).

89 Vasey to Hopkins, 16 January 1943, Vasey Papers 2/9. Some idea of Vasey's frustration, and the way in which commanders felt, right to the end of the campaign, that they were under pressure, can be gained from his situation report. Under the 'American Troops' paragraph he wrote blasphemously: '163 Regt, 41st US Div, See Hebrews, Chap 13, Verse 8.' This read, 'Jesus Christ the same yesterday, and today, and for ever!' (F. Allchin, *Purple and Blue, The History of the 2/10th Battalion, AIF.* (Adelaide, 1958), p. 313. Also Eather to author, 29 April 1974, Lucas to author 20 February, 1975.)

90 War Diary HQ 7 Div, G Br, January 1943, AWM 1/5/14.

91 Eichelberger has written that MacArthur 'talked a great deal to me about General Eisenhower for whom at the time he had a very open dislike. I remember after the successful conclusion of the African campaign he said, "Well no one can touch him now."'.' (Eichelberger to S. Milner, 8 March 1954, Eichelberger Papers.)

92 Kenney, op. cit., p. 124.

93 See p. 215.

94 'Lilliput' was the code name for the fleet of luggers running supplies from Milne Bay to Oro Bay.

95 In July 1944 MacArthur attended a conference in Honolulu with President Roosevelt. MacArthur put forward his plan to take Luzon and the President said that it would cause heavy losses. MacArthur replied: 'My losses would not be heavy, anymore than they have been in the past. The days of the frontal attack should be over. Modern infantry weapons are too deadly, and frontal assault is only for mediocre commanders. Good commanders do not turn in heavy losses.' MacArthur, *Reminiscences,* p. 198.

96 Milner, op. cit., p. 375. Waldron commanded the artillery of the 32nd Division, before succeeding Harding as division commander.

97 Doe to Gavin Long, Biak 7 July 1944, G. Long Notes, AWM 577/732.

98 See correspondence between Eichelberger and General Krueger, June, November 1943, Eichelberger File of Walter Krueger Papers, USMA Library, Special Collection, West Point, New York. Doe finished the war as the commander of the 41st Division, and with many decorations.

99 G. Long Notes, loc. cit.

1 Herring to Eichelberger, 15 July 1957, letter found in Eichelberger's copy of Milner, in possession of J. Luvaas.

2 Eichelberger to Miss Em, 19 June 1943, Eichelberger Papers, Box 5.

3 On 15 July 1957 Herring wrote to Eichelberger: 'I agree with you as to the importance of the fight for the beachheads, and I believe it had to be fought out as it was, in fact, fought out, although the writer of *Victory in Papua* suggests that we could have left the Japanese to starve. I still believe we had to clear the area once and for all. So long as any pockets were left, there was always the danger of reinforcement, and we did want to get on with the development of Dobodura air base.' (Letter in Eichelberger's copy of Milner.)

4 Herring to Eichelberger, 13 December 1943, Eichelberger Papers, Box 6.

5 See D. McCarthy, op. cit., Appendix 3; The *National Times* 10-15 February 1975.

6 After an interview with Vasey in Melbourne on 21 April 1944, Gavin Long wrote: 'Vasey is still pessimistic about the US Army, doubts whether they will ever make good soldiers. He puts their defects down to their civilisation, specially the films. Mentioned "Stage Door Canteen" which he had seen in New Guinea, and which appeared to aim at convincing every recruit he would die if he went to the war. American troops appeared to have this obsession, that they would die as soon as they got into action. Our men didn't think that way. They were all convinced they would survive, having in the meantime knocked hell out of the enemy . . . Vasey is evidently still bitter about Buna, and the way in which he had to use Wootten's brigade there when the Americans had failed.' (G. Long Notes, 44/41-3, AWM 577/7/32.)

7 Herring to author, 25 June 1974.

8 In mid November 1942 Eichelberger went to New Guinea, with the full concurrence of MacArthur, to witness the beginning of the fighting. Sutherland ordered him back to Australia. Whitehead told Eichelberger . . . 'Sutherland has told me he is going to run you out of New Guinea.' (Eichelberger Dictations, Book 2, p. 19.)

9 Before the attack on Lae in 1943 MacArthur wrote to Blamey: 'The coordination of the New Guinea Force with the Allied Naval Forces and the Allied Air Forces can be effected only by the Commander-in-Chief at General Headquarters. The commanders of all three forces will be present in Port Moresby during the operation when they will be available for immediate consultation.' (MacArthur to Blamey, 30 August 1943, AWM 423/11/209.)

10 MacArthur's apologists have attempted to create the impression that he often visited the front line. For example Willoughby wrote that 'MacArthur made a habit of going himself or sending his staff officers to the front.' (Willoughby and Chamberlain, op. cit., p. 95.) This was followed by an account of a visit by staff officers to Buna. The implication is that MacArthur also visited Buna.

11 Blamey to Herring, 30 November 1942, Blamey Papers 43.631.

12 Vasey to his wife, 13 December 1943, Vasey Papers 3/1.

Chapter 11 p. 267

13 Willoughby and Chamberlain, op. cit., p. 88.
14 W. Slim, *Defeat into Victory* (London, 1956), p. 180.
15 Willoughby and Chamberlain, op. cit., p. 88.

Conclusion pp. 268-80

1 W. Krueger, *From Down Under to Nippon* (Washington, 1953), p. 10.
2 Long, *The Final Campaigns*, p. 599.
3 Diller to MacArthur, 17 May 1943, RG4, Box 1B, MacArthur Memorial.
4 Transcript of interview with F. M. Forde, 4 March 1971, TRC 121/8, NLA.
5 See Chapter 10, p. 236.
6 The 1st Division remained as a training organisation.
7 Summary of Australian Army War Effort at 13 March 1943, AWM 243/6/53.
8 Lavarack to Blamey, 5 November 1942, Blamey Papers 170.8; Northcott to Blamey, Blamey Papers 170.1.
9 Blamey to Lavarack, 4 March 1943, Blamey Papers 85.2.
10 He commanded the 3rd Armoured Division after Steele for about one month.
11 Hopkins, The Royal Australian Armoured Corps 1927-1972, p. 104.
12 Vasey to his wife, 7 June 1943, Vasey Papers 3/1.
13 Brig. K. A. Wills to Gavin Long, 29 October 1942, G. Long Diary No. 9, p. 37; Brigadier MacArthur-Onslow to Gavin Long, 5 October 1942, G. Long Diary No. 9; Maj.-Gen Burston to Brig. Johnston, 9 November 1942; War Diary DDMS HQ NGF, November 1942, AWM 11/1/49; Maj.-Gen. Cannan to author, 1 October 1974; Chapman op. cit., p. 292.
14 The *Bulletin*, 3 March 1943.
15 On 27 February 1943 Blamey wrote to Mackay about the move of Allen to Northern Territory; 'This will be something of a wrench for him I am sure, but I am equally sure he will appreciate the independent command', Blamey Papers 85.12.
16 Disher to DGMS, probably 25 January 1943, War Diary, DDMS, HQ NGF 1943, Confidential messages, Brig. H. C. Disher, AWM 11/1/49.
17 Long, *To Benghazi*, p. 25.
18 Major-General H. W. Lloyd, the Commander of the 2nd Division, had been a regular officer, but he had retired as a substantive lieutenant-colonel (honorary brigadier-general) in 1928. In May 1943, of the 105 brigadiers in the army 39 had graduated from RMC, 46 were militia, 12 were medical corps and eight were regulars who had not graduated from RMC.
19 R. A. Leonard (ed.), *A Short Guide to Clausewitz on War* (London, 1967), p. 85.
20 Long, *MacArthur as Military Commander*, p. 93.
21 Keogh, op. cit., pp. 142-4.
22 Ibid., p. 144.
23 Long, *The Final Campaigns*, p. 599.
24 Hetherington, op. cit., p. 297.
25 Shedden to MacArthur, 27 February 1945, RG4, Box 1A, MacArthur Memorial.
26 MacArthur to Curtin, 5 March 1945, loc. cit.
27 Blamey to Curtin, 24 September 1942, Blamey Papers 23.81.
28 Blamey to Curtin, 8 October 1942; Hetherington, op. cit., p. 299.
29 Blamey to Curtin, 27 December 1942, Blamey Papers 23.73.
30 Hetherington, op. cit., p. 299.
31 Wynter to Berryman, 29 March 1944, AWM 225/1/16. For a discussion of the 'Battle of the Barracks' or 'Red Tabs v Frock Coats', see Hetherington, op. cit., pp. 224-8.
32 D. MacCarthy, op. cit., p. 307.
33 Blamey's letter to MacArthur of 27 December 1942 (see Chapter 11, p. 251). sought to protect Herring, rather than Eichelberger, from MacArthur's interference.
34 Montgomery, op. cit., p. 25.

Conclusion pp. 280-1

[35] A. J. Sweeting, The War in Papua, *Stand To*, Vol. 6, No. 6, November 1958-January 1959.

[36] Eather to author, 29 April 1974.

[37] See the author's article, George Vasey, Australian Division Commander, in the UK *War Diary*, 1976.

[38] Liddell Hart, op. cit., p. 219.

Bibliography and Notes on Sources

1. *Unpublished Official Records*

a. *Australian War Memorial.* The most valuable primary sources were found at the Australian War Memorial. This material falls into two categories: official government documents, which are controlled by the Australian Archives, and documents that have been donated to the War Memorial by private citizens. The second category is covered under Unpublished Private Papers and Manuscripts.

Generally speaking, the government documents held at the War Memorial can be divided into three classes. These are:

(1) Written Record Files War 1939-1945, Multiple Number System, Series A2663. These consist of army files and files compiled by the Army Historical Section during and after World War II. They were of great value, but because of their volume it was impossible to look at all files. Consequently files had to be selected from the card index and then cleared by the Archives before they could be examined. Sometimes files were inaccurately indexed. However, it took some weeks for Archives officers to examine the files and it was only then that the inaccuracies were discovered. Furthermore some folios dealing with personnel were still closed, as were those containing material gathered after 1945, for example interviews by War Historians with senior officers. In all, over 170 files were examined. They are cited simply by the prefix 'AWM'.

(2) Unit War Diaries. Most unit war diaries relevant to the topic were examined. As with the Written Records, they had to be cleared by the Archives, and again some folios remained closed. They are cited as 'War Diary' with the AWM file number.

(3) Blamey Papers. These are government documents and had to be cleared by Archives. One hundred and sixteen files were examined and many provided valuable material. They are cited as 'Blamey Papers' with the file number.

(4) Gavin Long Notes and Diaries. These are the notes and diaries of the late Gavin Long. Since a majority of the notes and diaries were produced while

Long was the official war correspondent, and hence a public servant, they are classified as government documents. They are cited with the diary or note number except when they are included in the general Written Record Files and have the AWM prefix.

b. *Australian Archives*. Fortunately the Australian Government records covering the period 1942-1945 were released at the end of 1974. They afforded the necessary completeness to the investigation, but although they provided some valuable material, they were not vital. The Advisory War Council records of July to September 1942 were the most important. Files from the following series were examined:

(1) Parkes, ACT

CA3, Cabinet Secretariat (1901-1968)

CRS A2700, Curtin, Forde and Chifley Ministries — Folders of Cabinet Agenda, 1941-1949.

CA1468, War Cabinet Secretariat (1939-1946)

CRS A2670, War Cabinet Agenda, 1939-1946.

CRS A2671, War Cabinet Agenda Files, 1939-1946.

CRS A2673, War Cabinet Minutes [Books], 1939-1946.

CRS A2676, War Cabinet Minutes without Agenda Files, 1939-1946.

CA495, Advisory War Council (1940-1945)

CRS A2679, Advisory War Council Agenda, 1940-1945.

CRS A2680, Advisory War Council Agenda Files, 1940-1945.

CRS A2684, Advisory War Council Minutes Files, 1940-1945.

CA12, Prime Minister's Department (1911-1971)

CRS 1608, Correspondence Files, Secret and Confidential War Series (Fourth System), 1939-1945.

CRS 1567, Correspondence Files, Multiple Number Series (Classes 665/4 to 678) (Personnel).

CA37, Department of Defence Co-ordination (1939-1942) and CA 46, Department of Defence III (1942-   )

CRS A663, General Correspondence (Unclassified) Series, 'O' Multiple Number System, 1940-1957.

CRS A816, Correspondence Files, Multiple Number System (Class 301) (Classified), 1935-1957.

Unfortunately the Defence Committee Minutes 1941-1945 are not yet available. Note that files from Parkes are prefixed by 'CRS'.

(2) Brighton, Melbourne

CA36, Department of the Army (1939-1974)

MP 729/6, Department of Army, Secret Correspondence, 1937-1945.

MP 729/7, Department of Army, Australian Headquarters, AIF, Classified Correspondence, 1939-1942.

Note that files from Melbourne are prefixed 'MP'.

c. *Department of Defence (Army Office)*. The Military Board Minutes for 1939-1943 were examined. I was not permitted to see the files of Sir Frederick Shedden, nor the Minutes of the Defence Committee.

d. *USA Official Records*. In November 1974 I was able to visit the USA for a fortnight. This short period meant that I had to be selective about the records I wished to examine. Naturally there would have been many more files that lack of time precluded me from seeing. A number of files were examined from the following series:

(1) Records of the War Department and Special Staffs, RG165. National Archives of the United States, Washington, DC. These records are identified by their record group and 'Nat. Archives (Wash.)'.

(2) Records of GHQ SWPA, RG165. Washington National Records Center, Suitland, Maryland. These records are identified by their record groups and 'Nat. Archives (Suitland)'.

(3) Records of General Headquarters, United States Army Forces, Pacific 1942-1947, RG4. MacArthur Memorial, Norfolk, Virginia. Cited as 'RG4, MacArthur Memorial'.

Whilst I was in America, I also had valuable discussions with the staff of the Center of Military History (formerly OCMH) in Washington.

2. *Unpublished Private Papers and Manuscripts*

Allen Papers. Papers of Major-General A. S. Allen, Australian War Memorial, File No. 419/3/9.

Bennett Papers. Papers of Lieutenant-General H. Gordon Bennett, MSS 807, Mitchell Library.

Dwyer, D. H. Interlude with Blamey, unpublished MS, loaned by Mr Dwyer.

Eichelberger Dictations. The Dictations of Lieutenant-General R. L. Eichelberger. Four books on loan from Professor Jay Luvaas of Allegheny College, Meadville, Penn.

Eichelberger Papers. Letters of General Eichelberger. On loan from Professor Luvaas.

Forde Transcript. Transcript of an interview with F. M. Forde, 4 March 1971. TRC 121/8, National Library.

Gow, N. The Australian War Cabinet, 1939, unpublished paper, RMC, Duntroon, 1974.

Hasluck Papers. Documents used by Sir Paul Hasluck when writing the official histories. Australian War Memorial.

Hayes, G. P. Pearl Harbour Through Trident, Vol. I, USA Joint Chiefs of Staff, Historical Section, 1953. Unpublished, held at U.S. National Archives, Military Section, Washington.

Hopkins, R. N. L. Order of Battle — Allied Land Forces — Reorganisation Within the Army, 10 July 1942. From General Hopkins.

— The Royal Australian Armoured Corps 1927-1972, unpublished MS.

Kitamoto, M. A record of Marathon Adventures in the New Guinea War. MS in Australian War Memorial.

Morshead Papers. Papers of Lieutenant-General Sir Leslie Morshead, Australian War Memorial.

Lucas Diary. Wartime Diary of Brigadier L. C. Lucas, 1939-1941. On loan from Brigadier Lucas.

Krueger Papers. Papers of General Walter Krueger. Special Collection Division, West Point, New York.

Morshead Papers. Papers of Lt-General Sir Leslie Morshead, Australian War Memorial.

Northcott Papers. Papers of Lieutenant-General Sir John Northcott, ML MSS 1431, Mitchell Library. Unfortunately most of these papers have restricted access.

Okada, S. Lost Troops, unpublished MS, Australian War Memorial.

Page Papers. Papers of Sir Earl Page, Australian War Memorial.

Rowell Papers. Private papers of Lieutenant-General Sir Sydney Rowell. On loan from General Rowell. Additional papers were made available by the Executors of General Rowell's Estate.

Ryan, P. The Australian New Guinea Administrative Unit, June 1968, Australian War Memorial.

Savige Papers. Papers of Lieutenant-General Sir Stanley Savige, Australian War Memorial.

Smith Reports. Reports of F. T. Smith of Confidential Press Conferences given by Curtin 1942-1945, MS 4675, National Library of Australia.

Vasey Papers. Papers donated by Vasey family to National Library, MS 3782. These papers had not been catalogued or sorted properly. The author sorted the 11 boxes of the collection. The description, for example Vasey Papers 2/5, refers to box No. 2, file 5.

Ward Papers. Papers of E. J. Ward, MS 2396, National Library of Australia.

War History Room of Training Institute of Defence Agency. Naval Operations (Part of Japanese War Histories — Vol. 1, South East Asia). Photostat in Australian War Memorial.

White, T. D. The AAF in Australia to the Summer of 1942, prepared by Assistant Chief of Air Staff, Intelligence, Historical Division, July 1944, photostat of typescript in Australian War Memorial.

— Air Action in the Papuan Campaign, prepared by Assistant Chief of Air Staff, Intelligence, Historical Division, August 1944, photostat of typescript in Australian War Memorial.

Wills, K. A. Appreciation of Colonel K. A. Wills, 29 July 1942. From Brigadier Sir Kenneth Wills.

Wilmot, C. Observations on the New Guinea Campaign, 26 August-26 September 1942, Australian Broadcasting Commission Archives.

Yoshiwara, Kane. Southern Cross — An account of the Japanese Eastern New Guinea Campaign 1942-45, Australian War Memorial 423/4/154.

3. *Private Communications*

I endeavoured to communicate with most of the principal protagonists thought still to be alive. In most cases I wrote requesting an interview although in some cases I asked for a written reply to a short question. To some letters I received no reply whatsoever. In other cases, fortunately few, I found that the addressee had died. Often the replies exceeded my expectations.

a. *Interviews*. These proved the most interesting part of my research. In almost all cases I used a cassette recorder, and only one person being interviewed objected to its use. He obligingly provided me with pencil and paper and ended up by allowing me to take some documents away.

Having graduated from Duntroon and served in Vietnam, I had a distinct advantage when interviewing. A number of generals began by inquiring about Duntroon and comparing it to what it was like when they were there. Other comments like, 'I expect you found much the same in Vietnam', show the value of my background.

It was vital that I had a full knowledge of all aspects of the topics to be discussed. This did much to establish my credentials with the retired officers. When I had gained their confidence they told me a great deal. Sometimes they asked me to switch off the cassette recorder for short periods. Naturally I took particular care to remember the events related at those times, and wrote them down afterwards although I did not use them in the book.

Sometimes it was necessary for me to test the veracity of certain officers by asking questions to which I already knew the answer. In most cases the recall of the officers was very good. I was able to cross-check stories with different officers and also with documents. The integration of written history and oral testimony was important.

I was indeed fortunate to be able to record these interviews for posterity, particularly since a number of those interviewed have since died. The results of the interviews make a considerable contribution to the book. Those interviewed were:

Lieutenant-General Sir Frank Berryman, 1 May, 22 July 1974, Sydney.

Brigadier Sir Frederick Chilton, 3 May 1974, Sydney.

Mrs Beryl Daley, General Kenney's wartime secretary, 24 July 1974, Sydney.

Major-General Sir Ivan Dougherty, 23 July 1974, Sydney.

Colonel D. H. Dwyer, Blamey's Personal Assistant, 21 February 1975, Sydney.

Major-General K. W. Eather, 29 April 1974, Sydney.

Colonel J. C. Hay, 3 December 1974, Lae, New Guinea, 20 February 1975, Sydney.

Lieutenant-General Sir Edmund Herring, 25 June 1974, Melbourne.

The late Mr John Hetherington, Blamey's biographer, 24 June 1974, Melbourne.

Major-General R. N. L. Hopkins, 12 August 1974, Adelaide.

Brigadier D. R. Jackson, 3 July 1974, Canberra.

Brigadier L. C. Lucas, 20 February 1975, Sydney.

The late Colonel E. Mander-Jones, wartime intelligence officer, 12 August 1974, Adelaide.

Mr Dudley McCarthy, author of Southwest Pacific Area First Year, 23 February 1974, Canberra.

Captain (now Sir Robert) R. E. Porter, Blamey's ADC, 9 August 1974, Adelaide.

The late Brigadier J. D. Rogers, 25 June 1974, Melbourne.

The late Lieutenant-General Sir Sydney Rowell, 26 June 1974, Melbourne.

Lieutenant-Colonel L. K. Shave, wartime intelligence officer, 23 July 1974, Sydney.
Brigadier Sir Charles Spry, 8 August 1974, Melbourne.
Brigadier Sir Kenneth Wills, 9 August 1974, Adelaide.
General Sir John Wilton, 15 November 1974, New York.
Major-General Sir Victor Windeyer, 2 May 1974, Sydney.

b. *Letters.* Valuable letters were received from the following:
Mr J. P. Buckley, General Sturdee's son-in-law, 20 August 1974.
The late Major-General J. H. Cannan, 1 October 1974.
Mrs Beryl Daley, 6 June 1974.
Mr L. G. Darling, Rowell's wartime ADC, 7 August 1974.
Brigadier C. M. L. Elliott, 10 July 1974.
Rt Hon. F. M. Forde, 28 October 1974.
Major-General R. N. L. Hopkins, 25 April, 19 May, 13 July 1974.
Commander R. B. A. Hunt, wartime NOIC Port Moresby, 12, 21 February 1975.
The late Major-General B. M. Morris, 3 September 1974.
The late Lieutenant-General Sir Sydney Rowell, 14 February 1975.
Brigadier R. R. Vial, 25 August 1974.
Mr F. W. Winterbotham, author of *The Ultra Secret*, 3, 10 July 1975.

4. *Official Histories*
Casey, H. J., *Engineers of the Southwest Pacific 1941-1945*, Vol. 1, *Engineers in Theater Operations* (Tokyo, 1947).
Cline, R. S., *Washington Command Post. The Operations Division* (Washington, 1951).
Craven, W. F. and Cate, J. L. (eds.), *The Army Air Force in World War II*, Vol. 4 (Chicago, 1950).
Dexter, D., *The New Guinea Offensives* (Canberra, 1961).
Dod, K. C., *The Corps of Engineers: The War Against Japan* (Washington, 1966).
Gill, G. H., *Royal Australian Navy 1939-1942* (Canberra, 1957).
— *Royal Australian Navy 1942-1945* (Canberra, 1968).
Gillison, D., *Royal Australian Air Force, 1939-1942* (Canberra, 1962).
Hasluck, P., *The Government and the People, 1939-1941* (Canberra, 1952).
— *The Government and the People, 1942-1945* (Canberra, 1970).
Huston, J. A., *The Sinews of War: Army Logistics 1775-1953,* (Washington, 1966).
Kirby, S. W., *The War Against Japan*, Vol. II (London, 1958).
Long, G., *To Benghazi* (Canberra, 1952).
— *Greece, Crete and Syria* (Canberra, 1953).
— *The Final Campaigns* (Canberra, 1963).
— *The Six Years War* (Canberra, 1973).
McCarthy, D., *South-West Pacific Area — First Year* (Canberra, 1959).
Matloff, M. and Snell, E. M., *Strategic Planning for Coalition Warfare,*

1941-1942 (Washington, 1953).

Maughan, B., *Tobruk and El Alamein* (Canberra, 1966).

Miller, J. Jr, *Cartwheel: The Reduction of Rabaul* (Washington, 1959).

— *Guadalcanal: The First Offensive* (Washington, 1949).

Milner, S., *Victory in Papua* (Washington, 1957).

Morison, S. E., *Coral Sea, Midway and Submarine Actions May 1942-August 1942* (Boston, 1967).

— *Breaking the Bismarcks Barrier 22 July 1942-1 May 1944* (Boston, 1953).

— *The Two-Ocean War* (Boston, 1963).

Morton, L., *Strategy and Command: The First Two Years* (Washington, 1962).

Odgers, G., *Air War Against Japan 1943-1945* (Canberra, 1957).

Thompson, G. R. and Harris, D. R., *The Signal Corps: The Outcome* (Washington, 1966).

U.S. Strategic Bombing Survey (Pacific), *The Campaign of the Pacific War* (New York, 1969).

Walker, A. S., *The Island Campaigns* (Canberra, 1957).

Wigmore, L., *The Japanese Thrust* (Canberra, 1957).

Willoughby, C. A., *et al.*, (comps.), *Reports of General MacArthur*, Vol. 1, *The Campaigns of MacArthur in the Pacific* (Washington, 1966).

— Vol. 2, *Japanese Operations in the Southwest Pacific Area* (Washington, 1966).

5. *Other Secondary Sources*

Anonymous (ed.), *Khaki and Green* (Canberra, 1943).

Allchin, F., *Purple and Blue, The History of the 2/10th Battalion, AIF* (Adelaide, 1958).

Barbey, D. E., *MacArthur's Amphibious Fleet* (Annapolis, 1969).

Bateson, C., *The War with Japan* (Sydney, 1968).

Bean, C. E. W., *Two Men I Knew* (Sydney, 1957).

Blainey, G. (ed.), *If I Remember Rightly, The Memoirs of W. S. Robinson, 1876-1963* (Melbourne, 1967).

Bond, B. (ed.), *Chief of Staff, The Diaries of Lieutenant-General Sir Henry Pownall*, Vol. 2 (London, 1974).

Brigg, S. and L., *The 36th Australian Infantry Battalion, 1939-1945* (Sydney, 1967).

Brooks, Dame Mabel, *Memoirs* (Melbourne, 1974).

Buggy, H., *Pacific Victory* (Melbourne, 1945).

Burns, J., *The Brown and Blue Diamond at War* (Adelaide, 1962).

Chandler, A. D. Jr (ed.), *The Papers of Dwight David Eisenhower, The War Years: 1* (Baltimore, 1970).

Chapman, I., *Iven G. Mackay: Citizen and Soldier* (Melbourne, 1975).

Clausewitz, General C. von, *On War*, Vol. 1 (London, 1968).

Collins, J., *As Luck Would Have It* (Sydney, 1965).

Craig, W., *The Fall of Japan* (Heron Books, 1967).

Crooks, W., *The Footsoldiers* (Sydney, 1971).

Davidson, R., *With Courage High* (Melbourne, 1964).
Davis, B., *Get Yamamoto* (London, 1969).
Dawes, A., *Soldier Superb* (Sydney, 1943).
Drake-Brockman, G., *The Turning Wheel* (Perth, 1960).
Dulles, A., *The Craft of Intelligence* (New York, 1969).
Edwards, C., *The Editor Regrets* (Melbourne, 1972).
Eichelberger, R. L., *Jungle Road to Tokyo* (London, 1951).
Fadden, Sir A., *They Called Me Artie* (Milton, Qld, 1969).
Farago, L., *The Broken Seal, The Story of 'Operation Magic' and the Pearl Harbor Disaster* (London, 1967).
Frye, W., *Marshall, Citizen Soldier* (New York, 1947).
Fuchida, M. and Okumiya, M., *Midway, The Battle that Doomed Japan* (New York, 1955).
Fuller, J. F. C., *The Foundations of the Science of War* (London, 1925).
— *Generalship, Its Diseases and Their Cure* (London, 1933).
Griffiths, O., *Darwin Drama* (Sydney, c.1944).
Hart, B. H. Liddell, *Thoughts on War* (London, 1943).
Hartley, F. J., *Sanananda Interlude* (Melbourne, 1949).
Haugland, V., *The AAF Against Japan* (New York, 1948).
Hetherington, J., *Blamey, Controversial Soldier* (Canberra, 1973).
— *Australians, Nine Profiles* (Melbourne, 1960).
Horton, D. C., *New Georgia, Pattern for Victory* (London, 1972).
Hunt, F., *The Untold Story of Douglas MacArthur* (London, 1954).
Huntington, S. P., *The Soldier and the State* (Cambridge, Mass., 1957).
Ike, N., *Japan's Decision For War, Records of the 1941 Policy Conferences* (Stanford, California, 1967).
Ind, A., *A Short History of Espionage* (New York, 1963).
James, D. C., *The Years of MacArthur*, Vol. I (London, 1970).
— *The Years of MacArthur*, Vol. II (Boston, 1975).
Janowitz, M., *The Professional Soldier* (New York, 1960).
Johnston, G. H., *Australia at War* (Sydney, 1942).
— *New Guinea Diary* (Sydney, 1943).
— *Pacific Partner* (New York, 1944).
Jones, F. C., *Japan's New Order in East Asia, Its Rise and Fall 1937-45* (London, 1954).
Kahn, D., *The Code-Breakers: The Story of Secret Writing* (New York, 1967).
Kahn, E. J. Jr, *G.I. Jungle* (New York, 1943).
Kennedy, P., *Pacific Onslaught 7 December 1941-3, February 1943* (New York, 1972).
Kenney, G. C., *The MacArthur I Know* (New York, 1951).
— *General Kenney Reports* (New York, 1949).
Kent, G., *Guadalcanal, Island Ordeal* (London, 1972).
Keogh, E. G., *South West Pacific 1941-45* (Melbourne, 1965).
Krueger, W., *From Down Under to Nippon* (Washington, 1953).
Laffin, J., *Links of Leadership* (London, 1966).

Lauer, E. T., *32nd Infantry Division World War II* (Madison, Wisconsin, c.1956).

Leahy, W. D., *I was There* (New York, 1950).

Lee, C., *They Call it Pacific* (New York, 1943).

Lee, C. and Henschel, R., *Douglas MacArthur* (New York, 1952).

Lee, J. E., *Duntroon* (Canberra, 1952).

Legg, F., *The Gordon Bennett Story* (Sydney, 1965).

Leonard, R. A. (ed.), *A Short Guide to Clausewitz on War* (London, 1967).

Lockwood, D., *Australia's Pearl Harbour, Darwin 1942* (Melbourne, 1966).

Long, G., *MacArthur as Military Commander* (London, 1969).

Luvaas, J. (ed.), *Dear Miss Em, General Eichelberger's War in the Pacific 1942-1945* (Westport, Conn., 1972).

MacArthur, D., *Reminiscences* (London, 1964), also (Greenwich, Conn., 1965).

Marshall, A. J. (ed.), *Nulli Secundus Log* (Sydney, 1946).

Marshall, S. L. A., *Men Against Fire* (New York, 1947).

Mayer, S. L., *MacArthur* (London, 1973).

Mayo, L., *Bloody Buna* (New York, 1974).

McCartney, W. F., *The Jungleers, A History of the 41st Infantry Division* (Washington, 1948).

Menzies, R. G., *Afternoon Light* (Melbourne, 1967).

Meo, L. D., *Japan's Radio War on Australia, 1941-1945* (Melbourne, 1968).

Montgomery, B. L., *A History of Warfare* (London, 1968).

Norris, F. K., *No Memory for Pain* (Melbourne, 1970).

O'Brien, J. W., *Guns and Gunners* (Sydney, 1950).

Page, Sir E., *Truant Surgeon* (Sydney, 1963).

Paull, R. A., *Retreat from Kokoda* (Melbourne, 1958).

Phillips, T. R. (ed.), *Roots of Strategy* (London, 1943).

Pogue, F. C., *George C. Marshall: Ordeal and Hope 1939-1942* (New York, 1966).

Robinson, P., *The Fight for New Guinea* (New York, 1943).

Rovere, R. H. and Schlesinger, A., *The MacArthur Controversy and American Foreign Policy* (New York, 1965).

Rowell, S. F., *Full Circle* (Melbourne, 1974).

Russell, W. B., *There Goes a Man* (Melbourne, 1959).

— *The Second Fourteenth Battalion* (Sydney, 1948).

Rutherford, W., *Fall of the Philippines* (London, 1972).

Sakai, S., *Samurai* (New York, 1967).

Sherwood, R. E., *The White House Papers of Harry L. Hopkins*, two volumes (London, 1948).

Spender, Sir P., *Politics and a Man* (Sydney, 1972).

Stimson, H. L. and Bundy, McG., *On Active Service in Peace and War* (New York, 1948).

Thorpe, E. R., *East Wind, Rain* (Boston, 1969).

Toland, J., *The Rising Sun* (London, 1970).

Tuker, Sir F., *Approach to Battle* (London, 1963).

Smythe, Sir J., *Leadership in War 1939-1945* (London, 1974).
Spratt, E., *Eddie Ward, Firebrand of East Sydney* (Adelaide, 1965).
Uren, M., *A Thousand Men at War* (Melbourne, 1959).
Vader, J., *New Guinea: the Tide is Turned* (New York, 1972).
Wavell, Sir A., *Generals and Generalship* (London, 1941).
White, O., *Green Armour* (Melbourne, 1972).
Whitehouse, A., *Espionage and Counterespionage* (New York, 1964).
Willoughby, C. A. and Chamberlin, J., *MacArthur 1941-1951* (Melbourne, 1956).
Winterbotham, F. W., *The Ultra Secret* (London, 1974).
Wohlstetter, R., *Pearl Harbor, Warning and Decision* (Stanford, California, 1962).

6. *Articles*

Anonymous (possibly A. W. Bazley and/or A. J. Sweeting), We Will Remember Them, *Stand To*, Vol. 1, No. 6, July 1950.
— Brigadier F. O. Chilton, DSO, *Stand To*, Vol. 1, No. 9, December 1950.
— Duntroon's New Commandant, *Stand To*, Vol. 2, No. 1, January-March 1951.
— Australian High Commissioner in Pakistan, *Stand To*, Vol. 3, No. 3, March 1952.
— Basil Moorehouse Morris, *Stand To*, September 1957-October 1958.
Anonymous, Australia, *Round Table*, No. 127, June 1942.
— Australia — The American Impact, *Round Table*, No. 128, September 1942.
Bazley, A. W. and Long, G., Iven Giffard Mackay: Citizen Soldier, *Australian Army Journal*, July 1967.
Beavis, L. E., General Northcott: A Wartime Chief of Staff, *Australian Army Journal*, April 1967.
— Review of Long, G., *The Final Campaigns* in *Stand To*, Vol. 9, No. 1, January-February 1964.
Calwell, A. A., Australia at War: Paul Hasluck's History, *Meanjin Quarterly*, Vol. 30, No. 4, December 1971.
Cowie, D., The Defence of Australia, *Army Quarterly*, Vol. XXXVI, No. 1, April 1938.
— Australia's New Army, *Army Quarterly*, Vol. XXXIX, No. 1, October, 1939.
Dedman, J. J., The Return of the AIF From the Middle East, *Australian Outlook*, Vol. XII, No. 2, August 1967.
— The Brisbane Line, *Australian Outlook*, Vol. XXII, No. 2, August 1968.
— The Labor Government in the Second World War, Part II, *Labour History*, No. 22, May 1972.
— Defence. Policy Decisions before Pearl Harbour, *Australian Journal of Politics and History*, Vol. XIII, No. 3, December 1967.
Dwyer, D., Blamey: personal memoir, *Sydney Morning Herald*, 6 December 1972.

Encel, S., The Study of Militarism in Australia, in J. Van Doorn (ed.), *Armed Forces and Society* (The Hague, 1968).

Fadden, Sir A., Forty Days and Forty Nights. Memoir of a War-time Prime Minister, *Australian Outlook*, No. 27, 1973.

Grahamslaw, T., When Undisciplined, Poorly Led Troops Looted Port Moresby, *Pacific Islands Monthly*, Vol. 42, March 1971.

— Grim Retribution for Papuans who Backed the Losing Side, *Pacific Islands Monthly*, Vol. 44, May 1971.

Hastings, P., Inside the War Files, *Sydney Morning Herald*, 28 October, 25, 27, 28 November 1972.

Honner, R., The 39th Battalion at Isurava, *Australian Army Journal*, July 1967.

Long, G., Australia in the Second World War, in C. Hartley Grattan (ed.), *Australia* (Berkley, 1947).

Marsh, J., Churchill versus Curtin, February 1942, *Australian Army Journal*, January 1971.

McCarthy, J. M., Australia: A View from Whitehall 1934-1945, *Australian Outlook*, Vol. 28, No. 3, December 1974.

— Singapore and Australian Defence 1921-1942, *Australian Outlook*, Vol. 25, No. 2, August 1971.

— Australia and Imperial Defence: Co-operation and Conflict 1918-1939, *Australian Journal of Politics and History*, Vol. XIII, No. 1, April 1971.

O'Neill, R. J., Australia in the Second World War, *Historical Studies*, Vol. 16, No. 64, April 1975.

Perry, W., Sir Frederick Shedden, 1893-1971, *Victorian Historical Magazine*, Vol. 42, No. 3, August 1971.

— Lieutenant General Douglas Wynter, *Victorian Historical Magazine*, Vol. 43, No. 2, May 1972.

— Lieutenant General Sir John Dudley Lavarack, *Victorian Historical Magazine*, Vol. 46, No. 2, May 1975.

— The Late Major General L. E. Beavis — an appreciation. *Army Journal*, March 1976.

Rowell, S. F., General Sturdee and the Australian Army, *Australian Army Journal*, August 1966.

Sissons, D. C. S., Australia and New Guinea in Japanese Post Mortems of the Pacific War, *Australian Army Journal*, September 1957.

Sweeting, A. J., The War in Papua, *Stand To*, Vol. 6, No. 6, November 1958-January 1959.

Thorne, C., MacArthur, Australia and the British, 1942-1943: The Secret Journal of MacArthur's British Liaison Officer (Part 1), *Australian Outlook*, April 1975, Vol. 29, No. 1, Part 2, *Australian Outlook*, August 1975, Vol. 29, No. 2.

— When Dr Evatt drove Churchill to Bed, *Sydney Morning Herald*, 31 May 1974.

— A Nation of Strike-happy Thugs, *Sydney Morning Herald*, 1 June 1974.

— MacArthur in Australia, *Australian* 1, 2, 3, 4, 5, 6 June 1974.

Turner, L. C. F., The Crisis of Japanese Strategy, January-June 1942, *R.M.C. Historical Journal*, Vol. 1, March 1972.

7. *Theses*

Brown, G., The Kokoda Trail — Myth and Reality, BA (Hons.) Thesis, University of Newcastle, October 1971.

Cornish, J. A., General Douglas MacArthur and Australia, 1942-1945, MEc Thesis, University of Sydney, 1967.

Hamill, I., The Imperial Commitment: The Singapore Strategy in the Defence of Australia and New Zealand, 1939-1942, MA Thesis, ANU, September 1974.

McCarthy, J. M., Air Power and Australian Defence: A Study in Imperial Relations 1923-1954. PhD Thesis, ANU, 1971.

Robertson, A. D., Problems of Supply Encountered by the Australian and Japanese Forces on the Kokoda Trail, and the Question of Morale. BA (Hons.) Thesis, University of Melbourne, June 1973.

8. *Newspapers*

Newspapers have been of only marginal value to this study. War-time censorship forbade publication of controversial information about command relationships. Close study of a number of papers for all of 1942 revealed little information. The *Bulletin* and the *Sydney Morning Herald* were the most perceptive in their analysis of the war situation. There was perhaps some value in the papers when attempting to determine public reaction to the war. This was of value to the work only when the public reaction caused the government to put pressure on the generals. Information from the following papers has been used:

The *Age*
The *Argus*
The *Australian*
The *Bulletin*
The *Canberra Times*
The *Courier-Mail*
The *Daily Telegraph*
The *Mercury*
The *Sunday Telegraph*
The *Sydney Morning Herald*

9. *Visit to Battlefields*

Towards the end of 1974 I was able to visit most of the relevant battlefields in New Guinea. The information gained from this visit was not used directly in the work, but the experience was extremely valuable, for it enabled me to understand the problems posed by the terrain, the climate and the vegetation, and to understand the relative distances between important areas. My itinerary was as follows:

26 November   Departed from Canberra

27 November	Drove around Port Moresby and examined old HQs and airfields.
28 November	Drove to Ower's Corner and walked along Kokoda Trail.
29 November	Flew to Popondetta. Drove to Buna and Oro Bay, and walked over area.
30 November	Drove to Kokoda, walked over Oivi battlefield and examined site of Wairopi on the Kumusi River.
1 December	Drove to Sanananda and Cape Killerton. Walked over Sanananda battlefield. Flew to Lae and drove around the area.
2 December	Drove to Wau.
3 December	Flew to Finschhafen and drove to Sattleberg.
4 December	Flew to Port Moresby and drove around area.
5 December	Departed from Port Moresby.

10. *Potentially Valuable Sources not Used*

a. Manuscript of book by Sir Frederick Shedden. Lady Shedden will not allow it to be examined.

b. Files of Sir Frederick Shedden and Minutes of the Defence Committee. Not yet available from the Department of Defence.

c. Diaries of Sir John Northcott 1915, 1933-66, and Correspondence 1912-1966. MS 1421/3-11, 13-24, Mitchell Library. Restricted until 2000 AD.

d. Papers of Major-General S. J. Chamberlin, held at U.S. War College, Carlisle, Penn. I heard about these papers just before I was due to return to Australia.

e. Unpublished MS, Say Not the Struggle, by Brigadier J. D. Rogers. At every inquiry the MS was with a potential publisher.

f. MS of unpublished book by Major-General R. E. Jackson. Brigadier D. R. Jackson has not been able to locate the MS.

g. Papers of Sir Iven Mackay. Lady Mackay promised that I would have full access to the papers when she donated them to the AWM. Unfortunately she became ill and the papers had not been donated at the time I left Canberra.

Index

Major Horner is a regular officer in the Royal Australian Infantry. He graduated from the Royal Military College, Duntroon, where he had studied military history, in 1969. On his return to Australia after service as a platoon commander in South Vietnam he completed a M.A. degree (hons) at the University of New South Wales. In 1976 he was awarded a Churchill Fellowship to visit military history institutions overseas. He is at present working on a Ph.D. thesis at The Australian National University.

In writing the book Major Horner interviewed many retired officers throughout Australia, inspected the battlefields in New Guinea, and studied in various centres in USA.

Text set in 10 point English Times and printed on 90 gm^2 Scanoffset by Southwood Press Pty Limited, Marrickville, NSW, Australia.